LAWRENCE UCHILL

ANATOMY OF MORTGAGE LOAN DOCUMENTS

UNDERSTANDING AND NEGOTIATING KEY COMMERCIAL REAL ESTATE LOAN DOCUMENTS

THIRD EDITION

AMERICAN BAR ASSOCIATION
Real Property, Trust and Estate Law Section

Cover design by Andrew Alcala

Printed in the United States of America.

27 26 5 4 3

A catalog record for this book is available from the Library of Congress.

Contents

Acknowledgments

The genesis for this Book was a desire to provide basic, useful information to new lawyers, in order to introduce them to key loan provisions contained in mortgage loan documents relating to commercial real estate transactions; and to provide them with techniques and concepts to consider in order to successfully deal with these loan provisions when they are engaged to represent borrowers in connection with closing such loans. The original editions of this Book were based on a series of panel programs which dealt with mortgage loan provisions set out in a mortgage or deed of trust. Apparently much of the material used in these panel presentations was then adapted by its authors into the first edition of this Book. In the second edition of this Book, which was edited by me, I tried to adapt and supplement these materials using more than 40 years of experience as a transactional real estate lawyer to build upon a number of the basic elements used in the first edition of this Book, with the goal of helping new lawyers understand why these major loan provisions are used, and strategies they should consider when they are negotiating these provisions, in order to achieve successful results for their clients. In this edition of the Book, I am analyzing not just the form of the mortgage or deed of trust used in these transactions, but also a number of other key documents typically used when closing a commercial real estate loan. As the author of this edition of this Book, I would like to thank the authors of the original edition, R. Wilson Freyermuth, John P. McNearney, Debra Pogrund Stark, and Dale A. Whitman, as well as Pam Belleman, the Chairperson of the Workouts, Foreclosures, and Bankruptcies Committee, and the individuals who served as panelists for the programs that formed the basis for the original edition of this Book, Melanie Rovner Cohen, Alexandra R. Cole, Neil S. Kessler, Jeffrey Lenobel, James C. Ryan, Jr., Mark S. Shiembob, and Stanley P. Sklar.

About the Author

Lawrence Uchill is the principal and founder of Uchill Law, PLLC, a boutique law firm specializing in complex real estate and capital market transactions, as well as alternative energy transactions and corporate law. Mr. Uchill is also an Adjunct Lecturer of Law at Boston University School of Law, where (i) for more than twenty years he, along with two other colleagues, have taught a course on Securitization and Secured Transactions and (ii) since 2017, he and a colleague have been teaching a different course which simulates the preparation and negotiation of key documents used in a commercial real estate acquisition. He received a BA in Economics from Brandeis University and a JD with honors from the Boston University School of Law. Having been a Partner at several well-known national and international law firms, as well as VP of Legal Affairs at Cabot, Cabot & Forbes, a real estate development firm, Mr. Uchill has now been successfully practicing real estate transactional law for almost fifty years.

Introduction

This Book endeavors to provide the reader with an understanding of the basic concepts of real estate finance provisions that a lawyer must know and understand in order to provide effective counsel to borrowers in the context of closing a commercial real estate loan. This goal will be accomplished through the detailed analysis of key provisions contained in real estate mortgages and several other key mortgage loan documents. Lawyers new to the practice of real estate finance can benefit greatly from a highly practical evaluation of these key provisions, because in most instances they represent very important aspects of a mortgage transaction.

This Book uses many provisions that were previously utilized in the Federal National Mortgage Association ("Fannie Mae") Deed of Trust form for multifamily housing, but this Book embellishes on those provisions and adds others that are also commonly used in commercial real estate loan transactions. In addition, this Book examines a number of other key loan documents that are often used in commercial real estate transactions. The goal in undertaking these examinations is to expose new lawyers to loan provisions that are now commonly used in commercial real estate loan documentation. In selecting these provisions, I have made a few assumptions, for several reasons. First, the loan provisions used in this Book contemplate that the mortgaged property is an income-producing property, as distinguished from a loan secured by a residence that the borrower would live in and which would not generate any income. A number of these provisions thus relate to the "commercial" nature of the property, such as the treatment of property rents. Second, unlike provisions contained in forms that some counsel for lenders have created and use for their first draft in a loan negotiation, the loan provisions used in this Book are relatively evenhanded and sometimes contain points that the borrower's counsel would want to seek on behalf of his/her client. When applicable, I have attempted to point out advantages and deficiencies contained in any of these provisions that could be utilized if the reader were to be engaged as counsel representing a borrower in a mortgage loan transaction, and also to give the reader strategies for use when negotiating these provisions.

As indicated earlier, this Book is organized around the provisions of a mortgage and several other key documents, including the Letter of Intent, Note, and Carve Out Guaranty. Each part of this Book sets forth an introduction to, and then the verbatim text of, a specific provision of a given key loan document (which is set out in italic type), immediately followed by commentary on the italicized provision. My commentary explains what the applicable italicized loan provision means, what functions the provision serves, and any problems with the application or enforcement of the provision from a lender's or borrower's perspective. The commentary includes basic information that any lawyer new to mortgage transactions would find helpful, including potential pitfalls to watch out for from a borrower's counsel perspective, as well as suggested approaches for dealing with such pitfalls. This commentary also provides a thorough analysis that even a lawyer who is well-seasoned in commercial mortgage loan practice would find useful. At the end of this Book, in the Appendix section, I have included a full form Letter of Intent, Note, Carve Out Guaranty and Mortgage. Each of these Appendix documents includes all of the applicable provisions that have been included as an italicized excerpt in each applicable Section of this Book, so the reader can use them to better follow how these provisions fit into an actual document.

This Book can be read cover to cover, especially by someone new to the practice of commercial real estate mortgage transactions. I hope that this Book will provide useful insight both to lawyers handling their first mortgage transactions and to more seasoned mortgage lawyers looking for a useful reference source.

PART I

Letters of Intent

SECTION 1

What Is a Letter of Intent?

Explanation

A letter of intent (LOI) is often used by a lender in a commercial real estate transaction as a means to outline for a prospective borrower some of the major terms that a lender proposes be incorporated in the binding loan documentation that would be used in a potential future commercial real estate loan transaction with such borrower. By signing the letter of intent, the parties are confirming that they find these outlined terms to be notionally acceptable, and that the parties desire to proceed with the process of trying to close this prospective loan, but notwithstanding such confirmation, the parties are not yet ready to be obligated to close the loan, and the parties are acknowledging that the actual obligations relative to funding and receiving loan proceeds will only arise when and if the parties formally enter into a set of loan documents. The letter of intent is often the preliminary document that a lender and a prospective borrower will negotiate in connection with the closing of a commercial real estate loan. Usually the signing of the letter of intent is largely symbolic, and is undertaken to motivate each of the parties to proceed with providing all necessary information to each other and to start the process that will lead to the negotiation of all of the material terms to be contained in, and then to execute, the formal loan documents for the prospective loan. In each of the ensuing Sections of this Part I, I will now look at key terms (which will be shown in italicized type) that could be included in a letter of intent; these italicized key terms are also included, verbatim, in a sample form of letter of intent, which is attached at the end of this Book as Appendix A. Although the LOI creates its own defined terms, I have tried, as much as possible, to use the exact same defined terms as those used in the Mortgage set out in Appendix D (see Part IV Section 1 of this Book, entitled "Definitions").

A typical financing letter of intent includes a number of major terms that will be incorporated in greater detail in the loan documentation for a potential future commercial real estate loan transaction. These major terms are often presented in an outline form. With this approach, only a general description of these terms is actually provided in the letter of intent, with the understanding that the specific details, including the actual obligations, benefits, and restrictions relating to these terms, will be laid out in the final binding loan documentation, and it is only if and when such documentation is fully negotiated and executed that parties will become bound to perform these terms. The LOI that I have drafted is structured as a letter, which has an attached term sheet that lists in outline form several major terms that Lender would like to see incorporated in the final loan documents, should Lender and Borrower decide to proceed with closing the Loan. The cover-letter portion of the LOI includes a description of the goals of the parties, along with a clarification that the parties do not intend for the terms outlined in the term sheet to be binding on the parties yet, and that the LOI also includes several provisions that only apply prior to the parties' entering into the binding loan documents. (Please note that it is typically the case that letters of intent and/or the term sheet attached thereto will often contain a few provisions that the signing parties will want to become immediately binding on them, when such parties mutually execute and deliver the LOI).

As previously mentioned, it is usually the case that at the point when the parties are entering into a letter of intent, they are still at a very preliminary stage in their relationship, and they are not yet ready to firmly bind themselves into a contractual lending relationship with each other. Thus, as discussed later in this text, they take care that the letter of intent contain clear provisions and statements that by executing the LOI, they will not be creating any binding obligations with regard to having to fund, or to accept the proceeds, of a future prospective loan. Usually at the point of signing the LOI, one or both parties still need to look into various matters, and evaluate whether or not they are prepared to move forward and commit themselves to proceeding with a given pending transaction. In the case of Lender, at this stage it needs much more information about its collateral, Borrower, and any applicable guarantor, as Lender will not want to take the risk of funding the loan and entering into the final loan documentation until it believes it has received and evaluated all of this information, and that it is comfortable that it should make a legal commitment to undertake the risk of loaning money to Borrower. Likewise, at this stage Borrower is trying to confirm that the Lender's loan terms and conditions related to closing the loan are such that Borrower can proceed in pursuing the prospective loan transaction, and that it would be fruitful for the parties to continue to pursue efforts to try to close the loan transaction by entering into more formalistic and binding documentation. As a result, the letter of intent tends to cover only several big-picture matters of importance relating to a potential financing in general terms, because if the transaction should move forward, the parties will then have the opportunity to negotiate all of the specific details of the financing transaction in the later binding transactional documents that will be entered into at the time of the loan closing. In setting out each party's big-picture expectations with respect to a future possible loan transaction, a financing letter of intent will deal with some or all of the following terms:

a. The targeted loan amount;
b. The interest rate;
c. The maturity date of the loan;
d. The nature of any guaranty or guaranties, and the party (or the criteria of the financial attributes of a party) who will serve as guarantor;
e. A description of how the periodic debt service payments will amortize throughout the term of the loan; and
f. The target or outside date for the execution and delivery of the definitive loan documents and closing the loan.

Some of the advantages of the parties' employing a loan letter of intent are:

a. The parties can focus and agree in general terms on a few essential terms, which (i) will be covered in greater detail in one or more of the binding loan documents to be entered into at the loan closing and/or (ii) relate to what will be required during the closing process in order to achieve a loan closing;
b. By having the parties enter into this letter of intent, it encourages each of the parties to move forward with the prospective loan transaction, with regard to sharing information and negotiating in detail all of the terms needed for the final set of loan documents;
c. It most often is not intended to commit the parties to finalize the loan transaction; signing this letter of intent simply indicates that there is a mutual agreement on (i) some of the general major loan terms and (ii) the closing process, such that it is mutually worthwhile for the parties to move forward with negotiations and other activities geared toward closing the loan.

Some of the disadvantages of the parties employing a letter of intent are:

a. Borrower might use the signed letter of intent (i) as a means to pursue loan discussions with other lenders, and/or (ii) to improve the terms it can secure from another lender, in an effort to see if the other third-party lender would be willing to close the loan with Borrower on better terms than those outlined in the signed letter of intent. In the first instance, the fact that Lender has signed the letter of intent might allow Borrower to establish that it is in a position to be able to reach an agreement in principle with Lender (who has evidenced such agreement by signing the letter of intent), with the hope that by seeing that another lender had provided Borrower with a signed letter of intent, other prospective lenders would be more willing to enter into a letter of intent on equal or better terms than the terms set out in the signed letter of intent with Lender. Under this scenario, if the competitor lender were to offer Borrower better loan terms, then it is likely that Borrower would walk away from the

Lender who signed the initial letter of intent, and instead close its loan with the competitor lender who was prepared to proceed with the loan transaction on better terms.

b. Even if the letter of intent contains terms indicating that it is not a binding document, if it is executed and then later one of the parties chooses not to go forward with the loan transaction, the mere fact that the parties executed the letter of intent and then began a process to close the loan might act as a basis for a party to bring a lawsuit against the other party alleging that the parties had reached a binding agreement to close the prospective loan transaction, and that the execution of the letter of intent either (i) embodied a binding agreement, or (ii) indicated terms that were subsequently agreed upon by the parties in connection with their efforts to try to close the loan, with the result that the parties ended up with a binding agreement. In either instance, any effort by one of the parties to walk away from the loan transaction, by claiming that they had not entered into a binding obligation with regard to the funding of the prospective loan, could give rise to the other party claiming it was damaged by such action, and allow the aggrieved party to pursue litigation to recover such damages.

A well-written letter of intent will make it clear that most of the terms outlined in the letter of intent do not constitute a binding agreement on the parties, and that the only way the parties could find themselves having made a binding agreement on those terms with each other would be if they each entered into one or more future definitive documents which clearly recognize that those terms are in fact binding on the parties. However, it is usually the case that there are certain terms in the letter of intent which will be expressly confirmed as being binding on the parties immediately upon the signing of such letter of intent, including the following:

a. A confidentiality provision, which obligates the parties to keep confidential any confidential information passed on to either of the parties.
b. Any economic amounts which one or both parties are agreeing to expend prior to the execution by the parties of the applicable future binding loan documents.

Although the parties to a letter of intent will usually make an effort to specify that the terms outlined in the letter of intent relative to committing to having a lender/borrower relationship do not constitute a binding agreement on the parties, courts have sometimes made some surprising findings in litigations relating to letters of intent.

For starters, simply entitling a document "Letter of Intent" is generally not sufficient to convince a court that the obligations contained in the document with regard to having to fund, or to accept the proceeds, of a future prospective loan are intended not to be binding. This is particularly likely if the body of the document is silent on whether or not the terms contained in the letter related to the funding of the loan are intended to be binding, even if one of the parties claims it did not intend to enter into a binding contract. In such case, the court is likely to allow a legal proceeding to ensue, to see whether or not there is evidence outside of the letter of intent to prove whether or not both parties intended to create a binding contract.

In addition, even if the subject letter of intent clearly contains language specifying that the document does not give rise to binding obligations on the parties to fund, or to accept the proceeds; of a future prospective loan, courts sometimes will also look at the course of conduct of the parties following the execution of an otherwise non-binding letter of intent, and sometimes come to the conclusion that the nature of the parties' course of conduct following the execution of the a non-binding letter of intent permits the court to conclude that they entered into a binding contract as a result of such course of conduct. There apparently was a case in which, following the execution of the letter of intent, the parties held a press conference and indicated that a "deal had been made," with the result that the court found that they had entered into a binding contract as a result of what was said at the press conference. If the parties, in correspondence or in emails, appear to be acting as if they are bound by any of the obligations which the letter of intent had indicated were not binding, it is possible that such conduct could be taken as evidence that the relationship had evolved into one where the parties now were to proceed as bound contractual parties.

It is also true that merely indicating in the letter of intent that there are additional terms to be negotiated by the parties in the future is not sufficient evidence to prove that a letter of intent did not create a binding obligation between the parties, particularly if those terms to be negotiated are non-material. *See* A.J. Richard & Sons, Inc. v. Forest City Ratner Cos., LLC, 2019 N.Y. Slip Op. 30215(U) (Sup. Ct. Kings County Jan. 28, 2019). In that case, most of the terms related to a sale of real estate were outlined in the parties' letter of intent, and the court ruled that the letter of intent was "not rendered unenforceable simply because certain non-material terms [were] left for future negotiation" or because the letter of intent specified that the parties would in the future enter into a more formal agreement. The court felt that its holding in the case was supported by the fact that the letter of intent did not specify that in order for the parties to be legally bound, the parties would need to enter into such formal documentation in the future.

As indicated earlier, usually there are some terms set out in a loan letter of intent that are intended to be binding on the parties. With respect to those obligations, it is important for the letter of intent to be clear that the parties do intend to be legally bound by those obligations. In particular, if the lender is looking for the prospective borrower to be responsible for making any monetary payments (particularly pre-loan fees to be paid by the borrower) prior to the funding of the loan, or if parties envision that there are payments that one or more of the parties are to make regardless of whether or not the loan closes, then the letter of intent needs to specify that the parties do intend to require the applicable party or parties to be legally bound to make such payments when the letter of intent is executed.

SECTION 2

Letter of Intent Cover Letter

The following are the opening two paragraphs of a theoretical cover letter (for the form letter of intent I have drafted), with the complete text of the LOI (including the Term Sheet Exhibit) being set forth in Appendix A of this Book.

> *The undersigned is pleased to provide you with this letter of intent and to inform you that the undersigned may be interested in providing you or your affiliate ("**Borrower**") with a $____________ commercial real estate financing (the "**Loan**") for the captioned Project, which has as its address ________________. The undersigned currently contemplates that the Loan could have terms which are similar to those set out in the attached term sheet (the "**Term Sheet**"). Based on the information that you have provided to us to date, the undersigned, or an affiliate thereof (such entity, together with its assigns, agents and successors, "**Lender**") hereby expresses its interest in proceeding to obtain additional information and to conduct such investigations regarding the business, operations, condition (financial or otherwise) and prospects of Borrower's parent, the Guarantor (as defined in the Term Sheet) and Borrower and to seek credit approvals for the Loan. This letter, together with the Term Sheet (collectively, this "**LOI**") does not purport to summarize all the terms, conditions, representations, warranties and other provisions with respect to the transaction referred to herein and in the Term Sheet. Capitalized terms not otherwise defined herein have the meanings assigned thereto in the Term Sheet.*
>
> *The terms which the undersigned proposes in this LOI are based upon our present understanding of the Project, Borrower, and the Guarantor. As additional or changed facts and circumstances become known to us, we may impose additional terms and conditions. The terms and conditions which shall ultimately be required with respect to Lender's closing the Loan are not limited to terms set forth herein and in the Term Sheet attached hereto. Those matters which are not covered by or made clear in this LOI are subject to mutual agreement by each of the parties hereto.*

Explanation

Let us assume that Lender, when issuing this Letter of Intent ("LOI"), has had one or more meetings with Borrower and has received and evaluated a loan application and some preliminary due diligence information from Borrower, but has not received any formal approvals from Lender's loan committee to proceed with the Loan. By issuing the LOI and seeking to have Borrower sign it, a lender like this is typically sending a signal to Borrower that Lender would be receptive to having both parties begin making mutual efforts to start the process that could result in closing the Loan on the terms set out in the Term Sheet, based on the Lender's present understanding of the Project, Borrower, and Guarantor. However, at this point Lender likely needs much more due diligence information, and also loan committee approval (in addition, it will need to negotiate and reach mutual agreement with Borrower regarding all of the Loan terms, and conditions for funding the Loan) before Lender will be able to make a final decision about whether or not to proceed with the Loan, with the result that Lender does not want the LOI to create any impression with Borrower that Lender has obligated itself, or is now committed to closing the Loan. As a result of these concerns, Lender has taken care in these opening paragraphs of the LOI to couch its current position as possibly having an interest in making the Loan on terms similar to those outlined in the Term Sheet. In the second paragraph, Lender clarifies that if additional or changed facts and circumstances occur, then Lender reserves the right to impose additional or different terms and conditions.

The next paragraph of the LOI states:

> *You understand that Lender has not completed its due diligence of Borrower, the Guarantor, and/or the Project, and that the conduct, performance, and satisfactory conclusion of such due diligence is a condition of and essential to any commitment on the part of Lender to enter into a transaction on the terms described herein. This LOI is provided for discussion purposes only, and is being provided solely to indicate the undersigned's current interest in the proposed transaction described herein. This LOI is neither an express nor implied commitment by the undersigned to lend or otherwise provide or arrange any financing in connection with the transactions contemplated herein or purchase any loans or securities in connection with the transactions contemplated hereby or to provide or assist in providing any loans. Any such commitment by the undersigned will be subject to, among other things, (i) satisfactory transaction structure and documentation, (ii) satisfactory completion of due diligence, including third-party reports and business plan, (iii) requisite Lender internal approvals, and (iv) other standard conditions for transactions of this type.*

Explanation

Again, this paragraph also emphasizes that the LOI does not represent a commitment by Lender to make the Loan, and that if Lender were to make such a commitment in the future, it would do so based upon all of the following conditions being satisfied: (i) a satisfactory transaction structure and documentation; (ii) satisfactory completion of due diligence, including third-party reports and business plan; (iii) requisite Lender internal approvals; and (iv) other standard conditions for transactions of this type. Normally if and when a lender issues a commitment, it comes at a time when (a) it has completed a substantial amount of its due diligence review and (b) has received loan committee approval to proceed with funding the prospective loan. When and if it issues a commitment letter (which is different from a letter of intent, and usually occurs after the lender has received sufficient due diligence materials, and loan committee approval to issue the commitment letter), the lender will usually require its borrower to pay a commitment fee, and such issuance will be done with the understanding that the lender will thereafter be subject to a good faith obligation to endeavor to work with the borrower to negotiate the terms of the loan documents with a goal to fund the loan, subject to the satisfaction of all of the express conditions contained in the commitment letter for closing the loan.

The next paragraph of the LOI states:

> *The parties acknowledge that it is their intention that the ultimate closing of the Loan will be conditioned upon Lender determining that the following conditions have been fully satisfied:*
>
> (a) *Your making all payments required to be made prior to the closing of the Loan, as set forth in your Loan Application dated ______________ (the "Loan Application");*
>
> (b) *The preparation, execution, and delivery of legal documentation (the "Loan Documentation"; and the loan documents comprising said documentation are herein collectively referred to as the "Loan Documents") in form and substance satisfactory to Lender and its counsel incorporating substantially the terms and conditions outlined or referred to in this LOI;*
>
> (c) *The absence of any material adverse change in the financial condition, business, affairs, operations, or control of the special purpose entity which will serve as Borrower and the Guarantor, or their respective principals since the date of their respective financial statements most recently delivered to Lender;*
>
> (d) *The satisfaction of all conditions to be satisfied as a condition for the funding of the Loan as set forth in the Loan Documents;*
>
> (e) *The absence of a disruption or adverse change in financial, banking, or capital markets generally, or in the market for new issuances of commercial real estate loans in particular, in each case that, in the judgment of Lender, could reasonably be expected to impair the syndication or sale of the Loan; and*
>
> (f) *The absence of any material adverse change in any due diligence items relating to the Project, Borrower, and the Guarantor previously provided by you or any material adverse change in any new due diligence items hereafter reviewed by Lender or its counsel.*

Explanation

Again, care is taken here in the LOI to set out that it is the intention of the parties (and therefore not the obligation of the parties) that the foregoing specified conditions will have to be performed in order for the Loan to close. Note that condition (b) makes it only a condition that Lender and its counsel approve the terms of the Loan Documentation (this condition provides Lender with a lot of leeway, going forward, to elect not to proceed with the Loan). Borrower's counsel might well consider requesting that condition (b) should be modified so that Borrower and its counsel will also have the right to approve the terms of the Loan Documentation. Also note in condition (e) that if there is a significant disruption in any of the financial, banking, or capital markets generally, or in the market for new issuances of commercial real estate loans in particular, that such occurrence could be a reason for Lender not to proceed with closing the Loan. It is true that in 2021, which was in many respects a turbulent year, the credit markets remained relatively stable; but note over the past 25 years that there have been at least two major disruptions to the credit markets (in 1998 and 2007), and based on those experiences, some lenders are still leery about the need to make it clear to prospective borrowers that the particular lender will need to have the right to be excused from closing the loan if there is a major disruption in the U.S. credit markets. For large commercial real estate loans, the borrower's counsel might want there to be greater clarification with regard to what would constitute "a disruption or adverse change in financial, banking, or capital markets generally, or in the market for new issuances of commercial real estate loans in particular."

The next paragraph in the LOI provides:

> *By your acceptance of this LOI, you agree to be responsible for all costs and expenses incurred by Lender including, but not limited to, legal fees and disbursements, environmental, engineering, and appraisal costs and other expenses incurred by Lender in connection with the processing of the Loan and your payment to Lender of the fees and other expenses which are required under the Loan Application.*

Explanation

This paragraph, and the next 12 paragraphs that follow in the LOI, are all examples of provisions that one or both of the parties to the LOI might want to specify as being obligations on the applicable party immediately when the LOI is executed by both parties. This is an exception to the general rule that neither party (but most particularly Lender) wants the key terms of the LOI to be binding on the parties. In particular, Lender is looking for Borrower to be responsible for making any monetary payments (particularly pre-loan fees called for in the Loan Application to be paid by Borrower) prior to the funding of the Loan, and certainly Lender wants these items to be paid if owed regardless of whether or not the Loan closes.

The Loan Application referenced in this LOI is an application for a loan, which Borrower must complete, and which provides Lender with some preliminary information about (i) the type and amount of loan that Borrower is seeking, and (ii) some key background items concerning the Project, Borrower's sponsor signing the application, and possibly a prospective Guarantor.

SECTION 3

Letter of Intent Term Sheet

The Lender has attached, to the cover letter portion of the LOI, a Term Sheet as Exhibit A. This Term Sheet is a summary of several major terms Lender would like to see incorporated in the final loan documents, should Lender and Borrower eventually enter into these documents and as a result the execution of such future loan documents would cause both parties to be legally obligated to close the Loan. Similar to comparable provisions in the cover letter portion of the LOI, the Term Sheet in several places also specifies that neither Lender nor Borrower desire at this time to become, or to commence to become, legally bound to any of the terms specified in the Term Sheet. The first example of this approach is specified in the introductory paragraph of the Term Sheet, which contains the following language:

> *This Term Sheet is neither an expressed nor implied commitment by _______ or an affiliate of ____________ (such entity, together with its assigns, agents, and successors, "**Lender**") or any of its affiliates to provide any financing, to provide or purchase any loans or securities in connection with the transactions contemplated hereby or to provide or assist in providing any loans, which commitment, if any, shall only be as set forth in a separate commitment letter or other applicable type of agreement. This Term Sheet does not purport to summarize all the terms, conditions, representations, warranties, and/or other provisions with respect to the transactions referred to herein.*

Explanation

At the beginning of this introductory paragraph, there is a statement that Lender does not intend for any of the terms outlined in the Term Sheet to imply that this has created any commitment on the part of Lender to close the Loan with Borrower, and that the only way for such a commitment to become legally binding on Lender would be if Lender should in the future enter into a formal commitment letter with regard to closing such Loan. The introductory paragraph also specifies that the terms set out in the Term Sheet are not intended to be a comprehensive summary of all terms, conditions, representations, warranties, or other provisions with regard to the Loan. Both sentences are consistent with the premise that Lender, when issuing the LOI, does not want to give Borrower the argument that Lender has become legally obligated to make the Loan. Should Lender decide to make such a commitment, it would do so in a formal separate commitment letter (which would contain its own conditions and caveats); likewise, should Lender desire to become obligated to fund the Loan, it would do so in the formal loan documentation, which would have to be executed by Lender and Borrower in connection with the funding of the Loan in order for those obligations to become binding.

It would be very typical for the cover letter of the LOI or the Term Sheet to specify where the real estate is located. In addition, it would also be fairly typical for the cover letter of the LOI or the Term Sheet to specify Borrower's sponsor (i.e., the individual, entity, or group that will be in operational control of the ultimate borrowing entity). Each of these details is set out in the first two items outlined in the matrix of this Term Sheet, which is in Appendix A of this Book.

The next item in this Term Sheet is the identity of Borrower. Here the Term Sheet specifies its identification of Borrower as follows:

> ____________________ *("**Borrower**"). Borrower must be a single-purpose entity engaged in the rental and operation of the Project, which entity shall be governed by an operating agreement that complies with Lender's standard requirements for single-purpose entities.*

Explanation

In virtually all real estate mortgage loans made by sophisticated lenders, the applicable lender will require that the borrower that owns the real estate collateral for the Loan must be a single-purpose entity. This requirement will typically mandate that the borrower be an entity whose sole principal asset is the real estate, and that the borrower will not have incurred any financing indebtedness, other than the secured real estate loan with the lender. This requirement is important to lenders because, if in the future a borrower stops making debt service payments on its mortgage loan and elects to declare bankruptcy (in an effort to delay the lender's ability to foreclose its mortgage lien on a particular real estate property), the lender does not want any other competing creditors of its borrower (who have no relationship to the mortgaged property) to be involved in such a bankruptcy proceeding, particularly other lenders of borrower who have been granted mortgage security on unrelated real estate properties owned by its borrower. By requiring the borrower to be a single-purpose entity, the borrower will not be permitted to own other real estate properties, and therefore will not be in a position to receive mortgage loans from other lenders which in turn are secured by real estate collateral that involves unrelated real estate. As indicated in this definition, the lender will typically have a number of representations and covenants that it will require be included in the borrower's operating agreement (and also in the mortgage), which will provide comfort for the lender that the borrower at the time of closing the Loan, and throughout the term of the Loan, will be a single-purpose entity.

A number of the next few items in the Term Sheet deal with key business terms relating to the Loan, such as loan amount, interest rate, default interest rate, and maturity date. Although these items are by and large business items (which will have to be acceptable to Borrower), I would like to comment on a few of them.

The Term Sheet calls for the Loan Amount to be "the lesser of *(i) $____________ and (ii) 70% loan-to-value of the Project based on an as-complete appraisal ordered by Lender*." This means that although Lender is prepared to consider a certain amount for the proposed Loan, in the Term Sheet Lender is telling Borrower that this capped amount of the Loan will have to be lower if the Lender's appraisal for the Project ends up being less than 142.85% of such capped Loan Amount. Commercial lenders frequently use loan-to-value ratios as a means of assuring that they will have sufficient collateral for their mortgage loan. By utilizing this requirement in connection with fixing the amount of the loan, a lender is able to provide assurance to its loan committee that, at the time of the mortgage loan closing, the mortgage loan collateral is likely to be worth more than the loan amount (so that if during the loan term there is a Borrower default and Borrower is unable to pay off the mortgage loan at that time, then the Lender could foreclose on, and sell, the Loan's mortgage collateral, and have some realistic hope that the foreclosure price will be sufficient to cover the outstanding amount of the loan then owing to the mortgage lender). Thus, in analyzing this Term Sheet, Borrower and its counsel need to be satisfied that the market value of the Project prior to the loan closing is likely to reflect a high enough amount, when the Project is appraised, to meet this loan-to-value ratio requirement. Alternatively, if Borrower thinks that another lender might be willing to allow for a higher loan-to-value ratio requirement (such as a 75% loan-to-value ratio), then Borrower might consider pushing Lender to change this requirement in the Term Sheet to a more favorable loan-to-value ratio, more in line with the loan-to-value ratio requirement that Borrower believes to be available if Borrower were to seek a mortgage loan from other lenders.

The Term Sheet sets the rate of interest for the Loan as follows:

> *One Month LIBOR plus a spread of 500bps (calculated for the actual number of days elapsed on the basis of a 365-day year), payable monthly in arrears, provided that LIBOR shall never be calculated at less than 0.00%.*

Explanation

This interest rate for the Loan will be based on LIBOR. The initials LIBOR stand for London Interbank Offer Rate. LIBOR rates reflect the interest rates that United Kingdom banking institutions charge other banking and financial institutions for loans that have a short-term maturity. There are LIBOR rates for various short-term maturities, which are published on a daily basis. Most commercial real estate loans in the United States utilize LIBOR as a base benchmark for calculating interest rates, and most often 1-month maturities are the reference rate selected for U.S. commercial real estate loans. The LIBOR rate selected in the Term Sheet will change each month, and will vary to reflect general changes in short-term capital markets' interest rates. For this Loan, the interest rate that will be charged to Borrower will be the sum of (a) whatever the LIBOR rate then is in effect on the specified day of the applicable month (throughout the term of the Loan) when the LIBOR rate gets reset, plus (b) 5% (Note: 500 bps reflects 500 multiplied by a single basis point (which always equals .01%)). LIBOR is discussed in much greater detail later in this Book (see Part IV Section 6 of this Book, entitled "Variable Interest Rates in Mortgage Loans"). This provision in the Term Sheet also clarifies that the interest rate for this Loan can never be less than 5%, even if the applicable LIBOR rate should drop below zero. Through this use of the LIBOR rate, which will go up and down throughout the term of the Loan, Lender protects itself from the risk of interest rates rising. It is the strong preference of lenders in the United States funding commercial real estate loans to select a variable interest rate (such as LIBOR) because if a lender had selected a fixed interest rate, and if interest rates set for other new comparable loans were to rise prior to the maturity of the fixed-rate loan, the value of such fixed-rate loan as booked on the lender's balance sheet would fall; in general, if the value of a lender's loans as shown on a lender's balance sheet should fall, this could give rise to regulatory issues. The concept of interest rate variable loans is discussed in greater detail later on (see Part IV Section 6 of this Book, entitled "Variable Interest Rates in Mortgage Loans").

The Term Sheet then requires Borrower to purchase an interest rate swap or a cap. Either of these instruments will allow Borrower to protect itself should its interest rate rise due to the LIBOR rate benchmark component used to calculate the Loan's interest rate, as discussed in the immediately preceding paragraph. The nature of the interest rate swap instrument is discussed later on (see Part IV Section 6 of this Book, entitled "Variable Interest Rates in Mortgage Loans").

A little later on in the Term Sheet are the following terms for the payment of "breakage costs" should Borrower elect to prepay all or any portion of the Loan:

> *The Loan may be prepaid partially or in full, subject to Borrower also paying all "breakage costs" associated with Borrower making a prepayment of any portion of the Loan. Such "breakage costs" shall approximate the costs that are payable to any counterparty pursuant to the applicable interest rate swap or a cap or cap agreement as a result of such prepayment of principal by Borrower.*

Explanation

It is quite typical for a lender making a commercial real estate loan to require the borrower to pay some type of prepayment fee should the loan be fully or partially prepaid prior to maturity. Such a fee helps to compensate lender for a loss in interest rate income, particularly if interest rates in general have risen following the closing of the Loan. In this situation, because the interest rate is calculated using the variable reference rate LIBOR, should all or part of the Loan be prepaid, Lender does not need to be directly paid such a fee to protect it from any fluctuation in interest rates, because the use of the LIBOR benchmark will cause the interest rate at the time of prepayment to approximate then-current market interest rates. However, because contemporaneous with closing the Loan, Borrower must purchase an interest rate swap or a cap—which will entail having Borrower, along with Lender and a counterparty (who could be the lender or another bank or financial institution) enter into an instrument providing for such interest rate swap or a cap—the terms of the applicable interest rate swap or cap will include a requirement that should the underlying commercial real estate loan be fully or partially prepaid prior to maturity, then at the time of prepayment Borrower would be obligated to pay these "breakage costs" referenced in the Term Sheet. This payment of "breakage costs" is designed to compensate the counterparty under the applicable instrument for losing part or all of the benefits it could have otherwise achieved if no such prepayment had occurred, and if the then applicable LIBOR reference rate were to have remained unchanged throughout the balance of the term of such underlying commercial real estate loan. When it is calculated, this payment of "breakage costs" can often turn out to be an enormous amount of money, particularly if such applicable LIBOR reference rate had significantly increased from the rate that was in existence at the time that the payment of "breakage costs" closed. The nature of "breakage costs" will be discussed later on (see Part IV Section 6 of this Book, entitled "Variable Interest Rates in Mortgage Loans").

Later on in the Term Sheet there is a requirement that there be a Guarantor and that the Guarantor enter into the following guaranties and indemnities:

- Non-Recourse Carve Out Guaranty;
- Environmental Indemnity; and
- Carry Guaranty (including interest on the Loan, property taxes, insurance, and other carry costs associated with the Project).

Typically commercial real estate mortgage loans are only funded to a newly formed single-purpose bankruptcy remote borrower entity, and the loan documents for a given mortgage loan will then typically specify that the loan's lender will not be afforded any collection remedies that would allow the lender to enforce collection against any of the borrower's assets which are not specifically covered in the granting clauses contained in one or more of the loan documents entered into by such borrower to secure the applicable mortgage loan. This type of loan structure is considered to be non-recourse to the borrower. As we will learn later, the borrower in this case will have granted security liens that will attach to all of its assets associated with the commercial real estate that it owns, together with related personalty. Lenders favor this ownership structure relative to the commercial real estate to be mortgaged in a commercial real estate loan, because (a) the security liens for these loans, which will encumber the borrower's real estate related assets, will be senior to all other creditors of the borrower, and (b) the loan documents for such commercial real estate mortgage loans will prohibit the borrower from granting any other security interests that encumber the borrower's assets, should the borrower subsequently go bankrupt. With this structure the applicable lender believes that it is maximizing the possibility that (a) it will be the sole creditor holding a lien on the borrower's assets securing such Lender's financing throughout the term of the applicable loan, and (b) should the borrower subsequently become subject to a bankruptcy proceeding, then there will be no other competing secured creditors who will also be participating in such an ensuing bankruptcy proceeding. In this way, Lender hopes to be able to achieve its best opportunity to be granted a relief-from-stay order from the bankruptcy from the applicable bankruptcy judge, which would then allow the lender to proceed with its ability to foreclose on the borrower's assets, free and clear of the bankruptcy proceeding.

Despite the fact that these commercial real estate loans are usually non-recourse relative to any of the borrower's assets that have not been specified in at least one of the granting clauses given to secure the applicable loan, lenders will require, as part of the loan documentation, that various guaranties and/or indemnities will be given by one or more entities or individuals other than the borrower, each of whom will have a substantive balance sheet at the time the loan is closed. The three guaranties/indemnities referenced in the Term Sheet (a Carve Out Guaranty, an Environmental Indemnity, and a Carry Guaranty) are typically required in most commercial real estate loans (and in the case of a commercial real estate construction loan, it would be quite common for the lender to require a Completion Guaranty, but this Book will not deal with the particulars of that type of instrument).

With regard to the Carry Guaranty, such a guaranty will be primarily focused on having its guarantor provide a guarantee of some or all of the principal evidenced by the applicable note; in many cases this instrument will also have such guarantee cover all periodic payments of regular interest that are due and payable pursuant to the applicable note. Often when such a guaranty only relates to payments of principal and interest, that instrument is referred to as a "payment guaranty." Payment guaranties often also cover, in addition to interest and principal evidenced by the note, other payments owed to the lender, including default interest and late charges. In some cases, the lender may agree to place a limit on the aggregate amount of principal that the guarantor is covering under the applicable payment guaranty. When this type of guaranty also has the guarantor's guarantee obligations include covering the payment of operating costs and expenses incurred throughout the term of the loan with regard to the maintenance and operation of the real estate (including payment of real estate taxes and insurance premiums), that type of guaranty is commonly referred to as a "carry guaranty."

The Environmental Indemnity, which will be given by Borrower and Guarantor, will cover, among other things: (a) Borrower's obligations under the Loan Documents to remediate any release of hazardous materials on any portion of the Property, and (b) reimbursing Lender or any monetary expenditures that Lender may be required to make as a result of any release of hazardous materials on any portion of the Property, including any remediation expenditures incurred by Lender.

The Carve Out Guaranty, which will also be given by the Guarantor, will provide for coverage of, among other things: (a) any liabilities incurred by Lender as a result of Borrower committing various so-called "bad acts," including fraud, theft, and intentionally causing damage to the Improvements (as defined in the Mortgage), and (b) Borrower voluntarily going bankrupt, or transferring all or a material portion of the Property. The Carve Out Guaranty is discussed in detail later (see Part III of this Book, entitled "Carve Out Guaranty").

The final section of the Term Sheet sets out various conditions precedent to the closing of the Loan, which are the following:

(i) *Payment of the Origination Fee provided for in the Loan Application;*
(ii) *Receipt and satisfactory review of environmental assessment, appraisal, and physical needs assessment;*
(iii) *Receipt and approval of current title reports, covenants, restrictions, encumbrances, title insurance policies and surveys for the Project;*
(iv) *Satisfactory review of evidence that the zoning applicable to the Property permits the construction, development and operation of the Project as contemplated hereunder;*
(v) *Satisfactory review of judgment, lien, litigation, UCC, bankruptcy and related searches of Borrower, any members and/or principals thereof and each Guarantor;*
(vi) *Satisfactory review of all organizational documents of Borrower, the constituent members thereof and each Guarantor;*
(vii) *Evidence that Borrower, the constituent members thereof and each Guarantor is in compliance with applicable governmental rules and regulations (e.g., PATRIOT Act);*
(viii) *Receipt and satisfactory review of liability, builder's risk and property insurance for Borrower and the Property;*
(ix) *Satisfactory review of any management agreement, and the subordination of same to Lender;*
(x) *Receipt and satisfactory review of all governmental approvals, including, but not limited to, the certificate of occupancy for the Project;*
(xi) *Receipt and satisfactory review of any and all regulatory or other agreements pertaining to the Project with any governmental or quasi-governmental agency, including review and approval of deed restrictions or any ground leases;*
(xii) *Receipt and approval by Lender of financial information pertaining to each Guarantor, which may include, but not be limited to, financial statements and state and federal income tax returns (if applicable) and financing documents;*
(xiii) *Receipt and satisfactory review of executed leases with current tenants in the Project;*
(xiv) *Receipt and approval at least 10 business days prior to the Closing Date of all information required from Borrower and each Guarantor under "know-your-customer" and anti-money laundering rules and regulations, including the PATRIOT Act;*

(xv) *Satisfaction of any additional Property-related due diligence or documents required by Lender;*

(xvi) *Receipt of approval of the Loan from all applicable committees of Lender; and*

(xvii) *Lender satisfaction with due diligence review of the Sponsor, Borrower and the Project, including any third-party reports, business plan and budget.*

Predominantly, this list of conditions precedent includes a variety of due diligence items, which Lender and its counsel will need to examine in order for Lender to formulate an opinion as to whether it can recommend to its loan committee that Lender should fund this particular Loan. Though I will not discuss each of these particular conditions precedent, I will highlight several of them below.

The initial condition precedent in this section of the Term Sheet is that Borrower must pay the Origination Fee, which will be provided for in the Loan Application (which, as indicated earlier, is an application for the Loan which must be submitted to Lender by Borrower). The requirement that Borrower must pay this "Origination Fee" is quite typical in the lending industry. For a number of lenders who make commercial loans, particularly those who will then sell their commercial loans into the secondary market immediately following the closing of such loans (which is especially common for commercial real estate loans that are to be bundled and sold as collateral for, or pooled together and will provide the payment source for, rated securities that will be issued to investors as part of a securitization), this Origination Fee will be the primary source of compensation that the originating lender will receive in connection with funding the commercial real estate loan. By selling off the commercial real estate loans into the secondary market shortly after they are originated, the originating lender eliminates the possibility of suffering losses from any risks associated with holding the commercial real estate loan for an extended period of time (which risks include (a) the occurrence of a future default by the borrower, and (b) any changes in value of the commercial real estate loan as a result of instability in the capital markets or any shifts in the interest rate environment during the term of the commercial real estate loan). Often lenders who are funding commercial real estate loans will require the borrower to provide a refundable payment at the time a letter of intent is executed in connection with the possible future funding of a given real estate loan (with the lender usually reserving the right to deduct certain third-party due diligence costs, such as attorneys' fees, appraisal fees, and payments owed to environmental engineers or firms, should the loan not close). In addition, it is often the case that at the time a lender is prepared to lock in an interest rate for the commercial real estate loan prior to the loan's closing, such lender will commemorate that decision by entering into a commitment letter with the borrower, and one of the terms of such commitment letter is usually a requirement that the borrower must then pay a so-called commitment fee in connection with lender's agreement to fund the loan utilizing such interest rate, as set forth in such a commitment letter (with the effect that, should the commercial real estate loan eventually be funded, then at that time the borrower will pay any balance owed on account of the applicable Origination Fee, which will usually be set forth in such commitment letter or in the loan application).

The next conditions precedent set out in this section of the Term Sheet calls for the delivery and satisfactory review of the following:

a. an environmental assessment;
b. an appraisal; and
c. a physical needs assessment.

Each of these items is usually a key due diligence item for a lender making a commercial real estate loan.

Per the Term Sheet, Lender will require that an environmental assessment of the Property be performed by a duly licensed environmental engineer or environmental engineering firm, because if a material release of a hazardous substance on any part of the Property shall have occurred, or if there is a material risk that such a release could occur, then Borrower, who will be owner of the contaminated real estate, will be required under applicable environmental laws and regulations to implement a comprehensive remediation program, which could be very costly. In particular, Lender will likely have the understandable concern that if Borrower should default under the applicable Loan Documents, and if, as a result Lender directly or indirectly takes title to the real estate (by foreclosure or deed in lieu of foreclosure), then if the Property is contaminated because such a release of a hazardous substance has occurred, it will be Lender's direct or indirect responsibility to implement such remediation, which could be very costly (and until such remediation is completed, the need to complete such remediation would have a highly negative impact on Lender's ability to sell the Property to a third party). This initial environmental assessment will usually be a Phase I environmental assessment, which generally involves an environmental engineering firm preparing this assessment through an examination and analysis of historical and public state environmental records, maps, and photos of the Property, as well as such firm doing a physical inspection of the Property, and possibly meeting with occupants and neighbors of the Property. This investigation will not involve taking any core dirt samples from the Property. Because it will be Borrower's responsibility to pay for this environmental assessment, it would be a good idea for counsel for Borrower, when negotiating the terms of this provision in the Term Sheet, either to specify the actual identity of the environmental engineering firm (to be engaged by Borrower) that will conduct the initial environmental assessment, or else specify that Borrower will have the right to select and engage the environmental engineering firm which will be producing this Phase I assessment (subject to Lender's approval (not to be unreasonably withheld or delayed)). In some cases, Lender may resist allowing Borrower to select the environmental engineering firm, and ultimately Lender will have ample leverage on a point like this to require that it should be Lender who selects the environmental engineering firm. In any event, if at all possible, prior to allowing Lender to see the initial Phase I environmental assessment report, Borrower and its counsel should review this report, and also have it reviewed by an environmental expert, and then try to make sure that the report gives the most favorable assessment possible with regard to environmental issues. In particular, Borrower and its counsel should attempt to avoid having the environmental engineering firm suggest in its Phase I report that there should be a Phase II assessment (which usually occurs when the environmental engineering firm determines, after conducting its Phase I investigation, that there is a reasonable risk that there has been a release of a hazardous substance which is affecting all or a portion of the Property). Should the Phase I report contain a recommendation that there be a Phase II assessment, then Lender will almost always insist that such a Phase II assessment be performed, and that assessment will usually involve the environmental engineering firm taking core samples of dirt from various suspected locations where a release of a hazardous substance might have occurred. After taking these samples, the environmental engineering firm will then do an analysis of such core samples of dirt to determine whether or not a release of hazardous substances has occurred on the Property, and the extent of any such release. If it is determined that such a release has occurred, then usually, under applicable state laws, such a release must be reported to applicable state environmental authorities. Such a release and reporting will then usually trigger the need for Borrower to prepare and submit a comprehensive remediation plan to the applicable state environmental authorities. Once that plan is approved by such authorities, Borrower will then be obligated to implement such plan and fully remediate the applicable contamination. The preparation of this plan and then its implementation can be very costly.

As indicated earlier, the Term Sheet also calls for an appraisal of the Property's fair market value which is satisfactory to Lender. In this instance, Lender will insist that it be the party that selects the appraiser who will be preparing this appraisal (although it will be Borrower who will be paying for the cost of the appraisal). The final fair market value determination of the Property is a critical due diligence item for Lender. Typically a key factor in determining the amount of the Loan which Lender will be prepared to fund will be the so-called loan-to-value ratio ("LTV"). The LTV is basically a percentage, based on a fraction where the numerator is the loan amount and the denominator is the appraised fair market value of the Property (except in the case where the financing is occurring at the time when the Property is being acquired by Borrower, and in that case the denominator will be the lesser of (a) such appraised fair market value or (b) the Property's acquisition cost). Usually at the time Lender's loan committee is determining whether or not to proceed with funding, the Loan will have a maximum LTV percentage for the commercial real estate asset class that the particular property falls into (e.g., Lender might be prepared to provide commercial real estate loans with a 75% LTV on a bank building that will be fully leased by a creditworthy bank, but in the case of a commercial real estate asset class of higher risk, such as a casino, Lender's maximum commercial real estate loan amount might be capped at a 60% LTV). In negotiating the Term Sheet with regard to this type of provision, Borrower's counsel might want to consider requiring Lender to allow Borrower to have a copy of the appraisal (which would be understandable, particularly since Borrower will be paying for the preparation of this appraisal). Another consideration for Borrower is that it might be able to obtain a lower interest rate for the Loan if is prepared to accept a lower LTV (and this could be appealing to Lender, since a lower LTV will translate to lower risk from the Lender's perspective, because this will result in a lower initial loan amount and therefore, in the event of a Borrower default, there is a better opportunity that a foreclosure sale could result in the full repayment of the then-outstanding principal balance owed to Lender).

Also as indicated earlier, the Term Sheet calls for Lender to receive a "physical needs assessment." This type of report, which is also sometimes called a "property condition report," will be prepared to inform Lender about whether or not there is an immediate concern about the need for repair of any element of the Improvements or any of the equipment supporting the Improvements, and whether Borrower's maintenance program for the Improvements is adequate. This type of report is usually prepared by an engineer or an engineering firm (selected by Lender) that is unaffiliated with either Borrower or Lender. This report will provide Lender with an analysis of the physical condition of the Improvements and the major equipment components servicing the Improvements, and will also provide Lender with the author's opinion on any immediate and future anticipated repairs or need for any maintenance activities with respect to the Improvements and any such equipment which are being recommended by the author. Usually the author providing this report will do (a) a thorough inspection of the Improvements and the related material building systems supporting the Improvements, (b) an examination of the plans for the Improvements, (c) interviews with the parties currently responsible for the maintenance of the Improvements, and (d) such other research and document review of the public records maintained by the various state and local authorities having jurisdiction over the Improvements, as the author thinks are appropriate for this type of study. After receiving this type of report, Lender will look to see whether there is a need for any immediate repairs, whether there is a likely possibility of the need for repairs during the term of the Loan, and whether or not there should be some adjustments in the maintenance activities relative to the Improvements that Borrower should undertake so as to adequately maintain the Improvements and any such equipment. Frequently if Lender determines that any such repairs are or will be needed, Lender will specify in the Loan Documents that Borrower must establish a cash reserve account, which will be pledged to Lender and then will be available to pay for, or reimburse Borrower for, the cost of any such repairs.

The Term Sheet also calls for Borrower delivering to Lender, for its review, the organizational documents of Borrower and each Guarantor. Lender and its counsel will review these documents so that Lender can be assured that Borrower and Guarantor have the adequate authority to execute and deliver the applicable Loan Documents, in line with the applicable entity purposes set out therein, and that the parties executing these documents on behalf of these entities likewise have the appropriate authorizations specified in such organizational documents. Lender and its counsel will want to be sure that the organizational documents for Borrower include provisions confirming that Borrower is a "special purpose" entity. [Note: this bankruptcy remote requirement is summarized in Part IV Section 21 of this Book, entitled "Borrower Bankruptcy Remoteness; Separateness Covenants."] These provisions will limit Borrower's activities so that such activities will solely relate to the ownership and operation of the Mortgaged Property (and therefore will not permit Borrower to acquire any other unrelated assets, nor participate in any other unrelated businesses). In addition, Lender will want to be certain that there are appropriate covenants which will prevent Borrower from undertaking any activities that would result in Borrower having to be consolidated with any constituent members of Borrower, should any such members be subject to a bankruptcy (see Part IV Section 21 of this Book, entitled "Borrower Bankruptcy Remoteness; Separateness Covenants").

PART II

Note

SECTION 1

Key Note Provisions

Explanation

Historically there is evidence that something approximating a promissory note existed and was used in ancient China. This view is supported by an old book written by Marco Polo, which indicated that he introduced to Europe the concept of utilizing Chinese notes. See generally Marco Polo, *The Travels of Marco Polo, a Venetian, in the Thirteenth Century: Being a Description, by That Early Traveller, of Remarkable Places and Things, in the Eastern Parts of the World* (1818). In any event, it appears that in Europe, these early notes were primarily given to wealthy travelers at the time they were about to depart on a long journey: each such traveler received the note in exchange for the traveler's turning over their valuables to the maker of the note (the purpose of this exchange was to decrease the risk that a given traveler might otherwise lose these valuables as a result of some adverse event occurring during the course of the traveler's journey). Then, when the traveler who held such a note reached the traveler's destination, the traveler would redeem the note with an employee or agent of the maker of the note (who resided at or near such destination point), and who would give the traveler tangible assets having value comparable to the value of the assets that the traveler had originally turned over to the maker of the note.

In today's modern world, a *promissory note* is a written instrument executed by the borrower which specifies that the borrower promises, among other things, to (a) repay to the holder of the note the full amount of the principal indebtedness advanced to the borrower by the note holder, and (b) pay such holder interest which accrues on such unpaid principal indebtedness that is outstanding during the term of the note, which payments are required to be paid on or before a date certain (which is typically referred to as the note's "maturity date"). For some loan transactions, such unpaid principal indebtedness must be paid by the borrower at any time when the borrower receives a payment demand from the holder of the note. Thus, a note is very similar to an IOU (which is usually just a promise by a party borrowing the funds to repay the borrowed funds to the holder of the borrower's IOU). In addition, it is quite common for promissory notes to provide for, among other things: (a) the timing for the periodic debt service payments that will be payable throughout the term of the applicable note (which periodic payments are usually either monthly or quarterly), (b) lender protections relative to state usury law requirements, and (c) a designation of which state laws will govern the obligations set forth in the applicable note.

Attached at end of this Book as Appendix B is a form Promissory Note (the "Note"). This Note is secured by a mortgage (the "Mortgage"). At its beginning, the Note clearly specifies (both prior to, and in, the first paragraph) the specific principal amount of the loan evidenced by the Note, which in this case is being fully advanced at the time the Note is being executed and delivered to the note holder. Sometimes the principal amount of a loan (to be evidenced by a promissory note) will be advanced in stages to Borrower (as hereinafter defined). For certain loans, such advances will be subject to the satisfaction of a number of preconditions; an example of this type of loan is a construction loan, where at different times a portion of the loan is advanced to Borrower periodically (usually on a monthly basis) so as to allow the parties who are directly building the improvements, or providing either related support services or building supplies for the construction of particular improvements, to be paid out of these advances for their work, services, and/or supplies, as the case may be. For other types of loans, funds will be advanced by the note holder simply upon the demand of Borrower; an example of this type of loan is the so-called "line of credit loan." The first paragraph of the Note also defines the term "Borrower," and specifies that interest will accrue on the unpaid principal balance of the loan (the "Loan") evidenced by the Note at the "Interest Rate" (which is defined later in the Note).

We can see in the Note that part of the definition of "Note" is: *"this Note ..., as the same may be amended, supplemented, extended, restated, or otherwise modified, from time to time."* This approach—of including within a definition of each of the transactional loan documents that is referenced within a given loan document language which clarifies that the capitalized term for such document will include not only the original document but also any and all changes to that document that could arise in the future—is good practice and should in almost all cases be implemented by lawyers when providing such definitions. The benefit of using this approach is that should a given loan document actually be modified in the future, the author(s) of such modification will not need to be concerned about whether or not they will remember to make a corresponding change to the definition of that loan document to reflect such modification, because the author of the original definition of such capitalized term previously had been careful enough to have included in such original definition the concept that the defined term would automatically encompass all future modifications when that author drafted the original definition. The effect is that when such document is actually modified in the future, then each time such capitalized term is used within a given loan document, such term will automatically reflect that loan document as modified (rather than just reflecting the original unmodified loan document).

Section 3 of the Note calls for the payment of principal and interest by Borrower. In Section 3 (a) of the Note, the term "Interest Rate" is defined as being *"either (i) Variable Rate or (ii) LIBOR Based Rate on the outstanding principal balance which is evidenced by this Note from time to time, as selected by Borrower pursuant to Section 6.1 (a) of the Security Agreement . . . ."* Accordingly, pursuant to the terms of Section 3 (a) of the Note, Borrower is given the right to select as the Interest Rate (which will be used to calculate periodic monthly interest payments to be made by Borrower throughout the term of the Loan) either (a) the Variable Rate (as defined in the Mortgage) or (b) the LIBOR Based Rate (as defined in the Mortgage), with the particulars of the selection process being set forth in Section 6.1 (a) of the Mortgage. Later on in this Book, there is an extensive discussion about the use of variable rates in promissory notes (see Part IV Section 6 of this Book, entitled "Variable Interest Rates in Mortgage Loans"). Oddly, both Variable Rate and LIBOR Based Rate are variable interest rates, in that each rate has the possibility of fluctuating upward or downward, from time to time, so as to reflect an interest rate on a particular given date that corresponds to a benchmark interest rate or index. As discussed in Part IV Section 6 of this Book, variable interest rates will fluctuate over a given period of time, and this trait marks a strong contrast to what is known as a "fixed interest rate," which is an interest rate that is established at the time of the execution of a given note and remains in effect throughout the term of such note. This is an important difference, as many institutional lenders have learned. In the 1970s and early 1980s, mortgage loan fixed interest rates on newly issued mortgage notes rose in lockstep with significant increases in annual inflation rates that occurred during this period. Many institutional lenders found that they were being put in severe financial jeopardy due to this rise in prevailing interest rates, for two important reasons:

> First, institutional lenders found that the notional fair market value of these fixed-rate loans on their books decreased, because the prevailing interest rates on newly issued mortgage notes increased. The reason for this loss in value of the fixed-rate loans they were holding in their loan portfolios is that, in a rising interest rate environment, should the holder of a fixed-rate loan have a need to sell that loan into the secondary market, the fixed-rate loan's interest rate will tend to be lower than the prevailing interest rate relative to the fixed interest rates for comparable new loans, which will mean that the price that a third-party buyer would be willing to pay for such an aging fixed-rate loan (with a lower fixed interest rate) will be less than the outstanding principal amount then evidenced by its note. It should also be kept in mind that during the 1970s and early 1980s, the ability of an institutional lender to sell any of its commercial loans into the secondary market was severely hampered in general because the securitization industry that then existed was still only a very small market, with the result that at this time it was difficult for institutional lenders to find secondary market buyers for fixed-rate commercial real estate loans.

Second, during the 1970s many of these institutional lenders, particularly savings and loans, depended on the money that was deposited into savings accounts opened with such lenders, because such deposits constituted a key source of their capital. However, during this time, in order to attract depositors, the institutional lenders had to offer depositors competitive interest rates on these deposit accounts. As a result, because the prevailing interest rates during this period continued to rise, the interest rate that a given savings and loan had to offer to depositors on their deposit savings accounts also needed to rise (so that the institutional lender could retain the applicable deposit). However, in many cases the interest rate that a savings and loan had to pay on its deposit accounts in order to retain its depositors began to exceed the interest income the savings and loan was receiving on many of the aging fixed interest rate commercial loans it was holding. This mismatch created a dilemma for many of the savings and loans.

As a result of these lessons, many institutional lenders began to use variable interest rates more often in connection with any new commercial real estate loans that they originated, so that if a given institutional lender elected to hold onto the commercial real estate loans after they were originated, the lender would not then be taking the risk that the prevailing interest rate would rise during the term of the loan. With a variable interest rate commercial real estate loan, when the prevailing interest rate increases, the interest rate on the variable interest rate loan would also rise, thereby maintaining the fair market value of the mortgage loans that these institutional lenders held in their portfolios.

Section 6.4 (f) of the Mortgage defines "LIBOR Based Rate" as follows:

> ***LIBOR Based Rate.*** *The term "LIBOR Based Rate" means the per annum rate of interest equal to the applicable LIBOR Rate, plus 225 basis points.*

This definition makes it clear that the "LIBOR Based Rate" is keyed to the LIBOR Rate (defined in Section 6.4 (d) of the Mortgage), which is a rate that is determined each day and is published by Reuters (generally, it is a rate that is being quoted by certain London banks to customers who are depositing U.S. dollars in such banks). Because this rate will fluctuate upward and downward over time, the LIBOR Rate and the LIBOR Based Rate are each a variable interest rate.

The alternative interest rate that Borrower could select pursuant to Section 3 (a) of the Note is the Variable Rate. The Variable Rate is defined in Section 6.4 (j) of the Mortgage as follows:

> ***Variable Rate.*** *The term "Variable Rate" means "a per annum rate equal at all times to the greater of (a) the Prime Rate or (b) the LIBOR Rate, plus __ basis points with changes therein to be effective simultaneously with any change in the Prime Rate without notice or demand of any kind."*

Clearly, one component of the Variable Rate is the aggregate of the LIBOR Rate plus a constant amount (which currently is a blank in the form of the Note), which usually will be anywhere from 1.5% to 4%, depending on how creditworthy Lender views the Mortgaged Property to be. That is, as Lender assesses the Mortgaged Property to be more creditworthy, Lender will allow this additional constant to be a lower percentage spread over the LIBOR Rate, because if Lender views the Mortgaged Property to be more creditworthy, then Lender will perceive less risk of the likelihood of default on the Loan by Borrower, with the result that Lender can be comfortable with using a lower constant to calculate the Variable Rate. The other component of the Variable Rate is the Prime Rate, which is defined in the Mortgage as *"the per annum rate of interest so designated from time to time by the Lender as its prime rate."* The prime interest rate for most institutional lenders is the interest rate that such lender will charge its most creditworthy customers, from time to time. The prime interest rate is reset periodically by each lender who utilizes a prime interest rate, with the result that a prime rate is a variable interest rate, because this rate can move up or move down over time. Usually the lender's prime interest rate is considerably higher than a short-term LIBOR Based Rate. Today, the most common measure of the prime rate is *The Wall Street Journal* prime rate, which surveys banks on their prime rates, and publishes its rate on a daily basis.

Section 3 (d) of the Note contains a provision that attempts to protect Lender from violating any state or federal usury law. It sets forth the following:

> (d) *Notwithstanding any provision to the contrary in this Note, in no event shall the Interest Rate charged on the outstanding principal balance which is evidenced by this Note from time to time exceed the maximum rate of interest permitted under applicable state and/or federal usury law. Any payment of interest that would be deemed unlawful under applicable law for any reason shall be deemed received on account of, and will automatically be applied to reduce, the principal sum outstanding and any other sums (other than interest) due and payable to Lender under this Note, and the provisions hereof shall be deemed amended to provide for the highest rate of interest permitted under applicable law.*

This Section 3 (d) in effect specifies that the Interest Rate will not be allowed to rise to a rate that would exceed the maximum rate of interest permitted under any applicable state and/or federal usury law. Thus, this provision places a hard cap on the Interest Rate. As previously mentioned, if we only looked at the definition of "Interest Rate," it is clear that it is a variable rate, which could theoretically have no limit regarding how high that rate could rise; thus, the hard cap placed on the Interest Rate in Section 3 (d) to prevent any usury law violations is particularly relevant. Violations of the usury rate law in certain instances can result not only in civil, but also in criminal, penalties, with the result that most promissory notes utilized by institutional lenders will contain this type of anti-usury law provision (which will protect a lender from inadvertently violating an applicable usury law). The particular state usury law that will typically be deemed applicable, should a court be asked to determine whether or not a usury law has been violated, will be the usury law in effect in the applicable state or commonwealth whose law is deemed to govern the Note. Section 16 of the Note specifies that it will be the laws of the jurisdiction in which the Land is located (which in this Note is defined as being the

"Property Jurisdiction") that will govern this particular Note. It is good practice for Lender's counsel (particularly if Lender's counsel is not licensed to practice law in the state or commonwealth whose laws will govern the Note) to have this type of provision reviewed by local counsel who is licensed to practice in the particular state or commonwealth whose laws will be governing the terms of the Note, and it is often the case that such local counsel can suggest helpful customary language that will make this provision more likely to be enforceable in that particular state or commonwealth should the provision become the subject of any future litigation. Usury laws do vary significantly from jurisdiction to jurisdiction. In general, it is also good practice to have such local counsel review the other provisions set forth in the Note, as well as any other provisions set out in any of the other Loan Documents that are to be governed by the jurisdiction in which such local counsel is licensed.

Section 3 (e) of the Note specifies that the debt service payments which Borrower will be paying pursuant to the Note will be paid on a monthly basis until the Maturity Date. Monthly payments of principal are to be made pursuant to a schedule that is attached to the Note. Requiring some type of periodic payments of principal is quite common, and by requiring such periodic partial prepayments of principal Lender can be sure that some or all of the initial amount of the Loan will be paid back through these mandatory installment payments. Section 3 (e) (iii) of the Note specifies that if Borrower fails to make a monthly payment of interest when due, the amount of such defaulted interest payment shall accrue interest at the Default Rate (which in the Note is 16% per annum). In today's world, a default rate of 16% per annum is somewhat higher than what is typically called for in commercial real estate loan documentation. As a result, counsel for Borrower probably should consider trying to negotiate with Lender's counsel for a somewhat lower Default Rate (something in the range of between 10% to 12% would be more typical today).

Section 8 of the Note sets out an extensive exculpation provision limiting Lender's ability to enforce the Note against personal assets of Borrower and certain related parties, to the extent such assets are encumbered by any of the lien granted by Borrower in any of the other Loan Documents, including the Mortgage. Part IV Section 28 of this Book provides an extensive discussion regarding the rationale for Lender allowing Borrower and these related parties to be permitted to have this type of exculpation, and Section 8 of the Note is essentially a restatement of Section 28 of the Mortgage with regard to these exculpation provisions.

PART III

Carve Out Guaranty

SECTION 1

Background; Bad-Boy Acts

As mentioned earlier, Lender is requiring that Borrower be a single-purpose bankruptcy remote entity whose sole assets are the Mortgaged Property (and Lender will be granted a lien that encumbers all of these assets). Because Borrower will only be permitted to own the assets comprising the Mortgaged Property, Borrower's net worth will be limited to these assets, and in general, Borrower will have limited liquidity in the form of cash or other liquid assets throughout the term of the Loan. Thus, if Borrower should face some major event (such as a major casualty or a litigation judgment that requires the expenditure of large sums of money), Borrower will have to look to other sources of liquidity to address these needs, such as insurance proceeds, payments from tenants occupying space in the Improvements, or Borrower capital calls that are paid to Borrower from some or all of the individuals or entities who can hold equity in Borrower. It is therefore understandable that Lender would require some other individuals or entities to provide guaranties or indemnities in favor of Lender, so that Lender will have the assurance that it will be able to look to, and can call on, such guarantor or guarantors (who have a strong balance sheet and significant assets and liquidity independent of Borrower's assets) to provide the cash necessary to pay for these types of costs and/or liabilities should they occur during the term of the Loan.

Earlier in this Book, I indicated that typically Lender will require that there be a Guarantor, who will be a creditworthy entity having a significant net worth and liquidity. This Guarantor will enter into the following guaranties and indemnities in connection with the Loan:

- Non-Recourse Carve Out Guaranty;
- Environmental Indemnity; and
- Carry Guaranty (including interest on the Loan, property taxes, insurance, and other carry costs associated with the Project).

In this Section I focus only on the Carve Out Guaranty, which is frequently referred to as the "bad-boy" guaranty. The Carve Out Guaranty will cover, among other things: (a) any liabilities incurred by Lender as a result of Borrower committing various so-called "bad-boy acts," including fraud, theft, and intentionally causing damage to the Improvements; and (b) Borrower voluntarily going bankrupt, or transferring all or a material portion of the Property. This type of "bad-boy" guaranty is very important to Lender, because these bad-boy acts are usually acts that Borrower can voluntarily prevent from happening and are of a particularly odious nature; thus, Lender will feel more comfortable entering into the loan transaction when it knows that a related party with significant and liquid assets is at risk of becoming personally liable to Lender should Borrower commit any of these bad boy acts. In addition, the existence of the Carve Out Guaranty discourages a Borrower, when an Event of Default occurs (and therefore is subject to the remedy of Lender foreclosing and selling the Mortgaged Property) from trying to siphon off cash from the Mortgaged Property prior to a foreclosure sale, or taking a radical defensive action such as declaring bankruptcy in an effort to fend off the foreclosure sale.

Since the early 1990s, commercial real estate lenders have typically required the execution and delivery of a guaranty that will compensate the lender if any "bad-boy" acts specified in such guaranty occur. The following are examples of such "bad-boy" acts (each of which are referenced in Sections 1.1 and 1.2 of the form Guaranty Agreement (the "**Carve Out Guaranty**") that appears in this Book as Appendix C):

(a) the failure of Borrower to account for security deposits, if any, or any other similar payment in lieu of a security deposit collected from any tenant demising space in the Improvements from time to time;

(b) any material misrepresentation made by Guarantor, Borrower, and/or the holders of beneficial or ownership interests in Borrower, in each case to Lender in connection with the financing evidenced by the Note, or as otherwise set forth in this Guaranty, the Note, the Mortgage, and/or the other Loan Documents;

(c) any attempt by Borrower to divert, misappropriate, or misapply, or otherwise cause to be diverted, misappropriated, or intentionally misapplied, any amounts payable by Borrower to Lender or which are to be paid by Borrower to Lender as set forth in any of the Loan Documents or are intended for the benefit of Lender;

(d) any misappropriation or misapplication of insurance proceeds or condemnation awards payable to or obtained by Borrower relating to the Mortgaged Property or Borrower's failure to maintain the Policies or the insurance coverages required by the Mortgage at all times in full force and effect;

(e) any environmental matter(s) affecting the Mortgaged Property which is introduced or caused by Borrower or any beneficial owner of Borrower, or which is otherwise covered by the Environmental Indemnity;

(f) any waste of, or damage to, the Mortgaged Property caused by the willful misconduct or wanton acts or omissions of Borrower or its agents, officers, Affiliates, directors, equity owners, or employees;
(g) any willful or grossly negligent material violation by Borrower of any law, ordinance, rule, or regulation applicable to Borrower or the Mortgaged Property;
(h) any failure of Borrower to obtain Lender's prior written consent to any subordinate financing or other voluntary lien caused by Borrower or its agents encumbering the Mortgaged Property as required by the Security Instrument;
(i) any failure on the part of Borrower, or of any Person acting by, through, or under Borrower, to pay charges for labor or materials that results in material liens on any portion of any of Borrower's interest in the Mortgaged Property;
(j) any misappropriation of funds in connection with the funding of the loan proceeds evidenced by the Note or otherwise in connection with the Indebtedness (as defined in the Security Instrument);
(k) so long as an Event of Default exists, any failure of Borrower to deliver 100% of all net income (i.e., for any applicable period of time, all revenues directly or indirectly derived from the Mortgaged Property, net of all accrued operating expenses relating to the Mortgaged Property) received by Borrower, in accordance with the terms of the Security Instrument and/or any of the other Loan Documents;
(l) any failure of Borrower to comply with separateness and bankruptcy-remoteness covenants in this Security Instrument and/or in the other Loan Documents;
(m) any material fraud committed by Borrower;
(n) any failure of Borrower to obtain Lender's prior written consent to any Transfer;
(o) the adjudication of Borrower or Guarantor as bankrupt as a result of:
    (i) any direct or indirect voluntary Insolvency Activity (as defined in the Security Instrument) caused or approved by Borrower or Guarantor and/or the holders of beneficial or ownership interests in Borrower or Guarantor or actions taken by any officer, director, or Person employed by Borrower or Guarantor (each a "**Restricted Entity**"); and
    (ii) any direct or indirect involuntary Insolvency Activity caused or approved by any other Person, if either (x) such Person was acting at the direction or request of, or in collusion or by agreement with a Restricted Entity, or (y) if such Person caused any such Insolvency Activity to occur at the direction or request of, or in collusion or by agreement with, a Restricted Person; and
(p) any adjudication of Borrower or Guarantor as bankrupt as a result of any formal filing in a legal proceeding by a Person who is not a Restricted Person, if Borrower or Guarantor, as the case may be,

fails to oppose in court such filing in good faith, or Borrower, Guarantor, or any Restricted Entity of either of them otherwise consents to, acquiesces in, agrees with, files court papers in any way supportive of, or joins in such filing.

As indicated in Part IV Section 28 of this Book, these "bad-boy" acts are typically embodied in the carve out provisions in the exculpation provisions of the Note, Mortgage, and/or Loan Agreement. [Note: Typical carve out provisions are set out in Part IV Section 28 of this Book.]

The liability of the Guarantor for carve out guaranty "bad-boy" acts usually falls into one of two categories. The first type of liability that is usually set out in a Carve Out Guaranty (which I will refer to as "**Damage Liability**") is one that covers the damages which Lender incurs as a result of the breach of any of the applicable "bad-boy" acts by Borrower. The second type of liability (which I will refer to as "**Springing Liability**"), sometimes referred to as "Springing Recourse," amounts to Guarantor becoming fully liable for the entire unpaid Indebtedness should any of the relevant acts occur.

In Section 1.1 of the attached Carve Out Guaranty, the Guarantor would incur Damage Liability with respect to those "bad-boy" acts referenced in the nonrecourse provisions of the Note, Mortgage, and/or Loan Agreement that involve misdeeds committed by Borrower, Guarantor, or an affiliate of either of them, and typically would include such matters as: employee theft, misapplication of rents, following the occurrence of an Event of Default, fraud, gross negligence, willful misconduct, misapplication of insurance proceeds or condemnation awards, failure to discharge mechanic's liens, waste, misrepresentations, failure to pay real estate taxes or insurance premiums, environmental discharges caused by Borrower or related parties, Borrower failure to comply with separateness and bankruptcy-remoteness covenants set out in the Loan Documents, not obtaining Lender consent for any subordinate financing, and/or breaches of representations and/or warranties contained in the Loan Documents. Recently some lenders have also attempted to provide for Springing Recourse if Borrower commits a criminal act or fails to permit Lender to inspect the Mortgaged Property and/or fails to provide required financial reports.

It would also be typical in an initial draft of a carve out guaranty for the Guarantor to incur Springing Liability if Borrower or Guarantor committed any voluntary bankruptcy act, or colluded with others to commence a bankruptcy case against Borrower, or to permit a transfer of all or any part of the Mortgaged Property or equity in, or indirectly relating to, Borrower in violation of the Loan Documents, or to breach any of the separateness covenants contained in the Loan Documents. [Note: these separateness covenants were discussed in Part IV Section 21 of this Book.] More recently there has been a trend for sophisticated commercial real estate lenders to require Springing Recourse if (i) substantive consolidation occurs as to Borrower, (ii) any of Borrower, Guarantor, or any of their affiliates initiates an action that would prevent or obstruct Lender's exercise of its remedies under any of the Loan Documents, (iii) Borrower commits a criminal act or fails to permit Lender to inspect the Mortgaged Property and/or fails to provide required financial reports, and/or (iv) any of Borrower, Guarantor, or any of their affiliates contests or opposes Lender's actions or motions to obtain relief from the automatic stay in Borrower's bankruptcy or other similar relief efforts attempted by Lender in such bankruptcy. In addition, some lenders have also attempted to provide for Springing Recourse if Borrower commits a criminal act or fails to permit lender to inspect the Mortgaged Property and/or fails to provide required financial reports (but when a lender attempts to do this, it is always good practice for Borrower's counsel to try to negotiate with such lender to have these types of activities only trigger Damage Liability).

It has now become clear that the courts will allow Lender to enforce against Guarantor, under a carve out guaranty, each of those provisions that would trigger either Damage Liability or Springing Liability, which in the latter case could result in Guarantor having to pay off the full liability then owed by Borrower to Lender under the Loan Documents. In *Heller Financial, Inc. v. Lee*, 2002 WL 1888591 (N.D. Ill., Aug. 16, 2002), the court held that the lender could collect for damages relating to a mechanic's lien that had been filed against the mortgaged property, which was in line with a corresponding carve out provision set out in the nonrecourse section of the note. The court found that such enforcement did not constitute a penalty, because the section of the note dealing with this nonrecourse carve out provided the lender with a means to recover its unpaid debt, which correlated to its actual damages (i.e., the amount of the unpaid indebtedness) and therefore such enforcement was not related to recovering liquidated damages. *See generally* Andrew H. Levy, *"Bad Boy" Guarantees—Courts Are Enforcing Non-Recourse Carve-Outs*, N.Y.L.J., July 30, 2003. In *Westheimer Mall, LLC v. Okun*, 2008 WL 3891257 (S.D.N.Y., Aug. 21, 2008), the court, in granting summary judgment in favor of the lender, held that the guarantors under a carve out guaranty, given in connection with a real estate mortgage loan made by two real estate borrowers who owned a mall in Houston, Texas, and who violated the plain language set out in such a guaranty (when each borrower filed for a voluntary bankruptcy), were subject to the full liability of their Springing Liability under such guaranty.

These cases, as well as many others that follow these holdings, make it clear that courts will allow lenders to enforce carve out provisions in accordance with the terms, even if it results in the defendant having to pay off the balance of the loan, where applicable. Therefore, it is imperative that each of these provisions be scrutinized carefully before they are entered into, and where possible be limited in scope. In addition, to avoid unwanted liability, all mortgage borrower related parties, most particularly guarantors under carve out guaranties, need to be careful that actions not be taken which could trigger this liability, and not to take this risk exposure lightly.

In *Blue Hills Office Park LLC v. J.P. Morgan Chase Bank*, 477 F. Supp. 2d 366 (D. Mass. 2007), the court faced an issue where several guarantors had executed a carve out guaranty in connection with a $33,149,000.00 nonrecourse loan secured by a mortgage. The borrowers had received a $2 million settlement in connection with a zoning dispute involving a neighboring property, and the settlement proceeds were wired to a trust account held by the law firm representing the borrowers. The borrowers did not notify their lender of such transfer of the settlement proceeds, and subsequently they defaulted on their real estate loan. One of the carve out provisions in the loan documents, which, if violated, could expose the guarantors to Springing Liability, was if the borrowers made an unauthorized transfer of mortgaged property. Ultimately, the court held that the settlement proceeds were a part of the mortgaged property that was subject to the lien of the mortgage held by the lender, and that the transfer of this property to the trust account constituted a plain violation of the transfer provisions, with the effect that the court gave full effect to the Springing Liability provisions of the carve out guaranty against the guarantors. Consequently, the guarantors were held to be fully liable for the entire indebtedness, which sum significantly exceeded the $2 million in settlement proceeds that had been transferred.

In *Wells Fargo Bank, N.A., v. Cherryland Mall Limited Partnership and David Schostak*, 2011 WL 6785393 (Mich. App.), and *51382 Gratiot Avenue Holdings, LLC v. Chesterfield Development Company, LLC and John Damico v. Morgan Stanley Mortgage Capital Holdings, LLC*, 2012 U.S. Dist. LEXIS 11617, each court held that the guarantor was fully liable for the Springing Liability under the applicable carve out guaranty (which meant that each guarantor was fully liable for the mortgage indebtedness). In each case this liability arose due to the failure of each borrower to remain solvent and to pay its debts as they became due (specifically, the failure to timely pay the required mortgage payment), which was one of these separateness covenants of each borrower contained in the applicable loan documents. Each of these courts found that because each borrower had defaulted in making its periodic debt service payment with respect to its mortgage loan, such failure was clear evidence that each borrower was "insolvent" and that they had failed to pay their respective debts when due in violation of the specific applicable separateness covenant in each of the applicable loan documents which required that borrower pay its debts when due and remain solvent throughout the term of the applicable mortgage loan. Although subsequently the Michigan legislature changed Michigan law to prevent Michigan courts from following these holdings, it has become common for counsel representing borrowers in commercial real estate loans to be sure that these separateness covenants on insolvency only mandate that borrower pay its liabilities and debts from available net cash flow arising from the mortgaged property, and specifically excusing the parent or parents of the mortgage borrower from having to contribute additional capital in order to keep the mortgage borrower solvent at all times, so as to comply with this separateness covenant.

Borrower's counsel, after reviewing the carve out guaranty for Borrower's commercial real estate loan, will want to carefully focus on the potential liabilities that Guarantor will be facing under the provisions dealing with (i) Springing Liability, and (ii) Damage Liability. Clearly, the greater risk to Guarantor will be its liability under the Springing Liability provisions, as this exposes Guarantor to the risk of having to pay off the entire indebtedness. As we saw in the *Blue Hills* case, even though the lender in that case suffered what was arguably approximately $2 million in damages (the amount of settlement proceeds that was diverted into a separate trust fund account by the borrowers in that case), the court gave full effect to the Springing Liability provisions contained in the *Blue Hills* carve out guaranty, and awarded summary judgment against guarantors under such guaranty in the full amount of the indebtedness, which amount was considerably higher than such damages.

One approach Borrower's counsel can take, when dealing with Springing Liability provisions, is to attempt to negotiate with Lender's counsel and convert those provisions into Damage Liability provisions, such that Lender can recover from Guarantor only to the extent that Lender incurs damages in connection with the violation of such provisions. For example, if Lender includes failure to pay real estate taxes, failure to remove mechanic's liens in a timely manner, or breach of representations or warranties as Springing Liability provisions, then Borrower's counsel can argue that these provisions should be changed to be treated as Damage Liability provisions. It is also worthwhile, if Lender is insisting on categorizing the commission of fraud as giving rise to Springing Liability, for Borrower's counsel to argue that a breach of this covenant should only give rise to Damage Liability. Nevertheless, it is quite unlikely that Lender will change the treatment of a voluntary commencement of a bankruptcy action or a breach of the material transfer provisions as anything but a Springing Liability provision.

With regard to a breach of the separateness covenants (which are discussed in Part IV Section 21 of this Book), if Lender wants to insist that a breach of such covenants gives rise to full Springing Liability, Borrower's counsel should limit such an outcome to only those situations in which such a breach results in a court determining that a substantive consolidation occurred in connection with a bankruptcy case involving the parent or an affiliate of Borrower.

With regard to a breach of the other "bad-boy" covenants that typically give rise to just Damage Liability, Borrower's counsel should attempt to limit those covenants to only situations in which the acts giving rise to such a breach were either intentional or willful. In the case where a breach of representations and/or warranties gives rise to Damage Liability, Borrower's counsel should resist having all representations and/or warranties set forth in the Loan Documents be susceptible to triggering such liability. Instead, Borrower's counsel should go through all of the Loan Documents and attempt to restrict the representations and/or warranties that could trigger such liability to a defined set of material representations and warranties, which in fact if breached sustain a minimum dollar amount of liability incurred by Lender. In addition, Borrower's counsel should strive to make it clear that Guarantor should have a minimum cure period in order to eradicate any such breach as being a trigger for liability under the carve out guaranty. If that fails, Borrower's counsel should attempt to make each applicable representation and/or warranty only triggered to the extent that at the time of the making of such representation and/or warranty Borrower had knowledge that the facts being represented or warrantied were false. Another approach would be to try to limit breaches of representations and/or warranties to only those situations where such breach was intentional.

SECTION 2

Other Comments on the Carve Out Guaranty

The first paragraph of the form Carve Out Guaranty (which appears as Appendix C at the end of this Book) contemplates that Guarantor could be one or more parties. It is often the case that Lender will require that Guarantor be more than a single individual or entity. This is not unusual, particularly if the direct or indirect parent entity or entities of Borrower include at least two or more individuals/entities who each (a) have a substantial net worth and (b) directly or indirectly own an equity interest in Borrower. It is certainly in Lender's interest in such a situation to have each such creditworthy individual or entity serve in the role of a Guarantor, since obviously their combined net worth will be higher than if only one of them served as the sole Guarantor. When there are multiple entities who are to serve as Guarantor, usually Lender will want each of them to be individually fully liable for the guaranty liabilities set out in the applicable guaranty. To achieve this result, Lender will usually require that each Guarantor be jointly and severally liable for such guaranty liabilities. If there is more than a single Guarantor for the applicable guaranty, this will generally result in placing the burden on each Guarantor of being solely responsible for paying up to 100% of the monetary obligations owed to Lender under such guaranty, regardless of the fact that there are multiple Guarantors. This approach allows Lender to have the option to sue, and/or collect from, only one of the Guarantors for the entire monetary obligation that is owed to Lender under the applicable guaranty, or to sue multiple Guarantors in an effort to try to collect from them what is owed to Lender. By having a joint and several guaranty, Lender then is indifferent as to whether the Guarantors elect to come up with a contractual arrangement that they will share in the burden of paying any monetary obligations owed to Lender, should any such monetary obligations become due and payable to Lender, because such a sharing arrangement is generally not binding on Lender.

However, it is often the case that when there are multiple Guarantors who are parties to a given guaranty, one or more of such Guarantors would prefer not to have their individual liabilities under the applicable guaranty be joint and several. It is also frequently the case that the amount of the net worth of each of the Guarantors will not be similar, and/or that the respective direct or indirect percentage equity interests in Borrower owned by such Guarantors will likewise not be similar. It is also the case that the risk profile appetite of each of the Guarantors with respect to embracing the potential personal liability under the applicable guaranty may not be similar, and one of the potential Guarantors might initially be unwilling to enter into the applicable guaranty if such Guarantor is forced to accept unrestricted joint and several liability relative to guaranty liabilities set out in such guaranty, which would then theoretically expose such Guarantor to the risk of having to pay to Lender 100% of the monetary obligations that might become due and payable under the applicable guaranty. Accordingly, it is a threshold question for Borrower's counsel to find out if each Guarantor is willing to accept the burden of being jointly and severally liable for the guaranty liabilities set out in such guaranty. Should this be an issue, particularly if it is one that will have to be addressed in the applicable guaranty by limiting in any way Lender's ability to pursue each Guarantor separately for 100% of the monetary obligations that might become due and payable under the applicable guaranty, then it is usually a good idea for Borrower's counsel to raise this issue as soon as possible with the Guarantors, because restricting Lender's ability to pursue such full recourse against each Guarantor on a separate basis might be a deal breaker for Lender (e.g., a good time to raise this issue is when a letter of intent for the Loan is being negotiated [see Part I of this Book, entitled "Letters of Intent"]). Here are a few approaches that could be used to deal with this multiple-guarantor situation, and have results that lower the risk that a single Guarantor might have to pay 100% of the monetary obligations owed to Lender under an applicable guaranty:

(a) An attempt can be made to convince Lender to have only a single Guarantor be party to the guaranty. If this approach is accepted by Lender, then only one individual/entity will be exposed to the guaranty liability recourse that Lender could pursue should any monetary obligations arise under the guaranty. This approach might be acceptable to Lender if only one of the potential Guarantors has a substantial net worth, or if a particular potential Guarantor has such an enormous net worth that Lender is comfortable with having only that Guarantor sign on to the applicable guaranty. Thus, in either of these scenarios, it is possible that Lender might conclude that there is no need to have multiple Guarantors in this transaction, because Lender will have adequate credit backing the Guaranty and therefore would not be losing much by foregoing having multiple Guarantors as parties to the applicable guaranty. If Lender can be convinced to have only a single Guarantor as a party to the applicable guaranty, such Guarantor (who is now taking on the full risk exposure posed by such guaranty) would be wise to enter into a side cost-sharing arrangement (which would be an agreement that Lender would not be a party to) with any other creditworthy entity (not related to such Guarantor) who directly or indirectly holds an equity interest in Borrower and who was not required to join in the guaranty. Such a side agreement would typically provide for the non-Guarantor to reimburse the single Guarantor, should such Guarantor have to make any payments to Lender pursuant to such guaranty. As an example of how this cost-sharing agreement could operate, hypothetically this side agreement might require that the non-Guarantor would reimburse the Guarantor for 20% of the aggregate payments made by Guarantor to Lender pursuant to such guaranty in the future (e.g., if Guarantor makes an aggregate of $100,000 of such payments to Lender pursuant to such guaranty, then pursuant to the side cost-sharing agreement, the non-Guarantor would have to make a $20,000 reimbursement to the Guarantor).

(b) Another approach would be to attempt to have the applicable guaranty impose a cap on the aggregate amount that Lender could collect from one or more of the Guarantors under such guaranty, should any of the monetary obligations under such guaranty become due and payable. This could be done by Lender adding a simple sentence to the guaranty indicating that there would be an aggregate maximum cap amount which Lender agrees it could collect from the applicable Guarantor getting the benefit of this limitation, notwithstanding any of the other provisions contained in that Guaranty to the contrary. Again, this approach might be acceptable to Lender if only one of the potential guarantors has a substantial net worth (in which case Lender would probably want to clarify in the guaranty that each Guarantor's liability under the guaranty is joint and several, and that notwithstanding the cap on liability that Lender is affording to one of the Guarantors, Lender could elect to collect up to 100% of any liability for monetary obligations arising under the guaranty solely from the Guarantor with the substantial net worth). If Lender provided this accommodation in the guaranty, it is likely that the Guarantor with the substantial net worth would again want the other Guarantors to enter into a side cost-sharing arrangement (similar to what was described in the immediately preceding clause (a)), but in this case it is likely that the Guarantor who is getting the benefit of the maximum cap amount on monetary liability under the guaranty would want to have that cap limitation on the amount that such Guarantor would be liable for paying under the guaranty, such side agreement, or under both documents. To accomplish this, the side cost-sharing arrangement would provide for a corresponding maximum cap amount that the applicable Guarantor could be called on to contribute as reimbursement under this agreement (and the Guarantor getting the benefit of this cap would also want to have the side agreement provide that it would receive, as a credit toward achieving such maximum cap amount, all actual payments made by such Guarantor to Lender under the applicable guaranty).

(c) Another approach similar to the one described in the immediately preceding clause (c) would be to attempt to limit the aggregate amount that Lender could collect from each of the Guarantors, splitting the 100% Guarantor obligation owed to Lender under the applicable guaranty, such that each Guarantor is allocated a fixed percentage of the amount owed from time to time by each Guarantor to Lender (with the aggregate of such percentage allocations totaling 100%). This approach might be acceptable to Lender in recognition that each Guarantor only directly or indirectly owns a fixed percentage interest in Borrower. Usually this approach will only be acceptable to Lender if (i) among the Guarantors, one or several of the Guarantors own a small percentage interest in Borrower (such as, say, 5%); (ii) each of the Guarantors with the small percentage interest in Borrower has a large enough net worth to make it reasonable for Lender to conclude that this Guarantor will have adequate capital to cover its obligations under the applicable guaranty, should monetary obligations under such guaranty become due and payable; and (iii) the Guarantor(s) with the large percentage interest in Borrower each has a large enough net worth to make it reasonable for Lender to conclude that each such Guarantor will have adequate capital to cover its obligations under the applicable guaranty, should monetary obligations under such guaranty become due and payable. If Lender provided this accommodation in the guaranty, it is likely that one or more of the Guarantors would again want all the Guarantors to enter into a side cost-sharing arrangement (similar to what was described in the preceding clause (a)).

(d) Another approach that is sometimes used would be to have the applicable guaranty start off as being a comprehensive joint and several guaranty relative to each Guarantor's liability thereunder, but then also have such guaranty provide that if some specified milestone is achieved, then such achievement would result in having the guaranty automatically implement one or more of the limitations on the liability of one or more of the Guarantors. This approach is sometimes used in a construction loan situation, when the particular guaranty provides for guarantied obligations to initially encompass the full payment and performance of Borrower with respect to all of Borrower's obligations under the Loan Documents. In such a case, such guaranty might specify that upon the achievement of a milestone—such as (i) the substantial completion of the construction of the project being built by Borrower, or (ii) the achievement of both such substantial completion and the successful lease-up of the project so as to meet some specified standard (such as having not less than 90% of the project's leasable area be under lease at some specified standard of an average annual rent per square foot)—then automatically there would be a cap on the aggregate amount that

Lender could collect from the Guarantors under the applicable guaranty should any of the monetary obligations under such guaranty become due and payable. (For example, such guaranty could provide that when the applicable project was substantially completed and a certificate of occupancy was issued, then the maximum aggregate liability of a Guarantor under the applicable guaranty for the payment of monetary obligations would be capped at a particular specified dollar amount). Notwithstanding the foregoing, this "burn-off" approach is virtually never used in a carve out guaranty.

Should Lender require that there be multiple Guarantors, and that each Guarantor be jointly and severally liable for the guaranty liabilities under an applicable guaranty, it is quite common for one or more of the Guarantors to require that all of the Guarantors enter into a side cost-sharing arrangement (similar to what was described in the preceding clause (a)), which side agreement would provide for some type of mutually agreeable allocation of the scope of the Guarantors' respective responsibilities for paying their monetary obligations. Often such allocation of these monetary obligations under such guaranty are based on the respective fixed percentage interest in Borrower that each Guarantor directly or indirectly owns.

As previously mentioned (see Section I of Part III of this Book, entitled "Carve Out Guaranty"), Section 1.1 of the Carve Out Guaranty (which appears as Appendix C at the end of this Book) specifies those "bad-boy" acts which, should they occur, due to an action by Borrower and/or certain related parties, would cause Guarantor to incur Damage Liability. Here are the "bad-boy" acts of Borrower listed in said Section 1.1 of the attached Carve Out Guaranty that comprise "bad-boy" acts which, should they occur, would give rise to such Damage Liability:

1.1.1. *the failure of Borrower to account for security deposits, if any, or any other similar payment in lieu of a security deposit collected from any tenant demising space in the Improvements* [as defined in the Security Instrument], *from time to time;*

1.1.2. *a material misrepresentation made by Guarantor, Borrower, and/or the holders of beneficial or ownership interests in Borrower, in each case to Lender in connection with the financing evidenced by the Note, or as otherwise set forth in this Guaranty, the Note, the Security Instrument, and/or the other Loan Documents;*

1.1.3. *any attempt by Borrower to divert, misappropriate, or misapply, or otherwise cause to be diverted, misappropriated, or intentionally misapplied, any amounts payable by Borrower to Lender or which are to be paid by Borrower to Lender as set forth in any of the Loan Documents or are intended for the benefit of Lender;*

1.1.4. *the misappropriation or misapplication of insurance proceeds or condemnation awards payable to or obtained by Borrower relating to the Mortgaged Property or Borrower's failure to maintain the insurance policies or the insurance coverages required by the Security Instrument at all times in full force and effect;*

1.1.5. *any environmental matter(s) affecting the Mortgaged Property which is introduced or caused by Borrower or any beneficial owner of Borrower, or which is otherwise covered by the Environmental Indemnity (as defined in Exhibit B);*

1.1.6. *any waste of, or damage to, the Mortgaged Property caused by the willful misconduct or wanton acts or omissions of Borrower or its agents, officers, Affiliates, directors, equity owners, or employees;*

1.1.7. *any willful or grossly negligent material violation by Borrower of any law, ordinance, rule, or regulation applicable to Borrower or the Mortgaged Property;*

1.1.8. *any failure of Borrower to obtain Lender's prior written consent to any subordinate financing or other voluntary lien caused by Borrower or its agents encumbering the Mortgaged Property as required by the Security Instrument;*

1.1.9. *any failure on the part of Borrower, or of any Person acting by, through, or under Borrower [other than any tenant under any applicable Lease], to pay charges for labor or materials that results in material liens on any portion of any of Borrower's interest in the Mortgaged Property [(unless such liens are being contested in accordance with the terms of Section 5.1(c) of the Loan Agreement)];*

1.1.10. *any misappropriation of funds by Borrower in connection with the funding of the loan proceeds evidenced by the Note or otherwise in connection the Indebtedness (as defined in the Security Instrument;*

1.1.11. *so long as an Event of Default exists, the failure of Borrower to deliver 100% of all net income (i.e., for any applicable period of time, all revenues directly or indirectly derived from the Mortgaged Property, net of all accrued operating expenses relating to the Mortgaged Property) received by Borrower, in accordance with the terms of the Security Instrument and/or any of the other Loan Documents;*

1.1.12. *any failure of Borrower to comply with separateness and bankruptcy-remoteness covenants in this Security Instrument and/or in the other Loan Documents; and*

1.1.13. *any material fraud committed by Borrower.*

There are several common themes relating to these "bad-boy" acts that give rise to such Damage Liability. The first is that each relates to acts committed only by Borrower or individuals or entities related to Borrower. This is important because arguably Borrower can only exercise control over Borrower or individuals or entities related to Borrower, and here Lender is using Damage Liability as a strong incentive to force Borrower to use restraint in taking any steps, or authorizing individuals or entities related to Borrower to take any steps, that could damage Lender and/or impede Lender from receiving the monetary benefits which Lender is expecting to receive from the Loan. Therefore, even if Borrower is successful in implementing a "bad-boy" act that could otherwise impair the collateral securing the Loan, the Carve Out Guaranty provides Lender with a means to have monetary recourse to a creditworthy party, without regard to the mortgage collateral. As a result of the fact that Lender has this power, Lender through the use of the Carve Out Guaranty hopes to discourage Borrower from ever pursuing such "bad-boy" acts, since Lender will have the ability to recover its monetary damage from the applicable Guarantor. Nevertheless, it is pretty clear that Borrower cannot directly prevent a third party from coming onto the Mortgaged Property and committing waste or damage to the Improvements. Likewise, it is clear that Borrower cannot prevent an earthquake from occurring and causing damage to the Improvements. Should those acts occur, the Loan Documents should, and usually do, provide for Borrower to repair any resulting damage to the Improvements caused by such occurrences, and if Borrower fails to effect such repair, then the Loan Documents should provide Lender with the appropriate remedy or remedies to deal with that situation. However, when an unrelated third party or an act of God causes such damage, there is usually very limited Borrower culpability associated with such activity. It is a different story should Borrower willfully commit waste or damage to the Improvements, because arguably Borrower could control that situation, and it is understandable that Lender would insist that such an act be deemed a "bad-boy" act under the Carve Out Guaranty.

A second common theme is that for these "bad-boy" acts to give rise to Damage Liability under this Carve Out Guaranty, the liability is generally not triggered simply by the commission of the act, or simply because the act was committed out of mere negligence. In most cases the party committing the act must be acting in a grossly negligent manner, or willfully. The point here is that generally this Damage Liability is not triggered by a minor error in judgment or a simple misstep. In most cases, it requires the party committing the "bad-boy" act to be acting well outside of the bounds of normal behavior and reasonable judgment, or else taking an action that threatens the Lender's security interest in the Mortgaged Property (such as failing to pay charges for labor or materials that results in material liens on any portion of any of Borrower's interest in the Mortgaged Property).

In general, under any of the Loan Documents it is an event of default not only (a) if a "bad-boy" act occurs, but that in addition, (b) such default must remain uncured following the duration of some specified grace period. Because this is usually the case, it is reasonable for Borrower's counsel to try to require in the Carve Out Guaranty that the corresponding "bad-boy" act should not trigger any Damage Liability under such guaranty until the same grace period called for in the Loan Documents expires before such act would allow Lender to pursue monetary remedies under the Carve Out Guaranty.

In Section 1.1.2 of the form of Carve Out Guaranty, it is a "bad-boy" act (creating Damage Liability) if there is a *"material misrepresentation made by Guarantor, Borrower, and/or the holders of beneficial or ownership interests in Borrower . . . [under] this Guaranty, the Note, the Security Instrument, and/or the other Loan Documents."* In this provision, it is interesting that Lender does not include the occurrence of a simple Borrower misrepresentation as a trigger that would result in Damage Liability (but, of course, it is still likely that such a simple misrepresentation by Borrower would trigger a default under at least one of the other Loan Documents). Instead, this provision requires that a Borrower misrepresentation must be material in order to trigger this liability, and this approach is consistent with the standard I referenced in the immediately preceding paragraph (i.e., that each such "bad-boy" act should involve something more than (a) just a simple breach or (b) that a party is simply acting in a negligent manner, in order to trigger Damage Liability). Here it is clear that in order for such a misrepresentation to qualify as being a "bad-boy" act," it must also be material. However, this particular provision would be even clearer if this guaranty defined or specified what it would take to qualify as a "material misrepresentation." In any event, if a Lender had instead chosen in this provision to try to make any misrepresentation (made by Guarantor, Borrower, and/or the holders of beneficial or ownership interests in Borrower) such a "bad-boy" act, regardless of whether such representation is material, or non-material, then in my view it would be reasonable for Borrower's counsel to at least try to make Lender modify such a provision so as to require that it would only constitute a "bad-boy" act if Guarantor, Borrower, and/or the holders of beneficial or ownership interests in Borrower had made a material misrepresentation. It would also be reasonable for Borrower's counsel to try to make Lender modify such a provision to provide that such a material misrepresentation clause should not be triggered if Lender had knowledge of the breach prior to the effective date of the representation, or if the facts giving rise to such breach had been disclosed to Lender in written materials received by Lender prior to the existence of such breach.

Section 1.1.5 of the form of Carve Out Guaranty states that it is a "bad-boy" act (creating Damage Liability) if *"any environmental matter(s) affecting the Mortgaged Property [occurs] which is introduced or caused by Borrower or any beneficial owner of Borrower, or which is otherwise covered by the Environmental Indemnity."* This provision specifies that it is a "bad-boy" act if any environmental matter which is covered by the Environmental Indemnity occurs that affects the Mortgaged Property. It is highly likely that the Environmental Indemnity will cover not only environmental matters caused by Borrower, but also environment matters that are not caused by Borrower or any party related to Borrower. Accordingly, it would be reasonable for Borrower's counsel to at least try to make Lender delete this provision on the basis that it is duplicative, since Guarantor will be signing the Environmental Indemnity, and therefore Guarantor will have already incurred the liability for dealing with all such environmental matters, by virtue of Guarantor having executed the Environmental Indemnity. At the very least, Borrower's counsel could try to make Lender modify this provision in the Carve Out Guaranty, so that it only applies to environmental matters caused by Borrower, since the matters triggering liability under this guaranty should only be matters caused by Borrower, and therefore such liability could be avoided if Borrower refrained from the conduct that would cause such matters to occur. Alternatively, Borrower's counsel might try to get Lender to modify this provision so that it only applies in the case where the cost of remediating the applicable environmental matter is either material, or exceeds some specified amount.

In Section 1.1.9 of the form of Carve Out Guaranty, it is a "bad-boy" act (creating Damage Liability) if *"Borrower, or . . . any Person acting by, through, or under Borrower, [fails] to pay charges for labor or materials that results in material liens on any portion of any of Borrower's interest in the Mortgaged Property."* In many jurisdictions, the filing of a mechanic's lien will allow such lien to have priority over the Mortgage lien; thus, in the case of a foreclosure sale of the Mortgaged Property, the proceeds of such sale would first go to pay the holder of any such mechanic's lien, before such proceeds could be used to pay Lender the sums it is entitled to as a result of its Mortgage lien. In addition, the holder of a mechanic's lien would be entitled to a secured creditor's status in a bankruptcy proceeding of Borrower. Accordingly, Lender has valid reasons for wanting to require Borrower to avoid allowing mechanic's liens to ever occur, and the principal reason that such a mechanic's lien would occur would be the failure of Borrower to pay in a timely manner an individual or entity providing services or materials used to construct the Improvements. Given that the language in this provision includes the failure of *"any Person acting by, through, or under Borrower"* to make such payments, it would be reasonable for Borrower's counsel to try to have Lender modify this provision so that it does not apply to any tenant under any Lease, given that (a) if a mechanic's lien arises because of a tenant's failure to make a payment that could give rise to a mechanic's lien, such lien would only attach to the tenant's leasehold estate (and accordingly would not gain priority over Lender's lien on Borrower's interest in the Mortgage Property [which is usually the fee interest in such property]), and (b) although a tenant does enter into a lease with Borrower, Borrower cannot in any meaningful way exercise control over an unrelated tenant. In addition, it is fairly common for the Loan Documents to contain a provision that gives Borrower the right to contest the filing of a mechanic's lien, and if the Mortgage or any other Loan Document should permit such right of contest, then it would be reasonable for Borrower's counsel to try to have Lender modify this provision so that before such act actually constitutes a "bad-boy" act under this guaranty, Lender would first allow Borrower to contest any such mechanic's lien filing in accordance with the applicable contest provision set forth in the Mortgage or any other applicable Loan Document, before any failure to make an applicable payment would constitute a "bad-boy" act (creating Damage Liability).

Whereas Section 1.1 of the form of Carve Out Guaranty relates to certain "bad-boy" acts that give rise to Damage Liability, Section 1.2 of the form of Carve Out Guaranty relates to certain actions that give rise to Springing Liability. Should Guarantor be liable for Damage Liability under the Carve Out Guaranty, it would then be obligated to reimburse Lender for any monetary damages Lender incurs as a result of Borrower committing any of the "bad-boy" acts enumerated in Section 1.1 of the form of Carve Out Guaranty. On the other hand, if Guarantor becomes liable for Springing Liability under the Carve Out Guaranty, it would then be obligated to potentially repay the entire Loan, and all other monetary obligations then owed to Lender. Accordingly, the risk exposure is much greater for Guarantor should it commit an act that would trigger Springing Liability, since that would mean that Lender could then demand that Guarantor pay the entire outstanding balance of the Loan and all accrued interest and other monetary obligations then owed to Lender under the Loan Documents. As a result, although Borrower's counsel would prefer to eliminate or restrict as much as possible each act that Lender tries to include in the Carve Out Guaranty from being a liability trigger, in almost all cases, if an act is to be included in the Carve Out Guaranty as a liability trigger, it would be better from Borrower's perspective to have the act trigger Damage Liability (rather than Springing Liability), because the monetary risk exposure to Guarantor is much more likely to be less if Damage Liability is triggered. It is often the case that Lender will be willing to downgrade an act as being a trigger for Damage Liability (rather than Springing Liability), particularly if the act in question does not involve an adjudication of bankruptcy, or the sale of substantially all of the Mortgage Property, without Lender's consent.

PART IV

Mortgage

SECTION 1

Definitions

Explanation

The following definitions of key terms are taken from the definition section of a typical real estate mortgage, mortgage loan agreement, and/or other key loan document. They are presented here for reference so that the reader will have a single place to look as a reference point to understand the meaning of these terms as used throughout this Book. It is typical for a real estate mortgage, and/or loan agreement, and/or other key loan document, to include a section that lists definitions of defined terms at the beginning of, or as an exhibit to, such document for easy reference. When Borrower's counsel is given a set of loan documents from Lender's counsel, that counsel should be careful to check that the definitions used in the various loan documents are consistent with one another. Definitions often contain terms that are controversial and need to be negotiated. Frequently, these definitions for a given defined term are not exactly the same when such term is used in different documents. It is usually best to have each term defined in only one document and then cross-reference that definition if that same capitalized term is used as a defined term in another loan document (otherwise, each time the same capitalized term is defined in a different loan document, borrower's counsel will need to cross-check and be sure that the applicable definition used in each applicable loan document for that capitalized term is word for word the same definition). I have assumed that each of these definitions is contained in a mortgage that is currently being negotiated.

> *"**Affiliate**" of any specified Person shall mean any other Person directly or indirectly controlling or controlled by or under direct or indirect common control with such specified Person and any immediate family member of such specified Person and/or any of his/her respective Affiliates. For the purposes of this definition, "control" when used*

with respect to any specified Person means the power to direct the management and policies of such Person, directly or indirectly, whether through the ownership of voting securities, by contract, or otherwise; and the terms "controlling" and "controlled" have meanings correlative to the foregoing.

"Assignment of Leases and Rents" *shall mean that certain Assignment dated as of the Closing Date between Borrower and Lender, as the same may be amended, restated, supplemented, or otherwise modified from time to time.*

"Assignment of Management Agreement" *shall mean that certain Assignment and Management Agreement dated as of the Closing Date among Borrower, Lender, and ________ [Manager], as the same may be amended, restated, supplemented, or otherwise modified from time to time.*

"Banking Day" *as defined in Section 6.3(a) of this Mortgage.* [Note: See Part IV Section 6 of this Book.]

"Borrower" *means all persons or entities identified as "Borrower" in the first paragraph of this Mortgage, together with its successors and assigns.*

"Borrower's Knowledge" *means with respect to any applicable representation and/or warranty provided for in any of the Loan Documents and that are subject to Borrower's Knowledge, such knowledge of applicable facts as ________* [Note: List applicable individuals] *had with respect to any applicable matter as of the date any such representation and/or warranty shall be deemed to have been given pursuant to the express terms of the Loan Documents.*

"Breakage Costs" *as defined in Section 6.3(b) of this Mortgage.* [Note: See Part IV Section 6 of this Book.]

"Cash Management Agreement" *means any separate agreement between Borrower, Lender, and an institutional bank or trustee, which is entered into for the purpose of, among other things, (i) establishing various reserves for the Mortgaged Property, (ii) collecting and depositing all revenues from the Mortgaged Property, and/or (iii) dealing with the distribution of such revenues and deposits in the various reserves, as the same may be amended, restated, supplemented, or otherwise modified from time to time.*

"Change in Law" *means the occurrence, after the date of this Mortgage, of any of the following: (a) the adoption or taking effect of any Legal Requirement; (b) any change in any Legal Requirement or in the administration, interpretation, implementation, or application thereof by any governmental authority; or (c) the making or issuance of any request, rule, guideline, or directive (whether or not having the force of law) by any governmental authority provided that notwithstanding anything herein to the contrary, (x) the Dodd-Frank Wall Street Reform and Consumer Protection Act and (y) all requests, rules, guidelines, or directives promulgated by Lender for International Settlements, the Basel Committee on Banking Supervision (or any successor or similar authority), or the United States or foreign regulatory authorities, in each case pursuant to Basel III regulations published by the Basel Committee on Banking Supervision,* *shall in each case be deemed to be a "Change in Law" regardless of the date enacted, adopted, or issued.*

"Closing Date" *shall mean the date of this Mortgage.*

"Default Rate" *as defined in Section 23.2 of this Mortgage.* [Note: See Part IV Section 23 of this Book.]

"Environmental Claim" *as defined in Section 18.12 of this Mortgage.* [Note: See Part IV Section 18 of this Book.]

"Environmental Inspections" *as defined in Section 18.7 of this Mortgage.* [Note: See Part IV Section 18 of this Book.]

"Environmental Permit" *means any State or Commonwealth, Federal, or local governmental permit, license, or other authorization issued under any Hazardous Materials Law with respect to any activities or businesses conducted on or in relation to the Mortgaged Property that relates to the use, handling, storage, and/or release of Hazardous Materials or other similar substances.*

"ERISA" *as defined in Section 8.1(g) of this Mortgage.* [Note: See Part IV Section 8 of this Book.]

"ERISA Plan" *as defined in Section 8.1(g) of this Mortgage.* [Note: See Part IV Section 8 of this Book.]

"Event of Default" *means the occurrence of any event listed in Section 24 of this Mortgage.* [Note: See Part IV Section 24 of this Book.]

"Fixtures" *means all property that is so attached to any portion of the Mortgaged Property so as to constitute a fixture under applicable State law in the State or Commonwealth where the Mortgaged Property is located, including machinery, equipment, engines, boilers, incinerators, and installed building materials; systems and equipment for the purpose of supplying or distributing heating, cooling, electricity, gas, water, air, or light; antennas, cable, wiring, and conduits used in connection with radio, television, security, fire prevention, or fire detection or otherwise used to carry electronic signals; telephone systems and equipment; elevators and related machinery and equipment; fire detection, prevention, and extinguishing systems and apparatus; security and access control systems and apparatus; plumbing systems; water heaters, ranges, stoves, microwave ovens, refrigerators, dishwashers, garbage disposers, washers, dryers, and other appliances; light fixtures, awnings, storm windows, and storm doors; pictures, screens, blinds, shades, curtains, and curtain rods; mirrors; cabinets, paneling, rugs, and floor and wall coverings; fences, trees, and plants; swimming pools; and exercise equipment.*

"Governmental Authority" *means any board, commission, department, or body of any municipal, county, State, or Federal governmental unit, or any subdivision of any of them, that has or acquires jurisdiction over the Mortgaged Property or the use, operation, or improvement of the Mortgaged Property.*

"Guarantor" *as defined in Section 8.1(a) of this Mortgage.* [Note: See Part IV Section 8 of this Book.]

"Hazardous Materials" *means petroleum and petroleum products and compounds containing them, including gasoline, diesel fuel, and oil; explosives; flammable materials; radioactive materials; polychlorinated biphenyls ("**PCBs**") and compounds containing them; lead and lead-based paint; asbestos or asbestos-containing materials in any form that is or could become friable; underground or above-ground storage tanks, whether empty or containing any substance; any substance the presence of which on the Mortgaged Property is prohibited by any Federal, State, or local authority; any substance that requires special handling; and any other material or substance now or in the future defined as a "hazardous substance," "hazardous material," "hazardous waste," "toxic substance," "toxic pollutant," "contaminant," or "pollutant" within the meaning of any Hazardous Materials Law.*

"Hazardous Materials Laws" *means all Federal, State, and local laws, ordinances, and regulations and standards, rules, policies, and other governmental requirements, administrative rulings, and court judgments and decrees in effect now or in the future and including all amendments that relate to Hazardous Materials and apply to Borrower or to the Mortgaged Property. Hazardous Materials Laws include, but are not limited to, the Comprehensive Environmental Response, Compensation and Liability Act, 42 U.S.C. Section 9601,* et seq.*; the Resource Conservation and Recovery Act, 42 U.S.C. Section 6901,* et seq.*; the Toxic Substance Control Act, 15 U.S.C. Section 2601,* et seq.*; the Clean Water Act, 33 U.S.C. Section 1251,* et seq.*; and the Hazardous Materials Transportation Act, 49 U.S.C. Section 5101,* et seq.*; and their State analogs.*

"Imposition" *means any obligation owed by Borrower to any governmental and quasi-governmental entity as a periodic and on-going payment that is owed because of Borrower's ownership of the Mortgaged Property and, if not paid, would become a lien against the Mortgaged Property.*

"Imposition Deposits" *as defined in Section 10.1 of this Mortgage.* [Note: See Part IV Section 10 of this Book.]

"Improvements" *means the buildings, structures, improvements, and alterations now constructed or at any time in the future constructed or placed upon the Land, including any future replacements and additions.*

"Indebtedness" *means the principal of, interest on, and all other amounts due and payable to Lender at any time under the Note, this Mortgage, or any other Loan Document and all other Obligations, including prepayment premiums, late charges, default interest, and advances as provided in Section 6 to protect the security of this Mortgage.*

"Initial Owners" *as defined in Section 22.3(a) of this Mortgage.* [Note: See Part IV Section 22 of this Book.]

"Interest Period" *as defined in Section 6.4 of this Mortgage.* [Note: See Part IV Section 6 of this Book.]

"Key Principal" *means the natural person(s) or entity identified as such in Exhibit __ of this Mortgage and any person or entity that becomes a Key Principal after the date of this Mortgage and is identified as such in an amendment or supplement to this Mortgage.*

"Land" *means the land described in Exhibit A attached to this Mortgage.*

"Leases" *means all present and future leases, subleases, licenses, concessions, grants, or other possessory interests now or hereafter in force, whether oral or written, covering or affecting the Mortgaged Property, or any portion of the Mortgaged Property (including proprietary leases or occupancy agreements if Borrower is a cooperative housing corporation), and all modifications, extensions, or renewals as each such written agreement documenting such lease, sublease, license, concession, grant, or other possessory interest may be amended, restated, supplemented, or otherwise modified from time to time.*

"Legal Requirements" *means all Federal, State, city, municipal, and other governmental statutes, laws, rules, orders, regulations, ordinances, judgments, decrees, and injunctions of any governmental or quasi-governmental body or agencies affecting the acquisition, ownership, development, leasing, operation, and/or use of the Mortgaged Property or any part thereof, whether now or hereafter enacted and in force, and all permits, licenses, and authorizations and regulations relating thereto, and all covenants, agreements, restrictions, and encumbrances contained in any instruments at any time in force affecting the Mortgaged Property or any part thereof.*

"Lender" *means the entity identified as "Lender" in the first paragraph of this Mortgage and its successors and assigns or any subsequent holder of the Note.*

"LIBOR" *as defined in Section 6.4(d) of this Mortgage.* [Note: See Part IV Section 6 of this Book.]

"LIBOR Advance Rate" *as defined in Section 6.4(e) of this Mortgage.* [Note: See Part IV Section 6 of this Book.]

"LIBOR Based Rate" *as defined in Section 6.4(f) of this Mortgage.* [Note: See Part IV Section 6 of this Book.]

"LIBOR Rate" *as defined in Section 6.4(d) of this Mortgage.* [Note: See Part IV Section 6 of this Book.]

"Limited Liability Agreement" *means that certain Operating Agreement dated _______, entered into by ________, which among other things constitutes the primary organizational document of Borrower, as the same may be amended, extended, or modified from time to time.*

"Loan" *means the loan made by Lender to Borrower that is evidenced by the Note and includes all obligations owed by Borrower to Lender pursuant to all guaranties, all indemnity agreements, the Note, and all other Loan Documents.*

*"**Loan Advance**" means each advance of proceeds of any portion of the Loan that shall be made from time to time by Lender to Borrower.*

*"**Loan Agreement**" means the loan agreement entered into on the date of this Mortgage between Borrower and Lender, which, among other things, provides for the funding of the Loan, as the same may be amended, extended, or otherwise modified from time to time.*

*"**Loan Documents**" means the Note, this Mortgage, the Loan Agreement, all guaranties, the Cash Management Agreement, all indemnity agreements, other collateral agreements, O&M Programs, and any other documents now or in the future executed by Borrower, Key Principal, any guarantor or any other person in connection with the Loan evidenced by the Note, as each such document may be amended, modified, or extended from time to time.*

*"**Loan Servicer**" as defined in Section 34.1 of this Mortgage.* [Note: See Part IV Section 34 of this Book.]

*"**Maturity**" as defined in Section 6.4(h) of this Mortgage.* [Note: See Part IV Section 6 of this Book.]

*"**Maturity Date**" as defined in Section 6.4(h) of this Mortgage.* [Note: See Part IV Section 6 of this Book.]

*"**Mortgage**" means this Mortgage and Security Agreement, which is entered into on the date hereof by Borrower for the benefit of Lender, as the same may be amended, extended, or otherwise modified from time to time.*

*"**Mortgaged Property**" means all of the following, as applicable:*

(1) *the Land;*
(2) *the Improvements;*
(3) *the Fixtures, including goods, materials, supplies, chattels, furniture, fixtures, equipment, and machinery now or later to be attached to, placed in or on, or used in connection with the use, enjoyment, occupancy, or operation of all or any part of the Land and/or the Improvements, whether stored on the Land and/or the Improvements or elsewhere, including all pumping plants, engines, pipes, ditches, and flumes, and all gas, electric, cooking, heating, cooling, air conditioning, lighting, refrigeration, and plumbing fixtures and equipment, all of which shall be considered to the fullest extent of the law to be real property for purposes of this Mortgage, and any manufacturer's warranties with respect thereto;*
(4) *the Personalty;*
(5) *all current and future rights, including air rights, development rights, zoning rights, and other similar rights or interests, easements, tenements, rights-of-way, strips and gores of land, streets, alleys, roads, sewer rights, waters, watercourses, and appurtenances related to or benefiting the Land or the Improvements, or both, and all rights-of-way, streets, alleys, and roads that may have been or may in the future be vacated;*

(6) *all existing and future appurtenances, privileges, easements, franchises, and tenements of the Land held by Borrower from time to time, including all minerals, oil, gas, other hydrocarbons and associated substances, sulphur, nitrogen, carbon dioxide, helium, and other commercially valuable substances that may be in, under, or produced from any part of the Land, all development rights and credits, air rights, water, water rights (whether riparian, appropriative, or otherwise and whether or not appurtenant) and water stock, and any portion of the Land lying in the streets, roads, or avenues, open or proposed, in front of or adjoining the Land and Improvements;*

(7) *all building materials, equipment, work in process, or other personal property of any kind owned by Borrower, whether stored on the Mortgaged Property or elsewhere, that have been or later will be acquired for the purpose of being delivered to, incorporated into, or installed in or about the Land and/or the Improvements;*

(8) *all current and future rights, including air rights, development rights, zoning rights and other similar rights or interests, easements, tenements, rights-of-way, strips and gores of land, streets, alleys, roads, sewer rights, waters, watercourses, and appurtenances owned by Borrower related to or benefiting the Land or the Improvements or both and all rights-of-way, streets, alleys, and roads that may have been or may in the future be vacated;*

(9) *all rights of Borrower to the payment of money, accounts, accounts receivable, reserves, deferred payments, refunds, cost savings, payments and deposits, whether now or later to be received from third parties (including all earnest money sales deposits) or deposited by Borrower with third parties (including all utility deposits and Imposition Deposits), contract rights, development and use rights, governmental permits and licenses, applications, architectural and engineering plans, specifications and drawings, as built drawings, chattel paper, instruments, documents, notes, drafts and letters of credit, which arise from or relate to construction on the Land and/or Improvements or to any business now or later to be conducted on it, or to the Land and/or Improvements generally, and any builder's or manufacturer's warranties with respect thereto;*

(10) *all insurance policies owned by Borrower pertaining to the Mortgaged Property and all proceeds payable to Borrower, including all claims to and demands for them, of the voluntary or involuntary conversion of any of the Land, Improvements, or the other property described above into cash or liquidated claims;*

(11) *all proceeds paid or to be paid by any insurer of the Land, the Improvements, the Fixtures, the Personalty or any other part of the Mortgaged Property whether or not Borrower obtained the insurance pursuant to Lender's requirement;*

(12) *all awards, payments, and other compensation made or to be made by any municipal, State, or Federal authority with respect to the Land, the Improvements, the Fixtures, the Personalty or any other part of the Mortgaged Property, including any awards or settlements resulting from condemnation proceedings or the total or partial taking of the Land, the Improvements, the Fixtures, the Personalty or any other part of the Mortgaged Property under*

the power of eminent domain or otherwise and including any conveyance in lieu thereof;

(13) *all contracts, options, and other agreements for the sale of the Land, the Improvements, the Fixtures, the Personalty or any other part of the Mortgaged Property entered into by Borrower now or in the future, including cash or securities deposited to secure performance by parties of their obligations;*

(14) *all of Borrower's books and records pertaining to any and all of the property described above, including computer readable memory and any computer hardware or software necessary to access and process such memory;*

(15) *all proceeds from the conversion, voluntary or involuntary, of any of the above into cash or liquidated claims and the right to collect such proceeds;*

(16) *all Rents and Leases;*

(17) *all earnings, royalties, accounts receivable, issues, and profits from the Land, the Improvements or any other part of the Mortgaged Property, and all undisbursed proceeds of the loan secured by this Mortgage and, if Borrower is a cooperative housing corporation, maintenance charges or assessments payable by shareholders or residents;*

(18) *all Imposition Deposits;*

(19) *all refunds or rebates of Impositions by any municipal, State, or Federal authority or insurance company (other than refunds applicable to periods before the real property tax year in which this Mortgage is dated);*

(20) *all tenant security deposits that have not been forfeited by any tenant under any of the Leases;*

(21) *all proceeds of, additions and accretions to, substitutions and replacements for, and changes in any of the property of Borrower described above;*

(22) *all "Equipment," as that term is defined in the Uniform Commercial Code, owned by Borrower;*

(23) *all "Goods," as that term is defined in the Uniform Commercial Code, owned by Borrower;*

(24) *all Borrower's "Accounts," as that term is defined in the Uniform Commercial Code"; and*

(25) *all names under or by which any of the above Mortgaged Property may be operated or known and all trademarks, trade names, and goodwill relating to any of the Mortgaged Property.*

"Note"/"Promissory Note" *means the Note secured by this Mortgage, and all schedules, riders, allonges, and addenda, as such Note may be amended, restated, supplemented, or otherwise modified from time to time.*

"Notice of Rate Selection" *means a written notice, given by cable, tested telex, telecopier (with authorized signature), or by telephone if immediately confirmed by such a written notice, from ________ (or such other individual who in a written notice to Lender from Borrower is authorized to act in such capacity) that (i) is irrevocable; (ii) is received by Lender not later than 10:00 A.M. Eastern Time: (a) if a LIBOR Based Rate is selected at least three (3) Business Days prior to the first day of the Interest Period to* *which such selection is to apply or (b) if a Variable Rate is selected on the first day of the Interest Period to which it applies; and (iii) as to each selected interest rate option sets forth the aggregate principal amount(s) to which such interest rate option(s) shall apply and the Interest Period(s) applicable to each LIBOR Advance.*

"Obligation(s)" *means, without limitation, all loans, advances, indebtedness, notes, liabilities, and amounts, liquidated or unliquidated, owing by Borrower in connection with the Loan to Lender at any time, of each and every kind, nature, and description, whether arising under this Mortgage or any of the other Loan Documents or otherwise, and whether secured or unsecured, direct or indirect (that is, whether the same are due directly by Borrower to Lender or are due indirectly by Borrower to Lender as endorser, guarantor, or other surety or as borrower of obligations due third persons that have been endorsed or assigned to Lender or otherwise), absolute or contingent, due or to become due, now existing or hereafter arising or contracted, provided any such debt or liabilities shall have arisen in connection with the Loan, including, without limitation, payment when due of all amounts outstanding from time to time under the Loan Documents. Said term shall also include (i) all interest and other charges chargeable to Borrower or due from Borrower to Lender from time to time and all costs and expenses referred to in this Mortgage or any of the other Loan Documents and (ii) any and all future advances made by Lender to protect or preserve the Mortgaged Property or the security interest created hereby on the Mortgaged Property or for Impositions or other taxes, assessments, or insurance premiums as hereinafter provided or for performance of any of Borrower's obligations hereunder or under the other Loan Documents (whether or not the original Mortgagor remains the owner of the Mortgaged Property at the time of such advances).*

"O&M Program" *as defined in Section 18.4 of this Mortgage.* [Note: See Part IV Section 18 of this Book.]

"Permitted Encumbrances" *means all matters of record set forth in Lender's title insurance policy that Lender received in connection with the closing of the Loan, together with any other title matters either approved by Lender or expressly permitted to be entered into by Borrower pursuant to this Mortgage.*

"Person" *means an individual, partnership, limited liability company, corporation, trust, or unincorporated organization.*

"Personalty" *means all furniture, furnishings, equipment, machinery, building materials, appliances, commercial tort claims, inventory, general intangibles, goods, supplies, tools, books, records (whether in written or electronic form), computer equipment (hardware and software), and other tangible personal property (other than Fixtures) that are used now or in the future in connection with the ownership, management, or operation of the Land or the Improvements or are located on the Land or in the Improvements and any operating agreements relating to the Land or the Improvements and any surveys, plans, and specifications and contracts for architectural, engineering, and construction services relating to the Land or the Improvements and all other intangible* *property and rights relating to the operation of, or used in connection with, the Land or the Improvements, including all governmental permits relating to any activities on the Land.*

"Prepayment Date" *as defined in Schedule A to the Note.* [Note: See Part IV Section 7 of this Book.]

"Prepayment Premium" *as defined in Schedule A to the Note.* [Note: See Part IV Section 7 of this Book.]

"Prime Rate" *as defined in Section 6.4(i) of this Mortgage.* [Note: See Part IV Section 6 of this Book.]

"Prohibited Activities or Conditions" *as defined in Part IV Section 18.1 of this Mortgage.* [Note: See Section 18 of this Book.]

"Property Jurisdiction" *as defined in Section 32.1 of this Mortgage.* [Note: See Part IV Section 32 of this Book.]

"Publicly-Held Corporation" *as defined in Part IV Section 22.3(c) of this Mortgage.* [Note: See Section 22 of this Book.]

"RCRA" *means the Resource Conservation and Recovery Act, 42 U.S.C. § 6901 et seq., which imposes a rigorous "cradle-to-grave" scheme that regulates hazardous wastes from generation to final disposal or destruction.*

"Remedial Work" *as defined in Part IV Section 18.8 of this Mortgage.* [Note: See Section 18 of this Book.]

"Rents" *means all rents (whether from residential or nonresidential space), revenues, and other income of the Land or the Improvements, including parking fees, laundry and vending machine income and fees, and charges for food, health care and other services provided at the Mortgaged Property, whether now due, past due, or to become due, and deposits forfeited by tenants.*

"Servicing Arrangement" *as defined in Part IV Section 37.1 of this Mortgage.* [Note: See Section 37 of this Book.]

"Significant Lease" *as defined in Part IV Section 5.6 of this Mortgage.* [Note: See Section 5 of this Book.]

"Taxes" *means all Impositions.*

"Transfer" *means (a) a sale, assignment, transfer, or other disposition (whether voluntary or involuntary or by operation of law); (b) the granting, creating, or attachment of a lien, encumbrance, or security interest (whether voluntary, involuntary or by operation of law); (c) the issuance or other creation of an ownership interest in a legal entity, including a partnership interest, interest in a limited liability company, or corporate stock; (d) the withdrawal, retirement, removal, or involuntary resignation of a partner in a partnership or a member or manager in a limited liability company; or (e) the merger,* *dissolution, liquidation, or consolidation of a legal entity. "Transfer" does not include (i) a conveyance of the Mortgaged Property at a judicial or nonjudicial foreclosure sale under this Mortgage or (ii) the Mortgaged Property becoming part of a bankruptcy estate by operation of law under the U.S. Bankruptcy Code. For purposes of defining the term "Transfer," the term "partnership" shall mean a general partnership, a limited partnership, a joint venture, and a limited liability partnership, and the term "partner" shall mean a general partner, a limited partner, and a joint venturer.*

"UCC Collateral" *as defined in Section 3.1 of this Mortgage.* [Note: See Part IV Section 3 of this Book.]

"Uniform Commercial Code" *or "UCC" means the Uniform Commercial Code of ___________ [the State or Commonwealth in which the Land is located], as the same may be amended and modified from time to time.*

"USTs" *means underground storage tanks containing regulated substances, including petroleum products.*

"Variable Rate" *as defined in Section 6.4(j) of this Mortgage.* [Note: See Part IV Section 6 of this Book.]

"Yield Rate" *as defined in Schedule A to the Note.* [Note: See Part IV Section 7 of this Book.]

SECTION 2

Grant of Real Estate Interests

Explanation

Commercial real estate loans in the United States are almost always secured by a lien on Borrower's real estate interests. In most jurisdictions of the United States, this lien is granted by Borrower to Lender in either (i) a mortgage, which is typically a security instrument executed by Borrower, for the benefit of Lender or (ii) a deed of trust, which is typically a two-party or three-party security agreement between Borrower or trustor and a trustee who is notionally granted collateral title to the real estate for the benefit of Lender as beneficiary (and such Lender may or may not be party to such deed of trust). When a deed of trust is used (and in some jurisdictions this is called a "deed to secure debt"), the trustee is usually domiciled and/or licensed to do business in the State or the Commonwealth where the Mortgaged Property is located (note, however, that in some jurisdictions, this security instrument may have a different name). Because the laws governing real property (in particular, real estate mortgages, deeds of trust, and the remedies set forth therein) vary widely from state to state, if the applicable Borrower whose project is located in a state or other jurisdiction where Borrower's counsel is not licensed to practice law, it is normal custom for Borrower's counsel to have Borrower authorize it to engage local counsel for the transaction (of particular importance with regard to providing Lender with a number of legal opinions, including the enforceability opinion for the mortgage or deed of trust, which a Lender will typically require, and usually involve having the knowledge of, and being licensed under, local law in order to render such opinions). Below are relevant sections of a theoretical Mortgage that deals with the granting of various property interests owned by Borrower, including its interest in the real estate project.

2.1 ***Mortgage.*** *For valuable consideration paid and for other good and valuable consideration, the receipt and sufficiency of which are hereby acknowledged,*

Borrower hereby irrevocably and unconditionally mortgages, grants, bargains, transfers, sells, conveys, sets over and assigns to Lender and its successors and assigns forever, with MORTGAGE COVENANTS, all of Borrower's right, title and interest in and to the "Mortgaged Property" more particularly defined below, to secure the prompt payment and performance of the Obligations, including, without limitation, all amounts due and owing and all obligations respecting the Note and all substitutions, modifications, extensions or amendments to any of the Loan Documents. The amount of principal obligations outstanding and evidenced by the Loan Documents and secured by this Mortgage total ________________ Dollars ($______________) as of the date of this Mortgage, but this Mortgage shall nevertheless secure payment and performance of all Obligations.

2.2 ***Conditions to Grant.*** *Lender shall have and hold the above granted Mortgaged Property unto and to the use and benefit of Lender, and its successors and assigns, forever; provided, however, the conveyances, grants and assignments contained in this Mortgage are upon the express condition that, if Borrower (i) shall irrevocably and indefeasibly pay and perform each Obligation in full, including, without limitation, all principal, interest and premium thereon and other charges, if applicable, in accordance with the terms and conditions in the Loan Documents and this Mortgage, (ii) shall pay and perform every other Obligation and (iii) shall abide by and comply with each and every covenant and condition set forth herein and in the Loan Documents, the conveyances, grants and assignments contained in this Mortgage shall be appropriately released and discharged.*

Explanation

When analyzing the granting provisions for real estate assets, which a Lender's counsel may include in a given mortgage or deed of trust, Borrower's counsel should look for and/or consider several things. First and foremost is that Borrower can grant a security interest only in property that Borrower owns. A well-written granting provision should specify that this grant relates only to Borrower's interest in the various property interests being referenced in these provisions, keeping in mind that other third parties—such as a landowner (in situations where Borrower does not own, but is ground-leasing the land), space tenants in Borrower's building (who hold occupancy rights therein pursuant to a lease with Borrower or a sublease with a space tenant in Borrower's building), and potentially other parties having easements or other real estate interests—in each case can simultaneously own a fee, leasehold, and/or easement interest in the same property that may be part of Lender's list of property interests that are included in the granting provisions of a given mortgage or deed of trust creating the lien on the collateral security for Lender's Loan. If Borrower for a particular mortgage loan transaction only holds a leasehold estate through a ground lease with the owner of the land, then in that case Borrower would lack the ability to grant a security lien that legally encumbers the fee interest in the land (because that fee interest would instead be owned by the landlord under such ground lease).

Invariably in these granting provisions, there will be a reference to an exhibit for a property description relating to the Land and/or other interests held by Borrower relating to the Land that will need to be attached as an exhibit. If Borrower holds a fee interest in the Land, then typically this property description exhibit will be a metes-and-bounds or platted legal description, although in some jurisdictions, this can vary. With regard to written legal descriptions, Borrower's counsel will want to obtain (i) a survey of the Land (created by a surveyor who has been licensed in the applicable jurisdiction), which should also include such a written legal description of the Land, (ii) copy of the last deed that conveyed title to the Land (which should also have a written legal description of the Land included in, or attached to, such deed), and (iii) a commitment for a title insurance policy insuring the priority of the lien of the Mortgage, which commitment likewise should have a written legal description of the Land. Upon receiving these materials, Borrower's counsel will need to verify that all of these legal descriptions (including the legal description attached as an exhibit to the mortgage or deed of trust obtained from Lender's counsel) exactly match one another (word for word), and if there are any discrepancies, then Borrower's counsel will need to reconcile such differences with the surveyor, the title company, and/or Lender's counsel so that at closing, the legal description in each of any new conveying deed, the mortgage or deed of trust, the title policy, and the survey match in all respects.

When the interest held by Borrower in the Land is different from a fee interest (i.e., when Borrower holds only a leasehold interest in the Land), a mere legal metes-and-bounds description of the Land as an exhibit to the mortgage or deed of trust is not enough to describe Borrower's relationship to the Land, and in this instance the focus of the legal description should be a clear description of Borrower's leasehold interest, which must be specified in the document so that it is clear to what interest the mortgage lien is attaching. In this case, it should be specified that the mortgage lien will be attaching to Borrower's leasehold interest arising under the applicable ground lease with the Land owner, and the date and any relevant recording information relating to such lease must be included in this description. It is often the case that in addition to referencing Borrower's interest in such document (like the ground lease), there will also be a metes-and-bounds description of the Land (and note that in many cases a similar metes-and-bounds description will also be set out in the actual ground lease). Usually, Borrower's counsel will be able to get helpful advice from the title company agent who will be providing a lender's title insurance policy for the project concerning the adequacy of the legal description and any necessary recording information that will need to be included in the applicable Loan Documents.

SECTION 3

Grant of Personal Property Interest

Explanation

Almost every income-producing real estate development includes some personal property which is owned by Borrower. Most often, Borrower owns some tangible property, such as equipment (lawn-mowing, pool-cleaning, computers, etc.) and furniture (office desks, chairs, etc.). Less obvious Borrower personal property assets are rents and other types of proceeds and revenues, which in most jurisdictions will be deemed to be personal property (more about these revenues later). In addition, bank accounts of Borrower which are granted as collateral to the Lender are also deemed to be personal property. When making a real estate mortgage loan, Lender will be seeking to perfect a security interest in all of the assets of Borrower (including personal property) as collateral security for its Loan. Generally speaking, personal property requires a somewhat different methodology for perfection than was the case with the granting of a perfected lien on the real estate assets, as previously discussed in Part IV Section 2 of this Book. [Note: A more detailed discussion concerning perfection of an interest in a deposit account is set out in Part IV Section 10 of this Book, as the methodology for perfection in this type of asset is somewhat different under the UCC.] Below are provisions which are also typically utilized in a Mortgage so that Borrower grants to Lender a security interest in most of Borrower's personal property:

3.1 *As a continuing security for the Obligations, Borrower hereby pledges, assigns and grants to Lender a security interest in any of the Mortgaged Property which, under applicable law, is deemed to be personal property or fixtures of Borrower, and all products and cash and non-cash proceeds thereof, whether acquired now or in the future (collectively, the **"UCC Collateral"**). This Mortgage is and shall be deemed to be a security agreement and financing* *statement pursuant to the terms of the Uniform Commercial Code as to the UCC Collateral, such that Lender shall have all of the rights and remedies of a secured party under the Uniform Commercial Code with respect the UCC Collateral. This Mortgage shall also constitute a financing statement filed as a fixture filing under Section ______ of the Uniform Commercial Code.* [Note: This is usually §9-502 of the Uniform Commercial Code covering any portion of the Mortgaged Property which now is or later may become a fixture, as determined by the laws of the State or Commonwealth in which the Land and Improvements are located.] *Borrower agrees that it shall execute and deliver to Lender, upon Lender's request, financing statements, continuation statements and amendments, in such form as Lender may require to perfect or continue the perfection of this security interest, and Borrower hereby agrees and designates that Lender may execute any such financing statements, continuation statements and amendments on Borrower's or Lender's behalf, without the necessity of Borrower executing any such documentation. Borrower shall pay all filing costs and all costs and expenses of any record searches for financing statements that Lender may require. Without the prior written consent of Lender, Borrower shall not create or permit to exist any other lien or security interest in any of the UCC Collateral. If an Event of Default has occurred and is continuing, Lender shall have the remedies of a secured party under the Uniform Commercial Code, in addition to all remedies provided by this Mortgage or existing under applicable law. In exercising any remedies, Lender may exercise its remedies against the UCC Collateral separately or together, and in any order, without in any way affecting the availability of Lender's other remedies.*

Explanation

For the last 25 years, in the United States, a Lender has typically required that a Borrower in a real estate transaction be a single-purpose entity, whose sole or primary purpose is to develop, manage, operate, finance and own only the Mortgaged Property, and therefore Borrower may not own any other assets, real estate or otherwise. The main purpose of this Lender and rating agency requirement is to prevent Borrower from owning an asset which may be granted as security to another lender, or may be subject to other claims of creditors who are otherwise unrelated to the Mortgaged Property. [Note: The existence of such creditors typically could pose an obstacle in a bankruptcy proceeding of Borrower, where a Lender holding a real estate mortgage loan will typically be looking for relief from the automatic foreclosure stay that is triggered by the commencement of such a bankruptcy proceeding, and within such proceeding Lender will typically be trying to obtain judicial relief from the restrictions that such proceeding places on Lender's ability to foreclose the Mortgage, as quickly following such commencement as possible.] As a result, in most cases, in order to qualify as being a single-purpose entity from a Lender's perspective, Borrower is typically required by Lender to be a newly formed special-purpose entity, who, in its organizational documents and in the Loan Documents, is not permitted to (a) own or control any assets other than the assets comprising the Mortgaged Property or (b) conduct any business other than the business of developing, managing, operating, financing and owning the Mortgaged Property.

As a result of this structure, Lender will want Borrower to grant to Lender a security interest in all, or virtually all, of Borrower's real estate, personal property assets, and any other interests of Borrower. To perfect its security interests in such real estate assets, Lender will require that the Mortgage be recorded in the appropriate registry of deeds having jurisdiction over the Land, Improvements, and other real estate interests of Borrower (and often Lender also will require a separate assignment of leases and rents from Borrower, but more on this later). To perfect its security interest in Borrower's personal property, Borrower will be required to take the appropriate steps mandated by the Uniform Commercial Code.

The Uniform Commercial Code provides that several different perfection steps must be taken for different types of personal property.

To provide Lender with a valid perfected interest in most of Borrower's personal property, Lender will typically require that Borrower enter into a security agreement as contemplated under Article 9 of the Uniform Commercial Code pursuant to which Borrower will grant to Lender a lien which shall cover such personal property. While some Lenders may prefer to employ a separate document as the security agreement, in most cases, the provisions for granting the security interest that would have been covered by a separate security agreement are instead built directly into the Mortgage. [Note: See the above Mortgage language in this Section of this Book, which deals with this point.] To perfect the Lender's security interest in most personal property, in addition to having Borrower grant such security interest to Lender, it is generally necessary also to file a financing statement with the Secretary of State where Borrower is domiciled. Lenders therefore routinely prepare and file (or have the title company file) such a statement in the appropriate county or state office of the Secretary of State where Borrower is domiciled. However, a different sort of filing is necessary with respect to Fixtures. Under §9-501(a)(1) of most state Uniform Commercial Codes, a "fixture filing" must be made "in the office designated for the filing or recording of a record of a mortgage on the related real property"—typically a county recorder's office where the Land is located.

There are certain distinct categories of personal property collateral that may require additional steps, such as perfecting an interest in a deposit account [Note: See Part IV Section 10 of this Book], in stock certificates, and in notes and other instruments, and the requirements for perfecting such interests are set out in the Uniform Commercial Code. [Note: If the applicable Borrower should own any of these types of assets, then those requirements will need to be adhered to in order for Borrower's counsel or Borrower's local counsel to be able to provide the necessary opinions which Lender will require in connection with closing the transaction; and obviously those requirements will be set out in the applicable Uniform Commercial Code.]

SECTION 4

Assignment of Rents

Explanation

It is quite common for a Mortgage to contain a provision which grants to Lender an assignment of Rents, or for Borrower to enter into a separate assignment of rents document. Some believe that Lenders might not bother to take assignments of Rents if mortgage foreclosure were always swift and certain. However, in reality, state law foreclosure proceedings may take from a few months to a year or more (with even lengthier periods to complete the foreclosure process being especially common in urban areas of states that still require foreclosure by judicial action). In addition, borrowers often file bankruptcy when faced with impending foreclosure, which can considerably lengthen the time before a foreclosure can be finalized (under the bankruptcy statute, a foreclosure proceeding is automatically stayed, pending the occurrence of certain judicial procedures and orders). As a result, it is quite important that Lender confirm that it is immediately entitled to the Rents following an Event of Default, while it waits for the foreclosure sale to occur. The following is a typical provision which might be contained in a Mortgage:

4.1 *As part of the consideration for the Obligations, Borrower absolutely and unconditionally assigns and transfers to Lender all Rents. It is the intention of Borrower to establish a present, absolute, unconditional and irrevocable transfer and assignment to Lender of all Rents and to authorize and empower Lender to collect and receive all Rents without the necessity of further action on the part of Borrower. Promptly upon request by Lender, Borrower agrees to execute and deliver such further assignments as Lender may from time to time require. Borrower and Lender intend this assignment of Rents to be immediately effective and to constitute a present absolute, unconditional and irrevocable assignment and not an assignment for additional security only.*

For purposes of giving effect to this present absolute, unconditional and irrevocable assignment of Rents, and for no other purpose, Rents shall not be deemed to be a part of the Mortgaged Property. However, if this present, absolute, unconditional and irrevocable assignment of Rents is not enforceable by its terms under the laws of the Property Jurisdiction, then the Rents shall be included as a part of the Mortgaged Property, and it is the intention of the Borrower that in this circumstance this Mortgage create and perfect a lien on Rents in favor of Lender, which lien shall be effective as of the date of this Mortgage.

Explanation

During the period between default and foreclosure, Borrower is unlikely to voluntarily pay any debt service payments to Lender. At the same time, during this period there is a significant risk that Borrower may try to "milk" or pocket all earned revenues of the Mortgaged Property, while deferring maintenance expenses, and payment of Impositions or other taxes, and other costs relating to the operation of the Mortgaged Property. Thus, the Mortgaged Property's value may be declining at the same time the Loan's accrued and unpaid interest is rising. As a result, the value of the Mortgaged Property, which might have been adequate security for the Loan when any applicable default occurred, may quickly become inadequate in these circumstances.

Prior to completing foreclosure, Lender's chief remedy to address this problem is to attempt to capture the rental cash flow and apply this money toward operating expenses and debt service. Even if the cash flow is inadequate to meet the full debt service, if a Lender can be successful in capturing this money, then such action will thwart Borrower's ability to "milk" the cash flow and avoid applying some or all of it to the Loan's debt service. *See* Julia Patterson Forrester, *A Uniform and More Rational Approach to Rents as Security for the Mortgage Loan*, 46 Rutgers L. Rev. 349 (1993).

Typically a rent assignment itself is similar to what was included in the above provisions and is intentionally configured so as to be an "absolute" assignment, as outlined above, but usually in the same document Borrower also is granted a "license" to administrate and manage the various obligations and conditions to be performed pursuant to each Lease as they relate to Rents (but with Lender reserving the right to cancel this license, and thereupon have the right to collect the Rents, when and if a default occurs). Thus, so long as a default does not exist, Borrower is expected to collect Rents and pay the Loan's debt service and Mortgaged Property's operating expenses. However, if there should exist any excess cash flow, then under these provisions, Borrower would have the right to retain such excess. This sort of assignment is sometimes described as "conditionally absolute," since the arising of a condition of default by Borrower under the Loan Documents must first occur in order to trigger the actual enforcement rights by Lender.

Although in the late 1980s and early 1990s there was some confusion concerning the concepts of "perfection" and "enforcement" of assignments of rents, during the latter part of the 1990s, the vast majority of bankruptcy court decisions have recognized that *perfection* of an assignment of rents (whether of the "security assignment" or the "conditionally absolute" type) is accomplished simply by recording it. *See, e.g., In re* Fairview-Takoma Ltd. P'ship, 206 B.R. 792 (D. Md. 1997). In addition, a number of states have recently enacted statutes providing that recording constitutes perfection.

SECTION 5

Assignment of Leases; Other Lease Covenants

Explanation

Lender will also want Borrower to grant to Lender a collateral assignment of Borrower's leasehold interest set out in the Leases with space tenants, in addition to receiving a collateral assignment of Rents (as discussed in Part IV Section 4 of this Book), because providing Lender with access to the Rents per se is not sufficient, and Lender also will want to have clear written permission which will allow Lender to modify the terms of a Lease, or to extend or terminate a Lease, once Borrower is in default under the Loan Documents. For example, if Lender, under the assignment of rents (following the occurrence of a default under the Loan Documents), commences collecting rents payable under the Mortgaged Property's Leases, and a particular tenant is delinquent, Lender would like to have the power to renegotiate some or all of the terms of the delinquent Lease, or to terminate such Lease if no satisfactory resolution can be achieved. Note that this is far from having complete authority to manage the Mortgaged Property, since such assignment does not per se permit Lender to enter into new Leases with respect to vacant space at the Mortgaged Property. To do that, Lender will probably either have to take the necessary steps to become a mortgagee-in-possession or get a receiver appointed.

The assignment of leases provision contained in the Mortgage will be characterized as an assignment in absolute terms for the same reasons discussed above regarding assignments of Rents. The statement that the assignment of leases is not "an assignment for additional security only" is as fictitious here as in the assignment of rents, because Lender's power over Leases is conditioned upon, and can only be exercised upon, the occurrence of a Borrower Event of Default.

Hence, it is in reality a security assignment. Below are some provisions which would typically be included in a Mortgage regarding the assignment of leases.

5.1 ***Assignment of Leases***. *As part of the consideration for the Obligations, Borrower absolutely and unconditionally assigns and transfers to Lender all of Borrower's right, title and interest in, to and under the Leases, including Borrower's right, power and authority to modify the terms of any such Lease, or extend or terminate any such Lease. It is the intention of Borrower to establish a present absolute, unconditional and irrevocable transfer and assignment to Lender of all of Borrower's right, title and interest in, to and under the Leases. Borrower and Lender intend this assignment of the Leases to be immediately effective and to constitute a present absolute, unconditional and irrevocable assignment and not an assignment for additional security only. For purposes of giving effect to this absolute assignment of the Leases, and for no other purpose, the Leases shall not be deemed to be a part of the Mortgaged Property. However, if this present, absolute, unconditional and irrevocable assignment of the Leases is not enforceable by its terms under the laws of the Property Jurisdiction, then the Leases shall be included as a part of the Mortgaged Property, and it is the intention of the Borrower that in this circumstance this Mortgage create and perfect a lien on the Leases in favor of Lender, which lien shall be effective as of the date of this Mortgage.*

5.2 **Borrower License to Exercise Landlord Rights**. *Until Lender gives notice to Borrower of Lender's exercise of its rights under this Section 5.2 of the Mortgage, Borrower shall have all rights, power and authority granted to Borrower under any Lease (except as otherwise limited by this Section or any other provision of this Mortgage), including the right, power and authority to modify the terms of any Lease or extend or terminate any Lease. Upon the occurrence of an Event of Default, the permission given to Borrower pursuant to the preceding sentence to exercise all rights, power and authority under Leases shall automatically terminate. Borrower shall comply with and observe Borrower's obligations under all Leases, including Borrower's obligations pertaining to the maintenance and disposition of tenant security deposits.*

5.3 **Borrower Recognition of Certain Lender Rights**. *Borrower acknowledges and agrees that the exercise by Lender, either directly or by a receiver, of any of the rights conferred under this Section 5.3 of the Mortgage, shall not be construed to make Lender a mortgagee-in-possession of the Mortgaged Property so long as Lender has not itself entered into actual possession of the Land and the Improvements. The acceptance by Lender of the assignment of the Leases pursuant to this Section 5 of the Mortgage shall not at any time or in any event obligate Lender to take any action under this Mortgage or to expend any money or to incur any expenses. Lender shall not be liable in any way for any injury or damage to person or property sustained by any person or persons, firm or corporation in or about the Mortgaged Property. Prior to Lender's actual entry into and taking possession of the Mortgaged Property, Lender shall not (i) be obligated to perform any of the terms, covenants and conditions* *contained in any Lease (or otherwise have any obligation with respect to any Lease); (ii) be obligated to appear in or defend any action or proceeding relating to the Lease or the Mortgaged Property; or (iii) be responsible for the operation, control, care, management or repair of the Mortgaged Property or any portion of the Mortgaged Property. The execution of this Mortgage by Borrower shall constitute conclusive evidence that all responsibility for the operation, control, care, management and repair of the Mortgaged Property is and shall be that of Borrower, prior to such actual entry and taking of possession.*

Explanation

This provision in the Mortgage attempts to give Lender the maximum possible authority over the landlord-tenant relationship without imposing on Lender the substantial responsibilities and risks of Lender undertaking "mortgagee-in-possession status," prior to the time that a Borrower Event of Default exists. However, it is unclear (and doubtful) whether a court will take this disclaimer language at face value. While the mere *acceptance* of the assignment of leases probably will not make Lender a mortgagee-in-possession, any actual *exercise* by Lender of authority over the Leases (e.g., renegotiation of their terms) probably will expose Lender to such responsibilities and risks, whether Lender has physically possessed the property or not. *See* Prince v. Brown, 856 P.2d 589 (Okla. Ct. App. 1993).

Likewise, it is clear that if a Lender becomes a mortgagee-in-possession, it could be liable for personal injuries to third parties caused by the mortgagee's management activities. *See* Skolnick v. E. Boston Sav. Bank, 29 N.E.2d 585, 130 A.L.R. 1519 (1940). It is extremely unlikely that a disclaimer of this duty in the mortgage would preclude a court from imposing liability on Lender. Obviously these concerns of Lender should not be too troubling to Borrower's counsel, but to the extent such provisions (which purport on their face to exempt Lender from incurring such liability) might not be enforceable and to the extent Borrower's counsel is rendering an enforceability opinion for the benefit of Lender in connection with the closing of the Loan, it would be wise for Borrower's counsel to expressly make such provisions subject to applicable law by starting them with: "to the extent permitted by applicable law," and then engage a counsel licensed to practice in the State where the Mortgaged Property is located to render an opinion on the enforceability of such local law matters.

As indicated in the prior Section, it is quite common for Lender to require a separate security document denominated as an "assignment of leases and rents" which will contain similar or expanded provisions relative to the provisions relating to the assignment of Leases and assignment of Rents contained in the Mortgage as set forth in the prior Section and in this Section. This separate Assignment of Leases and Rents will be in recordable form, and will need to be recorded in the registry where the Mortgaged Property is located (in order to perfect such interest).

Below are some other Mortgage covenant provisions that deal with Leases:

5.4 ***Lender's Right to Assert Its Assignment Rights***. *Upon delivery of notice by Lender to Borrower of Lender's exercise of Lender's rights under this Section 5.4 of this Mortgage at any time after the occurrence of an Event of Default, and without the necessity of Lender entering upon and taking and maintaining control of the Mortgaged Property directly, by a receiver, or by any other manner or proceeding permitted by the laws of the Property Jurisdiction, Lender immediately shall have all rights, powers and authority granted to Borrower under any Lease, including the right, power and authority to modify the terms of any such Lease, or extend or terminate any such Lease.*

5.5 ***Lender's Right to receive Leases***. *Borrower shall, promptly upon Lender's request, deliver to Lender an executed copy of each Lease then in effect. All Leases which are not Significant Leases shall either be on forms approved by Lender, and shall not include options to purchase,* ***provided*** *that any Lease which varies from the foregoing requirements shall require the prior written approval of Lender (which approval shall not be unreasonably withheld).*

Explanation

Lenders have a strong and legitimate interest in the Leases their Borrowers enter into with the Mortgaged Property's tenants. The value of a rental building is heavily dependent on the quality of its tenants leasing space, in the Improvements and their obligations under the Leases (particularly the obligation of such tenants to pay Lease rentals).

The following are some additional typical provisions relating to covenants concerning Leases that Lenders typically include in Loan Documents:

5.6 ***Certain Limitations upon Borrower's Rights to deal with Leases***. *Borrower shall not enter into a Lease of any portion of the Mortgaged Property in excess of _______ square feet (each a "****Significant Lease****"), except with the prior written consent of Lender and of the Tenant executing such Lease. Each Lease will be written on the approved Lease form which Borrower has previously delivered to Lender, or on another form approved in writing by Lender, in each case with such changes to the form as Lender shall approve in writing. Borrower shall not modify the terms of, or extend or terminate, any Significant Lease without the prior written consent of Lender. Borrower shall, without request by Lender, deliver an executed copy of each Lease to Lender promptly after such Lease is signed. All Leases, including renewals or extensions of existing Leases, shall specifically provide that (1) such Leases are subordinate to the lien of this Mortgage (unless waived in writing by Lender); (2) the tenant of such Lease shall attorn to Lender and any purchaser at a foreclosure sale, such attornment to be self-executing and effective upon acquisition of title to the Mortgaged Property by any purchaser at a foreclosure sale or by Lender* *in any manner; (3) the tenant of such Lease agrees to execute such further evidences of attornment as Lender or any purchaser at a foreclosure sale may from time to time request; (4) the Lease shall not be terminated by foreclosure or any other transfer of the Mortgaged Property; (5) after a foreclosure sale of the Mortgaged Property, Lender or any other purchaser at such foreclosure sale may, at Lender's or such purchaser's option, accept or terminate such Lease; and (6) the tenant shall, upon receipt after the occurrence of an Event of Default of a written request from Lender, pay all Rents payable under the Lease to Lender.*

Explanation

As the prior provisions indicate, Lender will likely insist on reviewing and approving all significant Leases and their respective tenants. The Mortgage usually contains a requirement that Borrower shall execute all leases only on a lender-approved form, or on another form approved in writing by Lender.

As indicated above, Borrower is almost always required to include in each Lease the subordination, nondisturbance, and attornment clauses referenced above. Subordination of each tenant's interest in each Lease is useful to Lender because it allows the purchaser of the Mortgaged Property at a foreclosure sale to terminate any given Lease and evict the tenant thereunder, if the purchaser views such tenant or Lease as being undesirable (however, many times a tenant's counsel will request that this form be modified to indicate that such termination right is only permitted if at the time it is being exercised, the tenant under the applicable Lease is then in default thereunder; with the result that as indicated below, Borrower's counsel will often try to negotiate for a provision in the Mortgage which provides each tenant with a nondisturbance assurance from Lender). Attornment by each tenant is useful because it allows the foreclosure purchaser, in the same situation, to insist that each tenant remain on its Lease if the purchaser views the Lease as desirable. In effect, Lender can choose whether to have its cake or eat it. In the above provisions, there is, however, no nondisturbance clause protecting any tenant from eviction in the event of foreclosure; and indeed, provision (5) expressly provides that the Lease may be terminated after foreclosure.

Many tenants, especially those with significant bargaining power, may find the absence of a nondisturbance assurance (in the event of a foreclosure sale) unacceptable. Borrower's counsel can try to negotiate with Lender's counsel to insert in the Mortgage such a non-disturbance covenant (particularly for new Significant Leases). Usually this type of covenant takes the form of Lender agreeing to enter into a "subordination, nondisturbance, and attornment agreement" with such tenants who are entering into the Significant Leases, or if Lender approves a request of Borrower to enter into such an agreement with any other tenant (to be perfected, these agreements must be in recordable form, and must be recorded in the registry which has jurisdiction over the Mortgaged Property).

Variable Interest Rates in Mortgage Loans

Explanation

Interest rates are used in Loan Documents to calculate the amount of annual interest which is to be paid throughout the term of the Loan. Historically, interest rates for commercial real estate loans have been either "fixed" or "variable." As indicated by its designated name, a "fixed" interest rate is generally a number (that is expressed as a percentage) which remains unchanged throughout the term of the Loan. "Variable" interest rates are also expressed as a percentage, but in this case the percentage interest rate will change periodically based on some type of agreed index (which is usually specified in the Note, Mortgage or Loan Agreement used in a given mortgage loan transaction) which is published regularly, and its rates are set to have such interest rate approximately keep pace with, and reflect, the then existing market interest rates for debt obligations which have varying terms (i.e., 30, 60, 90, 360 days, etc.).

Prior to the 1980s, banks, savings and loans, thrifts and other similar institutions in the United States, typically made shorter-term fixed-rate commercial mortgage loans and held them through the earlier of maturity or when they were paid off. Their experience with this business model was often disappointing because, following the loan closing, interest rates could go up, real estate values could go down, or both, with the effect, in either case, that the book value of the mortgage loans held by these lending institutions would go down. These circumstances gave rise to a negative impact on these loan assets, thereby impairing their ability to satisfy various government mandates regarding capital ratio requirements, which in turn jeopardized their ability to remain in business. These problems were particularly highlighted in the 1970s and early 1980s when there was a significant upward movement in inflation and in interest rates and also a significant nation-wide economic recession following the passage of the Federal Tax Reform Act in 1986 (which particularly hurt real estate values).

As a result of these circumstances, many of the commercial real estate loans which had closed in the United States following these recessionary periods have carried variable interest rates. With a variable interest rate, the book value of such variable rate loan held by a Lender would be less likely to fall when the interest rate environment was rising because the variable interest rate on the variable rate loan which previously closed also automatically would rise (so that the Loan's interest rate would continue to be at a level that would be somewhat comparable to the then increased market interest rate on newly originated loans).

However, a Borrower, when it is obtaining a mortgage loan, often does not want to be forced to take on the risk of a variable interest rate (because the rate may increase during the term of the Loan, and if it did, then such Borrower's interest payments would increase), and indeed a Lender is likewise often concerned about its Borrower being exposed to the risk of rising interest rates, which risk would exist if the mortgage loan should have a variable interest rate. The solution for addressing this problem, which has now become a very common feature in commercial mortgage lending in the United States, is for the Loan to require a variable interest rate, but at the same time, if Borrower or Lender do not want to expose Borrower to the risks associated with a variable interest rate, Borrower simultaneously with the loan closing could enter into an interest rate derivative contract, commonly known as an "interest rate swap." The interest rate swap (which is a contract between Borrower and a separate swap counterparty) allows a Borrower receiving a commercial real estate Loan with a variable rate, to basically only make monthly payments as if such Loan had carried a fixed interest rate. In short, under this structure, Borrower makes its monthly interest payments as if it were paying fixed interest, with the effect that if the then existing variable rate called for in the Loan Documents is higher than the fixed rate called for in the "interest rate swap," the swap counterparty will be obligated to pay Lender the difference on the Loan, and, conversely, if the existing variable rate called for in the Loan Documents is lower than the fixed rate called for in the "interest rate swap," Borrower will be obligated to pay the swap counterparty the difference on the Loan.

Starting in the mid-1980s, the British Bankers' Association, in conjunction with a number of other institutions, including the Bank of England, produced standardized contracts (which are commonly used in commercial real estate loan transactions) for interest rate swaps, which were based on an adjustable interest rate, which ultimately became known as the London Interbank Offered Rate ("LIBOR"). The LIBOR interest rate, which is recalculated each banking business day, is supposed to represent the interest rate which certain institutional banks would pay to borrow funds on a given business day (and actually represents an average of interest rates which are reported each Business Day to the entity which is calculating such average). After certain irregularities came to light regarding the fixing of LIBOR, the task of calculating LIBOR was transferred to a UK regulator in 2012, so that the calculation of LIBOR is currently regulated pursuant to several new laws passed by the British Parliament. Currently, when LIBOR is fixed each Business Day, such daily

LIBOR is reported by the Reuters news service. As will be discussed later on in this Section 6, following a more recent series of fraudulent actions, said UK regulator declared that it could not guarantee LIBOR's availability beyond the end of 2021.

Below are a typical variable rate set of provisions which are included in commercial real estate loan documents that use LIBOR as the interest rate:

6.1 ***Interest Rates.***

(a) ***Borrower's Options.*** *Principal amounts outstanding under the Loan shall bear interest at the following rates, at Borrower's selection, subject to the conditions and limitations provided for in this Mortgage or the Note: (i) Variable Rate or (ii) LIBOR Based Rate.*

(b) ***Selection to be Made.*** *Borrower shall select, and thereafter may change the selection of, the applicable interest rate, from the alternatives otherwise provided for in this Mortgage, by giving Lender a Notice of Rate Selection: (i) prior to each Loan Advance, (ii) prior to the end of each Interest Period applicable to a LIBOR Advance or (iii) on any Business Day on which Borrower desires to convert an outstanding Bank Rate Advance to a LIBOR Advance; provided, however, if an Event of Default exists, Borrower's right to select interest rate options other than ones based upon Bank Rates shall cease.*

(c) ***If No Notice.*** *If Borrower fails to select an interest rate option in accordance with the foregoing prior to a Loan Advance, or prior to the last day of the applicable Interest Period of an outstanding LIBOR Advance, any new Loan Advance made shall be deemed to be a LIBOR Advance.*

(d) ***Telephonic Notice.*** *Without any way limiting Borrower's obligation to confirm in writing any telephonic notice, Lender may act without liability upon the basis of telephonic notice believed by Lender in good faith to be from Borrower prior to receipt of written confirmation. In each case Borrower hereby waives the right to dispute Lender's record of the terms of such telephonic Notice of Rate Selection.*

(e) ***Limits on Options; One Selection Per Month.*** *Each LIBOR Advance shall be in a minimum amount of $_00,000. At no time shall there be outstanding a total of more than three (3) LIBOR Advances at any time. If Borrower shall make more than one (1) interest rate selection in any thirty (30) day period, excluding conversions of outstanding advances made at the end of an applicable Interest Period of any previously outstanding LIBOR Advance, Lender may impose and Borrower shall pay a reasonable processing fee for each such additional selection.*

6.2 ***Payment of Interest and Principal.***

(a) ***Payment and Calculation of Interest.*** *All interest shall be: (a) payable in arrears commencing [____________] 1, 20__ and on the same day of each month thereafter until the principal together with all interest and other charges payable with respect to the Loan shall be fully paid; and (b) calculated on the basis of a 360 day year and the actual number of days elapsed. Each change in the Prime Rate shall simultaneously change the Variable*

Rate payable under this Mortgage. Interest at the LIBOR Based Rate shall be computed from and including the first day of the applicable Interest Period to, but excluding, the last day thereof.

(b) ***Prepayment.*** *The Loan or any portion thereof may be prepaid partially or in full or in part at any time upon not less than [ten (10) days'] prior written notice to the holder of this Mortgage without premium or penalty other than any Breakage Costs. Any partial prepayment of principal shall first be applied to any installment of principal then due and then be applied to the principal due in the reverse order of maturity, and no such partial prepayment shall relieve Borrower of the obligation to pay each subsequent installment of principal when due.*

(c) ***Maturity.*** *At Maturity all accrued interest, principal and other charges due with respect to the Loan shall be due and payable in full and the principal balance and such other charges, but not unpaid interest, shall continue to bear interest at the Default Rate until so paid.*

(d) ***Application of Payments.*** *All payments shall be applied first to the payment of all fees, expenses and other amounts due to Lender (other than principal and interest), then to accrued interest, and thereafter to outstanding principal; provided, however, [after] during any Event of Default, payments will be applied to the Obligations of Borrower in such order and manner as Lender determines in its sole discretion.*

(e) ***Make Whole Provision.*** *Borrower shall pay to Lender, immediately upon request and notwithstanding contrary provisions contained in any of the Loan Documents, such amounts as shall, in the conclusive judgment of Lender (in the absence of manifest error), compensate Lender for the loss, cost or expense which it may reasonably incur as a result of (i) any prepayment of any then outstanding principal evidenced by the Note, under any circumstances whatsoever, whether voluntary or involuntary, of all or any portion of a LIBOR Advance on a date other than the last day of the applicable Interest Period of a LIBOR Advance, (ii) the conversion, for any reason whatsoever, whether voluntary or involuntary, of any LIBOR Advance to a Bank Rate Advance on a date other than the last day of the applicable Interest Period, (iii) the failure of all or a portion of a Loan Advance which was to have borne interest at the LIBOR Based Rate pursuant to the request of Borrower to be made under the Loan Agreement (except as a result of a failure by Lender to fulfill Lender's obligations to fund), or (iv) the failure of Borrower to borrow in accordance with any request submitted by it for a LIBOR Advance. Such amounts payable by Borrower shall be equal to any reasonable administrative costs actually incurred plus any Breakage Costs.*

6.3 ***Certain Definitions and Provisions Relating to Interest Rate.***

(a) ***Banking Day.*** *The term "Banking Day" means any day other than a Saturday, Sunday, legal holiday, or day on which banks are required or authorized by law to close in the city in which Lender's principal office is situated.*

(b) ***Breakage Costs***. *The term "Breakage Costs" means any actual loss or expense (including, without limitation, actual lost profit) that Lender sustains or incurs as a direct consequence of any prepayment (whether optional or mandatory) other than on the last day of the applicable Interest Period of a portion of the Note bearing interest at the LIBOR Based Rate by Borrower on and after the date hereof and through the Maturity, including, but not limited to, any loss or any interest payable by Lender to lenders of funds obtained by it in order to make or maintain the Loan at the LIBOR Based Rate or as provided in the Swap Documents.*

6.4 ***Interest Period***.

(a) *The term "Interest Period" means with respect to each LIBOR Advance: a period of one (1) month. Each such Interest Period shall commence on the Business Day so selected, or deemed selected, by Borrower and shall end on the numerically corresponding day in the first month thereafter, as applicable. Provided, however: (i) if there is no such numerically corresponding day, such Interest Period shall end on the last Business Day of the applicable month, (ii) if the last day of such an Interest Period would otherwise occur on a day which is not a Business Day, such Interest Period shall be extended to the next succeeding Business Day; but (iii) if such extension would otherwise cause such last day to occur in a new calendar month, then such last day shall occur on the next preceding Business Day.*

(b) *The term "Interest Period" shall mean with respect to each Bank Rate Advance consecutive periods of one (1) day each.*

(c) *No Interest Period may be selected which would end beyond the then Maturity Date of the Loan (as actually extended). If the last day of an Interest Period would otherwise occur on a day which is not a Business Day, such last day shall be extended to the next succeeding Business Day, except as provided above relative to a LIBOR Advance.*

(d) ***LIBOR Rate***. *The term "LIBOR Rate" shall mean, as applicable to any LIBOR Advance, the rate per annum equal to the London Interbank Offered Rate administered by the ICE Benchmark Administration (or any other Person that takes over the administration of such rate) ("LIBOR"), as published by Reuters (or other commercially available source providing quotations of LIBOR as designated by Lender from time to time in a manner consistent with any such designation by Lender generally under substantially similar credit facilities for which it acts as a lender) at approximately 11:00 a.m. London time on the date that is two (2) London Banking Days preceding the applicable Interest Period, for Dollars (for delivery on the first day of such Interest Period) with a term equivalent to such Interest Period; provided, however, if the rate described above does not appear on the Reuters screen on any applicable interest determination date, the LIBOR Rate shall be the rate determined on the basis of the offered rates for deposits in U.S. Dollars for a one-month period which are offered by four major banks in the London interbank market at* *approximately 11:00 a.m. London time, on the day that is two (2) London Banking Days preceding the first day of such LIBOR Advance as selected by Lender. The principal London office of each of the four major London banks will be requested to provide a quotation of its U.S. Dollar deposit offered rate. If at least two such quotations are provided, the rate for that date will be the arithmetic mean of the quotations. If fewer than two quotations are provided as requested, the rate for that date will be determined on the basis of the rates quoted for loans in U.S. Dollars to leading European banks for a period of time comparable to such LIBOR Advance offered by major banks in New York City at approximately 11:00 a.m. New York City time, on the day that is two London Banking Days preceding the first day of such LIBOR Advance. In the event that Lender is unable to obtain any such quotation as provided above, it will be deemed that LIBOR Rate for a LIBOR Advance cannot be determined. In the event that the Board of Governors of the Federal Reserve System shall impose a Reserve Percentage with respect to LIBOR Rate deposits of Lender then for any period during which such Reserve Percentage shall apply, the LIBOR Rate shall be equal to the amount determined above divided by an amount equal to 1 minus the Reserve Percentage. "Reserve Percentage" shall mean the maximum aggregate reserve requirement (including all basic, supplemental, marginal and other reserves) which is imposed on member banks of the Federal Reserve System against "Euro-currency Liabilities" as defined in Regulation D.*

(e) ***LIBOR Advance.*** *The term "LIBOR Advance" means any principal outstanding under the Note which pursuant to this Mortgage bears interest at the LIBOR Based Rate.*

(f) ***LIBOR Based Rate.*** *The term "LIBOR Based Rate" means the per annum rate of interest equal to the applicable LIBOR Rate, plus 225 basis points.*

(g) ***London Banking Day.*** *The term "London Banking Day" means any Banking Day on which dealings in deposits in Dollars are transacted in the London interbank market and banks are open for business in London.*

(h) ***Maturity.*** *The term "Maturity" means ____, 20__ ("Maturity Date"), or upon acceleration of the Loan, if the Loan has been accelerated by Lender upon an Event of Default.*

(i) ***Prime Rate.*** *The term "Prime Rate" means the per annum rate of interest so designated from time to time by Lender as its prime rate. The Prime Rate is a reference rate and does not necessarily represent the lowest or best rate being charged to any customer.*

(j) ***Variable Rate.*** *The term "Variable Rate" means a per annum rate equal at all times to the greater of (a) the Prime Rate or (b) the LIBOR Rate, plus ___ basis points with changes therein to be effective simultaneously with any change in the Prime Rate without notice or demand of any kind.*

(k) ***Variable Rate Advance.*** *The term "Variable Rate Advance" means any principal amount outstanding under the Note which pursuant to this Mortgage bears interest at the Variable Rate.*

6.5 ***Additional Provisions Related to Interest Rate Selection.***

(a) ***Increased Costs.*** *If, due to a Change in Law, there shall be an increase in the cost to Lender of agreeing to make or making, funding or maintaining LIBOR Advances, including without limitation changes which affect or would affect the amount of capital or reserves required or expected to be maintained by Lender, with respect to all or any portion of the Loan, or any corporation controlling Lender, on account thereof, then Borrower from time to time shall, upon written demand by Lender, pay Lender additional amounts sufficient to indemnify Lender against the increased cost. A certificate as to the amount of the increased cost and the reason therefor submitted to Borrower by Lender, in the absence of manifest error, shall be conclusive and binding for all purposes. Notwithstanding any provision hereof to the contrary, in no event shall Borrower be required to pay any amounts in respect of income or franchise taxes payable by Lender.*

(b) ***Illegality.*** *Notwithstanding any other provision of this Mortgage or the Note, if the introduction of or change in or in the interpretation of any law, treaty, statute, regulation or interpretation thereof shall make it unlawful, or any central bank or government authority shall assert by directive, guideline or otherwise, that it is unlawful, for Lender to make or maintain LIBOR Advances or to continue to fund or maintain LIBOR Advances then, on written notice thereof and demand by Lender to Borrower, (a) the obligation of Lender to make LIBOR Advances and to convert or continue any Loan Advances as LIBOR Advances shall terminate and (b) Borrower shall convert all principal outstanding under the Note into Variable Rate Advances.*

(c) ***Additional LIBOR Conditions.*** *The selection by Borrower of a LIBOR Based Rate and the maintenance of Loan Advances at such rate shall be subject to the following additional terms and conditions:*

(d) ***Availability.*** *If, before or after Borrower has selected to take or maintain a LIBOR Advance, Lender notifies Borrower that:*

   (i) *dollar deposits in the amount and for the maturity requested are not available to Lender in the London interbank market at the rate specified in the definition of LIBOR Rate set forth above, or*

   (ii) *reasonable means do not exist for Lender to determine the LIBOR Rate for the amounts and maturity requested,*

   then the principal which would have been a LIBOR Advance shall be a Variable Rate Advance.

(e) ***Payments Net of Taxes.*** *All payments and prepayments of principal and interest under this Mortgage and the Note shall be made net of any taxes and costs first imposed after the date hereof resulting solely from having principal outstanding at or computed with reference to a LIBOR Based Rate.*

Without limiting the generality of the preceding obligation, illustrations of such taxes and costs are taxes, or the withholding of amounts for taxes, of any nature whatsoever including income, excise, interest equalization taxes (other than United States or state income taxes) as well as all levies, imposts, duties or fees whether now in existence or as the result of a change in or promulgation of any treaty, statute, regulation, or interpretation thereof or any directive guideline or otherwise by a central bank or fiscal authority (whether or not having the force of law) or a change in the basis of, or the time of payment of, such taxes and other amounts resulting therefrom.

(f) ***Variable Rate Advances.*** *Each Variable Rate Advance shall continue as a Variable Rate Advance until Maturity of the Loan, unless sooner converted, in whole or in part, to a LIBOR Advance, subject to the limitations and conditions set forth in this Mortgage and the Note.*

Explanation

Notice that in these provisions, Borrower is given the option to select either (i) the Variable Rate (which in these provisions is keyed to the prime rate being periodically offered to Lender's best customers) or (ii) the LIBOR Based Rate. If Borrower has also entered into an interest rate swap arrangement, then pursuant to the applicable swap contract documenting such arrangement, Borrower will be mandated to always select the LIBOR Based Rate (which is equal to the aggregate of (i) the LIBOR Rate as it corresponds to a one-month period (and then which must always be reselected at the end of such monthly period throughout the term of the Loan), plus (ii) a fixed percentage spread (which in the case of the above provisions is 225 basis points). The reason that the swap contracts impose this requirement is that the swap counterparty is anticipating that Borrower under its Loan Documents will at all times only be utilizing a LIBOR Based Rate throughout the term of the Loan (which will also be the term of such swap contract) for the purposes of the interest rate swap contract. As a result, it is highly unlikely that Borrower, assuming it has elected to enter into such a swap contract, will ever voluntarily select the option in the Loan Documents that results in using the Variable Rate. In any event, in almost all circumstances, throughout the term of the Loan, the actual LIBOR Base Rate at all times will be lower than the Variable Rate, and therefore it will be a better selection for Borrower even if Borrower did not enter into an interest rate swap.

Most of the language used in these LIBOR interest provisions in the Loan Document is pretty much non-negotiable. Borrower's counsel should not be put off by the fact that the provisions seem to be talking about multiple advances of loan proceeds, because usually there will only be a single advance of loan proceeds from Lender to Borrower, and the effect of the language calling for multiple advances is simply a vehicle that allows a separate new LIBOR Based Rate to be selected at the end of each one-month period (and note that the one-month LIBOR Rate is the corresponding period for LIBOR Based Rates which is specified as the LIBOR Based Rate that is used in Borrower's swap contract). It is important for Borrower's counsel to confirm that the spread over the LIBOR Rate (which then forms the basis of the LIBOR Based Rate) that is specified in the Loan Documents, is the same as the spread that is set out in the interest rate swap documents (which, in the case of the foregoing Mortgage provisions set out above in this Section of this Book, has a spread equal to 225 basis points).

Borrower's counsel should be aware that if the Loan has to be prepaid earlier than the Maturity Date, there is the real possibility that such prepayment could come at a hefty price. If Borrower has entered into an interest rate swap, and depending on where U.S. Treasury interest rates then currently stand in the market at the time of such prepayment, there could be a significant prepayment penalty that would have to be paid by Borrower in connection with the payoff of the Loan. In the above Mortgage LIBOR interest provision, this prepayment penalty concept is captured in the definition of "Breakage Costs" in Section 6.3(b). This definition, as written, is too broad. The Breakage Costs in these provisions (where an interest rate swap agreement is in effect) should only include the costs in excess of then outstanding principal, which are payable pursuant to the swap documents as a result of any prepayment (and therefore, Borrower's counsel should insist that this definition not also include "lost profits"). The "Breakage Costs" provided for in the interest rate swap agreement must be paid by Borrower at the time of Prepayment of the Loan unless the then current rate of the applicable US Treasury security shall have risen higher than the spread provided for in the definition of LIBOR Based Rate. Note that if such rise in such rate shall have occurred, then at the time of the payoff of the Loan, Borrower will be entitled to a payment from the swap counterparty pursuant to the interest rate swap documentation. To the extent that Borrower's counsel is successfully able to negotiate a waiver of prepayment penalties in the Loan Documents, such as mandatory prepayment in the case of total condemnation, or, if applicable, total destruction of the Mortgaged Property, or mandatory prepayments required by Lender in connection with certain regulatory changes of law, then Borrower's counsel will want to be sure that such a waiver of prepayment penalties is also reflected in the interest rate swap documentation.

In certain cases where the LIBOR Based Rate is being used to determine the interest rate under the Loan, but where there is no corresponding interest rate swap arrangement in effect, then it is quite common for Borrower to negotiate the option to select from a number of different Interest Periods (such as two-month, three-month, quarterly, semiannually and annual periods).

With regard to Part IV Section 6.5(b) above in this Section 6 of this Book, which deals with illegality and which would result in requiring the interest rate to be calculated utilizing only the Variable Rate, Borrower's counsel should realize that if such future change in laws occurs, then under such circumstance it is likely that the swap contract documentation would mandate that the Breakage Costs would then have to be paid (because Borrower would no longer be obligated under the Loan Documents to pay the LIBOR Based Rate). In this instance, Borrower's counsel should try to require that if such illegality occurred and if Borrower made a prompt full prepayment of the Loan, then the Breakage Costs should be waived, since Borrower cannot control the occurrence of such illegality. However, I have found that rarely will such a suggested change be successfully accepted by Lender.

Whenever there is a provision in the Loan Documents relating to adjustable interest rates, or other compensation payable to Lender which could be viewed as supplemental interest, there is a danger that such a provision could run afoul of the Property Jurisdiction's usury laws. Inasmuch as Lender will be requiring enforceability opinions relative to the Loan Documents, and oftentimes such opinion must contain a usury opinion, with the effect that if Borrower's counsel is not licensed to practice under the Property Jurisdiction, Borrower's counsel will need to get local counsel to review the Loan Documents and provide such local law opinions (and if necessary require necessary changes to the Loan Documents so as to cause them to comply with the laws of the Property Jurisdiction, particularly in respect of usury). In some jurisdictions, Lenders are exempted from the restrictions contained in the usury laws of the Property Jurisdiction, if Lenders are licensed or regulated by federal or state governmental authorities.

As previously mentioned in this Section 6.1, as a result of several serious fraudulent actions involving the manipulation of the LIBOR Rate, said UK regulator declared that it could not guarantee LIBOR's availability beyond the end of 2021. Obviously there will need to be a transition from the use of LIBOR in mortgage real estate loans and interest rate swap contracts. The U.S. Federal Reserve convened a working group called the Alternative Reference Rates Committee ("**ARRC**") to help facilitate the likely transition away from LIBOR. ARRC has recommended the utilization of an index called the Secured Overnight Financing Rate ("**SOFR**") as its recommended alternative to LIBOR and has published a transition plan to promote the use of SOFR on a voluntary basis. Many newer mortgage loans now provide for the usage of SOFR, when and if the LIBOR Rates cease to be published.

SECTION 7

Other Prepayment Premiums

Explanation

As indicated in the preceding Section 6, many commercial real estate loans have a variable interest rate, and many of these variable interest rates are currently based on LIBOR. However, quite a few longer-term commercial real estate loans and most residential real estate loans continue to have a fixed annual interest rate. With a fixed annual interest rate, particularly if the term of the Mortgage is more than a few years, Lender will be concerned about allowing Borrower to have the option to prepay the Loan prior to Maturity, as this will allow a Borrower the option to refinance the Loan with another lender if interest rates should fall in the future (while at the same time costing the initial Lender the benefit of its bargain to receive the fixed rate for the term of the Loan). Clearly, if interest rates have fallen below the fixed annual interest rate provided for in the initial Loan, any Lender who is being paid off usually will not be able to redeploy the proceeds of such prepayment and make another loan at that time with those proceeds that will carry an interest rate comparable to the fixed interest rate that was part of the prepaid Loan. Indeed for most Lenders who permit interest rates to be fixed for longer-term loans, they are entering into this investment with the goal to have a reliable income stream for the term of the Loan. Therefore, permitting Borrower to have an option to refinance will be permissible only if Lender receives significant "kicker" compensation at the time of such prepayment. This excess compensation usually takes the form of a prepayment premium. This form of prepayment penalty often is very similar to the payment which I discussed in Part IV Section 6 of this Book which was payable in the case of variable interest rate loans where Borrower also entered into an interest rate swap agreement. In Section 6 it was noted if the swap contract was broken prior to the expiration of its term, Borrower could be liable to pay significant

Breakage Costs. As a result, most Loan Documents are not silent on the issue of prepayment. Below is a provision that is contained in a fixed interest rate note, which is somewhat typical for fixed interest rate loans and which provides that, if Borrower desires to voluntarily prepay a fixed interest rate Loan, Borrower will be obligated to pay Lender a prepayment premium to compensate Lender for the losses that it will or may incur in connection with the prepayment (the potential reinvestment loss described above and other losses and expenses that Lender may incur):

a. *A prepayment premium shall be payable in connection with any voluntary prepayment which Borrower elects to make of the then outstanding principal evidenced by the Note as provided below:*
    1. *Borrower may voluntarily prepay all (but not less than all) of the unpaid principal balance of the Note on the last Business Day of a calendar month if Borrower has given Lender at least 30 days prior notice of its intention to make such prepayment. Such prepayment shall be made by paying (A) the amount of principal being prepaid, (B) all accrued interest, (C) all other sums due Lender at the time of such prepayment, and (D) the prepayment premium calculated pursuant to Schedule A attached to this Note. For all purposes, including the accrual of interest, any prepayment received by Lender on any day other than the last calendar day of such month shall be deemed to have been received on the last calendar day of each month. For purposes of this Note, a* ***"Business Day"*** *means any day other than a Saturday, Sunday or any other day on which Lender is not open for business.*
    2. *Upon Lender's exercise of any right of acceleration under this Note, Borrower shall pay to Lender, in addition to the entire unpaid principal balance of this Note outstanding at the time of the acceleration, (A) all accrued interest and all other sums due Lender under the Note and the other Loan Documents, and (B) the prepayment premium calculated pursuant to Schedule A attached to this Note.*

b. *Any application by Lender of any collateral or other security to the repayment of any portion of the unpaid principal balance of this Note prior to the Maturity Date and in the absence of acceleration shall be deemed to be a partial prepayment by Borrower, requiring the payment to Lender by Borrower of a prepayment premium. The amount of any such partial prepayment shall be computed so as to provide to Lender a prepayment premium computed pursuant to Schedule A attached to this Note without Borrower having to pay out-of-pocket any additional amounts.*

c. *Notwithstanding the provisions of Paragraph __ of this Note, no prepayment premium shall be payable with respect to (A) any prepayment made no more than 90 days before the Maturity Date, or (B) any prepayment occurring as a result of the application of any insurance proceeds or condemnation award under this Note.*

d. *Schedule A is hereby incorporated by reference into this Note.*

e. *Any required prepayment of less than the unpaid principal of this Note shall not extend or postpone the due date of any subsequent monthly installments or change the amount of such installments, unless Lender agrees otherwise in writing.*

f. *Borrower recognizes that any prepayment of the unpaid principal balance of this Note, whether voluntary or involuntary or resulting from a default by Borrower, will result in Lender's incurring loss, including reinvestment loss, additional expense and frustration or impairment of Lender's ability to meet its commitments to third parties. Borrower agrees to pay to Lender upon demand damages for the detriment caused by any prepayment, and agrees that it is extremely difficult and impractical to ascertain the extent of such damages. Borrower therefore acknowledges and agrees that the formula for calculating prepayment premiums set forth on Schedule A represents a reasonable estimate of the damages Lender will incur because of a prepayment.*

g. *Borrower further acknowledges that the prepayment premium provisions of this Note are a material part of the consideration for the loan evidenced by this Note, and acknowledges that the terms of this Note are in other respects more favorable to Borrower as a result of the Borrower's voluntary agreement to the prepayment provisions.*

Explanation

The foregoing provisions do not require Borrower to pay a prepayment premium in the event of a casualty or condemnation when insurance proceeds or the condemnation award are applied to the debt (in these two instances the prepayment is beyond the control and fault of Borrower, and many Lenders have opted not to require a charge in that context), or when a prepayment is made within 90 days before the stated Maturity Date (this gives Borrower a window period to obtain and close on a refinancing). Also note that these provisions clarify that the prepayment charge applies whether the prepayment is "voluntary" or "involuntary" (i.e., a default by Borrower and acceleration of the Loan by Lender). It is also possible that Borrower's counsel may be able to negotiate a waiver of the prepayment premium in instances where the Loan Documents require a mandatory prepayment of the Loan due to changes in legal requirements or regulations relating to Lender. An example of this is where a change of law or regulation requires Lender to maintain additional reserves, such that the Loan Documents mandate a full or partial prepayment of the Loan should this event occur.

Below is the form of Schedule A to the Note which is referenced by the above provisions contained in this Section.

Schedule A

Prepayment Premium. *Any prepayment premium (a "**Prepayment Premium**") payable under this Note shall be computed as follows:*

If any applicable prepayment of the then outstanding principal evidenced by the Note is made before the 90 day period that immediately precedes the Maturity Date, the prepayment premium shall be the greater of:

i. *1% of the then unpaid principal balance evidenced by the Note; or*

ii. *The product obtained by multiplying:*

   A. *the amount of principal being prepaid, by*

   B. *the difference obtained by subtracting from the fixed interest rate on the Note the yield rate (the "Yield Rate") on the __% U.S. Treasury Security due ____________________ (the "Specified U.S. Treasury Security"), as selected by Lender, as such Yield Rate is reported in The Wall Street Journal on the fifth Business Day preceding (x) the date notice of prepayment is given to Lender where prepayment is voluntary, or (y) the date Lender accelerates the Loan, by*

   C. *the present value factor calculated using the following formula:*

   $\frac{1 - (1 + r)^{-n}}{r}$

   [r = Yield Rate

   n = the number of 365-day years (or 366-day years, if applicable), and any fraction thereof, remaining between the Prepayment Date and the expiration of the Yield Maintenance Period]

In the event that no Yield Rate is published for the Specified U.S. Treasury Security, then the nearest equivalent U.S. Treasury Security shall be selected at Lender's discretion. If the publication of such Yield Rate in The Wall Street Journal is discontinued, Lender shall determine such Yield Rate from another source selected by Lender.

For purposes of subparagraph (ii), the ***"Prepayment Date"*** *shall be (x) in the case of a voluntary prepayment, the date on which the prepayment is made, and (y) in any other case, the date on which Lender accelerates the unpaid principal balance of this Note.*

Explanation

It is important from a Lender perspective that the Loan Documents clarify that a prepayment premium will apply and be payable in an "involuntary" prepayment situation (i.e., any voluntary or mandatory prepayment made when a default or Event of Default shall occur and then be continuing). In the past, when Loan Documents have failed to clarify this, courts have refused to enforce the prepayment premium when Borrower has defaulted and Lender has accelerated the debt. *See, e.g.*, Slevin Container Corp. v. Provident Fed. Sav. & Loan Ass'n, 424 N.E.2d 939 (Ill. App. Ct. 1981); *In re* LHD Realty Corp., 726 F.2d 327 (7th Cir. 1984). However, when Loan Documents clearly require a prepayment charge in a default/acceleration situation, courts have enforced the imposition of such charges. *See, e.g.*, Pacific Trust Co. TTEE v. Fidelity Fed. Sav. & Loan Ass'n, 184 Cal. App. 3d 817, 824, 229 Cal. Rptr. 269, 274 (1986); Village of Rosemont v. Maywood-Proviso State Bank, 149 Ill. App. 3d 1087, 501 N.E. 2d 859 (1986); Eyde v. Empire of Am. Fed. Sav. Bank, 701 F. Supp. 126 (E.D. Mich. 1988).

There are other ways in which prepayment charges have been calculated. Older forms of Loan Documents frequently provided for a prepayment charge based upon a specified percentage multiplied against the then outstanding balance of the Loan being paid off (e.g., 5 percent). Typically, the percentage would decline as the Loan became closer to maturing (the idea being that as the Loan got closer to maturing, the lender's damages from prepayment declined). Under this approach you might have the prepayment charge be 5% of Loan in year 5, 4% of Loan in year 4, etc. This method was obviously imprecise (e.g., if interest rates had actually risen, then Lender would have no pure reinvestment losses; conversely, if interest rates had dropped significantly, it is possible that Lender could suffer losses in excess of 5 percent of the balance of the loan in year 5). Due to this imprecision, and the need to more accurately guarantee that the yields to maturity in the loan documents be maintained even if the loans were paid off early, lenders began to use a "yield maintenance formula" to calculate the prepayment charge.

The Schedule A to the Note, as shown above, provides for a typical yield maintenance formula that is used for a fixed interest rate note. Under this formula, to determine the prepayment fee, one multiplies the principal amount then being prepaid, by the difference between the fixed interest rate on the Note and the yield rate on a specified U.S. Treasury security (having a comparable term as the then remaining term of the Note) which an investor will receive if it purchases such specified U.S. Treasury security at the time of such prepayment or acceleration of the Loan. The theory behind using this formula is that upon repayment of the Loan from the proceeds paid by Borrower, Lender will be in a position to reinvest such proceeds (the aggregate of the prepaid principal of the Loan, plus the prepayment amount) to purchase a sufficiently large U.S. Treasury security, so as to enable Lender to receive the aggregate amount of principal and interest payments that such Lender would have received for the period following prepayment under the debt service payments which otherwise would have been payable had the Loan not been prepaid. If the U.S. Treasury security in the preceding example should accrue interest at the same or a higher interest rate than the interest rate that would have been payable under the Note, then Lender suffers no lost opportunity cost as a result of the prepayment, and thus no charge is owed. If the U.S. Treasury security is accruing interest at a lower interest rate than the interest rate that would have been payable under the Note, Borrower must pay a prepayment charge under this formula that will be equal to that difference in rates (as between the U.S. Treasury security and the Note), multiplied by the balance of the Loan to compensate Lender for that difference. Then under the terms of the prepayment provision formula, this amount is discounted to its present value to account for the fact that Lender will be receiving the money in a lump sum today, which allows Lender the ability to invest the money now and receive a return on such investment over the remaining term on the Loan that has been prepaid, so as to afford Lender the opportunity to be in the same financial position as if the Loan had not been prepaid. It should be noted, however, that the calculation of the prepayment charge which is used in this prepayment provision, also provides for Lender to receive the greater of 1 percent of the unpaid balance of the loan or the difference in interest rates described above.

Consequently, even if interest rates have risen since the Loan was funded, Lender would still pocket at least the 1 percent charge should the Loan be prepaid, regardless of how interest rates had moved in the interim period. It should also be noted that under such prepayment provision, the yield maintenance formula applies only to a set number of years of the loan (it is a blank in the form), which would normally correspond to the term of the Loan. Also note that this yield maintenance approach is highly favorable to Lender, because it allows Lender to get the credit of the United States Government (who is the obligor under the national U.S. Treasury security which Lender will have the right to purchase), which presumably is a much better credit than Borrower, and with the result that to achieve a comparable interest rate yield as embodied in the fixed interest rate under the Note, Borrower will be obligated to pay Lender, as part of this prepayment premium, a significant excess sum of money, in order to enable Lender to purchase a sufficient amount of U.S. Treasury securities so as to make this formulation work.

SECTION 8

Representations and Warranties

Explanation

Virtually all Loan Documents contain representations and warranties that are given by Borrower to Lender, and the bulk of these representations in a commercial mortgage loan are usually contained in the Mortgage and/or the Loan Agreement. Representations and warranties are needed by Lender, because to be comfortable funding the Loan, Lender will want certain factual information concerning the Mortgaged Property, Borrower and other matters relevant to the Loan to be confirmed, and often Borrower is the only one in a practical position to provide these representations and warranties. However, it is often the case that notwithstanding that Borrower may not be in a position to have knowledge of some of the facts that they are being called on in the Loan Documents to represent as being true and correct, or that this information is otherwise being provided to Lender by third-party experts, or is readily obtainable in the document file which Borrower will be providing Lender in connection with closing the Loan (so that Lender is in a position to determine the status of these facts through its review), Lender will still try to have Borrower make representations that such facts are true and correct, in order to provide Lender with the additional level of comfort with regard to closing the Loan. As we will see, in many cases Borrower's counsel needs to be concerned that Lender should not overreach with regard to these representations and warranties, since a Borrower misrepresentation could lead to a default, which in turn could cause the Loan to accelerate to the determent of Borrower. Below is a typical set of representations and warranties which a Lender might request in a Loan:

8.1 ***Representations and Warranties***.

Borrower warrants and represents to Lender for the express purpose of inducing Lender to enter into this Mortgage, to advance the proceeds of the Loan, and to otherwise complete all of the transactions contemplated hereby, that as of the date of this Mortgage:

(a) ***Financial Information.***

*True, accurate and complete, in all material respects, financial statements of Borrower [and each Person who shall have executed any guaranty or indemnity in favor of Lender, which shall be included as a Loan Document ("**Guarantor**")] have been delivered to Lender and the same fairly present the financial condition of Borrower and Guarantor as of the dates thereof and no material and adverse change has occurred in such financial condition since the dates thereof. All financial statements of Borrower and Guarantor hereafter furnished to Lender shall be true, accurate and complete in all material respects and shall fairly present the financial condition of Borrower and Guarantor as of the dates thereof.*

(b) ***No Violations.***

The consummation of the Loan and the subsequent payment and performance of the Obligations evidenced and secured by the Loan Documents shall not constitute a violation of, or conflict with, any law, order, regulation, contract, agreement or organizational document to which Borrower or Guarantor is a party or by which Borrower or Guarantor, or the Mortgaged Property, may be bound.

(c) ***No Litigation.***

There is no material litigation now pending, or to Borrower's Knowledge threatened, against Borrower, Guarantor or the Mortgaged Property which if adversely decided could reasonably be expected to materially impair the ability of Borrower, Guarantor or the Mortgaged Property to pay and perform its obligations hereunder or under the other Loan Documents. There is no other litigation, whether or not material, pending, or to Borrower's Knowledge threatened, against Borrower, Guarantor or the Mortgaged Property.

(d) ***Good Title and No Liens.***

Borrower is the lawful owner of the interest [and/or a leasehold interest] in the Mortgaged Property and of areas over, under or on which utility or passage easements are required to make use of the Improvements and parking as contemplated hereby and by the documents referred to herein, and is the lawful owner of the Improvements, free and clear of all liens and encumbrances of any nature whatsoever, except for the matters, if any, which are listed as permitted title exceptions in the Mortgage.

(e) ***Loan Proceeds.***

The proceeds of the Loan shall be used solely and exclusively for the payment of costs relating to the closing of the Loan, refinancing of any prior mortgage loan encumbering the Mortgaged Property, or other relevant costs as set forth in answer to the project budget (as the same may be amended from time to time in accordance with this Mortgage or otherwise with Lender's prior written approval in each instance where such approval is required by the terms of this Mortgage). No portion of the proceeds of the Loan shall be used directly or indirectly, and whether immediately, incidentally or ultimately (i) to purchase or carry any margin stock, or to extend credit to others for the purpose thereof, or to repay or refund indebtedness previously incurred for such purpose, or (ii) for any purpose which would violate or is inconsistent with the provisions of regulations of the Board of Governors of the Federal Reserve System including, without limitation, Regulations G, T, U and X thereof.

(f) ***Loan Documents Legal and Binding.***
Each of the Loan Documents constitute legal, valid and binding obligations of Borrower and, where applicable, Guarantor; in each case in accordance with the respective terms thereof, subject to bankruptcy, insolvency and similar laws of general application affecting the rights and remedies of creditors and, with respect to the availability of the remedies of specific enforcement, subject to the discretion of the court before which any proceeding therefore may be brought.

(g) ***ERISA.***
*Borrower does not have any pension, profit sharing, stock option, insurance or other arrangement or plan for employees covered by Title IV of the Employment Retirement Security Act of 1974, as now or hereafter amended ("**ERISA**") except as may be designated to Lender in writing by Borrower from time to time ("**ERISA Plan**") and no "Reportable Event" as defined in ERISA has occurred and is now continuing with respect to any such ERISA Plan. The granting of the Loan, the performance by Borrower of its obligations under the Loan Documents and Borrower's conducting of its operations do not and will not violate any provisions of ERISA.*

(h) ***No Material Adverse Change.***
There has been no material adverse change in the financial condition, business, affairs or control of Borrower or Guarantor since the date of their respective last financial statements most recently delivered to Lender. No Default exists under any of the Loan Documents. There is no Default on the part of Borrower or Guarantor under this Mortgage or any of the other Loan Documents and no event has occurred and is continuing which could constitute a Default under any Loan Document. Borrower has filed all required federal, state and local tax returns and has paid all taxes due pursuant to such returns or any assessments against Borrower or the Mortgaged Property.

(i) ***No Dealings with Brokers.***
Neither Borrower, nor Guarantor, nor anyone on behalf thereof, has dealt with any broker, finder or other person or entity who or which may be entitled to a broker's or finder's fee, or other compensation, payable by Lender in connection with this Loan.

(j) ***Condemnation/Casualty.***
There are no condemnation proceedings or the like pending or, to Borrower's Knowledge, threatened in writing against the Mortgaged Property or

any portion thereof nor has there occurred any casualty at the Mortgaged Property.

(k) ***Special Assessments.***

Except as may be set forth in the Title Policy, as of the date hereof there are no pending, or to the Borrower's Knowledge, proposed special or other assessments for public improvements or otherwise affecting the Mortgaged Property.

(l) ***Solvency.***

Neither Borrower nor any Guarantor is insolvent and neither Borrower nor any Guarantor will be rendered insolvent by the transaction contemplated under the Loan Documents.

(m) ***Flood Zone.***

No portion of the Mortgaged Property is located in any special flood hazard area designated as such by any public authority.

(n) ***Compliance with Anti-Terrorism, Embargo, Sanctions and Anti-Money Laundering Laws.***

Borrower and, to Borrower's Knowledge after having made diligent inquiry, (a) each Person owning an interest of 20% or more in Borrower, (b) each Guarantor, and (c) the property manager engaged by Borrower to manage the operation of the Mortgaged Property: (i) is not currently identified on OFAC List (as defined in Borrower's commitment letter), and (ii) is not a person with whom a citizen of the United States is prohibited to engage in transactions by any trade embargo, economic sanction, or other prohibition of United States law, regulation, or Executive Order of the President of the United States.

Explanation

Representations and warranties should address factual matters which exist as of, or prior to, a certain date (but they should not deal with facts or events to occur in the future, since at the time given, Borrower can have no certain knowledge of future events). Later on, in Part IV Section 24 of this Book, there is a discussion of defaults and Events of Default, and we will see that much of the time when Borrower breaches a representation or warranty contained in the Loan Documents, the event of default provisions will not provide Borrower any opportunity to cure such breach. However, in contrast to this approach, often in other types of Event of Default provisions when Borrower breaches most other types of covenants contained in the Loan Documents, Borrower will be given a grace period to cure such breaches. Therefore, limiting the scope of representations and warranties is important in order to avoid having Borrower face unanticipated acceleration of the Loan if it should commit a breach of a representation and then not be permitted to take any action to cure the breach.

Clearly the first sentence in Section 8.1(a) above is a legitimate representation and warranty, since Borrower is in the best position of knowing whether or not the information contained in its and in Guarantor's financial statements are accurate, and whether or not there have been any new changes which would have a material and adverse effect upon Borrower's financial condition. However, the second sentence is also characterized as a representation and warranty, but it deals with actions to be taken by Borrower in the future. It is a good rule of thumb that representations and warranties should not cover any future actions and events, but instead, for provisions which deal with the occurrence of future acts or events, Borrower can provide assurances to Lender in the form of one or more covenants (rather than styling them as a representation or warranty, which can be risky since oftentimes a representation in a given Loan Document does not have the benefit of permitting Borrower a grace period to cure a misrepresentation). In this case, rather than being a representation, Borrower's counsel could try to get this provision recharacterized to become a covenant and added to the covenant portion of the Mortgage, where it could provide that with regard to future financial statements Borrower would be obligated to provide Lender, with true, accurate, and complete copies of such statements (with the effect that this provision would become a promise or a covenant and not a representation).

With regard to the representations contained in Section 8.1(b) above, it could be argued that if Lender is requiring Borrower to provide a corporate opinion (to be given by Borrower's counsel as a condition to close the Loan) which will likewise confirm in the opinion that no such violations exist, then Borrower's counsel could argue to delete such representation from the Mortgage, because Lender should be able to rely on such required opinion, which fully covers this. However, I have rarely found that this argument will persuade a Lender to delete this representation. Instead, it could be pointed out to Lender's counsel that Borrower cannot be expected to have full command of all legal requirements, and so this entire representation should be revised so that it is expressly subject to "Borrower's Knowledge." By making the representation subject to Borrower's Knowledge, it will mean that a breach of this representation will only be deemed to have occurred if not only the representation is factually inaccurate, but also that at the time given, those individuals referenced in the definition of "Borrower's Knowledge" had actual knowledge that such facts were inaccurate.

With regard to the representations contained in Section 8.1(c) above, it could be argued that Lender should rely upon the litigation search which it will require for the closing of the Loan (which is a search typically completed and delivered to Lender at Borrower's expense). Unfortunately, this argument rarely works. Assuming that Lender insists on including this representation in the Mortgage, the entire representation should be subject to Borrower's Knowledge (and not just the portion of such representation dealing with threatened litigation). It is possible that Borrower may not be aware of any then existing litigation, if the service of process of a lawsuit did not come to the attention of the key individuals referenced in the definition of "Borrower's Knowledge," and sometimes it is possible that such key individuals may think that a lawsuit had been settled or terminated, when such termination may not have actually yet been fully implemented. In addition, Lender should only be concerned about material litigation, with the effect that the litigation suits referenced in this representation should probably be limited to controversies in excess of an agreed-upon amount, (e.g., $1 million) and should not relate to lawsuits which are otherwise covered by Borrower's existing liability insurance or which have been otherwise disclosed to Lender.

With regard to the representation contained in Section 8.1(d) above, I have frequently argued with Lender's counsel that this representation is not needed, since Lender is going to obtain a title policy from a creditworthy title company that will be providing these same assurances with regard to Borrower's title ownership of the Mortgaged Property. Again, in most instances Lender will not accommodate a request to delete this representation. Borrower is rarely in a position to know, with any certainty, what does and doesn't affect title to the Mortgaged Property, so Borrower's counsel should try to make this entire representation subject to "Borrower's Knowledge."

With regard to the representation contained in Section 8.1(f) above, given that this will be covered by a legal opinion, if Lender insists on this representation, it should be subject to "Borrower's Knowledge," as these matters are primarily legal in nature.

With regard to the ERISA representation contained in Section 8.1(g) above, it would probably be a good idea for Borrower's counsel to consult with a lawyer who has some experience in dealing with ERISA matters, which may be particularly important depending upon who Lender is and the structure and parties owning a direct and indirect ownership interest in Borrower. If this approach is taken, Borrower's counsel should provide ERISA counsel with a copy of the Loan Document containing the representation, to see if the ERISA counsel has any questions or comments.

The provisions contained in Section 8.1(h) above are overly broad, and Borrower's counsel should request the provisions at least be made subject to "Borrower's Knowledge."

With regard to the representation contained in Section 8.1(i) above, Borrower's counsel should question its client to determine if there are any brokers who are being paid in connection with the Loan transaction, and if so, then this representation should expressly exclude any brokerage fees payable in respect of such brokers.

With regard to the representation contained in Sections 8.1(k) and 8.1(m) above, an effort should be made to have this representation be made subject to "Borrower's Knowledge."

SECTION 9

Taxes; Operating Expenses

Explanation

It is important for Lender to make sure that, throughout the term of the Loan, Borrower has paid all operating expenses associated with the Mortgaged Property, particularly the real estate taxes and insurance premiums. If real estate taxes are not paid prior to delinquency, such a failure will typically afford the local governmental taxing authority a "priming" lien on the Mortgaged Property—i.e., a lien that is superior in priority to the security lien on the Mortgaged Property granted by Borrower under the Mortgage.

By adding a specific covenant to the Mortgage requiring Borrower to pay the real estate taxes, Lender affords itself a right to cure Borrower's failure to pay such taxes under the default and other provisions of the Mortgage, and to add the costs of cure to the Indebtedness secured by the Mortgage. In addition, Lender, and most commercial real estate loan transactions, will require following a default by Borrower (and in many cases prior to a default by Borrower), that operating cash flow from the Mortgaged Property be paid into an escrow deposit account to assure that these real estate taxes will be paid. Below is a Mortgage provision that deals with the payment of operating expenses, particularly real estate taxes, as well as typical Lender requirements concerning periodic payments into an escrow deposit account to cover real estate taxes and insurance premiums:

9.1 ***<u>Taxes; Operating Expenses</u>***.

(a) *Subject to the provisions of Section 5(c) and Section 9.1(d) of this Mortgage, Borrower shall pay, or cause to be paid, all Taxes when due and before the addition of any interest, fine, penalty or cost for nonpayment.*

(b) *Subject to the provisions of Section 5(c), Borrower shall pay the expenses of operating, managing, maintaining and repairing the Mortgaged Property (including insurance premiums, utilities, repairs and replacements) before the last date upon which each such payment may be made without any penalty or interest charge being added.*

(c) *As long as no Event of Default exists and Borrower has timely delivered to Lender any bills or premium notices that it has received, Borrower shall not be obligated to pay Taxes, insurance premiums or any other individual Imposition to the extent that sufficient Imposition Deposits are held in the deposit account controlled by Lender for the purpose of paying that specific Imposition pursuant to Section 10 of this Mortgage. If an Event of Default exists, Lender may exercise any rights Lender may have with respect to Imposition Deposits without regard to whether Impositions are then due and payable. Lender shall have no liability to Borrower for failing to pay any Impositions to the extent that any Event of Default has occurred and is continuing, insufficient Imposition Deposits are held by Lender at the time an Imposition becomes due and payable or Borrower has failed to provide Lender with bills and premium notices as provided above.*

(d) *Borrower, at its own expense, may contest by appropriate legal proceedings, conducted diligently and in good faith, the amount or validity of any Imposition other than insurance premiums, if (1) Borrower notifies Lender of the commencement or expected commencement of such proceedings, (2) the Mortgaged Property is not in danger of being sold or forfeited, (3) Borrower deposits with Lender reserves sufficient to pay the contested Imposition, if requested by Lender, and (4) Borrower furnishes whatever additional security is required in the proceedings or is reasonably requested by Lender, which may include the delivery to Lender of the reserves established by Borrower to pay the contested Imposition.*

(e) *Borrower shall promptly deliver to Lender a copy of all notices of, and invoices for, Impositions, and if Borrower pays any Imposition directly, Borrower shall promptly furnish to Lender receipts evidencing such payments.*

Explanation

The above Section 9.1(a) of the Mortgage is an affirmative covenant on Borrower's part to pay all "Taxes" (which this Mortgage defines as being "Impositions"). The term "Impositions" has been very broadly defined in the definition section of the Mortgage [See Part IV Section 1 of this Book], to include governmental and quasi-governmental impositions against the land and improvements constituting the security for the Loan that, if not paid, would become a lien against the Mortgaged Property (so clearly the definition of the term "Impositions" includes real estate taxes).

The above Section 9.1(b) of the Mortgage is an affirmative covenant on Borrower's part to pay all costs associated with operating and maintaining the Mortgaged Property, and is a way for Lender to require that the Mortgaged Property be well-maintained and well-operated. A well-maintained and well-operated Mortgaged Property is very important to Lender for several reasons. Most obviously, Lender wishes to avoid waste and deterioration of the Mortgaged Property during the term of the Loan, so that if at any time Lender has to enforce its foreclosure remedies and acquire the Mortgaged Property, it will be acquiring an asset which can then be resold at the highest price that can be paid for the asset in order to allow Lender to recover all or a substantial portion of the Indebtedness then owed to it by Borrower. Just as important, however, is the ability of the Mortgaged Property to attract and retain tenants leasing space in the Improvements. Typically, the cash flow, necessary to make Loan debt service and other sums payable to Lender under the Loan Documents, is predominantly obtained through the payment of Rents pursuant to the Leases. If the Mortgaged Property is not properly managed and maintained, it will be difficult to attract and retain tenants, and this may jeopardize the ability of Borrower to pay Loan debt service and other operating expenses related to the Mortgaged Property. Failure to maintain the Mortgaged Property may also provide tenants with an opportunity to terminate their Leases and/or expose the landlord under the Leases (and Lender succeeding to the interest of the landlord through foreclosure of its Mortgage) to potential liability, if tenants have the right to cure a failure by landlord to maintain the leased premises and seek reimbursement from landlord. In addition, if another party (such as a tenant) engages a third party to make repairs or improvements to any portion of the Mortgaged Property and such third party then fails to make payment for those repairs, this failure may (depending upon the jurisdiction) provide the repairing party with a lien for the costs of such repairs, and this lien may be superior to the lien granted by the Mortgage.

Similar to the treatment of Impositions in the above Section 9.1(a), the above Section 9.1(b) provides Lender with an opportunity to (i) declare a default if the costs of operating and maintaining the Mortgaged Property are not paid, and (ii) cure such default. Lender will typically give itself the right to add the costs of cure to the Indebtedness secured by the Mortgage.

The above Section 9.1(c) clarifies many of Lender's rights and obligations with respect to the Imposition Deposits addressed later in the Mortgage and relieves Borrower of the responsibility to pay Taxes to the extent Lender has received escrow deposits for such Impositions, so long as Borrower is not in default.

Section 9.1(c) also limits Lender's liability for failure to perform its obligation to pay moneys out of any escrow established for Lender's benefit, so long as an Event of Default exists, or if Borrower has failed to provide Lender with any required bills and premium notices. In addition, Section 9.1(c) permits Lender to apply the Imposition Deposits to Borrower's Indebtedness so long as an Event of Default exists, if permitted under the laws of the applicable jurisdiction. Should an Event of Default occur and continue to exist, then this provision specifies that Lender will not be responsible for failing to pay any Taxes from the Imposition Deposits that were to be paid if no Event of Default existed, particularly to the extent Lender has depleted the Imposition Deposits by applying the escrowed deposits to the Indebtedness during the existence of an Event of Default.

The above Section 9.1(e) of the Mortgage places an affirmative obligation upon Borrower to provide Lender with notice of the amount and due date of such Impositions.

Borrower should make sure that at least one of the Loan Documents (usually the Mortgage) contain provisions that allow Borrower to contest payment of any Impositions in the event Borrower believes that the government or other party has improperly levied any Imposition against the Mortgaged Property. Lender will typically permit Borrower to have the opportunity to contest such Impositions, provided Lender is comfortable that its security in the Mortgaged Property will not be impaired due to Borrower pursuing such contest. The above Section 9.1(d) of the Mortgage permits Borrower to contest Impositions (other than insurance premiums, which are a matter of contract between Borrower and insurer), provided that: (i) Borrower notifies Lender of the contest, (ii) the Mortgaged Property is not in jeopardy of being lost as a result of Borrower pursuing such contest, and (iii) Borrower provides Lender with security against a determination that the Imposition was properly assessed. With such notice and security, Lender can monitor the contest to ensure that its security is not impaired, and if there is any impairment, then the security will be a source of collateral to enable Lender to be made whole as a result of any such impairment. In the event the contest is determined adversely to Borrower, Borrower may be liable for interest and penalties. Lender will want to make sure that the amount of security received from Borrower is sufficient to cover any such amounts. Among the types of security routinely accepted by Lender are cash deposits, bonds, and letters of credit.

Note also that in the above sections, care has been taken when referring to an Event of Default as a condition for triggering rights and remedies of Lender; that in each case such condition requires either the existence of the Event of Default, or that the Event of default has both occurred and is continuing (rather than having that condition simply be triggered by the "occurrence" of an Event of Default). This is an important distinction because it is possible that an Event of Default can be cured, or can be waived, and when such waiver or cure happens, Borrower does not want Lender to continue to have such rights and/or remedies following the waiver or curing of such Event of Default. Therefore, Borrower's counsel should be careful to negotiate in the Loan Documents for express provisions that the relevant remedies and rights of Lender be triggered when an Event of Default both occurs and continues to exist.

SECTION 10

Deposits for Taxes, Insurance, and Other Charges

Explanation

Loan Documents frequently contain provisions which require Borrower to pay Lender monthly escrow deposits for a wide variety of items. Usually Lender has this requirement because the payments for the items being escrowed are critical to the operation and/or ownership of the Mortgaged Property, and in some cases if such payments are not made on a timely basis, the defaulted payment results in an automatic lien being placed against the title to the real estate elements of the Mortgaged Property. Below is a provision which is representative of mandatory escrow payments being required of Borrower in a Mortgage:

10.1 *Borrower shall deposit with Lender on the day monthly installments of principal or interest, or both, are due under the Note, until the Obligations are paid in full, an additional amount sufficient to accumulate in an escrow with Lender the entire sum required to pay, when due (based on estimates to be determined by Lender in accordance with provisions hereinafter set forth in this Section 10.1) the following: (1) any water and sewer charges which, if not paid, may result in a lien on all or any part of the Mortgaged Property, (2) the premiums for fire and other hazard insurance, rent loss insurance and such other insurance as Lender may require under Section 19 of the Mortgage, (3) Taxes, and (4) amounts for other charges and expenses which Lender at any time reasonably deems necessary to protect the Mortgaged Property, to prevent the imposition of liens on the Mortgaged Property, or otherwise to protect Lender's interests, all as reasonably estimated from time to time by Lender. The amounts to be deposited under the preceding sentence are collectively referred to in this Mortgage as the* ***"Imposition Deposits."*** *The amount of the Imposition Deposits shall be paid to Lender monthly, and such* *monthly sums, as estimated by Lender, shall be in an amount so as to be sufficient to enable Lender to pay each of the Impositions before the date when such applicable Imposition shall first be due and payable.*

Any waiver by Lender of the requirement that Borrower remit the Imposition Deposits to Lender must be by written notice given to Borrower, and may only be revoked by Lender, in Lender's discretion, at any time upon written notice given to Borrower.

Explanation

Lenders will frequently require that all revenues from the Mortgaged Property be deposited in escrow with a cash manager, and in the Loan Agreement require that a portion of such revenues be deposited in special escrow accounts to cover current or future key operating expenses, which often include payments for Taxes and Borrower insurance premiums. Different Lenders place different levels of importance on the maintenance of Imposition and insurance escrow accounts. For example, it is common for a Lender to agree to require that these items be escrowed with Lender only so long as an Event of Default continues to exist, but sometimes these escrowed amounts must be deposited throughout the term of the Loan. For Loans which are closed with a plan to sell them into a securitization, it is usually the case that a portion of these revenues will be held in an escrow account, even without the existence of a default, so that Lender can be certain that items critical to Lender or the operation of the Improvements will be paid (such as the Loan's interest, Impositions, insurance premiums, and future capital repair expenses). The bottom line is that Borrower's counsel should ask about Lender's policies regarding the maintenance of escrows. It is obviously preferable for Borrower to have escrows become payable into an escrow account for payment of such items as Impositions and/or other material expenses only during the existence of an Event of Default. In contrast to Impositions, water and sewer charges do not often result in the water or sewer authorities having the ability to impose priming the lien of the Mortgaged Property. Moreover, these charges are typically payable frequently, such as monthly or quarterly. Thus, there is often less justification for Lender to insist on an escrow for water or sewer charges, since each individual payment will be for a relatively small amount of money. Note that under the above Mortgage escrow provisions, Lender also has the right to include an escrow for "amounts lender deems necessary to protect the property." This particular escrow requirement is very broad and could include escrow payments for funding future repairs of capital improvements (which could prove to be quite expensive). For instance, Lender could decide that new roofs, air conditioning units, signage, or windows are in order. This provision does not require that nonpayment of any future payments to be covered by escrowed deposits would result in priming the lien of the Mortgage (and the amount of the periodic escrow payments could be a significant portion of the Mortgaged Property's cash flow). Borrower's counsel should request that this provision be deleted, or if not deleted, ask Lender to reduce or more strictly define this broad escrow power.

> 10.2 *Imposition Deposits when received by Lender shall be deposited in a deposit account. Lender shall apply the Imposition Deposits to pay Impositions so long as no Event of Default has occurred and is continuing. Unless applicable law requires, Lender shall not be required to pay Borrower any interest, earnings or profits on the Imposition Deposits. Borrower hereby pledges and grants to Lender a security interest in the Imposition Deposits and the account in which they are being deposited as additional security for all of Borrower's obligations under this Mortgage and the other Loan Documents. Any amounts deposited with Lender under this Section 10.2 shall not be trust funds, nor shall they operate to reduce the Indebtedness, unless applied by Lender for that purpose.*

Explanation

The above Section 10.2 of the Mortgage obligates Lender to apply the Imposition Deposits to the Mortgaged Property operating expenses for which Lender is escrowing. In many states the real estate taxes are payable annually by December 31 each year and if they are timely paid, Borrower will have a sizable income tax deduction by reason of payment. Under this sub-section, Lender is not promising to make the escrow payment with respect to Taxes prior to December 31 so as to insure that Borrower gets its allowable income tax deduction for that calendar year. Borrower's counsel should try to negotiate the requirement that such Tax payment is made by Lender before December 31.

The above Section 10.2 of the Mortgage also provides that Borrower grants Lender a security interest in the Imposition Deposits and the account in which they are held. This grant of a security interest does not mean that Lender necessarily has a perfected security interest in the account which holds the Imposition Deposits. Where Lender is itself a depository institution, retention of the Imposition Deposits will likely be in a deposit account with Lender. If Lender is not a depository institution, the Imposition Deposits will have to be deposited in a deposit account at another financial institution.

In 2001, there were revisions to Article 9 of the Uniform Commercial Code (the "**UCC**"). Included in these revisions were provisions to expand the collateral that could be perfected under Article 9 to include deposit accounts. Prior to these revisions, deposit accounts could not be perfected under Article 9. Section 9-312 now provides that a security interest in a deposit account may be perfected only by Lender having acknowledged control of the liened account by Lender, all as specified in Section 9-314. Section 9-314 specifies a security interest in a deposit account is only perfected when Lender has taken the necessary steps to obtain control over the deposit account, and such lien only remains perfected so long as such control is retained by Lender. The filing of a UCC-1 Statement will not perfect a security interest in a deposit account under Article 9. In order to obtain a perfected interest under Article 9, Lender must take a number of specific steps, so that just the granting of a security interest in deposit accounts will not be sufficient to enable Lender to obtain such a security interest (and therefore if Lender only grants a security interest in Borrower's deposit accounts, but has failed to take the other necessary steps to obtain control, Lender will not have perfected its security interest in such deposit accounts), and if these steps are not taken, then Borrower's counsel must be careful in rendering its enforceability and/or perfection opinions relative to the Loan Documents (because Lender will not have a perfected lien on such accounts, notwithstanding that the Mortgage grants a security interest in them).

Section 9-104 (a) specifies that in order for Lender obtain "control" of a Borrower deposit account, Lender must utilize one of the following three methods to obtain such "control":

- (i) if the Borrower deposit account has been opened with the depository institution which is Lender, then Lender is deemed to have achieved such "control"; or
- (ii) if the Borrower deposit account has not been opened with the depository institution which is Lender, then Article 9 requires that one of the following two methods must be employed to have achieved such "control":
  - (a) Lender must be deemed to become the depository institution's customer with respect to such deposit account (Note that this approach is rarely taken, since it requires Lender to actually own the account); or
  - (b) such deposit account may be opened in the name of Borrower, but Lender and the depository institution in which the deposit account is opened must agree in an authenticated record that such institution will comply with future Lender instructions that direct the disposition of the funds on deposit in such account, and that such instructions will not also require consent of Borrower. Usually this written instruction is included in a three party agreement, commonly called a "Control Agreement" which is entered into by Lender, such depository institution and Borrower.

Many banks that allow customers to open deposit accounts object to having a customer's deposit account be subject to a Control Agreement, as required by the UCC. If Lender (i) is not a financial institution which offers deposit accounts, and (ii) in the Loan Documents is requiring Borrower's deposit accounts be subject to a security lien, then often times Borrower must locate a bank that will enter into a Control Agreement. Once such a bank agrees to enter into a Control Agreement and is selected to hold the Imposition Deposits, the process begins to enter into a Control Agreement. Many depository banks have a form of Control Agreement that the depository bank will insist be used. Usually such banks will tolerate some small non-substantive changes to this form. If the bank does not have a form, the Business Law Section of the American Bar Association has a form which could be used as a model, although it might need to be adapted somewhat, as it is intended to be used for securitizations. The Article 9 of most states require, when using a Control Agreement as the means for perfecting a security interest in a deposit account, that the Control Agreement must contain a provision where Lender notifies the depository bank of its security interest in the deposit account, and where depository bank acknowledges and consents to such security interest. In Delaware, the requisite control may be obtained by simply a notice of the security interest being sent to the depository bank, so long as the escrow deposit accounts are sufficiently identified.

Even if a deposit account is subject to a Control Agreement, such that Lender has obtained a security interest in such deposit account, it is possible for Borrower to retain some direct use of such deposit account, as Section 9-104(b) allows Borrower to retain such right of use without destroying Lender's "control" over the account for perfection purposes.

If Borrower desires the right to have the monies in the secured account utilized to purchase investments such as CDs or treasury securities which will be held in the account, then such investments will be deemed to be a separate class of security called "investment property" and will require that additional steps be taken under Article 8 of the Uniform Commercial Code to perfect interests in such investment property.

Because perfection in a deposit account is somewhat complex, Borrower's counsel can often be successful in negotiating with Lender's counsel to accept a Lender's UCC insurance policy, which several major title companies now issue and which insures that Lender has a senior priority lien on the deposit account (which policy must be paid for by Borrower), and in such event, Lender will usually allow Borrower's counsel to exclude from its enforceability opinion any implication that it covers perfection in deposit accounts. This UCC insurance policy is similar to obtaining Lender's mortgagee title policy, and because Lender will have the credit of the title insurer insuring Lender's senior priority lien on the Mortgaged Property, Lender will then permit Borrower's counsel opinion to exclude that such opinion is covering good title to the Mortgaged Property or the perfection of the Mortgage lien on the Mortgaged Property, since these matters are covered by the title policy. Most Lenders are happy in employing this approach. By taking this approach, Borrower's counsel will then be able to utilize some of the expertise of the title company and its counsel when Borrower's counsel is putting together the Control Agreement for the Loan.

10.3 *If Lender receives a bill or invoice for an Imposition, Lender shall pay the Imposition from the Imposition Deposits held by Lender. Lender shall have no obligation to pay any Imposition to the extent it exceeds Imposition Deposits then held by Lender. Lender may pay an Imposition according to any bill, statement or estimate from the appropriate public office, insurance company or other vendor without inquiring into the accuracy of the bill, statement or estimate or into the validity of the Imposition.*

Explanation

Under the above Section 10.3, Lender is protected in paying any bills from appropriate public offices or vendors without inquiring into their accuracy. Lender is not obligated to pay bills if the escrow account is short. In effect, this provision gives Lender the right to decide whether or not it is in Lender's best interest to make a payment from the escrow account for the benefit of Borrower or to protect the Mortgaged Property, if the amounts on deposit are not sufficient to fully cover the amount then due.

> 10.4 *If at any time the amount of the Imposition Deposits held by Lender for payment of a specific Imposition exceeds the amount reasonably deemed necessary by Lender, the excess shall be credited against future installments of Imposition Deposits. If at any time the amount of the Imposition Deposits held by Lender for payment of a specific Imposition is less than the amount reasonably estimated by Lender to be necessary, Borrower shall pay to Lender the amount of the deficiency within 15 days after notice from Lender.*

Explanation

Under this Section 10.4, if Lender has collected more escrow funds than needed to pay the escrow items, not only does Lender not have to pay interest as provided in Part IV Section 10.2 of this Book, but it does not have to return the monies to Borrower. At the same time, if Lender "reasonably estimates" that the escrow monies will be insufficient to pay the anticipated invoices for the escrow items, Lender can demand that Borrower pay more funds to Lender to be deposited into the escrow account. If Borrower fails to make the demanded payment, such failure constitutes a default under the Mortgage. If a Borrower is a commercial borrower, it is not protected against overcharging for escrows by this Section 10.4 or by any federal law. In contrast, in the residential loan context, the Real Estate Settlement Procedures Act provides that a Lender may not require a Borrower to deposit in any escrow account an aggregate sum in excess of a sum that will be sufficient to pay such charges in accordance with a statutory formula. 12 U.S.C. § 2609. Regulation X sets out a very lengthy and complex regulatory protection scheme for the protection of Borrowers. 61 Fed. Reg. 10,440 (1996).

> 10.5 *If an Event of Default has occurred and is continuing, Lender may apply any Imposition Deposits, in any amounts and in any order as Lender determines, in Lender's discretion, to pay any Impositions or as a credit against the Indebtedness. Upon payment in full of the Indebtedness, Lender shall refund to Borrower any Imposition Deposits held by Lender.*

Explanation

This Section 10.5 provides that if an Event of Default is continuing, Lender can apply escrowed Imposition Deposit monies as Lender determines (and in particular, Lender may apply some or all of such escrowed Imposition Deposit monies to prepay the Loan) until the Loan is paid in full. This approach is typical, and Lender usually will not negotiate this type of provision, because the provision is predicated on there being an outstanding Event of Default.

SECTION 11

Application of Payments

Explanation

Typically the Mortgage (or the Loan Agreement, if a Loan Agreement is included as part of the Loan Documents) and/or the Note will contain provisions calling for Borrower to make various payments (including debt service payments) to Lender in certain amounts and at certain times. Often, however, a Borrower will not pay exactly those amounts at exactly those times and therefore by failing to pay the full amount then due, Borrower will be in breach of its payment obligations under the Loan Documents, even if it makes a partial payment. These breaches in such payment obligations can occur at any time during the term of the Loan—and often such breaches occur when Borrower is in financial trouble. When Borrower makes a partial payment, the acceptance by Lender of such partial payment or irregular payments can arguably create a course of dealing or waiver against that Lender at common law. Accordingly, Lender frequently inserts the following provision in the Loan Documents to deal with this type of situation:

> 11.1 *If at any time Lender receives, from Borrower or otherwise, any amount applicable to the Indebtedness which is less than all amounts due and payable at such time, then Lender may apply that payment to amounts then due and payable in any manner and in any order determined by Lender, in Lender's discretion. Neither Lender's acceptance of an amount which is less than all amounts then due and payable nor Lender's application of such payment in the manner authorized shall constitute or be deemed to constitute either a waiver of the unpaid amounts or an accord and satisfaction. Notwithstanding the application of any such amount to the Indebtedness, Borrower's obligations under this Mortgage and the Note shall remain unchanged.*

Explanation

This Section 11.1 when used in the Mortgage, attempts to protect Lender from common-law waiver and/or other similar arguments which Borrower could make if Lender receives partial payments required by the Loan Documents. Here Borrower agrees that Lender's acceptance of less than the amount due does not constitute a waiver by Lender, relative to any deficient amount which is not included in the current payment. Borrower agrees that Lender can apply partial payment monies it receives from Borrower in any manner determined by Lender, instead of in a manner designated by Borrower or as previously applied by Lender. Again, this is a fairly typical provision which is usually not subject to negotiation.

SECTION 12

Compliance with Laws

Explanation

Lender has a legitimate concern that Borrower must continue to comply with all applicable laws and regulations throughout the term of the Loan. If Borrower does not comply with all laws affecting the Mortgaged Property, and then if Lender has to foreclose and ultimately purchase the Mortgaged Property at foreclosure sale, Lender will then have to take over the operation of the Mortgaged Property; and if at that time the Mortgaged Property is out of compliance with any laws, then Lender will be faced with the problem. For example, if Borrower builds a capital improvement or maintains the Mortgaged Property in such a way that it comes out of, or otherwise it is not in, compliance with any applicable legal requirements, then Lender, if it purchases the Mortgaged Property at foreclosure sale, may not be able to resell the Mortgaged Property for maximum value without bringing such property into compliance with the laws, which could be an expensive and/or time-consuming proposition. Below is a typical provision in a Mortgage dealing with compliance with laws, and the obligation of Borrower to use the Mortgaged Property for permitted purposes under the law.

12.1 *Borrower shall comply with all laws, ordinances, regulations and requirements of any Governmental Authority and all recorded lawful covenants and agreements relating to or affecting the Mortgaged Property, including all laws, ordinances, regulations, requirements and covenants pertaining to health and safety, construction of improvements on the Mortgaged Property, fair housing, zoning and land use, and Leases. Borrower also shall comply with all applicable laws that pertain to the maintenance and disposition of tenant security deposits. Borrower shall at all times maintain records sufficient to demonstrate compliance with the provisions of this Section. Borrower shall take appropriate measures to prevent, and shall not engage in or knowingly permit, any illegal activities at the Mortgaged Property that could endanger tenants or visitors, result in damage to the Mortgaged Property, result in forfeiture of the Mortgaged Property, or otherwise materially impair the lien created by this Mortgage or Lender's interest in the Mortgaged Property. Borrower represents and warrants to Lender that no portion of the Mortgaged Property has been or will be purchased with the proceeds of any illegal activity.*

Explanation

In addition to requiring Borrower to comply with laws, this Section 12.1 of the Mortgage also attempts to protect Lender against illegal activities occurring on the Mortgaged Property. Such illegal activities could also result in lowering the value of the Mortgaged Property (because the Mortgaged Property might acquire a bad reputation as a result of such activities), and the ability of Lender to get its Loan fully repaid. These activities also could result in liens being filed against the Mortgaged Property or in some cases, the revocation of government permits and/or licenses needed for the operation of the Mortgaged Property.

SECTION 13

Use of Property

Explanation

At the time Lender funds the Loan, it has done so on the assumption that the Mortgaged Property will be used for a specific purpose, as indicated in the Loan application, and such use is a significant element in determining the fair market value of the Mortgaged Property and Lender's estimate of anticipated cash flow that will be generated from the Mortgaged Property's operations, a portion of which will be used throughout the Loan's term to fund all payments due Lender under the Loan Documents. Accordingly, Lender wants to make certain that it can maintain control over and prevent any changes in the Mortgaged Property, or its use, that might devalue the Mortgaged Property as security for the Loan, or impair the anticipated cash flow from the Mortgaged Property's operations. The following is a typical provision that might be included in the Mortgage regarding the use of the Mortgaged Property.

> 13.1 *Unless required by applicable law, Borrower shall not (a) except for any change in use approved by Lender, allow changes in the use for which all or any part of the Mortgaged Property is being used at the time this Mortgage was executed, (b) initiate or acquiesce in a change in the zoning classification of the Mortgaged Property, or (c) establish any condominium or cooperative regime with respect to the Mortgaged Property.*

Explanation

By having the power to approve any changes in Borrower's use of the Mortgaged Property, Lender will have the ability to veto a use which could, in Lender's opinion, be deleterious to the value of the Mortgaged Property, which of course is security for Lender. This type of provision is generally not negotiable to any great degree.

SECTION 14

Inspection

Explanation

In underwriting a given commercial mortgage loan, Lender will look to various underlying criteria—but one of the most important due diligence reports will be the appraisal which establishes the fair market value of the Mortgaged Property as of the time Lender closes the Loan. Lender will want such value to remain as high as it can be throughout the term of the Loan, because Lender is looking to the Mortgaged Property as the primary collateral security for the Loan, so that if Borrower should default, Lender can realize the highest amount of proceeds at a foreclosure sale of the Mortgaged Property, which in turn will then be used to pay down the Indebtedness. Such Mortgaged Property value is a function of many factors, but the physical condition and state of repair of the Mortgaged Property are always relevant in establishing this value. In order to proceed with funding the Loan, Lender has initially underwritten the Loan based on the Mortgaged Property having a certain value and being in a certain physical condition. It therefore is understandable that periodically throughout the term of the Loan, Lender will want the right to inspect the Mortgaged Property at Lender's convenience to confirm that the Mortgaged Property's value and state of repair continues to remain consistent with Lender's underwriting assumptions. Below is a typical provision which reserves for Lender the ability to inspect the Mortgaged Property.

> 14.1 *Lender, its agents, representatives, and designees may make or cause to be made entries upon and inspections of the Mortgaged Property (including environmental inspections and tests) during normal business hours, or at any other reasonable time.*

Explanation

This provision is fairly typical. Usually Borrower's counsel can require in this provision that Lender provide Borrower with advance notice for each inspection (other than in the case of an emergency). It is also fairly common to require Lender to take reasonable steps not to interfere with the use and enjoyment of any space being leased by a tenant when Lender is conducting such inspection.

SECTION 15

Books and Records; Financial Reporting and Other Reports

Explanation

Another criterion Lender will use to underwrite the Loan, since it is secured by commercial real estate property, is the on-going ability of the Mortgaged Property to produce adequate net cash flow to cover debt service and other payments that will be owed to Lender throughout the term of the Loan, as well as the Mortgaged Property's operating expenses that will be payable during such period. Lender will want to be sure that the Mortgaged Property generates, or has the prospect of generating, annual net income in excess of the amount needed to cover annual debt service and other sums payable to Lender under the Loan Documents, and all operating and capital costs relating to the Mortgaged Property (as well as reasonable reserves). The following section of the Mortgage requires Borrower to maintain accurate books of account and authorizes Lender to inspect those records:

> 15.1 *Borrower shall keep and maintain at all times at the Mortgaged Property or the management agent's offices, and upon Lender's request shall make available at the Mortgaged Property, complete and accurate books of account and records (including copies of supporting bills and invoices) adequate to reflect correctly the operation of the Mortgaged Property, and copies of all written contracts, Leases, and other instruments which affect the Mortgaged Property. The books, records, contracts, Leases and other instruments shall be subject to examination and inspection at any reasonable time by Lender.*
>
> 15.2 *Borrower shall furnish to Lender all of the following:*
>
> (a) *within 120 days after the end of each fiscal year of Borrower and Guarantor, financial statements of Borrower and Guarantor, which in the case of Borrower will include a statement of income and expenses for Borrower's*

operation of the Mortgaged Property for that fiscal year, a statement of changes in financial position of Borrower relating to the Mortgaged Property for that fiscal year and a balance sheet showing all assets and liabilities of Borrower relating to the Mortgaged Property as of the end of that fiscal year, all prepared in accordance with GAAP, and reviewed by a certified public accountant reasonably acceptable to Lender;

(b) *within 120 days after the end of each fiscal year of Borrower, and at any other time upon Lender's request, a rent schedule for the Mortgaged Property showing the name of each tenant, and for each tenant, the space occupied, the lease expiration date, the rent payable for the current month, the date through which rent has been paid, and any related information requested by Lender;*

(c) *within 120 days after the end of each fiscal year of Borrower, and at any other time upon Lender's request, an accounting of all security deposits held pursuant to all Leases, including the name of the institution (if any) and the names and identification numbers of the accounts (if any) in which such security deposits are held and the name of the person to contact at such financial institution, along with any authority or release necessary for Lender to access information regarding such accounts;*

(d) *within 20 days following the end of each calendar quarter, (i) an operating statement showing the results of operation of the Mortgaged Property for the prior quarter and on a year-to-date basis for the period just ended; (ii) a detailed, current rent roll of the Mortgaged Property, containing such details as Lender may reasonably request, (iii) cash flows from the Mortgaged Property for the quarter just ended, (iv) leasing reports for the quarter just ended, and (v) aging and accounts receivables report for the Mortgaged Property for the quarter just ended;*

(e) *concurrently with the filing thereof, complete copies of all federal and state tax returns and supporting schedules of Borrower; and*

(f) *within a reasonable period of time and from time to time such other financial data or information as Lender may reasonably request with respect to the Mortgaged Property, or Borrower, including, but not limited to, rent rolls, aged receivables, aged payables, leases, budgets, forecasts, reserves, cash flow projections, physical condition of the Mortgaged Property, pending lease proposals, evidence of payment of all real estate taxes due from time to time and to the extent in Borrower's possession or reasonably available to Borrower such other financial data or information as Lender may reasonably request.*

15.3 *Each of the statements, schedules and reports required by this Section 15.3 shall be certified to be complete and accurate by an individual having authority to bind Borrower, and shall be in such form and contain such detail as Lender may reasonably require. Lender also may require that any statements, schedules or reports be audited at Borrower's expense by independent certified public accountants acceptable to Lender.*

15.4 *If Borrower fails to provide in a timely manner the statements, schedules and reports required by this Section 15, Lender shall have the right to have Borrower's books and records audited, at Borrower's expense, by independent certified public accountants selected by Lender in order to obtain such statements, schedules and reports, and all related costs and expenses of Lender shall become immediately due and payable and shall become an additional part of the Indebtedness.*

15.5 *If an Event of Default has occurred and is continuing, Borrower shall deliver to Lender upon written demand all books and records relating to the Mortgaged Property or its operation.*

Explanation

This section of the Mortgage requires Borrower to provide Lender with various annual and monthly financial reports relating to the Mortgaged Property and other items. In addition, this section also allows Lender to request certain reports relating to the Mortgaged Property whenever it chooses. The reports included in Section 15.2 above allow Lender to monitor the financial health of the Mortgaged Property and include income and expense statements, balance sheets, rent schedules, an accounting of security deposits held, and financial statements of those holding equity interests in Borrower.

Section 15.3 above requires that all of the Mortgaged Property financial statements "be certified to be complete and accurate by an individual having authority to bind Borrower." This certification is designed to create liability if the person who certifies statements provides materials that turn out not to be true or accurate (and if such certification is false, then such misrepresentation would constitute an Event of Default under the Mortgage). In addition, Section 15.2(a) above requires that the annual financial statements be reviewed by a certified public accountant (such a review by a qualified third party provides Lender with greater confidence that the statements are true and accurate, since the accountant could have liability to Lender if it turned out that the accountant colluded with Borrower in the preparation of such statements, or negligently failed to provide a proper review of such statements). Section 15.3 above also allows Lender to require that any statement be audited at Borrower's expense. This audit level of review can be expensive, and frequently Borrower's counsel will try to negotiate that such financial material either be only certified by the appropriate financial officer of Borrower or that the applicable financial statements only be reviewed (but not audited) by the accountant.

Under Section 15.4 above, if Borrower "fails to provide [to Lender] in a timely manner the statements," then Lender has the right to have Borrower's books and records audited. To a large degree, the value of commercial real estate is not the real estate itself, but the net income the real estate is able to generate on an ongoing basis. A failure on the part of Borrower to provide a requested financial report should set off a warning bell. The Mortgage gives Lender the right to protect itself against the threats signaled by that warning bell by having the right to declare a Loan default if Borrower fails to provide such financial statements in a timely manner. Nevertheless, Section 15.4 is unlikely to be useful, because if there are serious financial issues facing the Mortgaged Property, such that Borrower is not turning over required reports, such failure would give rise to an Event of Default, with the result that Borrower will be unlikely to open its door to and allow Borrower's auditor to cooperate with Lender, absent a court order or other legal proceedings.

Section 15.5 is also unrealistic. What Borrower is going to default on its Loan and then go to the time, trouble, and effort to deliver its books and records to Lender? Both Part IV Sections 15.4 and 15.5 are really designed to enhance Lender's position in litigation. Their inclusion in the Mortgage may be a sufficient basis to enable Lender to obtain a receivership order that includes an audit right and delivery of books and records.

SECTION 16

Liens; Encumbrances

Explanation

Lender wants to discourage Borrower from allowing any other liens or encumbrances from attaching to title on any portion of the Mortgaged Property, so typically Lender will require provisions like those contained in the following section, which makes it an Event of Default for Borrower to permit any lien to attach to the Mortgaged Property:

> 16.1 *Borrower acknowledges that, to the extent provided in Section 22 of the Mortgage, the grant, creation or existence of any mortgage, deed of trust, deed to secure debt, security interest or other lien or encumbrance (a "Lien") on the Mortgaged Property (other than the lien of this Mortgage) or on certain ownership interests in Borrower, whether voluntary, involuntary or by operation of law, and whether or not such Lien has priority over the lien of this Mortgage, is a "Transfer" which constitutes an Event of Default.*

Explanation

By adding this section in the Mortgage, it will become an Event of Default if Borrower permits any lien to attach to the Mortgaged Property beyond any applicable grace periods. In the event Borrower commits a default with respect to such section, then, following the expiration of any applicable grace periods, Lender may exercise its remedies for the default permitted by the Loan Documents, including the right to accelerate the Indebtedness as permitted following the occurrence of an Event of Default under the Loan Documents. Usually the Mortgage or Loan Agreement will allow for a grace period (which is usually 30 days) to cure the attachment of a mechanic's lien or certain other encumbrances, so Borrower's counsel should try to modify this Section 16.1 so that the requirement that the attachment of liens result in an Event of Default, should be made subject to any expressly permitted grace periods relating to such attachments set forth in the Loan Documents. Lender's rationale for this section is that any lien on the Mortgaged Property (other than the Mortgage lien), whether prior to or subordinate to the lien of the Mortgage, may (i) impair (x) the value of the Mortgaged Property or (y) Lender's ability to foreclose or deal with a Borrower's bankruptcy or (ii) allow for a new entity to enforce such lien and acquire title to the Mortgaged Property, thereby allowing such entity who has not been underwritten by Lender to operate the Mortgaged Property which could impair the value of the Mortgaged Property. Also, Lender will wish to avoid the situation where a lien may gain priority over the lien of the Mortgage, as (for example) in the event of a modification of the Mortgage. Practically, then, Lender may use this Section 16.1 as a way to afford itself a right to approve or reject any subsequent encumbrances or liens affecting any portion of the Mortgaged Property.

SECTION 17

Preservation, Management, and Maintenance of the Mortgaged Property

Explanation

Earlier in Part IV Section 15 of this Book, there was a discussion as to why it is important for the Mortgaged Property to be well maintained (i.e., a well maintained commercial property retains a higher market value and attracts tenants (thereby allowing the Mortgaged Property to generate more net cash flow from its operations), each of which is important to Lender). It is quite common for Borrower to have the Mortgaged Property managed, and to enter into a management contract with a third party or an affiliate of Borrower to manage the Mortgaged Property. Below are some sections which are usually found in the Mortgage to deal with the maintenance and management of the Mortgaged Property:

17.1 *Borrower (1) shall not commit waste or permit impairment or deterioration of the Mortgaged Property, (2) shall not abandon the Mortgaged Property, (3) shall restore or repair promptly, in a good and workman-like manner, any damaged part of the Mortgaged Property to the equivalent of its original condition, or such other condition as Lender may approve in writing, whether or not insurance proceeds or condemnation awards are available to cover any costs of such restoration or repair, (4) shall keep the Mortgaged Property in good repair, including the replacement of Personalty and Fixtures with items of equal or better function and quality, (5) shall provide for professional management of the Mortgaged Property by a property manager satisfactory to Lender under a management contract approved by Lender in writing, and (6) shall give notice to Lender of and, unless otherwise directed in writing by Lender, shall appear in and defend any action or proceeding purporting to affect the Mortgaged Property, Lender's security or Lender's rights under this Mortgage. Borrower shall not (and shall not permit any tenant or other person to) remove, demolish or alter the Mortgaged Property or any part of the Mortgaged Property except in connection with the replacement of tangible Personalty.*

17.2 *If, in connection with the closing of the Loan or at any later date, Lender waives in writing the requirement of Section 17.1(5) above that Borrower enter into a written contract for management of the Mortgaged Property and if, after the date of this Mortgage, Borrower intends to change the management of the Mortgaged Property, Lender shall have the right to approve in writing such new property manager and the written contract for the management of the Mortgaged Property and to require that Borrower and such new property manager enter into an Assignment of Management Agreement on a form approved by Lender. If required by Lender (whether before or after an Event of Default), Borrower will cause any Affiliate of Borrower who shall serve as property manager of the Mortgaged Property to enter into an agreement with Lender, in a form approved by Lender, providing for subordination of the fees of the Affiliate of Borrower and such other provisions as Lender may require.*

Explanation

Historically, the common-law doctrine of waste protected all mortgage lenders by, at a minimum, making it wrongful for Borrower to damage the Mortgaged Property. The above sections of the Mortgage impose upon Borrower the duties of repair or replacement of personal property, the use of a professional property manager, and the defense of any suit affecting the Mortgaged Property.

A commercial property owner often forms a subsidiary or a related entity to perform property management on its commercial real estate projects. Indeed, management fees paid to such related property management entity often provide the sponsor of Borrower with an important revenue stream mechanism.

The above section permits Lender to insist that fees to a Borrower-related management company be subordinated to all payments due throughout the term of the Loan to Lender under the Loan Documents. One should note that this right in the above section is *not dependent on the existence of an Event of Default*. The subordination mentioned here is not a subordination of a lien, because the management company typically has no lien on the property. Rather, it is a "debt subordination," and allows Lender to prevent any payment from being made to the management company unless all payments under the Loan documents are current. *See* Patrick Mears, *Who's on First? Negotiating Debt and Lien Subordination Agreements in Real Estate Transactions*, PROB. & PROP., Jan/Feb. 1999, at 19.

SECTION 18

Environmental Hazards

Explanation

Since 1970, Congress has enacted a flood of environmental statutes, including those listed specifically in the definition of "Hazardous Materials Laws" as set forth in Part IV Section 1 of this Book. These statutes sweep broadly, making thousands of substances—as well as the businesses, individuals, and others who handle or emit them—subject to extensive and burdensome regulation. These statutes also subject the real estate affected by the release of any such Hazardous Materials to the risk of being encumbered with a lien (which would secure future remediation efforts and other related government costs) that would have primacy over the lien of the Mortgage. For the most part, each of these federal statutes uses the same regulatory approach: A national permit program sets and imposes minimum national standards, preempting less restrictive state regulations. Each state is called upon to enact conforming state laws and regulations and to seek the approval of the U.S. Environmental Protection Agency (EPA) to administer the national program within its borders.

Explanation

The definition of "Hazardous Materials" is quite broad. Borrower's counsel might want to try to limit this to only those specific substances, which is defined as being a "hazardous substance," "hazardous material," "hazardous waste," "toxic substance," "toxic pollutant," "contaminant," or "pollutant" within the meaning of any Hazardous Materials Law, rather than naming other so-called problematic substances, which might not be regulated in a Hazardous Material Law by a governmental entity, so that arguably such substances should not be covered by this section (but note that it may be very difficult to get a Lender to agree to this type of change). In addition it is also quite common for the definition of "Hazardous Materials Laws" (set out in Part IV Section 1 of this Book) to also include a list of applicable state statutes.

A key Hazardous Materials Law is The Comprehensive Environmental Response, Compensation and Liability Act, 42 U.S.C. § 9601 *et seq.* ("**Superfund**" or "**CERCLA**"), which was enacted in 1980. CERCLA is a comprehensive federal statute that grants the federal government broad powers to force private parties to clean up hazardous waste sites. In addition, CERCLA requires parties to report and clean up any "release" of hazardous substances in excess of the applicable "reportable quantity" as soon as the release occurs. Federal regulations list thousands of hazardous substances and their reportable quantities.

Liability under CERCLA is strict; fault and negligence are irrelevant. Liability is retroactive: a party may be held liable for past activities—even those prior to CERCLA's enactment in 1980—that were legal at the time they occurred. The fact that a party complied with all laws and regulations and exercised all due care with regard to the substances does not protect it from liability. The commingling of wastes from different potentially responsible parties ("**PRPs**") generally renders the harm indivisible. Finally, CERCLA's standard of causation is minimal. The issue of causation is reduced to whether a release or threat of release has caused the EPA or a private party to incur response costs. A plaintiff in a CERCLA legal proceeding must, however, establish a causal link between the release and the response.

CERCLA imposes liability for the costs of cleanup of a contaminated site or facility on four categories of PRPs: (a) the owners or operators of the site at the time the wastes were deposited; (b) the present owners or operators of such a site; (c) the transporters who delivered hazardous substances to the site; and (d) the persons who arranged for disposal, treatment, or transport of wastes to the site (usually called "generators"). The last category includes businesses that generate and send wastes to off-site disposal locations.

Particularly relevant to a discussion of this section of the Mortgage are two "safe harbors" from CERCLA liability: (a) the "secured party" exemption for lenders; and (b) the "innocent purchaser" exemption.

From the beginning, CERCLA has included an exemption for any secured party that acted "primarily to protect its security interest." Nevertheless, courts have imposed liability on lenders who became "owners" by foreclosing on a deed of trust and buying the contaminated property at the foreclosure sale (*see, e.g.,* United States v. Maryland Bank & Trust Co., 632 F. Supp. 573 (D. Md. 1986)), or "operators" by participating in the day-to-day operational aspects of the business's hazardous waste activities (*see, e.g.,* United States v. Mirabile, 23 Env't Rep. Cas. 1511 (E.D. Pa. 1985)). Under this line of authority, once a lender bank became an owner through foreclosure, participated in management through control over its borrower, or became "involve[d] with the management of the facility [in a manner] sufficiently broad to support the inference that it could affect hazardous waste disposal decisions if it so chose" (United States v. Fleet Factors Corp., 31 Env't Rep.

Cas. 1465 (11th Cir. 1990)), the bank was no longer exempt from liability as a creditor and thus was liable for cleanup costs.

In 1996, Congress enacted the Asset Conservation, Lender Liability, and Deposit Insurance Protection Act. The purpose of the legislation was to clarify lender liability issues under CERCLA. The act amends CERCLA and creates safe harbors for lenders, trustees, and fiduciaries. Lenders who do not exercise decision-making control over contaminated property during the term of a loan or who foreclose on contaminated property and make reasonable attempts to sell the property to protect their security interest are not subject to CERCLA liability as owners.

An owner of real property, which was contaminated before it was purchased by such owner, may be excused from liability under CERCLA, if such owner can show that it had no reason to know of the contamination before it purchased such property. To make this showing, the landowner must have "undertaken, at the time of acquisition, all appropriate inquiry into the previous ownership and uses of the property consistent with good commercial or customary practice in an effort to minimize liability." *See* CERCLA §101(35)(A), 42 U.S.C. § 9601(35)(A). The standard is not absolute for all land purchasers: The greater the sophistication of the land purchaser, or the more obvious the contamination, the more difficulty one will have qualifying for this exception from liability. *See, e.g.,* New York v. Lashins, 91 F.3d 353 (2d Cir. 1996) (landowner held to have exercised "due care").

A standard practice has emerged, in connection with financing or purchasing commercial real estate, for requiring that an environmental due diligence assessment (commonly known as a "phase I assessment") be performed by a licensed engineering firm, in order to qualify for this exemption. *See* ASTM E1527.13, Standard Practice for Environmental Site Assessments: Phase I Environmental Site Assessment Process (American Society for Testing and Materials, 2013). In summary, this practice involves having a licensed environmental engineering firm conduct a review of real property title records for the property; a review of all public and agency records concerning compliance with environmental laws on the site and nearby properties; interviews with current and past owners, tenants, and neighbors concerning current and past uses and previous complaints concerning the property; and a site inspection by a competent environmental professional. The phase I assessment does not include any soil boring, monitoring well installation, or sample collection and analysis. Such activities are reserved for later investigations if evidence of possible contamination turns up from records, interviews, or observations during the site visit.

Another key Hazardous Materials Law is the Resource Conservation and Recovery Act, 42 U.S.C. § 6901 *et seq.* ("**RCRA**"), which imposes a rigorous "cradle-to-grave" scheme that regulates hazardous wastes from generation to final disposal or destruction. The term "generator" is defined as any person, by site location, whose act or process produces hazardous waste that is identified or listed in the regulations. If a generator determines that its waste is "hazardous waste," it must notify the EPA and the state of its activity and obtain an EPA identification number. Hazardous wastes cannot be stored on-site for more than 90 days without a permit, and must be shipped to a facility that is authorized to treat or dispose of the wastes.

Hazardous waste must be properly containerized, labeled, and manifested prior to shipment off-site. There are severe civil and criminal penalties for regulatory violations and disposal of hazardous wastes at unauthorized locations.

Underground storage tanks ("**USTs**") containing regulated substances, including petroleum products, are also subject to regulation under RCRA. New USTs must meet minimum federal standards. Existing USTs must be replaced or upgraded to specified standards that will prevent overfilling, spills, and leaks. Where spills or leaks have caused contamination of soils or groundwater with petroleum products, the owner or operator of the UST system must report and clean up the contamination under state supervision.

Below is the text of a section that might be found in a Mortgage with respect to Hazardous Materials:

> 18.1 *Except for matters covered by an O&M Program or matters described in Section 18.4 below, Borrower shall not cause or permit any of the following:*
>
> (a) *the presence, use, generation, release, treatment, processing, storage (including storage in above ground and underground storage tanks), handling, or disposal of any Hazardous Materials on or under the Mortgaged Property or any other property of Borrower that is adjacent to the Mortgaged Property;*
>
> (b) *the transportation of any Hazardous Materials to, from, or across the Mortgaged Property;*
>
> (c) *any occurrence or condition on the Mortgaged Property or any other property of Borrower that is adjacent to the Mortgaged Property, which occurrence or condition is or may be in violation of Hazardous Materials Laws; or*
>
> (d) *any violation of or noncompliance with the terms of any Environmental Permit with respect to the Mortgaged Property or any property of Borrower that is adjacent to the Mortgaged Property.*
>
> *The matters described in subsections (a) through (d) above are referred to collectively in this Section as "**Prohibited Activities or Conditions.**"*

Explanation

Lender will not rely solely on government enforcement to protect its interests in the Mortgaged Property. This section of the Mortgage, which deals with Hazardous Materials, requires Borrower to comply with all Hazardous Materials Laws and Environmental Permits, and makes failure to do so an Event of Default. Moreover, these "prohibited activities or conditions" bar the presence of, and any lawful and permitted activities involving, Hazardous Materials on the Mortgaged Property, even if such presence or activity would not violate hazardous materials laws. The only exceptions to this broad prohibition are those activities that Lender may approve in a written operations and maintenance program.

18.2 *Prohibited Activities and Conditions shall not include the safe and lawful use and storage of quantities of (1) pre-packaged supplies, cleaning materials and petroleum products customarily used in the operation and maintenance of comparable multifamily properties; (2) cleaning materials, personal grooming items and other items sold in pre-packaged containers and used by tenants and occupants of demised spaces within the Mortgaged Property; and (3) petroleum products used in the operation and maintenance of motor vehicles from time to time located on the Mortgaged Property's parking areas, so long as all of the foregoing are used, stored, handled, transported and disposed of in compliance with Hazardous Materials Laws.*

Explanation

Section 18.2 above provides a narrow exemption from the broad prohibition in Section 18.1, and constitutes an acknowledgment that many substances found at commercial properties (e.g., cleaning products) contain hazardous materials such as chlorine and ammonia. Lender allows the presence of these categories of materials (which are necessary for the efficient operation of the Mortgaged Property), provided they are handled in accordance with Hazardous Materials Laws.

As reflected in Section 18.3 below, this Mortgage requires Borrower to impose the same requirements concerning prohibited activities and conditions on its employees, agents, contractors, tenants and occupants.

18.3 *Borrower shall take all commercially reasonable actions (including the inclusion of appropriate provisions in any Leases executed after the date of this Mortgage) to prevent its employees, agents, and contractors, and all tenants and other occupants from causing or permitting any Prohibited Activities or Conditions. Borrower shall not lease or allow the sublease or use of all or any portion of the Mortgaged Property to any tenant or subtenant for any use by any user that, in the ordinary course of its business, would cause or permit any Prohibited Activity or Condition.*

Explanation

Below is (a) a provision that has been inserted into this Mortgage to reflect that Borrower has established an O&M Program to deal with an issue concerning Hazardous Materials with respect to the Mortgaged Property, and (b) some typical Borrower representations and warranties that are included in the Loan Documents with respect to Hazardous Materials. Obviously the provision relating to the O&M Program would not be necessary if such existing condition did not exist.

18.4 *If a Borrower establishes a program pursuant to a written protocol approved by Lender which sets out a plan of training, cleaning, work practices, and surveillance to deal with and/or maintain Hazardous Materials (an "**O&M Program**"), then Borrower shall comply in a timely manner with, and cause all employees, agents, and contractors of Borrower and any other persons present on the Mortgaged Property to comply with, the O&M Program. All costs of performance of Borrower's obligations under any O&M Program shall be paid by Borrower, and Lender's out-of-pocket costs incurred in connection with the monitoring and review of the O&M Program and Borrower's performance shall be paid by Borrower upon demand by Lender. Any such out-of-pocket costs of Lender which Borrower fails to pay promptly shall become an additional part of the Indebtedness as provided in Section __.*

18.5 *Borrower represents and warrants to Lender that, except as previously disclosed by Borrower to Lender in writing:*

(a) *Borrower has not at any time engaged in, caused or permitted any Prohibited Activities or Conditions;*

(b) *to the best of Borrower's knowledge after reasonable and diligent inquiry, no Prohibited Activities or Conditions exist or have existed;*

(c) *except to the extent previously disclosed by Borrower to Lender in writing, the Mortgaged Property does not now contain any underground storage tanks, and, to the best of Borrower's knowledge after reasonable and diligent inquiry, the Mortgaged Property has not contained any underground storage tanks in the past. If there is an underground storage tank located on the Property which has been previously disclosed by Borrower to Lender in writing, that tank complies with all requirements of Hazardous Materials Laws;*

(d) *Borrower has complied with all Hazardous Materials Laws, including all requirements for notification regarding releases of Hazardous Materials. Without limiting the generality of the foregoing, Borrower has obtained all Environmental Permits required for the operation of the Mortgaged Property in accordance with Hazardous Materials Laws now in effect and all such Environmental Permits are in full force and effect;*

(e) *no event has occurred with respect to the Mortgaged Property that constitutes, or with the passing of time or the giving of notice would constitute, noncompliance with the terms of any Environmental Permit;*

(f) *there are no actions, suits, claims or proceedings pending or, to the best of Borrower's knowledge after reasonable and diligent inquiry, threatened that involve the Mortgaged Property and allege, arise out of, or relate to any Prohibited Activity or Condition; and*

(g) *Borrower has not received any complaint, order, notice of violation or other communication from any Governmental Authority with regard to air emissions, water discharges, noise emissions or Hazardous Materials, or any other environmental, health or safety matters affecting the Mortgaged Property or any other property of Borrower that is adjacent to the Mortgaged Property.*

The representations and warranties in this Section 18.5 shall be continuing representations and warranties that shall be deemed to be made by Borrower throughout the term of the loan evidenced by the Note, until the Indebtedness has been paid in full.

Explanation

Borrower's representations and warranties set out in Section 18.5, concerning Borrower's confirmation of facts relating to the environmental history of the Mortgaged Property, provides Lender with important assurances that Lender needs in order to be comfortable with making its decision to authorize and proceed with the funding of the Loan. While Lender will also be relying on an environmental report or reports issued by licensed experts, only Borrower may be in a position to ascertain whether or not there are some environmental concerns relating to the Mortgaged Property which would have a bearing on Lender's underwriting of the Loan. The above provision of the Mortgage obligates Borrower to represent and warrant unequivocally, inter alia, that Borrower has not conducted any prohibited activities or conditions on the Mortgaged Property. As is the case with any representation made by Borrower in the Loan Documents, it is entitled to provide a written schedule of exceptions to these representations for known instances of any fact that would render any given representation false (and often these exceptions will provide critical information to Lender). As to activities that occurred on the Mortgaged Property before Borrower owned it (e.g., the presence of underground tanks), Borrower should insist that any such representations are qualified based on Borrower's actual knowledge (since if some act occurred before Borrower acquired the Mortgaged Property, Borrower does not want to be held to have breached a representation because a fact that is unknown to Borrower occurred which is at odds with such representation). In most instances, Borrower or Lender will have required a licensed engineer to produce one or more environmental reports, so that with respect to the above representations, Borrower's counsel should consider requesting that such representations be qualified to be made subject to the facts and disclosures set forth in such reports, which then puts the burden on Lender to read and assimilate the facts and disclosures. Note that the above Section 18.5 requires that Borrower make these representations and warranties continuously throughout the term of the Loan—which is not reasonable, inasmuch as Borrower cannot predict with any accuracy events that might occur in the future, so that with regard to future activities, Borrower should only be providing Lender with covenants that Borrower will not commit actions which violate reasonable environmental requirements imposed by Lender and/or that if a future environmental condition arises, then Borrower will take the appropriate action to mitigate any adverse impacts on the Mortgaged Property arising from such future environmental condition.

It is not uncommon for the Loan Documents to require Borrower to provide Lender with notice of the occurrence of future events which impact on the environmental condition of the Mortgaged Property. Below is an example of this type of provision.

> 18.6 *Borrower shall promptly notify Lender in writing upon the occurrence of any of the following events:*
>
> (a) *Borrower's discovery of any Prohibited Activity or Condition;*
>
> (b) *Borrower's receipt of or knowledge of any complaint, order, notice of violation or other communication from any Governmental Authority or other person with regard to present or future alleged Prohibited Activities or Conditions or any other environmental, health or safety matters affecting the Mortgaged Property or any other property of Borrower that is adjacent to the Mortgaged Property; and*
>
> (c) *If any representation or warranty in this Section 18 becomes untrue after the date of this Mortgage.*
>
> *Any such notice given by Borrower shall not relieve Borrower of, or result in a waiver of, any obligation under this Mortgage, the Note, or any other Loan Document.*

Explanation

Section 1.6 of the Mortgage above places the burden on Borrower to remain abreast of, and report to Lender, any developments that may result in a governmental enforcement action or require some cleanup activity. Borrower's compliance with this reporting obligation does not relieve Borrower of other obligations in the Loan Documents.

Below is a provision dealing with Lender's right to perform environmental inspections of the Mortgaged Property.

> 18.7 *Borrower shall pay promptly the costs of any environmental inspections, tests or audits ("**Environmental Inspections**") required by Lender in connection with any foreclosure or deed in lieu of foreclosure, or as a condition of Lender's consent to any Transfer under Section 22 of this Mortgage, or required by Lender following a reasonable determination by Lender that Prohibited Activities or Conditions may exist. Any such costs incurred by Lender (including the fees and out-of-pocket costs of attorneys and technical consultants whether incurred in connection with any judicial or administrative process or otherwise) which Borrower fails to pay promptly shall become an additional part of the Indebtedness. The results of all Environmental Inspections made by Lender shall at all times remain the property of Lender and Lender shall have no obligation to disclose or otherwise make available to Borrower or any other party such results or any other information obtained by Lender in connection with its Environmental Inspections. Lender hereby reserves the right, and Borrower hereby expressly authorizes Lender, to make available to any party, including any prospective bidder at a foreclosure sale of the Mortgaged*

Property, the results of any Environmental Inspections made by Lender with respect to the Mortgaged Property. Borrower consents to Lender notifying any party (either as part of a notice of sale or otherwise) of the results of any of Lender's Environmental Inspections. Borrower acknowledges that Lender cannot control or otherwise assure the truthfulness or accuracy of the results of any of its Environmental Inspections and that the release of such results to prospective bidders at a foreclosure sale of the Mortgaged Property may have a material and adverse effect upon the amount which a party may bid at such sale. Borrower agrees that Lender shall have no liability whatsoever as a result of delivering the results of any of its Environmental Inspections to any third party, and Borrower hereby releases and forever discharges Lender from any and all claims, damages, or causes of action, arising out of, connected with or incidental to the results of, the delivery of any of Lender's Environmental Inspections.

Explanation

Despite the protections for secured parties, no lender should foreclose on and take title to mortgaged property before satisfying itself that the property remains free of contamination that could lead to CERCLA liability. Therefore, the above Section 18.7 reserves to Lender the right to order an environmental assessment of the Mortgaged Property— to be conducted at Borrower's expense— when the Mortgaged Property is subject to foreclosure or transfer of title, or at any time Lender reasonably believes that contamination may be present. This sub-section also permits Lender to choose the consultants to perform such assessments and to control the scope and conduct of such assessments.

Further, this Section 18.7 reserves to Lender the right to withhold or disclose the information generated as Lender sees fit to protect its interests, whether or not Borrower objects. Lender may wish to have its lawyers direct such assessments and protect the work product from disclosure to third parties under the attorney-client and attorney work product privileges. Granting Borrower the right to the information might destroy these privileges and lead to disclosure of the information to other third parties. In contrast, this section authorizes Lender to disclose any information discovered to any governmental agency to which reports must be made, or to prospective buyers, even if Borrower objects because its interest will be adversely affected.

18.8 *If any investigation, site monitoring, containment, clean-up, restoration or other remedial work (“**Remedial Work**”) is necessary to comply with any Hazardous Materials Law or order of any Governmental Authority that has or acquires jurisdiction over the Mortgaged Property or the use, operation or improvement of the Mortgaged Property under any Hazardous Materials Law, Borrower shall, by the earlier of (1) the applicable deadline required by*

Hazardous Materials Law or (2) 30 days after notice from Lender demanding such action, begin performing the Remedial Work, and thereafter diligently prosecute it to completion, and shall in any event complete the work by the time required by applicable Hazardous Materials Law. If Borrower fails to begin on a timely basis or diligently prosecute any required Remedial Work, Lender may, at its option, cause the Remedial Work to be completed, in which case Borrower shall reimburse Lender on demand for the cost of doing so. Any reimbursement due from Borrower to Lender shall become part of the Indebtedness.

Explanation

Section 18.8 of the Mortgage authorizes Lender to require Borrower to undertake and complete "remedial work" to comply not only with governmental cleanup orders, but also with Lender's directions to correct noncompliance problems on the Mortgaged Property. Section 18.8 reserves the latter right because Lender cannot rely on any governmental authority to require Borrower to conduct needed remedial actions, or to prosecute an effective enforcement action if Borrower fails to comply. Alternatively, if Borrower fails to act, said Section 18.8 of the Mortgage permits Lender to perform the cleanup at Borrower's expense, and to add the cost to the Indebtedness.

18.9 *Borrower shall cooperate with any inquiry by any Governmental Authority and shall comply with any governmental or judicial order which arises from any alleged Prohibited Activity or Condition.*

18.10 *Borrower shall indemnify, hold harmless and defend (i) Lender, (ii) any prior owner or holder of the Note, (iii) the Loan Servicer, (iv) any prior loan servicer, (v) the officers, directors, shareholders, partners, employees and trustees of any of the foregoing, and (vi) the heirs, legal representatives, successors and assigns of each of the foregoing (collectively, the* ***"Environmental Indemnitees"****) from and against all proceedings, claims, damages, penalties and costs (whether initiated or sought by Governmental Authorities or private parties), including fees and out-of-pocket expenses of attorneys and expert witnesses, investigatory fees, and remediation costs, whether incurred in connection with any judicial or administrative process or otherwise, arising directly or indirectly from any of the following:*

(a) *any breach of any representation or warranty of Borrower in this Section 18 of this Mortgage;*
(b) *any failure by Borrower to perform any of its obligations under this Section 18 of this Mortgage;*
(c) *the existence or alleged existence of any Prohibited Activity or Condition;*
(d) *the presence or alleged presence of Hazardous Materials on or under the Mortgaged Property or any property of Borrower that is adjacent to the Mortgaged Property; and*
(e) *the actual or alleged violation of any Hazardous Materials Law.*

18.11 *Counsel selected by Borrower to defend Environmental Indemnitees shall be subject to the approval of those Environmental Indemnitees. However, any Environmental Indemnitee may elect to defend any claim or legal or administrative proceeding at the Borrower's expense.*

18.12 *Borrower shall not, without the prior written consent of those Environmental Indemnitees who are named as parties to a claim or legal or administrative proceeding (an "**Environmental Claim**"), settle or compromise the Environmental Claim if the settlement (1) results in the entry of any judgment that does not include as an unconditional term the delivery by the claimant or plaintiff to Lender of a written release of those Environmental Indemnitees, satisfactory in form and substance to Lender; or (2) may materially and adversely affect Lender, as determined by Lender in its discretion.*

18.13 *Lender agrees that the indemnity under this Section 18 shall be limited to the assets of Borrower and Lender shall not seek to recover any deficiency from any natural persons who are general partners of Borrower.*

18.14 *Borrower shall, at its own cost and expense, do all of the following:*

(a) *pay or satisfy any judgment or decree that may be entered against any Environmental Indemnitee or Environmental Indemnitees in any legal or administrative proceeding incident to any matters against which Environmental Indemnitees are entitled to be indemnified under this Section of the Mortgage;*

(b) *reimburse Environmental Indemnitees for any expenses paid or incurred in connection with any matters against which Environmental Indemnitees are entitled to be indemnified under this Section of the Mortgage; and*

(c) *reimburse Environmental Indemnitees for any and all expenses, including fees and out-of-pocket expenses of attorneys and expert witnesses, paid or incurred in connection with the enforcement by Environmental Indemnitees of their rights under this Section of the Mortgage, or in monitoring and participating in any legal or administrative proceeding.*

18.15 *In any circumstances in which the indemnity under this Section of the Mortgage applies, Lender may employ its own legal counsel and consultants to prosecute, defend or negotiate any claim or legal or administrative proceeding and Lender, with the prior written consent of Borrower (which shall not be unreasonably withheld, delayed or conditioned), may settle or compromise any action or legal or administrative proceeding. Borrower shall reimburse Lender upon demand for all costs and expenses incurred by Lender, including all costs of settlements entered into in good faith, and the fees and out-of-pocket expenses of such attorneys and consultants.*

18.16 *The provisions of this Section of the Mortgage shall be in addition to any and all other obligations and liabilities that Borrower may have under applicable law or under other Loan Documents, and each Indemnitee shall be entitled to indemnification under this Section 18 of this Mortgage without regard to whether Lender or that Indemnitee has exercised any rights against the Mortgaged Property or any other security, pursued any rights against any guarantor, or pursued any other rights available under the Loan Documents or applicable law. If Borrower consists of more than one person or entity, the obligation of those persons or entities to indemnify the Environmental Indemnitees under this Section 18 of this Mortgage shall be joint and several. The obligation of Borrower to indemnify the Environmental Indemnitees under this Section 18 of this Mortgage shall survive any repayment or discharge of the Indebtedness, any foreclosure proceeding, any foreclosure sale, any delivery of any deed in lieu of foreclosure, and any release of record of the lien of this Mortgage.*

Explanation

Environmental provisions in real estate and financial documents commonly include indemnity rights. Current and past property owners and tenants, as well as their lenders, have been subjected to lawsuits seeking cleanup actions. In the liability phase of such litigation, a defendant may be unable to defend by arguing that another party is or should be entirely responsible for the contamination. Instead, it is a common occurrence that a number of parties will be "caught in the net" of liability as potentially responsible parties, and will incur large litigation expenses. In the relief or damages phase of the case, if the case is not settled first, the share of liability to be borne by each party will be established. Also, while the governmental cleanup action is threatened or pending, the lender may undertake some cleanup action, either voluntarily or involuntarily. The foregoing indemnity provisions enable Lender to recover these costs directly from Borrower. It is quite likely that in addition to this indemnity, Lender will require Guarantor to enter into a separate environmental indemnity, which will mean that as an alternative to foreclosing on the Mortgaged Property, Lender would have the alternative option to either (a) attempt to force Guarantor to remediate any hazardous environmental condition that at any time might be affecting the Mortgaged Property, or (b) sue Guarantor in an amount sufficient to cover the cost of remediation (prior to Lender pursuing its foreclosure remedies).

SECTION 19

Property and Liability Insurance

Explanation

Adequate casualty property insurance coverages is essential to both a Lender and Borrower; and without such insurance, a casualty loss which impacts the Mortgaged Property could easily result in very expensive repair damage. If such damage occurs and is not repaired because Borrower does not have adequate funds to pay for the needed repairs, then such damage could result in the Mortgaged Property's value being significantly reduced, and this could mean that if Lender needed to foreclose, then the resulting foreclosure sale proceeds might not be sufficient to cover the then outstanding Indebtedness. The following provision contains typical language set out in Loan Documents with regard to Borrower's obligation to maintain casualty insurance:

19.1 *Borrower shall keep the Improvements insured at all times against such hazards as Lender may from time to time require, issued by companies authorized to do business in the State of _______, having a Best's Rating of not less than A-VIII and otherwise reasonably acceptable to Lender in its sole discretion and which insurance shall include but not be limited to the following:*

(a) *commercial property insurance on an all-risk or Special Causes of Loss basis without exception (including, without limitation, flood, required if Mortgaged Property is in a "Special Flood Hazard Area" A or V, pursuant to the Federal Flood Disaster Protection Act of 1973, as amended, vandalism and malicious mischief, flood, earthquake, windstorm, collapse, boiler explosion, machinery breakdown, sprinkler leakage coverage, cost of demolition, increased costs of construction and the value of the undamaged portion of the building and soft costs coverage) covering all the real estate, fixtures and personal property to the extent of the full insurable* *value thereof, having replacement cost valuation and no coinsurance, with deductibles not in excess of $100,000 (or as otherwise reasonably acceptable to Lender). If at any time the Property and Collateral are undergoing construction or renovation, the property insurance required herein shall be written on a builder's risk/course of construction non-reporting form prior to completion and a Permission to Occupy Endorsement, if not otherwise covered under the borrower commercial property insurance; and*

(b) *rent loss or business interruption insurance in an amount equal to one year's projected rentals then being derived by the Mortgaged Property, plus an extended period of indemnity of no less than 180 days.*

Borrower acknowledges and agrees that Lender's insurance requirements may change from time to time throughout the term of the Indebtedness. If Lender so requires, such insurance requirements, to the extent applicable, shall also include sinkhole insurance, mine subsidence insurance and, if the Mortgaged Property does not conform to applicable zoning or land use laws, building ordinance or law coverage.

Explanation

These provisions are fairly typical requirements relating to what a Lender will want included in commercial property insurance coverages for the Mortgaged Property. Borrower's counsel, upon receiving Loan Documents which contain requirements for insurance coverages, should always request that Borrower send these provisions to its insurance agent or insurance advisor, so that the onus is placed on Borrower to be sure that Borrower will be able to obtain in the market the insurance so requested by Lender. Frequently, the insurance agent and/or insurance advisor of Borrower will be engaged by Borrower to review these provisions so that such agent or advisor can be in a position to provide Borrower with helpful suggested changes to the insurance language that will better serve Borrower's interests. In reading the above provision, in addition to requiring that the insurer issuing this insurance meet certain typical financial rating standards issued by the firm A.M. Best Company, Inc., the provision indicates that the insurer must be reasonably acceptable to Lender, in its sole discretion. Arguably if the standard is to be reasonably acceptable to Lender, then the added language "in its sole discretion," cuts against the reasonability standard; so that when a provision in the Loan Documents contains a reasonableness standard, subject to the sole discretion of Lender, it would not be unreasonable for Borrower's counsel to request that the sole discretion language be deleted. However, often times, Lender will refuse to this, and I don't think it is productive for Borrower's counsel to make a major issue over this point.

This provision also does not permit Borrower to have "deductibles" in excess of $100,000, without Lender's consent. This would mean that if a casualty were to occur, the first hundred thousand dollars of loss would have to be paid by Borrower, and only the excess of that loss would be covered by the insurance policy. The larger the deductible, the less Borrower has to pay for the annual premium, but obviously, a higher deductible means that Borrower will be taking a risk that it will have to pay a higher amount if a substantial loss occurs. Borrower wants to avoid having Lender impose a deductible limit which is too low, as that will cause Borrower's annual insurance premiums to be higher than they would be if the deductible were set as a higher amount. In this case, $100,000 would seem reasonable for a commercial real estate transaction involving an asset worth more than $2 million (so that if the real estate asset was worth more than $500 million, then Borrower should consider asking for a higher deductible in order to save on its insurance premium).

This provision also calls for "rent loss or business interruption" insurance. This insurance will require the insurance company to pay Borrower an amount equal to lost revenues attributable to a given casualty, subject to the terms of the insurance coverage. The one year's projected rentals required by this provision for such insurance is fairly typical.

Here Lender is also reserving the right to require additional insurance coverages at a later time. In response to this request, Borrower's counsel should consider limiting any such insurance to insurance consistent with customary insurance obtained in accordance with the practices of prudent owners of similar properties, and the requirement for additional insurance coverage should be permitted only to the extent the premiums payable in respect of such additional insurance are commercially reasonable.

Below are some additional insurance coverages that are typically required in a commercial real estate loan:

> 19.2 *Borrower shall at all times provide and maintain the following additional insurance coverages issued by companies authorized to do business in the State of the Property Jurisdiction, having a Best's Rating of not less than A-VIII:*
>
> (a) *commercial general liability insurance, with not less than $1,000,000 per occurrence and $2,000,000 in the aggregate, per location or such other amounts as may be determined by Lender from time to time;*
>
> (b) *automobile liability insurance (including non-owned automobile) with a coverage of $1,000,000 per occurrence;*
>
> (c) *worker's compensation, employer's liability and other insurance required by law;*
>
> (d) *excess liability insurance in an amount no less than $50,000,000 each occurrence and in the aggregate; and*
>
> (e) *such other insurance coverages in such amounts as Lender may request consistent with the customary practices of prudent developers and owners of similar properties.*
>
> *All premiums on insurance policies required under this Section 19.2 shall be paid by Borrower. All such policies shall also be in a form approved by Lender. All policies of property damage insurance shall include a non-contributing, non-reporting mortgage clause in favor of, and in a form approved by, Lender.*

Explanation

These provisions are also fairly typical. Note, however, that Lender is requesting additional liability coverage in the amount of at least $50 million. This amount of additional coverage is high, and would be expensive, so it would not be uncommon for Borrower's counsel to request that this minimum amount be lowered. In any event, Borrower's counsel should consult with Borrower and/or Borrower's insurance agent or consultant regarding this provision. Note that at the end of the above provision, Lender is reserving the right to request additional insurance coverages and insurance amounts, but this request is conditioned upon such coverages and amounts being consistent with customary practices of prudent owners of similar properties. This is a reasonable approach for Lender to take and Borrower usually will not be successful in getting Lender to agree to delete this provision. However, it would be reasonable for Borrower's counsel to press that the insurance should only be obtainable to the extent the premiums payable in respect of such insurance is commercially reasonable. In addition, if possible Borrower's counsel should try to change the portion of the above provision which allows Lender in the future to make changes to the insurance coverages or the amount limits, at Lender's sole discretion. Again, it would be better if such provisions were specifically limited to such coverages and/or such amounts as would be consistent with customary practices of prudent owners of similar properties.

Below are provisions which are also typically contained in the insurance section of the Loan Documents.

19.3 *An actual insurance policy or certified copy thereof, or a binder, certificate of insurance, or other evidence of property coverage in the form of Acord 27 (Evidence of Property Coverage), Acord 25 (Certificate of Insurance), or a 30-day binder in form acceptable to Lender with an unconditional undertaking to deliver the policy or a certified copy within sixty (60) days, shall be delivered at closing of the Loan. Lender shall be named as first mortgagee on policies of all-risk-type insurance on the Mortgaged Property, as loss payee on the Improvements and its contents, and as first mortgagee on rent-loss or business interruption coverages related thereto. Except with respect to commercial general liability insurance, as to which Lender shall be named as an additional insured, on forms acceptable to Lender, with respect to the Mortgaged Property, all other required insurance coverages shall have a so-called "Mortgagee's endorsement" or "Lender's loss-payable endorsement," in form and substance reasonably satisfactory to Lender.*

19.4 *Borrower shall comply with all insurance requirements and shall not permit any condition to exist on the Mortgaged Property that would invalidate any part of any insurance coverage that this Mortgage requires Borrower to maintain.*

Explanation

Again these provisions are fairly typical. By and large, Borrower's counsel will not be successful in being able to substantially remove or materially negotiate these provisions.

19.5 *In the event of a casualty loss which damages any portion of the Mortgaged Property, Borrower shall give immediate written notice to the insurance carrier and to Lender. Borrower hereby authorizes and appoints Lender as attorney-in-fact for Borrower to make proof of loss, to adjust and compromise any claims under policies of property damage insurance, to appear in and prosecute any action arising from such property damage insurance policies, to collect and receive the proceeds of property damage insurance, and to deduct from such proceeds Lender's expenses incurred in the collection of such proceeds. This power of attorney is coupled with an interest and therefore is irrevocable. Subject to the provisions contained in Section 19.5 of this Mortgage, Lender may, at Lender's option, (1) hold the balance of such proceeds to be used to reimburse Borrower for the cost of restoring and repairing the Mortgaged Property to the equivalent of its original condition or to a condition approved by Lender (the "**Restoration**"), or (2) apply the balance of such proceeds to the payment of the Indebtedness, whether or not then due. To the extent Lender determines to apply insurance proceeds to Restoration, Lender shall do so in accordance with Lender's then-current policies relating to the restoration of casualty damage on similar multifamily properties.*

19.6 *Notwithstanding the foregoing provisions of Section 19.6 of this Mortgage to the contrary, Lender shall not exercise its option to apply insurance proceeds and/or condemnation awards to the payment of the Indebtedness if all of the following conditions are met:*

(a) *no Event of Default (or any event which, with the giving of notice or the passage of time, or both, would constitute an Event of Default) has occurred and is continuing;*

(b) *Lender determines, in its discretion, that there will be sufficient funds from the proceeds or awards that are paid pursuant to the applicable insurance, or are otherwise paid to Lender by Borrower, in either case to complete the Restoration;*

(c) *Lender determines, in its discretion, that the rental income from the Mortgaged Property after completion of the Restoration will be sufficient to meet all operating costs and other expenses, Imposition Deposits, deposits to reserves and loan repayment obligations relating to the Mortgaged Property;*

(d) *Lender determines, in its discretion, that the Restoration will be completed before the earlier of (A) one year before the maturity date of the Note or (B) one year after the date of the loss or casualty;*

(e) *to the extent plans and specifications are customarily prepared in connection with implementing the repairs necessary to complete the Restoration ("**Cost To Repair**"), Lender shall have approved, in its discretion, in writing any such plans and specifications;*

(f) *Borrower shall have provided to Lender such waivers of lien, architect's certificates, contractor's sworn statements and other evidence of payments required to be made, from time to time, until the Restoration has been fully completed, as Lender shall reasonably require; and*

(g) *upon Lender's request, Borrower provides Lender evidence of the availability during and after the Restoration of the insurance required to be maintained by Borrower pursuant to this Mortgage.*

19.7 *If the aggregate actual cost of making the necessary repairs, restorations or replacement needed to complete the Restoration does not exceed $100,000, the insurance proceeds or condemnation award shall be released to Borrower to pay for the Costs To Repair, but only to the extent of such costs, as estimated by Lender. Otherwise, funds shall be released upon final completion of the Restoration, unless Borrower requests earlier funding, in which event partial monthly disbursements equal to 90% of the value of the work completed shall be made prior to final completion of the repair, restoration or replacement and the balance of the disbursements shall be made upon full completion and the receipt by Lender of satisfactory evidence of payment and release of all liens. Notwithstanding the foregoing, Lender will release the portion of such retained amount being held with respect to any contractor, subcontractor or materialman engaged in the Restoration as of the date upon which Lender has determined that such contractor, subcontractor or materialman has satisfactorily completed all work and has supplied all materials in accordance with the provisions of such contractor's, subcontractor's or materialman's contract, such contractor, subcontractor or materialman delivers the lien waivers and evidence of payment in full of all sums due to such contractor, subcontractor or materialman as may be reasonably requested by Lender or by the title company issuing Lender's title insurance policy.*

Explanation

When a casualty loss to the Mortgaged Property occurs and the insurance company makes a payment under its policy, Borrower will want the insurance proceeds to be applied to pay for the Cost To Repair. As can be seen in the above provisions, the general rule is for such proceeds to be made available to Lender to apply, at its option, to repayment of the Indebtedness. In theory, applying the insurance proceeds toward the balance of the Loan could be economically beneficial to Borrower, depending upon where market interest rates then stand (if interest rates have gone down since the time of closing of the Loan, theoretically Borrower might be able to refinance with proceeds from a new loan that carried a lower interest rate than the Loan), but given that the Improvements are then damaged, and income may be impaired, such refinancing might prove to be difficult for Borrower to achieve, and that might certainly be the case if interest rates have risen from the time of the closing of the Loan. In addition, market conditions may be such that obtaining a new loan may not be practical for Borrower. As a result, it is important for Borrower's counsel to be sure that there are provisions in the Loan Documents which will compel Lender to allow the proceeds of insurance to be used to pay the Cost To Repair, as is the case with the above provisions.

The above provisions of the Mortgage are relatively generous to Borrower in respect of Lender's permitting insurance proceeds to be used to pay for the Cost To Repair. This provision requires Lender to allow Borrower to use casualty insurance proceeds to pay for Restoration if: no Event of Default then exists, the insurance proceeds are sufficient to complete the Restoration, the Mortgaged Property will generate sufficient income after Restoration to cover Borrower's debt service and all operating expenses, and the Restoration can be completed within a year from the date of the loss. These are all reasonable conditions, and courts would almost certainly uphold them. There is one further limitation: Lender need not release the insurance proceeds for Restoration if the Loan will mature within one year after the Restoration is completed. The rationale for this limitation is that Lender should not have to endure the trouble of restoration if the Loan has only one year or less to maturity, and it is not unreasonable for Lender to insist upon a provision like this.

SECTION 20

Condemnation

Explanation

Under State and Federal laws, the applicable Governmental Authorities have reserved the right to acquire private real estate interests and tear down and/or alter the improvements located on any taken land, so as to enable the applicable Governmental Authority to pursue its mandated course of action. Such an acquisition is typically known as a "condemnation" or a "taking," and when the applicable Governmental Authority so acquires title, it is obligated to pay a market price for the acquired real estate interest. The market price oftentimes is contested by Lender or Mortgagor in a court proceeding. Pursuant to the Mortgage, Lender will have a lien on these condemnation proceeds which, under the circumstances set forth in the Mortgage, may allow Lender to apply such proceeds to pay-down the Indebtedness, but in many cases, such provisions in the Mortgage will mandate that the proceeds be able to be used by Mortgagor to rebuild and/or restore the Improvements. Usually there are the following two types of takings: a total condemnation, and a partial condemnation. A total condemnation is one where all or substantially all of the Mortgaged Property is acquired by the applicable Governmental Authority in the taking. A partial condemnation is one where only a portion of the Mortgaged Property is acquired by the Governmental Authority in the taking. In the case of partial condemnations, so long as no Event of Default exists, Lender usually is required to permit condemnation proceeds to be utilized to rebuild the Mortgaged Property, subject to certain terms and conditions. Below is the first portion of a condemnation provision in a Mortgage, which deals with the occurrence of a Condemnation, and describes the circumstances under which Lender is mandated to permit the proceeds of the Condemnation to be utilized for restoration of the Mortgaged Property.

20.1 *Borrower shall promptly notify Lender of any action or proceeding relating to any condemnation or other taking, or conveyance in lieu thereof, of all or any part of the Mortgaged Property, whether direct or indirect (a "***Condemnation***"). Borrower shall appear in and prosecute or defend any action or proceeding relating to any Condemnation unless otherwise directed by Lender in writing. Borrower authorizes and appoints Lender as attorney-in-fact for Borrower to commence, appear in and prosecute, in Lender's or Borrower's name, any action or proceeding relating to any Condemnation and to settle or compromise any claim in connection with any Condemnation. This power of attorney is coupled with an interest and therefore is irrevocable. However, nothing contained in this Section 20.1 shall require Lender to incur any expense or take any action. Borrower hereby transfers and assigns to Lender all right, title and interest of Borrower in and to any award or payment with respect to (i) any Condemnation, or any conveyance in lieu of Condemnation, and (ii) any damage to the Mortgaged Property caused by governmental action that does not result in a Condemnation.*

20.2 *Except for those provisions expressly provided for in Section 19 of this Mortgage (which require Lender to allow the awards or proceeds of any such Condemnation to be applied to pay for applicable costs of Restoration), Lender may apply such awards or proceeds, after the deduction of Lender's expenses incurred in the collection of such amounts, to the payment of the Indebtedness, with the balance, if any, to be paid to Borrower. Unless Lender otherwise agrees in writing, any application of any awards or proceeds to the Indebtedness shall not extend or postpone the due date of any monthly installments referred to in the Note, or change the amount of such installments. Borrower agrees to execute such further evidence of assignment of any awards or proceeds as Lender may require.*

Explanation

The proceeds of a condemnation award are similar to casualty insurance proceeds, and are regarded as a substitute res to which the lien of the Mortgage attaches. *See* Grant S. Nelson, Dale A. Whitman, Ann M. Burkhart & R. Wilson Freyermuth, Real Estates Finance Law § 4.12 (6th ed. 2007); Harold D. Teague, *Condemnation of Mortgaged Property*, 44 Tex. L. Rev. 1535 (1966).

Usually as long as no Event of Default exists, following completion of any applicable restoration of the Mortgaged Property (in the case of a partial taking), and compliance by Borrower with any other relevant terms of the Mortgage (See Part IV Section 19 of this Book), the condemnation award will be applied first to pay for the costs of the restoration of the Mortgaged Property (but in all other cases, Lender has the right to apply the award first to pay down the Indebtedness). However, there is a major difference between the treatment of eminent domain awards here and the treatment of casualty insurance proceeds which was discussed in Part IV

Section 19 of this Book. When eminent domain awards are received, Lender has the absolute discretion as to whether to apply them toward the loan balance or toward restoration of the property. There is no affirmative duty on Lender's part to permit use of the funds for restoration, even if restoration is feasible. The reason for the difference is that when a condemnation occurs, unlike an insured casualty, at least part of the property is simply gone and literally cannot be restored. It is true that in some cases the taking may be of a minor part of the property, and it may be possible to restore the property's value to its pre-taking level by applying the eminent domain award. But these instances are probably rare, so borrowers are unlikely to complain much about the lender having discretion to allocate the award.

SECTION 21

Borrower Bankruptcy Remoteness; Separateness Covenants

Explanation

A major goal of modern lenders on commercial real estate properties is to make their borrowers, who own these properties that will secure their loans, "bankruptcy remote." This is desirable from Lender's viewpoint because it does not wish to see the Mortgaged Property becoming part of a Borrower's bankruptcy estate (and therefore become subject to the "automatic stay" which comes into effect once a bankruptcy case is commenced. The automatic stay results in Lender being precluded from exercising its foreclosure remedies pending the bankruptcy judge providing an order which provides Lender with "relief" of this stay; as well as associated incremental delays and additional legal expenses which are required if the Mortgaged Property becomes part of Borrower's bankruptcy estate). Lender will typically employ several strategies to cause Borrower and the Mortgaged Property to become bankruptcy remote. These strategies include: (i) requiring that Borrower's only directly owned real estate asset be the Mortgaged Property; (ii) requiring that Borrower take steps to prevent it from being able to be consolidated in the bankruptcy of its parent or any of its affiliates, by having Borrower enter into a series of covenants (commonly referred to as "separateness covenants") in the Mortgage or the Loan Agreement; and (iii) requiring that Borrower not be permitted to make an election which would cause Borrower to commence a bankruptcy case or take a similar step under state law which would effectively cause it to become bankrupt, without getting a formal approval from an independent party, who would be part of the group of individuals and/or entities who would be solely vested in the organizational documents of Borrower with the ability to veto an action by Borrower to commence such bankruptcy case, or take such similar bankruptcy step.

To accomplish Lender's requirement that the Mortgaged Property be the sole real estate asset owned by Borrower, the following is a Mortgage provision which seeks to require that the relationship between Borrower and the Mortgaged Property be kept totally free from entanglement with other real estate projects (that might otherwise drag the Mortgaged Property and/or Borrower into a bankruptcy case; or if such bankruptcy case is commenced, might involve other creditors competing with Lender and who will also have a secured position with respect to other real estate projects).

> 21.1 *Until the Indebtedness is paid in full, Borrower (a) shall not acquire any real or personal property other than the Mortgaged Property and personal property related to the operation and maintenance of the Mortgaged Property; and (b) shall not operate any business other than the management and operation of the Mortgaged Property.*

Explanation

If a voluntary or involuntary bankruptcy case is commenced against Borrower, Section 362(a) of the Bankruptcy Code requires that from the time such case is commenced, a broad statutory stay of litigation against Borrower and any enforcement proceedings by creditors of their respective liens against any of Borrower's property is also automatically stayed. This "automatic stay" affords the debtor an opportunity to focus its energy and resources on dealing with Borrower's bankruptcy litigation, and in the case of a chapter 11 proceeding, allows the trustee or debtor in possession to prepare and work through a reorganization plan, without having to expend resources on dealing with litigation or enforcement proceedings which might have been on-going prior to the commencement of the bankruptcy case. *See, e.g., In re* Siciliano, 13 F.3d 748, 750 (3d Cir. 1994). However, the Bankruptcy Code does provide a secured creditor with some way to deal with this situation (i.e., these creditors are given "adequate protection" against the deterioration of the Mortgaged Property's collateral value, as well as time limits with respect to the bankrupt's ability to utilize the extension period which a bankrupt is permitted when requesting the bankruptcy judge to modify a stay order).

Although the general rule is that unless modified by the bankruptcy judge, the automatic stay must remain in effect for the duration of the bankruptcy case, the bankruptcy judge has discretion as to whether to terminate, amend or condition the terms of a particular stay, if a party to the bankruptcy makes a motion for the bankruptcy judge to grant a stay modification. Section 362(d)(3) provides that secured creditors be allowed to commence foreclosure 90 days following the commencement of the bankruptcy case, unless the debtor prior to the expiration of such 90 day period either (a) has filed a confirmable plan of reorganization, or (b) has commenced making monthly payments to the secured creditor equal to interest at the then applicable non-default contract rate of interest on the value of such debtor's secured collateral. With regard to interest payments owed to Lender (which holds a lien on the Mortgaged Property), Borrower is permitted to make such payments from rents or other revenue which is generated from the Mortgaged Property.

The Bankruptcy Code at Section 362(e) mandates that the bankruptcy judge hold a preliminary hearing involving the parties within 30 days after a party in the bankruptcy case makes a motion that seeks leave to proceed against the property of the bankruptcy estate.

Due to bankruptcy concerns, the issuers of mortgage-backed securities and the rating agencies that evaluate such securitizations particularly insist that if any holder of a mortgage loan desires to sell such loan into a securitization pool, the loan documents for such mortgage loan contain provisions that will cause Borrower and the Mortgaged Property to be bankruptcy remote. A simple "single-asset borrower" clause like the one above is not considered a sufficient assurance of bankruptcy remoteness by such issuers or the rating agencies. These entities, and many other sophisticated lenders originating or acquiring commercial real estate loans, commonly take other steps as well, including the following: (a) imposing in the applicable loan documents covenants (i) against mergers and consolidations of Borrower; and (ii) which require Borrower "entity controls" such as independent third parties being appointed to Borrower's board (whose vote would be required in order to commence a bankruptcy case); and (b) requiring a "springing" guaranty by the borrower's principals that take effect only in the event of a bankruptcy filing; and (c) the use of a "hard lockbox" system for loan payments, with tenants depositing rents directly into an account controlled by mortgage lender. *See* Frederick Z. Lodge et al., *Bankruptcy Remote Structures in Mortgage Loans*, Prob. & Prop., May/June 1996, at 49.

So if the Loan were to be sold into a rated securitization, then with regard to structuring Borrower to make it "bankruptcy remote," rating agencies and issuers of mortgage-backed securities strongly prefer that a number of actions be taken to cause Borrower to be bankruptcy remote, including the concepts contained in the following numbered paragraphs (the "**Bankruptcy Remote Paragraphs**"):

1. Cause Borrower to (i) be newly formed, (ii) free from any indebtedness other than the Loan, and (iii) take title to the Mortgaged Property as its sole real estate asset, in each case at or about the time of the initial funding of the Loan (i.e., by so doing, there can be no claims from prior creditors, since Borrower neither existed nor had the opportunity to incur indebtedness with other creditors, prior to the funding of the Loan);
2. Cause Borrower to be incorporated in Delaware, or another jurisdiction which Lender approves;
3. At the time of the funding of the Loan, to only permit Borrower to own assets which are part of, and/or obtain financing related to, the Mortgaged Property (i.e., Borrower cannot own any other real estate assets which are not part of the Mortgaged Property and/or obtain financing that is unrelated to the Mortgaged Property, however this limitation on ownership of real estate assets and financing does not apply to the ability of Borrower's parent(s) and/or subsidiaries of such parent to own other real estate assets);

4. Require that at least one of Borrower's directors and/or managers be an independent individual whose vote would be needed in order for Borrower to be able to proceed with commencement of a bankruptcy case by Borrower; and
5. Subject Borrower in the Loan Documents to a number of special purpose entity warranties and covenants (discussed in greater detail later in this Section 21).

Even if Lender were to create requirements in its Loan Documents that are designed to make Borrower bankruptcy remote by requiring Borrower to satisfy or agree to honor each of the above referenced techniques, such provisions would not make it impossible for Borrower to commence a voluntary bankruptcy proceeding. In general, bankruptcy courts, as a matter of public policy, will not enforce covenants made by Borrower under the Loan Documents that require Borrower to agree to waive their right to commence a bankruptcy proceeding. *See, e.g.*, Klingman v. Levinson, 831 F.2d 1292, 1296 n.3 (7th Cir. 1987). The reason why issuers of mortgaged backed securities, the rating agencies, and most sophisticated commercial real estate lenders require bankruptcy remote provisions, is to make it far more unlikely for a voluntary or involuntary Borrower bankruptcy case to be commenced.

Many mortgage lenders, and the rating agencies rating mortgage loans, require as a general rule that when a mortgage loan is closed, the mortgage borrower be newly formed. With regard to confirming that Borrower is newly formed, Lender can require that as a condition of closing the Loan, Borrower provide Lender with the applicable Secretary of State records which will show when Borrower was formed (so that Lender can easily confirm whether or not Borrower was in fact newly formed), and in addition will want the opinion of Borrower's counsel to reaffirm that Borrower is newly formed. However, in certain cases, Borrower's counsel will be directed by its client, or will otherwise determine, that the Borrower entity which had been formed at some point prior to the funding of the Loan, will need to continue as Borrower for the Loan at the time of, and following when the Loan is closed, notwithstanding that during this prior period Borrower may have either held other real estate assets, or incurred other indebtedness (typically when Borrower is not a newly formed entity, it is called a "recycled" Borrower). Most often Lender will accommodate this need for a pre-existing Borrower entity to continue its existence when the Loan is closed, but usually, in order for Lender to permit this accommodation, prior to the funding of the Loan, Borrower will need to pay-off any pre-existing indebtedness and/or sell off and/or otherwise transfer any assets which are unrelated to the Mortgaged Property. [Note: further embellishment of provisions dealing with a recycled borrower are discussed more fully later on in this Section 21.]

Lender will prefer that Borrower be organized or incorporated in Delaware [Note: this is one of the previously referenced bankruptcy remote requirements, which in this case was summarized in Bankruptcy Remote Paragraph 2], because the Delaware laws provide lenders protections which are often superior to comparable protections under other State laws, and counsel for lenders are usually quite familiar with the inter-workings of Delaware law with respect to these protections. Often times, Borrower's counsel can negotiate with Lender's counsel to permit Borrower to be organized or unincorporated in a different State; but I have not seen in the last 20 years a mortgage loan closing (where the Mortgaged Property is located in the United States) where Lender permitted Borrower to be incorporated or formed in a jurisdiction located outside of the United States, and a foreign mortgage borrower would most likely disqualify a Loan from being able to be sold into a rated commercial real estate mortgage-backed securitization.

It is most common for the actual Borrower entity to be a domestic limited liability company because the selection of utilizing such an entity will provide limited liability for its equity parent(s), while at the same time passing the federal income tax liability attributable to net operating revenues from the Mortgaged Property through the Borrower entity, and onto its parent(s) (so as to avoid a "double tax"). In this regard, the Delaware limited liability company statute is very favorable to the equity owners of a limited liability company formed in Delaware, which adds to the popularity of using Delaware limited liability companies, and I suspect that the majority of commercial real estate property owners elect to use a Delaware limited liability company to own the Mortgaged Property when they are acquiring and financing commercial real estate properties. There are times when a given Borrower's parent finds it better to elect to utilize an entity that is not a limited liability company. In such instance, Borrower usually ends up selecting another entity that will afford income tax pass-through characteristics to the ultimate beneficial owners. Most frequently these other entities are either trusts or limited partnerships. Usually if a limited partnership is selected as the Borrower entity, Lender will require (i) Borrower's parent to be the sole equity owner in Borrower or in the general partner of Borrower, and (ii) both Borrower and its parent to be subjected to the bankruptcy remote requirements that Lender is requiring for the particular Loan. Because of the concerns relating to incurring a "double income tax" exposure which would arise if Borrower were formed as a corporation, Borrower's counsel rarely elects to utilize a corporation to be the entity which owns commercial real estate.

Once an entity for Borrower is selected, Borrower's counsel must either draft the organizational documents for Borrower, or modify them in a way to include provisions acceptable to Lender which will meet Lender's requirements that the Borrower entity be bankruptcy remote. One of these requirements will be that a provision be included in the Borrower's organizational documents which confirms that Borrower is a "special purpose" entity. This provision will limit Borrower's activities so that such activities will solely relate to the ownership and operation of the Mortgaged Property (thus, Lender, by requiring Borrower to restrict the scope of its permitted purposes in Borrower's organizational documents to the ownership and operation of the Mortgaged Property, has some comfort that future prospective creditors, who might be interested in extending credit to Borrower in connection with other real estate assets or other activities of Borrower, will likely want to examine Borrower's organizational documents, and will see that Borrower is subject to this type of restriction; a restriction which does not allow Borrower to own other real estate assets or conduct other business activities). Typical language, which could be included in such organizational documents which would meet this special purpose requirement, would be as follows:

> *The Company is formed for the sole purpose of acquiring, owning, leasing, operating, maintaining, financing, selling and taking other similar actions with respect to its ownership and operation of the Mortgaged Property and to otherwise engage in any lawful act or activity and/or exercise any powers which a ___________ [limited liability company] would be allowed to take under the laws of the State of Delaware, including, without limitation, those actions which are incidental or related to and which are otherwise advisable for the accomplishment of owning and operating the Mortgaged Property, including, without limitation, entering into the Loan Documents and/or entering into any modification, amendment or extension of the Loan.*

The foregoing provision restricts Borrower from owning and/or financing any other real estate assets which are not part of the Mortgaged Property. As previously mentioned, by restricting Borrower's ownership of assets to the Mortgaged Property, the foregoing provision effectively limits the nature of potential creditors who might otherwise be involved in extending credit to Borrower if Borrower were permitted to own other assets and then incur secured mortgage debt in connection with its acquisition and/or development of other real estate, or otherwise incur liabilities in connection with the operation of such other real estate assets.

Issuers of mortgaged backed securities, rating agencies and sophisticated commercial real estate lenders will usually require that the Borrower entity have one or two independent directors and/or managers. Depending upon the form of governance used in the organizational documents for Borrower; and for ease of reference, we will assume that the Loan Documents only require the Borrower entity to have one of these entities, which I will be referring to as the "independent director." In this Loan, Lender has included a provision in the Mortgage which requires that there be included in the organizational documents (for the Borrower entity) a provision which mandates that at all times the Borrower entity have in place an independent director, whose sole mandated function is to provide a supporting vote in the event Borrower's parent(s), and/or any of the officers or other directors of Borrower, desire to take an action which would result in the commencement of a Borrower bankruptcy case, or take other actions which would constitute an insolvency of Borrower under federal or state law. By requiring an independent party's vote to take such actions, Lender hopes to reduce the likelihood that Borrower will pursue an insolvency, which will result in Borrower being subject to a bankruptcy proceeding. A bankruptcy proceeding would immediately impose restrictions on Lender's ability to proceed with enforcement of its remedies under the Loan Documents, for the reasons discussed earlier in this Section 21. If Borrower is a Delaware entity, it is not uncommon for Lender to require that with respect to such a vote by an independent director, it need only consider what is in the best interests of Borrower. The purpose for this provision is to focus on the minimum standard which Delaware law requires be considered by directors, which is their need to employ good faith and fair dealing with respect to making decisions on behalf of Borrower.

Another concern which Lender has with regard to bankruptcy relates to the judicially created doctrine commonly referred to as "substantive consolidation." This doctrine is derived from the equitable powers which a bankruptcy judge has pursuant to the provisions of Section 105 (a) of the Bankruptcy Code. In certain circumstances, some bankruptcy judges have exercised equitable discretion and have ordered that with respect to a case involving the bankruptcy of an entity, that it is appropriate for the judge to consolidate that entity with other subsidiaries and/or related parties so as to treat the consolidated group as all being bankrupt and subject to the jurisdiction of the court in that bankruptcy case. The appropriateness of utilizing this "equitable discretion is determined on a case-by-case basis," thus making it difficult to predict with certainty whether or not in a given circumstance such substantive consolidation will be ordered by the court. In any event, under no circumstances does Lender want to permit a parent or another entity to be able to consolidate with Borrower in connection with that entity's bankruptcy, which would have the effect of immediately issuing the automatic stay with regard to Lender's ability to exercise its remedies under the Loan Documents, as discussed earlier. As a result, typically Lender will require that the Loan Documents and Borrower's organizational documents each contain provisions which will minimize the risk that Borrower will be subject to a substantive consolidation with its parent or another related entity. These provisions are typically called "separateness covenants," although while many of these covenants attempt to deal with substantive consolidation issues, some of them also deal with other bankruptcy remote issues previously discussed. The following are examples of separateness covenants:

21.2 *Borrower will not engage in any business or activity, other than the ownership, operation and maintenance of the Mortgaged Property and activities incidental thereto, including, without limitation, Borrower's obtaining of the Loan from Lender.*

21.3 *Borrower will not acquire, own, hold, lease, operate, manage, maintain, develop or improve any assets other than the Mortgaged Property and such Personalty as may be necessary for the operation of the Mortgaged Property and will conduct and operate its business as presently conducted and operated.*

21.4 *Borrower will preserve its existence as an entity duly organized, validly existing and in good standing (if applicable) under the laws of the jurisdiction of the State of Delaware and will do all things necessary to observe organizational formalities.*

21.5 *Borrower will not merge or consolidate with any other Person.*

Explanation

The separateness covenants set out in the above referenced Sections 21.2 and 21.3 of the Mortgage deal with the requirement that Borrower only be permitted to own and manage and operate the Mortgaged Property.

21.6 *Borrower will not take any action to dissolve, wind-up, terminate or liquidate in whole or in part; to sell, transfer or otherwise dispose of all or substantially all of its assets; to change its legal structure; transfer or permit the direct or indirect transfer of any partnership, membership or other equity interests, as applicable, other than Transfers permitted under this Mortgage; issue additional partnership, membership or other equity interests, as applicable, or seek to accomplish any of the foregoing.*

21.7 *if Borrower is a limited partnership, each general partner of Borrower must be a Person who is not an individual and must either be a corporation or a single-member Delaware limited liability company, in each case which must (x) have two (2) independent directors, and (y) must hold direct equity interests as a general partner in Borrower of not less than __ [1]%.*

21.8 *if Borrower is a corporation, Borrower shall at all times have at least two independent directors on its board.*

21.9 *if Borrower is a limited liability company, Borrower shall at all times remain organized under the laws of the State of Delaware; and Borrower (A) must have at least __ [1] independent director(s) serving as special independent manager(s) of Borrower, (B) shall not take any bankruptcy related action or shall not cause or permit the members or managers of Borrower to take any bankruptcy related action, unless its independent director(s), then serving as special independent manager(s) of Borrower, shall have consented in writing to such action, and (C) must have two natural individuals, or one entity that is not a member of Borrower, enter into the limited liability company agreement of Borrower, which shall contain a provision that under the terms of such limited liability agreement, such individuals or entity, as the case may be, shall become a member of Borrower immediately prior to withdrawal or dissolution of the last remaining member of Borrower.*

Explanation

The separateness covenants set out in the above referenced Sections 21.7 through 21.9 of the Mortgage deal with the requirement of Lender that the Borrower entity have independent directors and/or managers in order to reduce the risk that Borrower will commence a voluntary bankruptcy proceeding. Because Lender is only interested in requiring that no bankruptcy action on behalf of Borrower may be pursued without the written consent or vote of the independent directors, Lender does not require that the independent directors be given any rights to vote on any other actions of Borrower. Depending on which type of entity corresponds to the actual Borrower entity, Lender will also require a corresponding provision which would parallel the applicable section in the Borrower's organizational documents (i.e., if Borrower is a limited liability company, then Borrower's limited liability company agreement would need to contain a provision similar to the above referenced Section 21.9 of the Mortgage). As will be seen later in this Section 21, Lender may want to impose restrictions relating to the removal and/or replacement of the independent directors.

21.10 *Borrower will not, without the prior unanimous written consent of all of Borrower's partners, members, or shareholders, as applicable, and, if applicable, the prior unanimous written consent of 100% of the members of the board of directors or of the board of Managers of Borrower, take any of the following actions ("**Insolvency Activities**"):*

(a) *File any insolvency, or reorganization case or proceeding, to institute proceedings to have Borrower be adjudicated bankrupt or insolvent.*

(b) *Institute proceedings under any applicable insolvency law.*

(c) *Seek any relief under any law relating to relief from debts or the protection of debtors.*

(d) *Consent to the filing or institution of bankruptcy or insolvency proceedings against Borrower.*

(e) *File a petition seeking, or consent to, reorganization or relief with respect to Borrower under any applicable federal or state law relating to bankruptcy or insolvency.*

(f) *Seek or consent to the appointment of a receiver, liquidator, assignee, trustee, sequestrator, custodian, or any similar official for Borrower or a substantial part of its property.*

(g) *Make any assignment for the benefit of creditors of Borrower.*

(h) *Admit in writing Borrower's inability to pay its debts generally as they become due.*

21.11 *Borrower will not amend or restate its organizational documents if such change would cause the provisions set forth in those organizational documents not to comply with the requirements set forth in this Section 21 of this Mortgage.*

21.12 *Borrower will not own any subsidiary or make any investment in any other Person.*

21.13 *Borrower will not commingle its assets with the assets of any other Person and will hold all of its assets in its own name.*

21.14 *Borrower will not incur any debt, secured or unsecured, direct or contingent (including guaranteeing any obligation), other than, (A) the Indebtedness (and any further indebtedness as expressly permitted in this Mortgage) and (B) customary unsecured trade payables incurred in the ordinary course of owning and operating the Mortgaged Property provided the same are not evidenced by a promissory note, do not exceed, in the aggregate, at any time a maximum amount of two percent of the original principal amount of the Indebtedness and are paid within 60 days of the date incurred.*

Explanation

This Section 21.10 has been added to the Mortgage by Lender in order to provide greater assurance that Borrower can only make an election to take a bankruptcy action if it has obtained the necessary consents from the applicable independent directors and/or independent managers. Subsection (x) does not permit a modification of Borrower's organizational documents which would cause a change in these separateness covenants (and if there are some other provisions in the organizational documents which relate to the bankruptcy remoteness of Borrower, then quite often Lender will require that this limitation also apply to those additional provisions relating to bankruptcy remoteness). Section 21.14 of the Mortgage restricts Borrower from obtaining additional indebtedness because Lender wants to restrict the number of other Borrower creditors that exist at any time. Lender is particularly interested in limiting Borrower from utilizing any other creditors who will have as collateral security any of the Mortgaged Property. However, said Section 21.14 does permit Borrower to utilize customary unsecured trade payables incurred in the ordinary course of business, subject to a limitation (in this case, that maximum limit is 2% of the original principal amount of the Loan). The exact maximum limit is subject to negotiation, and Borrower's counsel can request that the maximum limit be reduced.

21.15 *Borrower will maintain its records, books of account, bank accounts, financial statements, accounting records and other entity documents separate and apart from those of any other Person and will not list its assets as assets on the financial statement of any other Person; provided, however, that Borrower's assets may be included in a consolidated financial statement of its Affiliate provided that (A) appropriate notation will be made on such consolidated financial statements to indicate the separateness of Borrower from such Affiliate and to indicate that Borrower's assets and credit are not available to satisfy the debts and other obligations of such Affiliate or any other Person and (B) such assets will also be listed on Borrower's own separate balance sheet.*

21.16 *Except for capital contributions or capital distributions permitted under the terms and conditions of its organizational documents, Borrower will only enter into any contract or agreement with any general partner, member, shareholder, principal or Affiliate of Borrower or any Guarantor, or any general partner, member, principal or Affiliate thereof, upon terms and conditions that are commercially reasonable and substantially similar to those that would be available on an arm's-length basis with third parties.*

21.17 *Borrower will not maintain its assets in such a manner that will be costly or difficult to segregate, ascertain or identify its individual assets from those of any other Person.*

21.18 *Borrower will not assume or guaranty (excluding any guaranty that has been executed and delivered in connection with the Note) the debts or obligations of any other Person, hold itself out to be responsible for the debts of another Person, pledge its assets to secure the obligations of any other Person or otherwise pledge its assets for the benefit of any other Person, or hold out its credit as being available to satisfy the obligations of any other Person.*

21.19 *Borrower will not make or permit to remain outstanding any loans or advances to any other Person except for those investments permitted under the Loan Documents and will not buy or hold evidence of indebtedness issued by any other Person (other than cash or investment-grade securities).*

21.20 *Borrower will file its own tax returns separate from those of any other Person, except to the extent that Borrower is treated as a "disregarded entity" for tax purposes and is not required to file tax returns under applicable law, and will pay any taxes required to be paid under applicable law.*

21.21 *Borrower will hold itself out to the public as a legal entity separate and distinct from any other Person and conduct its business solely in its own name, will correct any known misunderstanding regarding its separate identity and will not identify itself or any of its Affiliates as a division or department of any other Person.*

Explanation

The above referenced subsections 21.15 through 21.21 of the Mortgage are typical examples of separateness covenants designed to prevent a bankruptcy court from making a determination that the manner that Borrower conducted its business was such that third parties could believe that Borrower was operating in effect as a consolidated entity with another Person. Lender, at all costs, wants to avoid in the bankruptcy of another Person, that Borrower would be substantively consolidated with that Person and be subject to such bankruptcy.

21.22 *Borrower will maintain adequate capital for the normal obligations reasonably foreseeable in a business of its size and character and in light of its contemplated business operations and will pay its debts and liabilities from its own assets as the same become due.*

21.23 *Borrower (1) has paid and will pay its debts and liabilities as the same become due; (2) has maintained and will maintain adequate capital; (3) will at all times remain solvent; (4) will pay its debts and liabilities (including a fairly allocated portion of any personnel and overhead expenses shared with any affiliate); and (5) will maintain adequate capital for the normal operations reasonably foreseeable in a business of its size and character in light of its business operations.*

21.24 *Borrower will allocate fairly and reasonably shared expenses with Affiliates (including shared office space) and use separate stationery, invoices and checks bearing its own name.*

Explanation

The covenants in Sections 21.22 and 21.23 of the Mortgage are each potentially dangerous as neither identifies from where the source of required capital will need to come. As will be made clear in Part IV Section 28 of this Book, Borrower does not want there to be any covenant in the Loan Documents which gives the impression that Borrower's parent is obligated to fund capital deficiencies to keep Borrower solvent. A previous court case held that a Guarantor under a carve out guaranty which guarantees Borrower's performance under separateness covenants similar to those in Sections 21.22 and 21.23 above, is in fact enforceable, with the result that such Guarantor could be held liable for the payment of the entire Indebtedness. Borrower's counsel, in this instance, should attempt to clarify these subsections to make it clear that such capital would only be made available from the net cash flow arising from the Mortgaged Property. Because of these concerns, a better way to draft these two separateness covenants, would be as follows:

(xxi) *Borrower will maintain adequate capital out of the net cash flow from the Mortgaged Property in order to cover the normal obligations reasonably foreseeable in a business of its size and character and in light of its contemplated business operations and will, out of such net cash flow, pay its debts and liabilities from its own assets as the same become due; provided that the foregoing shall not require any member, partner or shareholder of Borrower to make any additional contributions to Borrower.*

(xxii) *Borrower has paid and will pay its debts and liabilities from its assets as the same become due; and in addition, Borrower will maintain adequate capital, to the extent there exists sufficient cash flow from the operations of the Mortgaged Property, so that it will at all times remain solvent and will pay its debts and liabilities (including, a fairly allocated portion of any personnel and overhead expenses which it shares with any affiliate), as the same become due, and will maintain adequate capital for the normal operations reasonably foreseeable in a business of its size and character in light of its business operations (in each case, to the extent there exists sufficient cash flow from the operations of the Mortgage Property; provided that the foregoing shall not require any member, partner or shareholder of Borrower to make any additional contributions to Borrower).*

Because of the findings of a certain case discussed in greater detail in Part IV Section 29 of this Book, it is extremely important to make such separateness covenants dealing with Borrower's ongoing solvency and/or its obligations to pay all third-party expenses relating to the operations of the Mortgaged Property subject to the availability of adequate net cash flow from the operations of the Mortgage Property.

21.25 *Borrower will not acquire obligations or securities of its partners, members, shareholders, or Affiliates, as applicable.*

21.26 *Except as contemplated or permitted by the property management agreement with respect to the Property Manager, Borrower will not permit any Affiliate or constituent party independent access to its bank accounts.*

21.27 *If Borrower is a single-member limited liability company, it must satisfy each of the following conditions:*

(a) *Have either one springing member that is a corporation whose stock is 100% owned by the sole member of Borrower and that satisfies the requirements for a corporate springing member set forth below in this Section or two springing members who are natural persons;*

(b) *Otherwise comply with criteria for single-member limited liability companies (including the delivery of Delaware single-member limited liability company opinions acceptable in all respects to Lender and to the Rating Agencies), as established by Standard & Poor's Ratings Services. If the springing member is a corporation, such springing member will at all times comply, and will cause Borrower to comply, with each of the representations, warranties and covenants contained in Section 21 of this Mortgage as if such representation, warranty or covenant were made directly by such corporation. If there is more than one springing member, only one springing member will be the sole member of Borrower at any one time, and the second springing member will become the sole member only upon the first springing member ceasing to be a member.*

(c) *At all times Borrower will have one and only one member.*

Explanation

Note that the preceding Section 21.27 of the Mortgage provides that if Borrower is a single-member limited liability company (which means that it only has one member which owns one hundred percent of the equity interest in Borrower), then, among other things, it must make provision in Borrower's limited liability company agreement that if its sole member should resign, or otherwise cease to exist, then automatically either a new member who is a corporation (whose stock is 100% owned by the current sole member of Borrower) or two individuals must be irrevocably committed to step in and automatically become the member or members, as the case may be, of Borrower. By adding this provision to Borrower's limited liability company agreement, should the single member of Borrower resign, or otherwise cease to exist, then because the departing member will automatically be replaced, this provision prevents Borrower from dissolving (which dissolution is often mandated under state law, should at any time a limited liability company have no equity members).

There are many more separateness covenants which can be suggested by Lender's counsel in its Loan Documents. Since the major purpose of the separateness covenants is to prevent substantive consolidation, one way to object to a suggested separateness covenant which seems atypical, would be to obtain a list of the particular requirements for single-purpose entities and separateness from one or more of the rating agencies, and then present this list to Lender's counsel, if Lender's counsel has embellished on the requirements beyond what the rating agencies would use in this regard. It has been previously mentioned that Borrower and/or its counsel may prefer to utilize a so-called recycled Borrower, rather than create a brand-new Borrower entity in connection with closing the Loan. The use of a recycled Borrower may be necessary in some jurisdictions due to costs, such as transfer taxes, associated with transferring the Mortgaged Property to a brand-new entity. If a recycled Borrower entity is used, it is critical that Borrower's counsel carefully scrutinize each of the separateness and/or bankruptcy remote covenants and representations, since by the very nature of Borrower being a recycled entity, it may be impossible to avoid being in breach of such representations and/or covenants without making necessary modifications to reflect the fact that this Borrower is in fact a recycled entity (and the fact that there may have been pre-existing indebtedness and/or extraneous real estate assets). In this regard, Lender legitimately will not permit the recycled Borrower to own any extraneous real estate assets and/or retain any pre-existing indebtedness (unless such pre-existing indebtedness is fully subordinated in a manner satisfactory to Lender). In such a case, it is likely that all extraneous real estate assets will have to be transferred to another entity and the pre-existing indebtedness will either have to be paid off in full, or the recycled Borrower entity will have to be released from any liability associated with such indebtedness.

SECTION 22

Transfers of the Mortgaged Property Interests in Borrower

Explanation

An important due diligence criteria which Lender must consider when deciding whether or not to agree to make the Loan, is making the decision that the creditworthiness, reputation, and experience of Borrower is adequate, since Lender will be looking to Borrower to successfully deal with all of the numerous adverse events that may occur during the term of the Loan and which could impact the value of the Mortgaged Property and the net cash derived from its operation. It is logical that Lender will have much more confidence in Borrower's ability to achieve success in dealing with these events if Borrower has prior history demonstrating its financial capacity and/or experience to effectively and quickly take the appropriate actions that might be needed to "fix" each of these potential adverse events, so that the value of the Mortgaged Property can be maintained (and which in turn will better ensure that there will be adequate cash flow to pay all Loan, operating and capital costs related to the Mortgaged Property and the Loan through Maturity). Consequently, it is important to Lender that during the term of the Loan, Borrower, and ultimately, the key people (which in this Mortgage is defined as the "Key Principal") who control Borrower and its sub-entities and related parties that are continuously involved with the operations of the Mortgaged Property, remain the same and that any change in this manpower is at all times subject to Lender's consent. The following are typical provisions which are included in a Mortgage that deal with either a transfer of the Mortgaged Property, or a transfer of interests in Borrower, which, if they are allowed to occur, could completely change who Borrower is, and/or the underlying key people who control Borrower, or who Borrower looks to operate the Mortgaged Property.

22.1 *The occurrence of any of the following events shall constitute an Event of Default under this Mortgage:*

(a) *a Transfer of all or any part of the Mortgaged Property or any interest in the Mortgaged Property;*

(b) *a Transfer of a Controlling Interest in Borrower;*

(c) *a Transfer of a Controlling Interest in any entity which owns, directly or indirectly through one or more intermediate entities, a Controlling Interest in Borrower;*

(d) *a Transfer of all or any part of Key Principal's ownership interests (other than limited partnership interests) in Borrower, or in any other entity which owns, directly or indirectly through one or more intermediate entities, an ownership interest in Borrower;*

(e) *if Key Principal is an entity, (A) a Transfer of a Controlling Interest in Key Principal, or (B) a Transfer of a Controlling Interest in any entity which owns, directly or indirectly through one or more intermediate entities, a Controlling Interest in Key Principal;*

(f) *if Borrower or Key Principal is a trust, the termination or revocation of such trust; and*

(g) *a conversion of Borrower from one type of legal entity into another type of legal entity, whether or not there is a Transfer.*

Lender shall not be required to demonstrate any actual impairment of its security or any increased risk of default in order to exercise any of its remedies with respect to an Event of Default under this Section.

22.2 *The occurrence of any of the following events shall not constitute an Event of Default under this Mortgage, notwithstanding any provision of this Section to the contrary:*

(a) *a Transfer to which Lender has consented in writing;*

(b) *a Transfer that occurs by devise, by descent, or by operation of law upon the death of a natural person, so long as the transferee is reasonably satisfactory to Lender;*

(c) *a Transfer of obsolete or worn out Personalty or Fixtures that are contemporaneously replaced by items of equal or better function and quality, which are free of liens, encumbrances and security interests other than those created by the Loan Documents or consented to by Lender;*

(d) *the grant of an easement, if before the grant Lender determines in writing that the easement will not materially affect the operation or value of the Mortgaged Property or Lender's interest in the Mortgaged Property, and Borrower pays to Lender, upon demand, all costs and expenses incurred by Lender in connection with reviewing Borrower's request; and*

(e) *the creation of a tax lien or a mechanic's, materialman's or judgment lien against the Mortgaged Property which is bonded off, released of record or otherwise remedied to Lender's satisfaction within 30 days of the date of creation.*

22.3 *For purposes of this Section, the following terms shall have the meanings set forth below:*

(a) *"**Initial Owners**" means, with respect to Borrower or any other entity, the persons or entities who on the date of the Note own in the aggregate 100% of the ownership interests in Borrower or that entity.*

(b) *A Transfer of a "Controlling Interest" shall mean, with respect to any entity, the following:*

(i) *if such entity is a general partnership or a joint venture, a Transfer of any general partnership interest or joint venture interest which would cause the Initial Owners to own less than 51% of all general partnership or joint venture interests in such entity;*

(ii) *if such entity is a limited partnership, a Transfer of any general partnership interest;*

(iii) *if such entity is a limited liability company or a limited liability partnership, a Transfer of any membership or other ownership interest which would cause the Initial Owners to own less than 51% of all membership or other ownership interests in such entity;*

(iv) *if such entity is a corporation (other than a Publicly Held Corpora tion) with only one class of voting stock, a Transfer of any voting stock which would cause the Initial Owners to own less than 51% of voting stock in such corporation;*

(v) *if such entity is a corporation (other than a Publicly-Held Corporation) with more than one class of voting stock, a Transfer of any voting stock which would cause the Initial Owners to own less than a sufficient number of shares of voting stock necessary to have the power to elect the majority of directors of such corporation; and*

(vi) *if such entity is a trust, the removal, appointment or substitution of a trustee of such trust other than (A) in the case of a land trust, or (B) if the trustee of such trust after such removal, appointment or substitution is a trustee identified in the trust agreement as approved by Lender.*

(c) *"**Publicly-Held Corporation**" shall mean a corporation, the outstanding voting stock of which is registered under Section 12(b) or 12(g) of the Securities and Exchange Act of 1934, as amended.*

Explanation

As indicated above, Lender has underwritten the Loan on the basis of the creditworthiness and experience of Borrower, the Key Principal, the Borrower parent, and other related entities and key people who are related to Borrower, in each case to the extent they relate to the operation of the Mortgaged Property and/or the ability of Borrower to perform its obligations under the Loan Documents and maintain the value of the Mortgaged Property. One way for Lender to assure itself that Borrower and such related entities and key people will continue their involvement with the Mortgaged Property throughout the term of the Loan is for the Loan Documents to prohibit any transfers of the Mortgaged Property or of any controlling interests in Borrower and sub-entities of Borrower, as set forth in Section 22.1 above.

Note that in Section 22.2 above, there are a list of permitted transferees to which Borrower is permitted to transfer the Mortgaged Property. These permitted transferees are the ones that borrowers commonly request and that lenders typically can accept, as they do not impinge upon the basic protections that Lender seeks to achieve using a "due-on-sale" provision. It is also not uncommon for Borrower's counsel to ask for greater flexibility in expanding who might be a permitted transferee. Frequently another category of permitted transferees would include entities in which Borrower, the Borrower parent, the Key Principal, or other key individuals maintain Control as well as a minimum percentage of equity interest in such entities (and in this regard, Lender will frequently require that such transferee be a bankruptcy remote, special purpose entity). In this way, Borrower can bring in new partners, and/or permit minor equity owners to transfer their interests without needing Lender's consent regarding transferring equity interests to such partners or equity owners.

When entering into the Loan Documents, it is frequently an important consideration of Borrower that it have the Loan Documents contain a provision that allows Borrower to be able to transfer the Mortgaged Property, subject to the Loan. This kind of provision can frequently afford Borrower a lot of flexibility in the future, particularly if the interest rate environment shall have risen materially from the time of the closing of the Loan. If this rise in interest rates should happen, the ability to transfer the Mortgaged Property subject to the Loan, which affords Borrower a relatively lower interest rate, will allow Borrower to transfer the Mortgaged Property for a considerably higher purchase price than would otherwise be the case if it had to sell the Mortgaged Property free and clear of the Loan (since without the provision, the Loan would have to be paid off and the new buyer would, if it needed financing for the acquisition, have to incur the market's higher interest rate (thereby lowering the Mortgage Property's net cash flow, which in turn results in the Mortgage Property having a lower market value)). Therefore, it is a particular advantage for Borrower's counsel to make his client think about trying to negotiate a provision which will allow for a future sale of the Mortgaged Property, subject to the Loan. The following Section 22.4 relates to this type of a permitted transfer, which would enable Borrower to transfer the Mortgaged Property, subject to the Loan.

22.4 *Lender shall consent, without any adjustment to the rate at which the Loan secured by the Note bears interest or to any other economic terms of the Loan, to a one time Transfer during the term of the Loan that would otherwise violate this Section, if, prior to the Transfer, Borrower has satisfied each of the following requirements:*

(a) *the submission to Lender of all information required by Lender to make the determination required by this Section;*

(b) *the absence of any Event of Default;*

(c) *the transferee meets all of the eligibility, credit, management and other standards (including any standards with respect to previous relationships between Lender and the transferee and the organization of the transferee) customarily applied by Lender at the time of the proposed Transfer to the approval of borrowers in connection with the origination or purchase of loans secured by similar mortgages, deeds of trust or deeds to secure debt on commercial real estate properties which are being used for similar purposes as Mortgaged Property;*

(d) *in the case of a Transfer of all or any part of the Mortgaged Property, or direct or indirect ownership interests in Borrower or Key Principal (if an entity), if transferor or any other person has obligations under any Loan Document, the execution by the transferee or one or more individuals or entities acceptable to Lender of a written assumption agreement that is acceptable to Lender and that, among other things, requires the transferee to perform all obligations of transferor or such person set forth in such Loan Document, and may require that the transferee comply with any provisions of this Mortgage or any other Loan Document which previously may have been waived by Lender;*

(e) *if a guaranty has been executed and delivered in connection with the Note, this Mortgage or any of the other Loan Documents, Borrower causes one or more individuals or entities acceptable to Lender to execute and deliver to Lender a similar guaranty in a form acceptable to Lender;*

(f) *the transferring Borrower ("Transferee") assumes and agrees to pay (subject to the non-recourse provisions of this Section 22 hereof) all the service payments payable under the Note and to perform all other obligations of Borrower arising under the Note, this Mortgage and the other Loan Documents and (provided that Borrower shall be relieved of such obligations from and after the date of such Transfer and Lender shall execute and deliver to such Borrower at the time of the Transfer a release to such effect) prior to or concurrently with the closing of such Transfer, the Transferee, as a condition to proceeding with such Transfer, shall execute, without any cost or expense to Lender, such documents and agreements as Lender shall reasonably require to evidence and effectuate said assumption and shall deliver such legal opinions (including a nonconsolidation opinion in substantially the same form as that delivered in connection with the closing of the Loan evidenced by the Note) as Lender may reasonably require;*

(g) *Transferee and Borrower authorize the filing of, without any cost or expense to Lender, new financing statements or financing statement amendments and any additional documents reasonably requested by Lender;*

(h) *Borrower shall cause to be delivered to Lender, without any cost or expense to Lender, such endorsements to Lender's title insurance policy, hazard insurance endorsements or certificates and other similar materials as Lender may deem necessary at the time of the Sale, all in form and substance reasonably satisfactory to Lender, including, without limitation, an endorsement or endorsements to Lender's title insurance policy insuring that the lien of this Mortgage constitutes a first lien on the Mortgaged Property subject only to the Permitted Exceptions, extending the effective date of such policy to the date of execution and delivery (or, if later, of recording) of the assumption agreement referenced above in sub-subsection (f) of this Section 22.4 and insuring that fee simple title to the Mortgaged Property is vested in the Transferee, or, in lieu thereof, such other documents or evidence as Lender may reasonably require in order to confirm the priority of this Mortgage;*

(i) *Borrower shall execute and deliver to Lender, without any cost or expense to Lender, a release of Lender, its officers, directors, employees and agents, from all claims and liability relating to the transactions evidenced by the Note, this Mortgage, and any of the other Loan Documents through and including the date of the closing of the Transfer, which agreement shall be in form and substance satisfactory to Lender and shall be binding upon the Transferee; and*

  (i) *Lender's receipt of all of the following:*

  (ii) *a non-refundable review fee in the amount of $______ and a transfer fee equal to one percent (1%) of the outstanding Indebtedness immediately prior to the Transfer.*

  (iii) *In addition, Borrower shall be required to reimburse Lender for all of Lender's out-of-pocket costs (including reasonable attorneys' fees) incurred in reviewing the Transfer request.*

22.5 *Any Transfer shall not be construed so as to relieve any current guarantor or indemnitor (collectively "**Indemnitor**") of its obligations under any existing guaranty or indemnity agreement, in favor of Lender which is in effect immediately prior to any such Transfer, as being part of the Loan Documents; and each such Indemnitor at the time of any such Transfer, as a condition to Lender's consenting to such Transfer, shall execute, without any cost or expense to Lender, such documents and agreements as Lender shall reasonably require to evidence and implement the ratification of each such guaranty or indemnity; provided that if any beneficial owner of, or related party to, the Transferee shall be approved by Lender in Lender's sole but reasonable discretion, not to be unreasonably withheld or delayed, and any such entity (which approval shall be deemed granted so long as Lender receives (1) a certified financial statement of such beneficial owner of Transferee showing that such entity has a liquid net worth of not less than $____________, and (2) a certification of such beneficial owner of Transferee, in form and substance reasonably satisfactory to Lender, which certifies that at no time during the ten (10) year period immediately prior to the date of such Transfer (A) has such entity been convicted of a felony, or (B) has such entity been adjudicated bankrupt or insolvent or filed, consented to or acquiesced in any petition of bankruptcy, reorganization or arrangement pursuant to any federal bankruptcy law, or any similar federal or state law), executes, without any cost or expense to Lender, each indemnity and guaranty,* *in form substantially the same as executed in connection with the execution of the original Loan Documents, then Lender shall execute and deliver to the current Indemnitor or, concurrently with such transaction, a full release of the current Indemnitor from all obligations related to, or arising under, the Loan Documents in connection with occurrences which happen from and after the closing of such Transfer.*

Explanation

By giving Borrower the right to elect to sell the Mortgaged Property subject to the Loan, as set forth in Section 22.4 above, arguably Lender is not giving up much economically, since both before and after any such Transfer, its collateral will remain exactly the same, and its risks regarding whether or not it will receive amortization payments for the remainder of the term of the Loan, and whether or not it has adequate collateral, also remains the same, because in both cases, the Loan remains secured by the Mortgaged Property and the income generated from the Mortgaged Property. Pursuant to this provision, there are parameters regarding who would be an acceptable Transferee. But even though this type of provision does not necessarily come with significant economic risks, a Lender will frequently be disinclined to include such a provision in the Mortgage, because in order to implement the Transfer, Lender must spend time and effort to assure itself of the satisfactory nature of (i) the Transferee, (ii) any new guarantor, and (iii) the documentation necessary to permit such Transfer. More importantly, if interest rates have moved up, and there are circumstances which require Borrower to pursue a Transfer when interests rates are higher, then Lender will be stuck with retaining the Loan at its relatively lower interest rate, and therefore, Lender will be forgoing the opportunity to use the prepayment proceeds to make a new mortgage loan at a higher interest rate. As a result, Lender may resist allowing Borrower to have this Transfer election.

If Lender does permit Borrower to have a Transfer election included in the Mortgage, similar to the provision contemplated by Section 22.4 above, it is understandable that Lender will only allow this election to be made by Borrower, if (i) no Event of Default then exists, and (ii) the new borrower is structured as a single purpose, bankruptcy remote entity. It is also understandable that Lender would require the Transferee to assume the obligations under the Loan Documents and the old Borrower to release Lender from all prior acts.

As part of these Transfer provisions, Lender is legitimately requiring that Borrower provide Lender with a release from any potential "lender liability claims" which might have arisen prior to the Transfer. Lender's requirement that its title policy be endorsed to reflect that the new owner is now the Transferee, is a reasonable requirement, since Lender legitimately wants assurance that following the Transfer, Lender will have evidence that the new Borrower actually owns Lender's primary collateral, the Mortgaged Property.

Also note that the Transfer provision in Section 22.5 above also contemplates that Lender is committed to enabling a substitution of the guarantor. Most often,

Lender will not commit to this type of provision. By obtaining this type of substitution right, Borrower will be able to require Lender at the time of the Transfer to permit such a substitution, which will usually be a precondition for Borrower's ability to proceed with the Transfer (although sometimes, if such provision does not exist, and if Lender refuses to permit such a substitution, Borrower will proceed with the Transfer and obtain an indemnification from a creditworthy related party of the Transferee).

A related type of provision would be for the Borrower's parent(s) to obtain a one-time right to transfer its equity interest in Borrower to a third party. This type of transaction could be beneficial to Borrower in States where such a transfer would not trigger a transfer tax, or where there may be key ownership rights in the name of the original Borrower which might be voided upon a transfer of the Mortgaged Property. Such a provision typically would include most of the provisions set out in the foregoing Section 22.4 and 22.5, but would not necessarily include some of the property due diligence or financing statement filings, because in this case Borrower would remain the same following such a transfer.

Another type of Transfer election which is not included in this Mortgage is a transfer provision which enables only part of the Mortgaged Property to be released and sold, while enabling Lender to maintain the lien of its Mortgage on the balance of the Mortgaged Property. It is often useful to Borrower if the Mortgaged Property includes vacant land, multiple facilities and/or condominium units, which ultimately Borrower hopes to sell off, to include a provision in the Mortgage which permits such a sale of part of the collateral (like vacant land and/or surplus condominium units). This type of provision, if permitted by Lender, frequently mandates a number of additional due diligence provisions requiring Lender's approval, including a new survey; and usually also requires that certain credit tests, such as minimum percentages for Loan to value ratio and annual debt service to annual net revenue ratio (with respect to the portion of the Mortgaged Property that will still be encumbered by the lien of the Mortgage), be achieved as a pre-condition to enabling such transfers to be implemented. This type of provision then would usually mandate that all or a portion of the net proceeds of any sale arising from such a Transfer be utilized to partially prepay the Loan.

It is very important for Borrower's counsel to discuss these various Transfer alternatives with its client, including various provisions in the Loan Documents that would permit Transfers and/or substitution of guarantors, because without them, Borrower is usually totally at the mercy of Lender, with regard to making a non-permitted transfer of all or part of the Mortgaged Property. Such a situation often leads to extended delay and cost in negotiating with Lender at the time of a future transfer, and at times Lenders will actually refuse to consent to such a transfer (particularly if the Loan has been sold into a securitization), leaving Borrower as its only recourse to pre-pay the entire amount of the Loan, which at the time can come with crippling prepayment penalties.

SECTION 23

Protection of Lender's Security

Explanation

Clearly Lender must be concerned about what actions it is permitted to take, pursuant to the provisions set out in the Loan Documents, should Borrower fail to perform its obligations under any of the Loan Documents. Because of these concerns, Lender needs to have express rights in the Loan Documents to deal with the situation where Borrower has failed to perform obligations under the Loan Documents, which, if not corrected, could adversely impair the collateral securing the Loan or the cash flow necessary to pay the debt service payments pursuant to the Note. As an alternative to being required to pursue litigation in order to remedy a Borrower breach, the Loan Documents usually contain provisions like the following, which enable Lender to step in and perform obligations under the Loan Documents which Borrower has failed to perform.

> 23.1 *If Borrower fails to perform any of its obligations under this Mortgage or any other Loan Document, or if any action or proceeding is commenced which purports to affect the Mortgaged Property, Lender's security or Lender's rights under this Mortgage, including eminent domain, insolvency, code enforcement, civil or criminal forfeiture, enforcement of Hazardous Materials Laws, fraudulent conveyance or reorganizations or proceedings involving a bankrupt or decedent, then Lender at Lender's option may make such appearances, disburse such sums and take such actions as Lender reasonably deems necessary to perform such obligations of Borrower and to protect Lender's interest, including (1) payment of fees and out-of-pocket expenses of attorneys, accountants, inspectors and consultants, (2) entry upon the Mortgaged Property to make repairs or secure the Mortgaged Property, (3) procurement of the*

insurance required by Section 19 of this Mortgage, and (4) payment of amounts which Borrower has failed to pay under other Section(s) of this Mortgage.

Explanation

Section 23.1 above provides Lender with a "self-help" right, so that Lender can take direct steps to protect its security and assure itself that its advances in this regard can be recovered from Borrower, with interest. The self-help remedy in Section 23.1 is a valuable tool in instances of code violations or failure of Borrower to maintain the Mortgaged Property, to maintain insurance, or to pay Taxes. These are all Borrower failures that Lender can meaningfully step in and perform. If Lender corrects these failures by Borrower, it helps to assure that Lender's collateral value will be maintained.

Said Section 23.1 also helps Lender by specifying that to the extent it incurs expenses of attorneys, accountants, inspectors, or consultants in any of these instances, Lender can recover those amounts from Borrower. Some states have statutory provisions that allow lenders to add such items to the debt regardless of whether the Loan Documents so provide. For example, a Missouri statute permits recovery of lawyers' fees expended to enforce a credit agreement, even if not provided for in the credit agreement, if: (1) the enforcing lawyer is a licensed member of the Missouri bar or is authorized to practice law in Missouri, (2) the fees do not exceed 15 percent of the outstanding credit balance in default, and (3) the credit was extended by a for-profit business or credit union. R.S. Mo. § 408.092.

In order to assure Lender that if it advances money to protect its security, it will earn interest on the money advanced, the Mortgage usually contains this type of provision.

23.2 *Any amounts disbursed by Lender under this Section, or under any other provision of this Mortgage or the other Loan Documents, shall be added to, and become part of, the principal component of the Indebtedness evidenced by the Note, shall be immediately due and payable and shall bear interest from the date of disbursement until paid at the "**Default Rate**" as defined in the Note.*

Explanation

As indicated above, if Lender has to advance its own money to maintain the Mortgaged Property, obtain insurance, pay for insurance premiums, pay Taxes, or perform other Borrower obligations under the Loan Documents, Lender is specifying in the above Section 23.2 that it is going to earn a premium interest rate for the inconvenience of having to make an additional advance of funds. Lender can also justify this result because it is having to advance these additional sums due to a default by Borrower, which means that at the time Lender is making this advance, the Loan is now a more risky loan than when the original Loan was funded, and lenders typically charge a higher rate of interest for a loan that has a higher risk to Lender.

Finally, Lender does not want Borrower to be under any misunderstanding or impression; that simply because the Mortgage authorizes Lender to take such actions and spend such monies as are needed to deal with the failure of Borrower to perform maintenance and/or performance obligations under the Mortgage and the other Loan Documents, does not mean that Lender is obligated to advance any monies or take any actions to correct Borrower's failures, and so the Mortgage typically includes a provision like the following:

> 23.3 *Nothing in this Section 23 of this Mortgage shall require Lender to incur any expense or take any action.*

Explanation

As Section 23.3 provides, Lender's performance of such actions is optional and may be exercised in Lender's sole discretion. In other words, Lender may decide whether or not expending any sums in a particular circumstance amounts to "throwing good money after bad." Lender may have no hope of recovery of its investment. Lender may conclude on its own that spending the additional monies will not increase the recovery by Lender and may only serve to increase the equity available to Borrower.

SECTION 24

Events of Default

Explanation

Lender's ability to exercise its legal remedies under the Mortgage, and very frequently with regard to other breaches relating to the other Loan Documents, will usually depend upon the occurrence of a defined concept called an "Event of Default." Below is a typical provision in a Mortgage which defines Event of Default for this Mortgage.

> 24.1 *The occurrence of any one or more of the following shall constitute an Event of Default under this Mortgage:*

Explanation

This Section lists a number of events which will constitute an "Event of Default," with many of them relating to the occurrence of events or circumstances that would tend to threaten (a) Lender's prospect of payment on the Note debt service or balloon payments at maturity, or other payments required under the Loan Documents, in each case in a timely fashion, (b) the physical integrity, prudent management, or financial value of the Mortgaged Property, (c) the financial integrity of Borrower (including cash flow from the operation of Mortgaged Property needed to pay operating expenses), or any applicable guarantor, indemnitor, or other related party involved in the management or operations of the Mortgaged Property, (d) Lender's senior lien priority position relative to the Mortgaged Property or

(e) Lender's ability to exercise its default remedies in a prompt and effective fashion following a default by Borrower.

(a) *any failure by Borrower to pay or deposit when due any amount required by the Note, this Mortgage or any other Loan Document;*

Explanation

This Section 24.1(a) of the Mortgage provides that Borrower's failure to make monetary payments required under any of the Loan Documents in a timely fashion will be an Event of Default (which then would justify Lender to make an election to accelerate the maturity of the Loan). Section 24.1(a) requires Borrower not only to pay debt service payments in a timely fashion, but also to pay all other monetary obligations payable by Borrower pursuant to the Loan Documents, including those payments integrally related to the preservation of the Mortgage lien, including real estate taxes and casualty insurance premiums.

As a threshold matter, what constitutes "timely" debt service payment is a function of whether or not the provisions of the Note and other Loan Documents require the payment to be made by a fixed date with no grace period, or whether there is a payment date provided for which also has a grace period (which extends the time by which Borrower needs to make such payment). Thus, as a starting point, Borrower's failure to make debt service payments within the time specified by the express language of the Note or Loan Agreement, as the case may be, generally would justify Lender's decision to declare a default and accelerate the maturity of the debt. It is quite typical for the Loan Documents to provide different time frames for the making of different types of monetary payments. Typically the payment due at maturity of the Loan must be paid on the maturity date (i.e., with Borrower being afforded no grace period with regard to that payment). It is also quite typical for Lender to permit some minor grace periods for the payment of monthly debt service or other monetary payments payable to Lender (usually something like 3 to 5 business days following the due date set forth in the Note or the Loan Agreement). With regard to most other monetary payments payable by Borrower under the Loan Documents, Lender frequently may allow a longer grace period (typically 10 to 30 days), and may permit such grace period to run from the date when Lender gives written notice of such default to Borrower.

(b) *any failure by Borrower to maintain the insurance coverage required by Section 19 of the Mortgage;*

Explanation

If Borrower fails to maintain the insurance required by the Loan Documents, and then if (a) a casualty occurs that would have been insured if the insurance had been procured, and (b) that casualty causes major damage to the Mortgaged Property, or otherwise creates a liability for which Borrower is responsible, then such occurrences could have devastating consequences for Lender, especially if the Loan is made on a nonrecourse basis. An example of this would be if a fire damages or destroys the Mortgaged Property. This Section 24.1(b) encourages Borrower to obtain the required insurance for the Mortgaged Property by allowing Lender to use a breach of this provision as a basis for declaring a default, which then would afford Lender the right to accelerate the Loan.

The approach used in Section 24.1(b) for dealing with insurance is actually extremely rare. The more typical event of default provision used in mortgage loan documentation usually requires the borrower to provide Lender with evidence of policy renewal 30 days prior to the policy's expiration. By utilizing this provision, the prudent Lender who fails to receive such evidence of insurance renewal within such time frames, is then given ample time and opportunity to directly secure substitute insurance coverage or take adequate steps to ensure Borrower's renewal of the existing insurance policy.

(c) *any failure by Borrower to comply with the bankruptcy remote special purpose provisions of Section 21 of the Mortgage;*

Explanation

The Bankruptcy Code provides significant constraints upon Lender's ability to enforce its default remedies following a Borrower's default. A very important constraint on Lender's ability to enforce its remedies occurs if a Borrower files a bankruptcy petition. Such filing under the Bankruptcy Code effects an automatic stay against creditor enforcement activity, which results in Lender not having the ability to implement foreclosure and other remedies under the Mortgage and other Loan Documents without first getting the bankruptcy judge to issue an order affording Lender relief from this automatic stay.

Single-asset real estate borrower entities, of course, are perhaps not the traditional bankrupt "debtor" that Congress envisioned in enacting the Bankruptcy Code. Currently, most Lenders require that its Borrower be structured to be a newly formed bankruptcy remote entity, in order to minimize the risk of Borrower being able to avail itself of the benefits of the Bankruptcy Code. One of the typical requirements of Lender in order to make Borrower a bankruptcy remote entity, is for Borrower to be a single-asset real estate entity, with the effect that it will only own the Mortgaged Property (but no other real estate assets). As a result of Borrower being a single-asset real estate entity, it will typically be allowed to have only one major creditor; and that creditor will be Lender. To the extent that a single-asset real estate Borrower does have trade creditors, those creditors will tend to hold monetary claims that are in percentage terms relatively insignificant as compared with the amount of the Loan, with the result that Lender will typically be holding most of Borrower's secured and/or unsecured debt at the time of the bankruptcy.

Although some courts concluded that single-asset real estate bankruptcy filings were bad-faith filings subject to dismissal, most courts prior to 1994 concluded that single-asset real estate debtors could file Chapter 11 petitions seeking to reorganize and/or restructure mortgage indebtedness. Erich J. Stegich, *The National Bankruptcy Review Commission: Proposals for Single Asset Real Estate,* 5 AM. BANKR. INST. L. REV. 530 (1997). Nevertheless, Congress perceived that single-asset real estate debtors were abusing the bankruptcy process by filing Chapter 11 petitions to delay mortgage foreclosures even when there was little chance that the debtors could successfully restructure their loans. In response to perceived abuses by real estate debtors, Congress amended the Bankruptcy Code to provide special rules governing single-asset real estate, which now has the Bankruptcy Code definition of real property constituting a single property or project, other than residential real property with fewer than 4 residential units, which generates substantially all of the gross income of a debtor and on which no substantial business is being conducted by a debtor other than the business of operating the real property and activities incidental thereto having aggregate non-contingent, liquidated secured debts in an amount no more than $4,000,000 [11 U.S.C. § 101(51B)].

These special Bankruptcy Code rules limit the scope of the automatic stay with regard to single-asset real estate. To ensure the continued protection of the automatic stay, the single-asset real estate debtor must file its reorganization plan within 90 days of the petition date, that plan must have a "reasonable possibility of being confirmed within a reasonable time," and the debtor must begin making monthly payments to the mortgage lender equal to the interest that would accrue at current market rates on the secured portion of the mortgage lender's claim. These rules thus enable a lender who is holding a mortgage loan which encumbers the debtor's single-asset real estate, with significantly more favorable and expedient treatment in bankruptcy than might otherwise result in a traditional Chapter 11 case. For example, in a traditional Chapter 11, the debtor would not be obligated to make interim "adequate protection" payments during the pendency of the bankruptcy unless the mortgaged land was depreciating in value. See United Sav. Ass'n of Texas v. Timbers of Inwood Forest Assocs., Ltd., 484 U.S. 365 (1988).

(d) *Breach of any representations or warranties contained in this Mortgage or any of the other Loan Documents;*

Explanation

Section 24.1(d) of the Mortgage does not afford Borrower any grace period, which will allow Borrower the ability to cure a breach misrepresentation, with the effect that as written, if any representation or warranty of Borrower contained in any of the Loan Documents should be incorrect, then Lender would have the option of immediately accelerating Borrower's obligation to repay the entire Loan in full. It is not uncommon for Lender to provide in its initial draft of the Loan Documents that there be no grace periods for the curing of a representation or warranty that turns out to be factually incorrect. However, in most instances, if pressed by Borrower's counsel, Lender will permit a 30-day cure period following Lender's giving of written notice to Borrower of any such breach, except that Lender often will not permit any grace period for a willful breach of a representation, particularly if such breach relates to a representation relating to the accuracy of Borrower's, the guarantor's or the Mortgaged Property's financial statements. If Lender is unwilling to provide for a grace period relating to a Borrower misrepresentation, then Borrower's counsel should attempt to carefully look at each representation made in the Mortgage and/or the other Loan Documents, as applicable, and attempt to limit the scope of such representation to being subject to Borrower's knowledge, since frequently Borrower is asked to make representations on matters that it is not in a position to know with certainty whether or not the factual matters included therein are in fact correct. Note the following examples of representations which typically are beyond what a Borrower can say with certainty: (i) Borrower has good title to the Mortgaged Property, free and clear of all liens (a Borrower is not in a position of knowing whether or not there were any errors in prior conveyances, or whether the registry of deeds has made any prior mistakes in filing title documents that could impact the Mortgaged Property); (ii) whether or not the Mortgaged Property complies with all legal requirements; (iii) whether or not there exists any releases of Hazardous Materials on or about the Mortgaged Property; and (iv) at the time of the execution of this Mortgage and the other Loan Documents, whether or not there exists a default under any of the Loan Documents. It is not unusual for Lender and Borrower to negotiate the scope of the meaning of the phrase "to the best of Borrower's knowledge." Frequently this will come down to Borrower and Lender agreeing that they are looking to the extent of knowledge then known to certain key individuals related to Borrower.

(e) *the existence of any collusion, fraud, dishonesty or bad faith by or with the acquiescence of Borrower, which in any material way relates to or affects the Loan or reduces the value of the Collateral;*

(f) *any breach by Borrower of its obligations with respect to Transfer set forth in Section 22 of this Mortgage;*

Explanation

As indicated in Part IV Section 22 of this Book, in making commercial real estate mortgage loans, lenders typically make a careful evaluation of the creditworthiness, reputation, and experience of the borrower, borrower's parent and related parties who will be involved with the operation of the mortgage collateral. Through this evaluation, if the decision is made to proceed with funding the mortgage loan, Lender has reached a conclusion to commit to enter into a significant long-term business relationship with Borrower, who Lender will be looking to manage and operate the mortgage collateral, and to be in a position to deal with any adverse event that arises during the term of the Loan, so that the mortgage collateral and the cash flow derived therefrom will be maintained and protected. Accordingly, Lender will typically want to include this type of provision in the Loan Documents, so that it can prevent the original Borrower from transferring the Mortgaged Property, and not be involuntarily forced to accept a new Borrower whom Lender has not approved. It is not uncommon for Lender to make the sale of the Mortgaged Property a Springing Liability event in the Carve Out Guaranty, which would allow Lender to be able to sue Guarantor for the entire unpaid Indebtedness that then existed at the time of such a sale (see Section 1.2 of the Carve Out Guaranty set out in Appendix C of this Book), which further demonstrates how strongly Lender is concerned about Borrower not making such a sale without Lender's consent.

Generally speaking, "due-on-sale" or "due-on-transfer" sections in mortgage documentation are enforceable by virtue of § 341 of the Garn–St. Germain Depository Institutions Act of 1982, 12 U.S.C. § 1701j-3.

(g) *any failure by Borrower to perform any of its obligations as and when required under any Loan Document other than this Mortgage which continues beyond the applicable express cure period, if any, specified in that Loan Document;*

(h) *any failure by Borrower to perform any of its obligations under this Mortgage (other than those specified in the immediately preceding subsections (a) through (g)), as and when required, which continues for a period of 30 days after written notice of such failure by Lender to Borrower, but no such notice or grace period shall apply in the case of any such failure which could, in Lender's judgment, absent immediate exercise by Lender of a right or remedy under this Mortgage, result in harm to Lender, impairment of the Note or this Mortgage or any other security given under any other Loan Document;*

Explanation

Although Lender's primary concern with regard to the performance by Borrower of obligations under the Mortgage and other Loan Documents will usually be Borrower's timely payment of its mortgage debt service payments and other monetary payments, a breach by Borrower of its "nonmonetary" obligations also can pose potentially unacceptable risks to Lender. For example, Borrower's failure to provide current financial statements may compromise Lender's ability to make sound judgments regarding administration and monitoring of the Loan. A decision by Borrower to change the use of the Mortgaged Property could threaten the fair market value of the Mortgaged Property and/or its ability to generate an adequate amount of net cash flow. Borrower's failure to maintain the Mortgaged Property in a proper fashion could have an obvious negative effect upon its fair market value, thereby potentially compromising Lender's ability to recover sufficient proceeds if it had to implement a foreclosure sale.

Mortgage loan documents typically require a lender to provide the borrower with written notice and a grace period in which to cure any non-monetary covenant breaches before the lender may use those breaches as a basis for accelerating the maturity of the mortgage debt. In many circumstances 30 days may not be sufficient time in which to cure a non-monetary default. Lenders will usually permit the borrower, if it commences cure within 30 days following receipt of written notice of default, but the nature of the default is such that it cannot be cured within such 30 day period, to have an additional period of time (usually an additional 90 to 150 days) to prosecute such cure, so long as the borrower prosecutes such cure with diligence.

(i) *any exercise by the holder of any other debt instrument secured by a mortgage, deed of trust or deed to secure debt on all or any part of the Mortgaged Property, or a pledge of equity interests in Borrower, in each case of a right to declare all amounts due under that debt instrument immediately due and payable.*

Explanation

If all or any part the Mortgaged Property is also covered by one or more other mortgages, a decision by another mortgagee to accelerate its mortgage debt could serve as a critical warning flag to Lender that there may be material problems with Borrower and/or the Mortgaged Property. In the unlikely event that the party accelerating this other debt is a mortgagee holding a superior mortgage lien, Borrower's default under such superior mortgage debt will create the risk that a foreclosure of such superior mortgage would result in the extinguishment of Lender's mortgage lien interest in the Mortgaged Property. Since that type of risk would be intolerable to Lender, the existence of such a default clearly would justify Lender taking swift action to declare a default under the Loan Documents and begin exercising its own default remedies. Typically Lender will not even permit any other subordinate mortgage lien to encumber the Mortgaged Property, in order to eliminate competing secured claims in a bankruptcy of Borrower. Usually the only supplemental type of secured debt which Lender will permit would be subordinate debt secured by a pledge by Borrower's parent of its equity interest in Borrower (this is otherwise known as a "mezzanine loan"). Generally the only ways that Borrower can secure mezzanine financing is to have the mezzanine financing be in place at the time of the making of the Loan, or if Borrower's counsel negotiates for provisions for the future funding of mezzanine financing to be expressly included in the Loan Documents. Typically Lender will insert a provision in the Loan Documents permitting mezzanine financing only if it is requested to do so by Borrower, and such a provision will then allow such mezzanine financing only if at the time Borrower's parent enters into such mezzanine financing various financial tests are met (usually in the form of examining the combined impact of the Loan and the prospective mezzanine financing, and making sure that this aggregate impact meets certain specified loan to value ratios and/or debt service coverage ratios, in each case calculated on the basis of the indebtedness being the aggregate of the Loan and the mezzanine loans), because Lender will want to be sure that the mezzanine financing will not have an adverse impact on the value of the Mortgaged Property and/or the net cash flow available to pay debt service on the Loan. In addition, Lender will almost always require that the mezzanine lender enter into a subordination, nondisturbance, and attornment agreement with Lender at the time Borrower's parent enters into such mezzanine financing (which subordination, nondisturbance, and attornment agreement will subordinate the right of the mezzanine lender to receive cash flow in the event of a default under the Loan, as well as imposing other limitations on the mezzanine lender, including its ability to foreclose on its security pledge of the equity in Borrower, and the mezzanine lender's rights during a bankruptcy case involving Borrower).

Some other typical Event of Default provisions are set forth below:

(j) *if Borrower:*
  (i) *shall file a voluntary petition in bankruptcy or for arrangement, reorganization or other relief under any chapter of the federal bankruptcy code or any similar Law, now or hereafter in effect;*
  (ii) *shall file an answer or other pleading in any proceedings admitting insolvency, bankruptcy, or inability to pay its debts as they mature;*
  (iii) *within sixty (60) days after the filing against it of any involuntary proceedings under the federal bankruptcy code or similar Law, now or hereafter in effect, such proceedings shall not have been vacated;*
  (iv) *have an order issued appointing a receiver, trustee or liquidator for it or for all or a major part of its property or the Land which is not vacated within sixty (60) days following entry thereof;*
  (v) *shall be adjudicated a bankrupt;*
  (vi) *shall make an assignment for the benefit of creditors or shall admit in writing its inability to pay its debts generally as they become due or shall consent to the appointment of a receiver or trustee or liquidator of all or the major part of its property, or the Land; or*
  (vii) *shall for any reason cease to exist.*

(k) *one or more final, unappealable judgments are entered against Borrower in amounts aggregating in excess of $200,000, and said judgments are not stayed or bonded over within thirty (30) days after entry and not otherwise fully insured; or*

(l) *if Borrower shall fail to pay any debt owed by it or is in default under any agreement with Lender or any other party and such failure or default continues after any applicable grace period specified in the instrument or agreement relating thereto.*

SECTION 25

Acceleration; Remedies

Explanation

The following Mortgage provision addresses a variety of issues associated with Lender's decision to accelerate the maturity of the Indebtedness following the occurrence of an Event of Default by Borrower.

25.1 *At any time during the existence of an Event of Default, Lender, at Lender's option, may declare the Indebtedness to be immediately due and payable without further demand, and may invoke the power of sale and any other remedies permitted by the laws of the Property Jurisdiction or provided in this Mortgage or in any other Loan Document. Borrower acknowledges that the power of sale granted by this Mortgage may be exercised by Lender without prior judicial hearing. Borrower has the right to bring an action to assert that an Event of Default does not exist or to raise any other defense Borrower may have to acceleration and sale. Lender shall be entitled to collect all costs and expenses incurred in pursuing such remedies, including attorneys' fees and costs of documentary evidence, abstracts and title reports.*

25.2 *If the applicable laws of the Property Jurisdiction permit the holder of a mortgage to invoke power of sale remedies, and Lender invokes the power of sale, Lender shall deliver a copy of a notice of sale to Borrower in the manner prescribed by the applicable laws of the Property Jurisdiction. In addition, Lender shall give public notice of the sale, to the extent such public notice is mandated by the applicable laws of the Property Jurisdiction, in the manner prescribed by such law, and in all events Lender shall sell the Mortgaged Property in accordance with the applicable provisions of the laws of the Property Jurisdiction. To the extent permitted by applicable law, Lender, without demand on Borrower, shall sell the Mortgaged Property at public auction to the highest bidder at the time and place and under the terms designated in the notice of sale in one or more parcels and in such order as Lender may determine. Lender may postpone the sale of all or any part of the Mortgaged Property by public announcement at the time and place of any previously scheduled sale or by advertising in accordance with the applicable laws of the Property Jurisdiction. Lender or Lender's designee may purchase the Mortgaged Property at any sale.*

Explanation

Courts have used a variety of rules to determine when acceleration of a mortgage debt becomes effective pursuant to an acceleration clause in the Mortgage. Most courts have held Lender must perform some overt affirmative act demonstrating an intention to accelerate the Indebtedness, but that this act need not involve notice to Borrower prior to acceleration. *See, e.g.,* Butter v. Melrose Sav. Bank, 435 N.E.2d 1057 (Mass. Ct. App. 1982) (requirement satisfied by a letter to mortgagor stating that acceleration had already occurred); United States Sav. Bank of Newark v. Continental Arms, Inc., 338 A.2d 579 (Del. Super. Ct. 1975) (institution of judicial foreclosure proceeding constituted sufficient evidence of an election to accelerate mortgage debt). In contrast, courts in Texas have required Lender to give Borrower *both* notice of intent to accelerate prior to acceleration *and* a separate notice of the acceleration itself. *See, e.g.,* Ogden v. Gibraltar Sav. Ass'n, 640 S.W.2d 232 (Tex. 1982); McLemore v. Pacific S.W. Bank, FSB, 872 S.W.2d 286 (Tex. Ct. App. 1994). In the view of these courts, a separate, pre-acceleration notice of the intent to accelerate is "necessary in order to provide the debtor an opportunity to cure his default prior to the harsh consequences of acceleration and foreclosure." *Ogden,* 640 S.W.2d at 234. Furthermore, the Texas courts have held that provisions in the loan documents allowing the mortgagee to accelerate "without prior notice or demand" are not effective to waive the mortgagor's right to notice of intention to accelerate prior to acceleration. See, e.g., Shumway v. Horizon Credit Corp., 801 S.W.2d 890 (Tex. 1991).

The *Restatement (Third) of Property: Mortgages* has attempted to provide some clarity by providing that "[a]n acceleration becomes effective on the date specified in a written notice by the mortgagee to the mortgagor delivered after default." Restatement (Third) of Property: Mortgages § 8.1(a). Under this approach, Lender must provide one (but not more than one) written notice after an Event of Default; the notice can specify that the acceleration is effective either upon delivery of the notice or at a later date specified in the notice. Further, the *Restatement* takes the position that the Loan Documents may not waive this written notice requirement. *Id.* § 8.1, cmt. b.

One might argue that, on its face, the above provision would permit Lender to accelerate the maturity of the Indebtedness without notice to or demand of Borrower. (Of course, a subsequent judicial foreclosure would require notice to

Borrower in order to obtain personal jurisdiction over Borrower, and a subsequent power-of-sale foreclosure would require notice of the sale to Borrower in order to satisfy the statute authorizing power-of-sale foreclosure.) Under this view, this Mortgage provision would be sufficient to allow Lender to accelerate the maturity of the Indebtedness without a separate pre-acceleration notice to Borrower, as long as Lender performs some additional act (such as instituting a foreclosure process) that evidences Lender's decision to accelerate the Indebtedness. One might also argue, however, that this Mortgage provision's use of the language "Lender . . . may *declare* the Indebtedness to be immediately due and payable" suggests that Lender must make a declaration to Borrower in the form of a written notice such as that contemplated by Restatement § 8.1. In a jurisdiction that adopts the Restatement view, Lender would thus be obligated to provide Borrower with written notice that it had accelerated the debt. In a jurisdiction such as Texas, it is doubtful that this Mortgage provision would be sufficient to waive Borrower's right to notice prior to acceleration.

In any event, regardless of whether the Loan Documents require written notice prior to acceleration, the prudent Lender generally chooses to provide Borrower with written notice and an opportunity to cure prior to acceleration, even if only out of courtesy and/or goodwill rather than any obligation imposed by the Loan Documents.

Note that this Mortgage provision contains no specific express language that affords to Borrower a contractual right to cure the applicable Event of Default, so as to have the effect of negating Lender's acceleration and reinstating Borrower's ability to continue to have the right to make periodic debt service payments through maturity of the Loan. As a result, Borrower's only ability to prevent Lender from proceeding with its exercise of its power of sale remedies, following the giving of such written notice, would be if Borrower were to redeem the Mortgaged Property from the lien created by the Mortgage by paying the full accelerated balance of the Indebtedness, along with any costs, fees, and expenses assessed to Borrower under the terms of the Loan Documents. This traditional result is reflected in *Restatement (Third) of Property: Mortgages* § 8.1(c) ("After an acceleration has taken place . . . a mortgagor may prevent foreclosure only by paying or tendering to the mortgagee the full accelerated mortgage obligation").

However, it is important to note that a number of states have enacted statutes permitting the mortgage borrower to reinstate the original maturity of the mortgage debt merely by curing the borrower's arrearages. *See, e.g.,* CAL. CIV. CODE ANN. § 2924c; COLO. REV. STAT. § 38-38-104; MINN. STAT. ANN. § 580.30; UTAH CODE § 57-1-31. In jurisdictions with these "arrearages" statutes, timely cure by the borrower obligates the mortgagee to reinstate the maturity of the debt and cease any further activities in foreclosing the mortgage.

In a number of States, judicial foreclosure, not Lender's exercise of a power of sale, is the exclusive method of foreclosing a mortgage lien. GRANT S. NELSON, DALE A. WHITMAN, ANN M. BURKHART & R. WILSON FREYERMOUTH, REAL ESTATES FINANCE LAW § 7.12 (6th ed. 2007). In such States, foreclosure under the power of sale contained in the above referenced Mortgage provision is not available.

In those states authorizing power-of-sale foreclosure (approximately 60 percent of the States), Lender generally may conduct a sale by complying with the notification requirements contained in the Mortgage and any other notification requirements provided in the statute authorizing power-of-sale foreclosure. In the overwhelming majority of these states, power-of-sale foreclosure occurs without any judicial supervision or proceedings. In these states, the above referenced Mortgage provision (which authorizes Lender to proceed "without prior judicial hearing") is enforceable according to its terms.

Because most power-of-sale foreclosure statutes do not require a hearing to be conducted prior to sale, some have argued that these power-of-sale foreclosure statutes violate the due process clause of the Fourteenth Amendment. Most courts have rejected this argument, on the ground that the mortgagor has the right to file a lawsuit seeking to enjoin the foreclosure and thus can obtain a hearing prior to sale in that fashion. Although commentators have challenged this view (*see* GRANT S. NELSON, DALE A. WHITMAN, ANN M. BURKHART & R. WILSON FREYERMOUTH, REAL ESTATES FINANCE LAW § 7.26 (6th ed. 2007)), most courts have concluded that the mortgagor's ability to seek judicial relief provides the mortgagor with sufficient opportunity to a hearing prior to sale and thus satisfies the Fourteenth Amendment. *See, e.g.,* Laughlin v. Walters, 718 F.2d 513 (1st Cir. 1983).

The above referenced Mortgage provision authorizes Lender to assess Borrower with the costs of pursuing its post-default remedies. Under the law of most states, such contractual provisions are freely enforceable against Borrower.

A limited number of States have statutory limitations upon Lender's ability to collect attorneys' fees from Borrower with respect to Lender's enforcement of its remedies under the Mortgage. In a few other States, statutes authorize the collection of attorneys' fees only after compliance with procedural "notice and cure period" protections. For example, in North Carolina, a creditor cannot enforce an attorneys' fees clause in a note without first giving the debtor a written "five-day notice" of the creditor's intention to enforce the attorneys' fees clause if Borrower does not repay the debt within that five-day period. If the creditor fails to give this notice, or if the debtor pays within the five-day period, the attorneys' fees provision is unenforceable. N.C. GEN. STAT. § 6-21.2(5).

Lender's ability to collect attorneys' fees expended in pursuing its default remedies may also be compromised, despite the express language of the above referenced Mortgage provision, in the event that Borrower commences a voluntary bankruptcy case. Under § 506(b) of the Bankruptcy Code, 11 U.S.C. § 506(b), a creditor holding a secured claim against a bankrupt debtor can recover its post-default attorneys' fees only if its claim is oversecured (i.e., only if the value of the collateral exceeds the balance of Borrower's claim). If market fluctuations have caused the Mortgaged Property to decline in value below the amount of the Indebtedness, Lender would be unable to recover attorneys' fees as a part of its secured claim if Borrower files a bankruptcy petition and its bankruptcy case is not thereafter dismissed.

The above referenced Mortgage provision requires Lender to provide notice of sale to Borrower and also requires Lender to "give public notice of the sale, to the extent such public notice is mandated by the applicable laws of the Property Jurisdiction, in the manner prescribed by such law" and to "sell the Mortgaged Property in accordance with such law." Thus, Lender must provide notice of sale to Borrower and to any other person that must receive notice pursuant to the state's power-of-sale foreclosure statute. Power-of-sale foreclosure statutes vary somewhat from State to State regarding the entitlement of parties other than Borrower and the record owner of the land (if different from Borrower) to notice of sale. Some states require that Lender must notify the holders of any junior liens or claims that appear on the public record or are known to Lender. *See, e.g.,* ALASKA STAT. § 34.20.070(c); IDAHO CODE § 45-1506(2) (c). Other states require Lender to notify only those junior claimants who have recorded a request for notice prior to sale. *See, e.g.,* MO. ANN. STAT. § 443.325; N.C. GEN. STAT. § 45-21.17A. Regardless of State law, a power-of-sale foreclosure will not be effective against a subordinate federal tax lien unless Lender gives the United States written notice of sale at least 25 days prior to sale. 26 U.S.C. § 7425(b), (c).

Some courts have concluded that the failure of Lender to give notice to Borrower as required by the power-of-sale foreclosure statute renders the sale void. *See, e.g.,* Shearer v. Allied Live Oak Bank, 758 S.W.2d 940 (Tex. Ct. App. 1988); Little v. CFS Serv. Corp., 233 Cal. Rptr. 923 (Ct. App. 1987). Under this view, the failure to provide notice to Borrower would allow Borrower to set aside the sale even against a bona fide purchaser at the sale. The possibility of collateral attack of foreclosure sales based upon defects in notice, however, has potentially significant consequences for the viability of power-of-sale foreclosure as a remedy. To the extent that foreclosure sale purchasers cannot receive some assurance of finality of title, potential purchasers may be dissuaded from bidding at foreclosure sales, thereby resulting in sales that would systematically produce fewer bidders and lower sale prices.

In general, the power-of-sale foreclosure process is somewhat analogous to the secured party's right to repossess and sell personal property under Article 9 of the Uniform Commercial Code. Each regime allows the secured lender to exercise its foreclosure rights in a non-judicial setting. Nevertheless, Article 9 holds the foreclosing secured party to a higher standard than the one real estate law places upon a mortgagee exercising a power of sale. Under § 9-504(3) of the 1972 text and § 9-610(b) of the 1999 revision, Article 9 requires that the foreclosing secured party conduct a sale that is "commercially reasonable" in every aspect, including "the method, manner, time, place, and other terms." Often, secured parties may publicly advertise foreclosure sales by nothing more than a legal notice in the classified advertisements of a legal or general-circulation newspaper. In some cases involving specialized collateral, however, courts have concluded that foreclosing secured parties must target their advertisements more meaningfully. For example, in *Contrail Leasing Partners, Ltd. v. Consolidated Airways, Inc.,* 742 F.2d 1095 (7th Cir. 1984), the court held that a secured party foreclosing on an airplane breached the "commercially reasonable" standard by running only one inconspicuous advertisement, when a "serious effort to interest potential buyers would have required a more conspicuous ad plus advertising in other trade publications as well." Under this view, the secured party conducting a foreclosure sale should take care to target its advertisement of the sale in a fashion likely to generate meaningful interest in the sale among potential buyers.

In contrast, power-of-sale foreclosure statutes typically do not impose an express duty of "commercial reasonableness" upon the foreclosing mortgagee. Instead, most of the statutes require only that Lender publish a limited number of notices in newspapers of general circulation in the county where the land is located. *See, e.g.*, Mo. Stat. Ann. § 443.320; N.C. Gen. Stat. § 45-21.17. Most courts have concluded that compliance with these minimum statutory requirements is sufficient, even if additional advertisements or advertisements in other forums might have generated wider interest in the sale and thereby might have produced a higher price. For example, Texas courts have held that "a mortgagee is under no duty to take affirmative action, beyond that required by statute or deed of trust, to ensure a 'fair' sale." Pentad Joint Venture v. First Nat'l Bank of La Grange, 797 S.W.2d 72, 76 (Tex. Ct. App. 1990). Indeed, the *Pentad* court expressly rejected the view that a foreclosure sale under a deed of trust had to be "commercially reasonable" and held that a failure to conduct a commercially reasonable foreclosure sale of land is not actionable. *See also* Huddleston v. Texas Commerce Bank–Dallas, N.A., 756 S.W.2d 343, 347 (Tex. Ct. App. 1988). Under this view, Lender's compliance with the minimum standards established by the power-of-sale foreclosure statute and the loan documents would insulate the sale from subsequent scrutiny.

Nevertheless, the Mississippi Supreme Court has borrowed the "commercially reasonable" standard from Article 9 and has applied it by analogy to foreclosure by power of sale. In *Wansley v. First National Bank of Vicksburg*, 566 So. 2d 1218 (Miss. 1990), the court held that every aspect of sale under a power of sale, "including the method, advertising, time, place and terms, must be commercially reasonable." *Wansley*, 566 So. 2d at 1127. Under this view, the requirements established by the statute and the loan documents would establish only a minimum "floor" below which the lender/trustee could not sink; the lender/trustee would also have to take any additional objectively reasonable steps to advertise and conduct the sale in a fashion designed to produce a sale reasonably calculated to produce a fair price for the land. Likewise, in sustaining a judgment for damages against a foreclosing mortgagee who purchased the property at its own sale for a below-market price, the New Hampshire Supreme Court observed that Lender could have "advertised commercially by display advertising in order to assure that bidders other than themselves would be present." Murphy v. Fin. Dev. Corp., 495 A.2d 1245, 1251 (N.H. 1985). The court's suggestion in *Murphy* should give Lender some pause, inasmuch as the mortgagee in that case had complied with all of the statutory requirements for advertising the sale.

Often, foreclosure sales produce little public interest and few (if any) bidders other than Lender, even in cases where there may exist equity in the land beyond the balance of the mortgage debt. In such a case, a mortgagee might be tempted to credit bid the balance of its debt and (if that remains the high bid) thereby capture any equity in the land for itself. Traditionally, mortgage law—which has been quite protective of Borrower's equitable interest in the mortgaged premises—looked unfavorably upon the potential for abuse inherent in allowing the mortgagee to purchase at its own foreclosure sale. To prevent such abuse, a number of decisions held that, where a mortgage contained a power of sale, the mortgagee exercising that power of sale could not purchase at its own sale. GRANT S. NELSON, DALE A. WHITMAN, ANN M. BURKHART & R. WILSON FREYERMOUTH, REAL ESTATES FINANCE LAW § 7.22 (6th ed. 2007).

In some jurisdictions, however, Borrower has either limited or extensive post-sale redemption rights that may complicate Lender's ability to deliver clear title to the foreclosure sale purchaser. *See, e.g.,* COLO. REV. STAT. § 38-38-302 (rights for 75 days; period expanded to six months for "agricultural real estate"); MO. REV. STAT. ANN. § 443.410 (one-year redemption period, though terminated by sale unless the mortgagor gives notice of its intention to redeem at or before sale and posts bond); MICH. COMP. LAWS ANN. § 600.3240(3) (six-month redemption period for mortgage on commercial property); N.C. GEN. STAT. § 45-21.27 ("upset bid" may be filed during a ten-day period following the sale; filing of upset bid necessitates resale, prior to which Borrower may redeem).

In a jurisdiction recognizing such post-sale redemption rights, the delivery by Lender of a deed to the Mortgaged Property to the purchaser at a foreclosure sale given pursuant to the exercise of a power of sale prior to the end of the redemption period will be insufficient to vest complete legal title in the purchaser. In Michigan, for example, if the mortgagee purchases at the foreclosure sale, the trustee's deed does not convey any right to possession upon the mortgagee until the end of the redemption period. *See, e.g.,* Lendzion v. Senstock, 1 N.W.2d 567 (Mich. 1942).

In addition to the unpaid principal balance of the mortgage debt, Lender may seek to collect additional sums pursuant to provisions authorizing the collection of default interest or involuntary prepayment charges. For example, for most Loans, the Loan Documents will provide that, in the case of any prepayment of the Indebtedness, Borrower will be obligated to pay, in addition to all of the Indebtedness, a prepayment fee, even in the case where such prepayment occurs as a result of Lender's exercise of any right of acceleration of the Indebtedness. As explained in the discussion of Part IV Sections 6 and 7 of this Book, when the Loan Documents (and the Note) clearly provide that a prepayment fee will apply to "involuntary" prepayments—such as the application of foreclosure sale proceeds to the accelerated debt—courts have generally enforced such provisions in accordance with the parties' agreement. *See, e.g.,* Pacific Trust Co. TTEE v. Fidelity Fed. Sav. & Loan Ass'n, 229 Cal. Rptr. 269 (Ct. App. 1986); Village of Rosemont v. Maywood-Proviso State Bank, 501 N.E.2d 859 (Ill. App. Ct. 1986); Eyde v. Empire of Am. Fed. Sav. Bank, 701 F. Supp. 126 (E.D. Mich. 1988). In the event of Borrower's bankruptcy, however, Lender's ability to collect such a fee would be dependent upon the bankruptcy court's judgment that the fee was a "reasonable" charge pursuant to 11 U.S.C. § 506(b).

Likewise, the Mortgage and the Note provide for Borrower to pay interest at the Default Rate, if debt service payments are not made on a timely basis. A significant majority of State court decisions have freely enforced contract default interest provisions (when not inconsistent with state usury limitations). *See, e.g.,* Mattvidi Assocs. L.P. v. NationsBank of Va., 639 A.2d 228 (Md. 1994) (collecting cases).

A decision of the New Jersey Superior Court, Appellate Division, *Metlife Capital Financial Corp. v. Washington Avenue Associates, L.P.*, 713 A.2d 527 (1998), had created significant concern among the lending community when it declared a mortgage default interest provision of 12.55 percent—3 percent over the contract interest rate of 9.55 percent—to be an unenforceable penalty rather than a valid liquidated-damages provision. In that case, the court held that the mortgagee had failed to prove that the 3 percent increase bore any relationship to the damages or actual administrative expenses incurred by the mortgagee. On June 30, 1999, however, the New Jersey Supreme Court reversed the lower court's ruling and concluded that the 3 percent rate was "a reasonable estimate of potential damages" and fell "well within the range demonstrated to be customary." Further, the court held that such a default interest provision, as a "stipulated damages clause negotiated between sophisticated commercial entities," should be treated as presumptively reasonable. Metlife Capital Fin. Corp. v. Washington Ave. Assocs., L.P., 732 A.2d 493 (N.J. 1999).

Where the difference between the contract interest rate and the default rate is 4 to 6 percent or less, it is very likely that, outside the bankruptcy context, the majority of courts will enforce the default interest rate in accordance with its terms. Where the difference between the contract interest rate and the default rate is significantly more than 4 to 6 percent, courts may view default interest provisions significantly more harshly and may be inclined to treat such provisions as an unenforceable penalty. *See, e.g.,* Feller v. Architects Display Bldgs., Inc., 148 A.2d 634 (N.J. App. 1959) (default interest rate of 33 percent—nearly twice the contract rate of 17 percent—was an unenforceable penalty).

Lender's ability to enforce a default interest provision after Borrower commences a voluntary bankruptcy case is less certain. During the pendency of bankruptcy, an undersecured lender is not entitled to collect interest on its secured claim at all. *See* 11 U.S.C. § 506(b); United Sav. Ass'n of Tex. v. Timbers of Inwood Forest Assocs., Ltd., 484 U.S. 365 (1988). The bankruptcy courts have split over whether an oversecured lender may collect default interest under 11 U.S.C. § 506(b) during the pendency of a bankruptcy case. *Compare In re* Terry Ltd. P'ship, 27 F.3d 241 (7th Cir. 1994) and *In re* Courtland Estates Corp., 144 B.R. 5 (Bankr. D. Mass. 1992) (default interest allowed) with *In re* Boulders on the River, Inc., 169 B.R. 969 (Bankr. D. Or. 1994) and *In re* Hollstrom, 133 B.R. 535 (Bankr. D. Colo. 1991) (default interest disallowed as unreasonable).

Remedies Cumulative

Explanation

When Borrower defaults in performing its obligations under the Loan Documents, there are numerous remedies potentially available to Lender seeking to be made whole (e.g., to receive payment of the entire amount of Indebtedness owed to it under the Loan Documents and to recover on any indemnities for any additional losses which Lender may have incurred). Below is a typical provision contained in the Mortgage which deals with the ability of Lender to enforce remedies following the occurrence of an Event of Default:

> 26.1 *Each right and remedy provided in this Mortgage is distinct from all other rights or remedies under this Mortgage or any other Loan Document or afforded by applicable law, and each shall be cumulative and may be exercised concurrently, independently, or successively, in any order:*
>
> (a) *Upon the occurrence and during the continuation of any Event of Default, Lender may take such action, without notice or demand, as it deems advisable to protect and enforce its rights against Borrower and in and to the Mortgaged Property, subject to applicable law, including, but not limited to, the following actions, each of which may be pursued concurrently or otherwise, at such time and in such order as Lender may determine, in its sole discretion, without impairing or otherwise affecting the other rights and remedies of Lender:*
>
> (i) *declare the entire Indebtedness to be immediately due and payable;*
>
> (ii) *institute proceedings for the complete foreclosure of this Mortgage in which case the Mortgaged Property or any interest therein may be sold for cash or upon credit in one or more parcels or in several interests or portions and in any order or manner;*

(iii) *with or without entry, to the extent permitted and pursuant to the procedures provided by applicable law, institute proceedings for the partial foreclosure of this Mortgage for the portion of the Indebtedness then due and payable, subject to the continuing lien of this Mortgage for the balance of the Indebtedness not then due;*

(iv) *sell for cash or upon credit the Mortgaged Property or any part thereof and all estate, claim, demand, right, title and interest of Borrower therein and rights of redemption thereof, pursuant to power of sale or otherwise, at one or more sales, as an entity or in parcels, at such time and place, upon such terms and after such notice thereof as may be required or permitted by law;*

(v) *institute an action, suit or proceeding in equity for the specific performance of any covenant, condition or agreement contained herein or in the Note;*

(vi) *recover judgment on the Note either before, during or after any proceedings for the enforcement of this Mortgage;*

(vii) *apply for the appointment of a trustee, receiver, liquidator or conservator of the Mortgaged Property, without notice and without regard for the adequacy of the security for the Indebtedness and without regard for the solvency of the Borrower, any guarantor or of any person, firm or other entity liable for the payment of the Indebtedness;*

(viii) *enter into or upon the Mortgaged Property, either personally or by its agents, servicers, nominees or attorneys and, to the extent Borrower is in occupancy of the Mortgaged Property, dispossess Borrower and its agents and servants therefrom, and thereupon Lender (or any receiver appointed pursuant to subsection (vii) above) may do or permit one or more of the following, successively or concurrently: (a) enter upon and take possession and control of any and all of the Mortgaged Property; (b) take and maintain possession of all documents, books, records, papers and accounts relating to the Mortgaged Property; (c) exclude Borrower and its agents, servants and employees wholly from the Mortgaged Property; (d) manage and operate the Mortgaged Property; (e) preserve and maintain the Mortgaged Property; (f) make repairs and alterations to the Mortgaged Property; (g) complete any construction or repair of the Improvements, with such changes, additions or modifications of the plans and specifications or intended disposition and use of the Improvements as Lender may, in its sole discretion, deem appropriate or desirable to place the Mortgaged Property in such condition as will, in Lender's sole discretion, make it or any part thereof readily marketable or rentable; (h) if the Lease has been terminated, conduct a marketing or leasing program with respect to the Mortgaged Property, or employ a marketing or leasing agent or agents to do so, directed to the leasing or sale of the Mortgaged Property under such terms and conditions as Lender may, in its sole discretion, deem appropriate or desirable; (i) employ such contractors, subcontractors, materialmen, architects, engineers, consultants, managers, brokers, marketing agents, or other employees, agents, independent contractors or professionals, as Lender may, in its sole discretion, deem appropriate or desirable to implement and effectuate the rights and powers herein granted; (j) execute and deliver, in the name of Lender as attorney-in-fact and agent of Borrower or in its own name as Lender, such documents and instruments as are necessary or appropriate to consummate authorized transactions; (k) affirm or modify any lease of any real property interest constituting a part of the Mortgaged Property, or enter such other leases, whether of real or personal property, or tenancy agreements, under such terms and conditions as Lender may, in its sole discretion, deem appropriate or desirable; (l) collect and receive the Rents from the Mortgaged Property; (m) eject tenants or repossess personal property, as provided by law, for breaches of the conditions of their leases or other agreements; (n) sue for unpaid Rents, payments, income or proceeds in the name of Borrower or Lender; (o) maintain actions in forcible entry and detainer, ejectment for possession and actions in distress for rent; (p) compromise or reduce Rents, payments, income or proceeds that may become due; (q) delegate or assign any and all rights and powers given to Lender by this Mortgage; and (r) do any acts which Lender, in its sole discretion, deems appropriate or desirable to protect the security hereof and use such measures, legal or equitable, as Lender may, in its sole discretion, deem appropriate or desirable to implement and effectuate the provisions of this Mortgage. Borrower hereby constitutes and appoints Lender, its assignees, successors, transferees and nominees, as Borrower's true and lawful attorney-in-fact and agent, with full power of substitution in the Mortgaged Property, in Borrower's name, place and stead, during an Event of Default, to do or permit any one or more of the foregoing described rights, remedies, powers and authorities, successively or concurrently, and said power of attorney shall be deemed a power coupled with an interest and irrevocable so long as any portion of the Indebtedness is outstanding. Any money advanced by Lender in connection with any action taken under this subsection (viii), together with interest thereon at the Default Rate from the date of making such advancement by Lender until actually paid by Borrower, shall be a demand obligation owing by Borrower to Lender and shall be secured by this Mortgage and by every other instrument securing all or any portion of the Indebtedness;*

(ix) *with or without taking possession of the Mortgaged Property, sue or otherwise collect the Rents, including those past due and unpaid; and*

(x) *exercise any other right or remedy available hereunder, under any of the other Loan Documents or at law or in equity.*

In the event of a sale, by foreclosure or otherwise, of less than all of the Mortgaged Property, this Mortgage shall continue as a lien on the remaining portion of the Mortgaged Property.

(b) *To the fullest extent permitted by law, the proceeds of any sale under this Mortgage shall be applied, to the extent funds are so available, to the following items in such order as Lender in its discretion may determine:*

(i) *To payment of the reasonable costs, expenses and fees of taking possession of the Mortgaged Property, and of holding, operating, maintaining, using, leasing, repairing, improving, marketing and selling the same and of otherwise enforcing Lender's rights and remedies hereunder and under the other Loan Documents, including, but not limited to, receivers' fees, court costs, attorneys', accountants', appraisers', managers' and other professional fees, title charges and transfer taxes.*

(ii) *To payment of all sums expended by Lender under the terms of any of the Loan Documents and not yet repaid, together with interest on such sums at the Default Rate.*

(iii) *To payment of the interest, principal, the Prepayment Consideration and all other obligations secured by this Mortgage, including, without limitation, interest at the Default Rate, in any order that Lender chooses in its sole discretion.*

(iv) *The remainder, if any, of such funds shall be disbursed to Borrower or to the person or persons legally entitled thereto.*

(c) *To the extent permitted by applicable law, Lender may adjourn from time to time any sale by it to be made under or by virtue of this Mortgage by announcement at the time and place appointed for such sale or for such adjourned sale or sales; and, except as otherwise provided by any applicable provision of law, Lender, without further notice or publication, may make such sale at the time and place to which the same shall be so adjourned.*

(d) *Upon the completion of any sale or sales made by Lender under or by virtue of this Section, Lender or an officer of any court empowered to do so, shall execute and deliver to the accepted purchaser or purchasers a good and sufficient instrument, or good and sufficient instruments, conveying, assigning and transferring all estate, right, title and interest in and to the property and rights sold. Any such sale or sales made under or by virtue of this Section shall operate to divest all the estate, right, title, interest, claim and demand whatsoever, whether at law or in equity, of Borrower in and to the properties and rights so sold, and shall be a perpetual bar both at law and in equity against Borrower and against any and all persons claiming or who may claim the same, or any part thereof from, through or under Borrower.*

(e) *Upon any sale made under or by virtue of this Section, Lender may bid for and acquire the Mortgaged Property or any part thereof and in lieu of paying cash therefor may make settlement for the purchase price by crediting upon the Indebtedness the net sales price after deducting therefrom the expenses of the sale and costs of the action and any other sums which Lender is authorized to deduct under this Mortgage.*

(f) *No recovery of any judgment by Lender and no levy of an execution under any judgment upon the Mortgaged Property or upon any other property of Borrower shall affect in any manner or to any extent the lien of this Mortgage upon the Mortgaged Property or any part thereof, or any liens, rights, powers or remedies of Lender hereunder, but such liens, rights, powers and remedies of Lender shall continue unimpaired as before.*

Explanation

The most obvious remedy for a Lender to employ in a mortgage loan situation is to foreclose the Mortgage, and then cause the Mortgaged Property to be sold pursuant to the related foreclosure sale (which is the end-part of the foreclosure process). If Lender is the successful bidder at the foreclosure sale, then Lender will own the Mortgaged Property and can resell it in order to recover the Indebtedness then owed to it from the net sale proceeds derived from such foreclosure sale. If another party is the successful bidder at such foreclosure sale, this ordinarily means that this party bid more than the amount of Indebtedness owed to Lender, which could be a good result for Lender, because with its senior lien position, netting out sales costs, the first priority for the application of the net sales proceeds will be to repay Lender up to the amount of the Indebtedness.

Sometimes, however, foreclosure of the Mortgaged Property does not generate sufficient net sale proceeds that will make Lender whole. If the value of the Mortgaged Property is less than the Indebtedness, then it is quite possible that the Indebtedness may also exceed the net proceeds which are payable to Lender from the foreclosure sale (or any subsequent sale of the Mortgaged Property by Lender, if it is the successful bidder at the foreclosure sale). In such circumstances, Lender may want to consider pursuing additional legal collection remedies against Borrower or any applicable guarantor (if the Loan is a recourse loan or if an applicable "carve out" to nonrecourse liability applies) who may have executed a guaranty of payment as part of the Loan Documents for the then remaining "deficiency" (i.e., the difference between the aggregate Indebtedness then owed to Lender and the amount of net proceeds paid to Lender in connection with the foreclosure sale). Furthermore, in some cases, Lender may elect not to foreclose on the Mortgage, or may be unable to pursue foreclosure if Borrower is the subject of a bankruptcy case and an "automatic stay" has been ordered by the bankruptcy judge (see Part IV Section 21 of this Book). For example, if there is a serious environmental contamination problem with respect to the Mortgaged Property, the value of the property will have declined, with the result that no one would bid a meaningful amount at the foreclosure sale. In this circumstance, Lender may prefer to sue Borrower (again if a recourse loan and if Borrower has other assets from which to recover) or the guarantors, if any, who may have executed a guaranty of payment with respect to the Indebtedness, rather than pursue the foreclosure remedy.

In jurisdictions that do not limit (or place few limitations upon) the remedies available to Lender after Borrower commits an event of default pursuant to the Mortgage, the clarification on remedies available to Lender is usually specified in the remedy provisions set forth in the Mortgage.

However, numerous jurisdictions limit the remedies available to Lender after Borrower's default. One key limitation involves the ability of Lender to pursue a deficiency action against Borrower. Some jurisdictions prohibit a deficiency action in certain circumstances, such as when Lender elects to foreclose through the swifter power-of-sale procedure rather than the judicial foreclosure procedure. Some jurisdictions will allow Lender to sue Borrower (for any recourse liability) or any guarantor, but will require that Lender foreclose on the Mortgage first. These limitations on remedies are immutable rules or rules of law (e.g., they cannot be modified by agreement of the parties at the time that the loan is first made) rather than default rules or rules of construction (which could be modified by agreement of the parties at the time the loan is first made).

SECTION 27

Forbearance

Explanation

Lenders sometimes insert in the Mortgage a provision which contemplates that at Lender's election, it may decide to provide Borrower with some relief of its obligations under the Loan Documents, such as extending the time when Borrower's payments may be paid, reducing one or more payments, or releasing one or more Persons from the liability to make obligated payments due under the Mortgage or any other Loan Document. A typical mortgage provision which reflects this concept is as follows:

> 27.1 *Lender may (but shall not be obligated to) agree with Borrower, from time to time, and without giving notice to, or obtaining the consent of, or having any effect upon the obligations of, any guarantor or other third-party obligor, to take any of the following actions: extend the time for payment of all or any part of the Indebtedness; reduce the payments due under this Mortgage, the Note, or any other Loan Document; release anyone liable for the payment of any amounts under this Mortgage, the Note, or any other Loan Document; accept a renewal of the Note; modify the terms and time of payment of the Indebtedness; join in any extension or subordination agreement; release any Mortgaged Property; take or release other or additional security; modify the rate of interest or period of amortization of the Note or change the amount of the monthly installments payable under the Note; and otherwise modify this Mortgage, the Note, or any other Loan Document.*

Explanation

This Section 27.1 of the Mortgage responds to court decisions that have released guarantors from liability when a lender and borrower have modified the terms of the mortgage loan without the guarantor's consent. These decisions have used the reasoning that it is unfair to the guarantor to change the loan in such a manner that it increases the chances that the borrower will default or increases the guarantor's liability under the loan without the guarantor's consent. Once such a modification has occurred without the guarantor's consent, the guarantor is released of all liability under the guaranty. *See, e.g.,* Regency Equities Corp. v. Reiss, 1995 WL 362496 (S.D.N.Y. 1995). In light of this risk, lenders attempt to obtain contractual assurance in the Loan Documents that they in fact have the right to make loan modifications (including releases of persons and collateral) without first notifying and obtaining the guarantor's consent.

When guarantors have signed agreements that waive objections to loan modifications made without notice to them and without their consent, courts have enforced such agreements. *See, e.g.,* Regency Equities Corp. v. Reiss, 1995 WL 362496 (S.D.N.Y. 1995).

The next provision of the Mortgage, addresses the situation that exists when Borrower has defaulted under the Loan, and Lender has failed to insist on on-going strict performance of all of the Loan terms, or where Lender has failed to exercise its remedies.

> 27.2 *Any forbearance by Lender in exercising any right or remedy under the Note, this Mortgage, or any other Loan Document or otherwise afforded by applicable law, shall not be a waiver of or preclude the exercise of any other right or remedy. The acceptance by Lender of payment of all or any part of the Indebtedness after the due date of such payment, or in an amount which is less than the required payment, shall not be a waiver of Lender's right to require prompt payment when due of all other payments on account of the Indebtedness or to exercise any remedies for any failure to make prompt payment. Enforcement by Lender of any security for the Indebtedness shall not constitute an election by Lender of remedies so as to preclude the exercise of any other right available to Lender. Lender's receipt of any awards or proceeds under Sections 19 and/or 20 of this Mortgage shall not operate to cure or waive any Event of Default.*

Explanation

The above Section 27.2 attempts to provide that any inaction by Lender to continue to insist upon strict performance by Borrower, neither constitutes a waiver by Lender of its remedies under any of the Loan Documents, nor does such an action constitute a Lender estoppel with respect to its right under the Loan Documents to insist upon on-going strict performance by Borrower of any of its obligations under the Loan Documents, or in any way prevent Lender at any time in the future from exercising remedies for any future defaults by Borrower under the Loan Documents. Lenders have included such language in loan documents because many courts have found that when a lender establishes a prior course of dealing in accepting late payments, Lender has waived its ability to declare a default or is estopped from accelerating the debt upon future defaults (at least until Lender makes clear to Borrower that it will in the future insist on strict performance). *See* Greenberg v. Service Bus. Forms Indus., Inc., 882 F.2d 1538, 1542 (10th Cir. 1989).

SECTION 28

Exculpation

Explanation

Prior to the 1990s, it was not uncommon for commercial real estate loans to be made on a "nonrecourse" basis (i.e., the property mortgaged was the sole asset the lender could look to for collection purposes in the event that the borrower defaulted in performing its obligations under the loan documents, and except for a Hazardous Material indemnity, no third party was at risk for being sued if a borrower default occurred). Lenders were willing to make nonrecourse loans to real estate projects that were fully constructed and profitably operating, loaning typically up to 80% of the appraised value of the mortgaged property (so in effect at the time of the loan closing, the borrower had at risk 20% of the appraised value of the mortgaged property). In the event of a default, the lender could accelerate the debt, foreclose on the property, and recover its investment. Prior to the 1990s, real estate investments frequently were "syndicated," so as to allow unrelated investors to the sponsoring entity to invest in these projects, and the non-recourse nature of the projects permitted these investors to participate in depreciation tax benefits, which could be allocated to them. However, these investors did not want to be personally responsible for the repayment of the mortgage loan, and the nonrecourse provisions blended well with the desires of these investors. The allocation of the depreciation tax benefits was reversed with the federal Tax Reform Act of 1986, which made it considerably more difficult for such investors to take advantage of these depreciation tax benefits.

The real estate recession of the late 1980s and early 1990s was in part brought on by the Tax Reform Act of 1986. This modification of the federal tax code contained provisions that took away the depreciation benefits from investors who had been investing in real estate projects, and brought about a decline in demand that crushed real estate valuations, so that numerous real estate projects began to fail and numerous real estate loans went into default. During this time, lenders learned many lessons as they attempted to enforce the mortgage loan documents that had gone into default. One common problem lenders encountered was that many borrowers would "milk" the mortgaged property (i.e., they would pocket the property's income, and not apply it to the expenses of the property and the debt service for the mortgage loan). Oftentimes these borrowers might divert a property's cash flow to other real estate projects on which the lender did not have a mortgage lien, or accumulated the cash as a "war chest" to fund a defense to the lender's foreclosure action (in particular, filing for bankruptcy relief). In reaction to this behavior, starting in the mid-1990s, lenders revised their loan documentation to provide "carve outs" to the nonrecourse nature of the loan (conditions which, if violated, would cause the borrower to be personally liable for such violations), and more importantly, lenders insisted with each new commercial real estate loan that a creditworthy related-party guarantor had to execute a guaranty (which became known as a "carve out guarantee"), pursuant to which the guarantor was personally liable to the lender for repayment of a portion of the debt equal to the loss or damage suffered by the lender as a result of violations of the carve out conditions. Below is a provision which deals with both making the Loan non-recourse, but permitting aforementioned "carve outs."

28.1 *Lender shall not be entitled to and shall not enforce the liability and obligation of Borrower to perform and observe the obligations contained in this Mortgage, the Note or in any of the other Loan Documents by any action or proceeding wherein a money judgment or personal liability shall be sought against Borrower or any members, beneficiaries, trustees, the economic and beneficial owner of Borrower or of any beneficial owners or trustees of Borrower or any managers, officers, shareholders or directors thereof (collectively, the "Released Parties"), except that Lender may bring a foreclosure action, an action for specific performance or any other appropriate action or proceeding to enable Lender to enforce and realize upon its interests under the Note, this Mortgage or the other Loan Documents or in the Mortgaged Property, or any other collateral given by Borrower pursuant to this Mortgage and the other Loan Documents; provided, however, that, except as specifically provided herein, for purposes of enforcing Lender's rights under this Section 28, any judgment in any such action or proceeding shall be enforceable against Borrower only to the extent of Borrower's interest in the Mortgaged Property and in any other collateral given to Lender, and Lender, by accepting this Mortgage, the Note and the other Loan Documents, agrees that it shall not sue for, seek or demand any deficiency judgment against Borrower or any of the Released Parties in any such action or proceeding under, or by reason of, or in connection with this Mortgage, the Note or the other Loan Documents. The provisions of this Section 28.1 shall not, however, (i) constitute a waiver, release or impairment of any obligation evidenced or secured by this Mortgage, the Note or any of the other Loan Documents; (ii) impair the right of Lender to name Borrower as a party defendant in any action or suit for foreclosure and sale under this Mortgage; (iii) affect the validity or enforceability of any guaranty made in connection with the Debt or guaranty of liability for the acts specified below or any of the rights and remedies of the Lender thereunder; (iv) impair the right of Lender to obtain the appointment of a receiver; (v) impair the enforcement of the Assignment of Leases and Rents executed in connection herewith; or (vi) constitute a waiver of the right of Lender to enforce the liability and obligation of Borrower, by money judgment or otherwise, to the extent of any loss, damage excluding consequential exemplary and punitive damages, cost, expense, liability, claim or other obligation incurred by Lender (including, without limitation, attorneys' fees and costs reasonably incurred) arising out of or in connection with the following:*

(a) *the misappropriation or conversion of Rents, if any, or any other similar payment collected, received or held by or on behalf of Borrower under any Lease;*

(b) *after notice of an uncured Event of Default and during the continuance of such Event of Default, the failure of Borrower to apply 100% of any and all income derived from the Mortgaged Property, and received by Borrower, to the repayment of the Indebtedness (except to the extent that Borrower did not have the legal right, because of a bankruptcy, receivership or similar judicial proceeding, to direct disbursement of such sums or payments);*

(c) *a material misrepresentation made by Borrower, or the holders of Controlling beneficial or ownership interests in Borrower, in connection with the Mortgaged Property, or the financing evidenced by the Note, this Mortgage or the other Loan Documents ("Control" shall mean, with respect to any Person, the possession, directly or indirectly, of the power to direct or cause the direction of the management and policies of such Person, whether through the ownership of voting securities or other beneficial interests, by contract or otherwise, and Control shall not be deemed absent solely because another Person shall have veto power with respect to major decisions. The terms "Controlled" and "Controlling" shall have correlative meanings);*

(d) *the misappropriation or misapplication of insurance or condemnation proceeds obtained by Borrower relating to the Mortgaged Property;*

(e) *any violation of an Environmental Law or any release or contamination affecting the Mortgaged Property, which is introduced or caused by Borrower or the holders of Controlling beneficial or ownership interests in Borrower or any parties Controlled by or under common Control therewith;*

(f) *any physical waste of or damage to the Mortgaged Property caused by the willful or wanton acts or omissions of Borrower or its agents;*

(g) *the failure of Borrower to comply with special purpose entity provisions contained in Section 21 of this Mortgage;*

(h) *Borrower fails to obtain Lender's prior written consent to any subordinate financing or other voluntary lien caused by Borrower or its agent encumbering the Mortgaged Property as required by this Mortgage;*

(i) *Borrower fails to obtain Lender's prior written consent to any Transfer if and to the extent required by this Mortgage;*

(j) *Borrower permits monthly Rent to be paid more than one (1) month in advance without depositing such Rent in an account earmarked for payment of the Debt;*

(k) *the failure of Borrower to cause the required insurance policies which Borrower is required to maintain pursuant to this Mortgage to at all times remain in full force and effect and to cause all Taxes and Premiums to be paid prior to delinquency thereof;*

(l) *the commission of any fraud by Borrower or the holders of beneficial or ownership interests in Borrower;*

(m) *the adjudication of Borrower, or any guarantor or indemnitor who shall have executed a guarantee or an indemnity for the benefit of Lender and which are part of the Loan Documents, as bankrupt as a result of any voluntary filing by Borrower, such guarantor or such indemnity, as the case may be; and*

(n) *Borrower, such guarantor or such indemnitor conspires with others to cause an involuntary filing of a bankruptcy proceeding against Borrower, such guarantor or such indemnitor, as the case may be.*

Notwithstanding anything to the contrary in this Mortgage, the Note or any other Loan Documents, Lender shall not be deemed to have waived any right which Lender may have under Sections 506(a), 506(b), 1111(b) or any other provisions of the Bankruptcy Code to file a claim for the full amount of the Indebtedness secured by this Mortgage or to require that all collateral shall continue to secure all of the Indebtedness owing to Lender.

Explanation

The lead-in paragraph of this Section of the Mortgage provides for the basic nonrecourse nature of the Loan. Since Borrower is a single-asset entity (with all of its assets being subject to the lien of the Mortgage, and therefore subject to recourse), the important element of this nonrecourse language is that Lender is agreeing that parties (i.e., the "Released Parties") related to Borrower (other than any applicable guarantor or indemnitor) will not be personally liable for the obligations of Borrower under the Loan Documents, except to the extent that they violate the carve out conditions. Legitimately, Lender makes an effort in this provision to preserve its rights to pursue foreclosure and specific performance remedies against the Mortgaged Property and/or Borrower, as the case may be.

Note that the carve out claims (in respect of which Lender reserves recourse rights against the respective Released Parties) are typically referred to as "bad-boy" acts. As you can see, these acts include misappropriations, fraud, and physical waste, each of which is fundamentally illegal. In addition, these acts also include a breach of the Transfer and single-asset covenants in the Mortgage, which, as I have discussed earlier, are very important to Lender. Finally, these acts also include a voluntary bankruptcy filing, or a bankruptcy filing which is organized by Borrower, or any applicable guarantor or indemnitor. Because a bankruptcy of Borrower would lead to an automatic stay of Lender's ability to proceed with foreclosure, this provision is of particular importance to Lender.

In this Mortgage a violation of any of the carve outs could result in potential liability and/or losses to Lender, particularly if Lender ends up purchasing the Mortgaged Property at a foreclosure sale, and then must deal with any loss or damage which is the result the occurrence of such acts. As a result, Lender will require a credit worthy Guarantor to execute a carve out guaranty to cover such losses or damage; and it is quite common for Lender to specify in such guaranty that rather than being restricted to just damages, that the Guarantor would become fully liable for the payment of the entire Indebtedness in connection with the occurrence of certain events, such as a voluntary bankruptcy filing, an involuntary bankruptcy filing which is promoted or encouraged by Borrower or any of the Released Parties, or a violation of the Transfer or separateness covenant provisions (all of which is covered in greater detail in Part III of this Book, entitled "Carve Out Guaranty").

SECTION 29

Waiver of Marshaling

Explanation

Marshaling is a doctrine that determines the order of foreclosure when a Mortgage lien encumbers multiple parcels of real estate properties. For example, if a Mortgage is secured by a lien on two parcels and one of said parcels is also encumbered by a junior lien securing another mortgage loan, while the other parcel is unencumbered by any other mortgage lien, the concept of marshaling would dictate that Lender first proceed with foreclosing its lien upon the parcel where its lien is the only mortgage lien encumbering the property. The rationale for the marshaling process is that the parcel which is solely encumbered by the Mortgage lien might bring a sufficient price at its applicable foreclosure auction such that the foreclosure sale proceeds would be sufficient to pay the Indebtedness in full, making the foreclosure of the Mortgage's lien encumbering the other parcel unnecessary. The basic purpose of marshaling, then, is to avoid unnecessary harm to the holders of junior interests in the mortgaged property. *See* Restatement (Third) of Property: Mortgages § 8.6 (1997); Grant S. Nelson, Dale A. Whitman, Ann M. Burkhart & R. Wilson Freyermouth, Real Estates Finance Law § 10.9 (6th ed. 2007). Below is a typical marshaling provision in a Mortgage.

29.1 *Notwithstanding the existence of any other security interests in the Mortgaged Property held by Lender or by any other party, Lender shall have the right to determine the order in which any or all of the Mortgaged Property shall be subjected to the remedies provided in this Mortgage, the Note, any other Loan Document or applicable law. Lender shall have the right to determine the order in which any or all portions of the Indebtedness are satisfied from the proceeds realized upon the exercise of such remedies. Borrower and any party who now or in the future acquires a security interest in the*

Mortgaged Property and who has actual or constructive notice of this Mortgage waives any and all right to require the marshaling of assets or to require that any of the Mortgaged Property be sold in the inverse order of alienation or that any of the Mortgaged Property be sold in parcels or as an entirety in connection with the exercise of any of the remedies permitted by applicable law or provided in this Mortgage.

Explanation

In the current commercial mortgage lending environment, the Mortgage lien usually only encumbers a single parcel, with the effect that the marshaling concept is irrelevant in this circumstance. (Note, however, that marshaling might still apply, at least in theory, because the Mortgage also contains a personal property security agreement—which employs "other property" besides the real estate as collateral.) If the Mortgage encumbers more than one real estate parcel, marshaling is quite likely to be an issue.

There is no real doubt that the right to marshal can be waived by language in the junior mortgage—a mortgage held by a lender with a right to request marshaling. *See, e.g.*, Raynor v. Raynor, 193 S.E.2d 216 (N.C. 1937). The question raised by the above Mortgage section is whether language in the senior mortgage can deprive a junior lienholder of the right to request marshaling. This question is largely unanswered in the case law. The argument that it can do so is based on the principle of notice: If the senior mortgage (with its "waiver of marshaling" clause) is recorded, any persons taking junior liens on the property are on constructive notice of that clause, and hence of the fact that they will not be able to assert marshaling. Under this logic, there is no unfairness to them in denying marshaling; if they considered the loss of the right to marshal to be unacceptable, one might argue, they should not have made junior loans on this property!

Comments in the *Restatement* take the position that this sort of "advance waiver" of the right to marshal is valid and enforceable. RESTATEMENT (THIRD) OF PROPERTY: MORTGAGES § 8.6.e; *accord* Platte Valley Bank v. Kracl, 174 N.W.2d 724 (Neb. 1970); Thompson v. Thomas, 195 P. 427 (Cal. Ct. App. 1919).

SECTION 30

Further Assurances

Explanation

It is not uncommon for Lender to include a provision in the Mortgage which requires Borrower to enter into such additional documents of record or to provide other assurances after the closing of the Loan as Lender shall reasonably require in order to better assure that Lender has received the rights that were intended to be granted to Lender by the Loan Documents. Below is a typical provision.

> 30.1 *Borrower shall execute, acknowledge, and deliver, at its sole cost and expense, all further acts, deeds, conveyances, assignments, estoppel certificates, financing statements, transfers and assurances as Lender may require from time to time in order to better assure, grant, and convey to Lender the rights intended to be granted, now or in the future, to Lender under this Mortgage and the Loan Documents.*

Explanation

This provision serves two distinct functions. First, it constitutes, on behalf of Borrower, a covenant for title analogous to the "covenant of further assurances" traditionally recognized by the common law as one of the six covenants for title provided in a general warranty deed. (The title warranties contained in the unnumbered introductory paragraphs of a mortgage do not expressly state such a covenant.) The common-law covenant of further assurances obligates the grantor to execute or cause to be executed, upon the grantee's request, any additional documents necessary to perfect the title that the grantor's original deed purported to convey to the grantee. William B. Stoebuck & Dale A. Whitman, The Law of Property § 11.13, at 910 (3d ed. 2000). Second, this provision obligates Borrower to perform any and all acts as Lender requires in order to provide Lender with assurance of the rights intended to be granted to it under the Mortgage and related Loan Documents. This covenant goes beyond matters of title.

SECTION 31

Estoppel Certificate

Explanation

Since Lender may desire in the future to get an updated status from Borrower about certain key items, the Mortgage usually contains a provision which requires Borrower to provide certain updated representations on Lender's request. These updated representations would be particularly useful to Lender if it desires to sell all or a part of its interest in the Loan to a third party. Below is a typical provision, which contains the required representations, and which are typically known in the industry as estoppel representations, because once made, if these statements are factually inaccurate, then Borrower risks being in default under the Loan Documents.

31.1 *Within 10 days after a request from Lender, Borrower shall deliver to Lender a written statement, signed and acknowledged by Borrower, certifying to Lender or any person designated by Lender, as of the date of such statement, (i) that the Loan Documents are unmodified and in full force and effect (or, if there have been modifications, that the Loan Documents are in full force and effect as modified and setting forth such modifications); (ii) the unpaid principal balance of the Note; (iii) the date to which interest under the Note has been paid; (iv) that Borrower is not in default in paying the Indebtedness or in performing or observing any of the covenants or agreements contained in this Mortgage or any of the other Loan Documents (or, if the Borrower is in default, describing such default in reasonable detail); (v) whether or not there are then existing any setoffs or defenses known to Borrower against the enforcement of any right or remedy of Lender under the Loan Documents; and (vi) any additional facts requested by Lender.*

Explanation

As indicated above, it is customary for a Lender to obtain these representations in order to facilitate a secondary market sale or pledge of the mortgage loan by Lender. Any party who might purchase the Loan or accept it as collateral for repayment of some other advance of credit is naturally concerned about the loan's status and whether Borrower has any defenses to payment.

The estoppel certificate described in this Section 31.1 of the Mortgage is designed to allay those concerns.

An estoppel certificate is effective whether or not the Note is negotiable. The estoppel certificate's primary purpose is not to act as a release of any defenses the maker of the Note might raise, but simply to get those defenses out "on the table" so that the secondary-market investor can examine them and determine whether they are serious enough to cause the investor to decide not to complete the purchase or loan. The matters that can be discovered in this way are sometimes called "patent equities," because they can be brought to light by means of an estoppel certificate. The certificate should recite that it will be relied upon by persons who are acquiring or lending on the security of the mortgage note.

In addition to bringing any defenses of the maker to light, the estoppel certificate is also useful to a secondary-market investor in verifying the lender's representations concerning the loan's documentation, the current principal and interest outstanding, and the absence of any default. The above section permits Lender to ask for "any additional facts" that Lender deems significant. For example, if the Note bears an adjustable interest rate, the investor may want confirmation of the current rate. The investor may also wish to confirm, through the estoppel certificate, the balance in any escrow or reserve accounts, the status of insurance coverage on the property, the status of existing leases, and the existence and unencumbered status of items of personal property. Finally, the investor may wish to confirm that Borrower still owns the real estate and associated personal property, and has not made any transfers in violation of the due-on-sale clause.

SECTION 32

Governing Law; Consent to Jurisdiction and Venue

Explanation

The Mortgage, the Note and the other Loan Documents almost always have a provision which specifies which State laws will govern the provisions of each such agreement. Below is a typical provision in the Mortgage which specifies this concept.

> 32.1 *This Mortgage, and any Loan Document which does not itself expressly identify the law that is to apply to it, shall be governed by the laws of the jurisdiction in which the Land is located (the "**Property Jurisdiction**").*

Explanation

It is often the case that the Mortgage and other Loan Documents which will be filed in the registry of deeds where the Mortgaged Property is located, will be governed by the laws of the State in which the Mortgaged Property is located. This choice-of-law provision conforms to the general approach taken by courts with respect to the construction, validity, and effect of the Mortgage. The express statement contained in Section 32.1 above can prove helpful in this regard, particularly when the Loan is negotiated, executed, or performed in one jurisdiction and/or one or more of the parties to the transaction reside in a different jurisdiction.

Sometimes, particularly with a Loan secured by Mortgaged Property which is located in multiple states, the Loan Documents contain a choice-of-law provision that selects a state other than the applicable forum state. In a multistate secured loan, lenders sometimes choose the laws of a jurisdiction of which they are more familiar. In addition, lenders sometimes hope to avoid problematic laws of a given jurisdiction (such as anti-deficiency laws or usury limitations) by providing for the choice of a more favorable jurisdiction's laws.

The above section's choice-of-law provision is clearly enforceable. The validity of the Mortgage and its construction, and the capacity of the parties to the Mortgage and their rights under it, are all governed by the laws of the forum state, even when the mortgage is executed in another state and the parties reside in another state. *See, e.g.*, Connor v. Elliot, 79 Fla. 524, 85 So. 164 (1920); Guardian Life Ins. Co. of Am. v. Rita Realty Co., 5 A.2d 45 (N.J. Super. Ct. 1939).

Selecting the law of the forum state to govern the transaction usually makes sense and will be enforceable. Sometimes, as with multistate loans, it may make sense to select the laws of another jurisdiction with respect to matters that do not directly affect title. If the provision at issue does not directly affect title matters, it is possible that a court will honor the choice of a different jurisdiction's laws if the provision does not contravene the fundamental policy of the forum state, and the chosen state bears at least a reasonable relationship to the parties and the transaction. *See, e.g.*, Hengel, Inc. v. Hot'N Now, Inc., 825 F. Supp. 1311 (N.D. Ill. 1993). In order to avoid potential usury issues, or certain issues which could impair the ability of Lender to choose between electing enforcement of foreclosure remedies and having to forgo the ability to enforce a payment guaranty (which sometimes occurs in certain jurisdictions where the Mortgaged Property is located), more favorable laws of a different State may sometimes be chosen in order to avoid these issues. Often in a transaction where the Loan is expected to be sold into a mortgaged backed securitization structure, there will be a strong preference by Lender and/or the rating agencies for the laws of Delaware or New York to be chosen. When a jurisdiction for the governing laws of one or more of the Loan Documents differs from the jurisdiction in which the Mortgaged Property is located, it would be prudent to have discussions with local counsel to be sure that such election will not interfere with the ability of Lender to enforce foreclosure remedies. Sometimes in the Mortgage the laws of a different jurisdiction than where the Mortgaged Property is located are selected with respect to all of the provisions of the Mortgage, except those relating to the enforcement of remedies (and with respect to enforcement of remedies, the Mortgage will specify that the laws of the State in which the Mortgaged Property is located will govern those provisions only).

If Borrower's counsel is not licensed to practice law in (i) any State whose laws are selected to govern any of the Loan Documents and/or (ii) the State(s) in which the Mortgaged Property is located, then Borrower's counsel should engage local counsel in those applicable States where Borrower's counsel is not licensed, with respect to the enforceability opinions which Lender will be requiring to close the Loan. Local counsel should be rendering all of those opinions which impact on the State in which such counsel is licensed to practice.

> 32.2 *Borrower agrees that any controversy arising under or in relation to the Note, this Mortgage, or any other Loan Document shall be litigated exclusively in the Property Jurisdiction. The state and federal courts and authorities with*

jurisdiction in the Property Jurisdiction shall have exclusive jurisdiction over all controversies which shall arise under or in relation to the Note, any security for the Indebtedness, or any other Loan Document. Borrower irrevocably consents to service, jurisdiction, and venue of such courts for any such litigation and waives any other venue to which it might be entitled by virtue of domicile, habitual residence or otherwise, and agrees that all litigation relating to the Loan shall be conducted in the state and federal courts which are located in the state which contains the Property Jurisdiction.

Explanation

The above Section 32.2 of the Mortgage provides for Borrower's consent to service of process, jurisdiction, and venue of the courts (state and federal) in the jurisdiction where the Mortgaged Property is located and the waiver of claims to the contrary based upon Borrower's domicile or residence elsewhere. As discussed above, the choice of the law and the courts of the forum state usually makes sense in the typical case, but may not make sense in a multistate mortgage loan. Although the laws of the respective forum states may govern certain matters, it may be best to litigate as many of the other issues as possible in a single jurisdiction. To increase the chances of this result, such Section 32.2 provides for consent to service of process, jurisdiction, and venue, including waiver of a claim to a different venue that may have connections to the loan transaction or the parties.

SECTION 33

Notice

Explanation

Effective monitoring of the loan requires effective communication between Borrower and Lender regarding the status of the Loan and in order to make various provisions of the Loan effective. Numerous provisions contained in the Loan Documents obligate the parties to provide written notice of information or events relevant to the status of the Loan. Below is a typical provision contained in a Mortgage which clarifies issues regarding both the form and timing of such written notices.

> 33.1 *All notices, demands and other communications ("**notice**") under or concerning this Mortgage shall be in writing. Each notice shall be addressed to the intended recipient at its address set forth in this Mortgage, and shall be deemed given on the earliest to occur of (1) the date when the notice is received by the addressee; (2) the first Business Day after the notice is delivered by a recognized overnight courier service, with arrangements made for payment of charges for next Business Day delivery; or (3) the third Business Day after the notice is deposited in the United States mail with postage prepaid, certified mail, return receipt requested.*

Explanation

Section 33.1 makes clear that any notice required under the Loan Documents must be in writing. This approach avoids the evidentiary and related problems associated with attempts by one party to provide notice orally (either in person or by telephone).

Where the obligation to provide notice arises, the provisions of the Mortgage generally refer only to "giving" notice or "delivering" notice; they do not specify that the intended recipient must actually receive the written notice. Section 33.1 provides that as long as the notice is directed to the recipient's address as specified in the Mortgage, any such notice is deemed given on the first Business Day after it is deposited for next-business-day delivery with a recognized overnight courier (such as Federal Express) or on the third business day after it is deposited into the United States mail (certified mail, return receipt requested). Under this provision, for example, suppose that Borrower fails to provide financial statements as required in the Mortgage (see Part IV Section 15 of this Book). Under the Event of Default provision of the mortgage form that has been used in this Book (see Part IV Section 24 of this Book), if Lender desires to declare a default for the failure of Borrower to deliver such financial statements, Lender has to give Borrower a written notice of such default, and then Borrower has 30 days from the giving of such notice to cure the failure before Lender can declare an Event of Default exists under the Mortgage. Under Section 33.1, if Lender deposits written notice of Borrower's failure to provide the financial statements into the U.S. mail on Monday, June 1, via postage-prepaid certified mail, return receipt requested, Lender will be deemed to have given notice on Thursday, June 4—thereby triggering Borrower's 30-day grace period— even if Borrower does not actually receive the notice.

SECTION 34

Sale of Note; Change in Service

Explanation

Most large commercial real estate mortgage loans on income-producing property are held by institutional lenders (e.g., life insurance companies and pension funds) or by trustees established to hold commercial real estate mortgages in connection with commercial real estate securitized mortgage pools. In both cases, the holder of the Loan usually engages one or more entities to perform the servicing, including collection and remittance of loan payments and maintenance of various reserve accounts. Below is a typical provision which contemplates that the Note may be sold, in whole or in part, and that the parties servicing the Loan may change, from time to time.

> 34.1 *The Note or a partial interest in the Note (together with this Mortgage and the other Loan Documents) may be sold one or more times without prior notice to Borrower. A sale may result in a change of the parties who service the loan (collectively the "**Loan Servicer**"). There also may be one or more changes of the Loan Servicer unrelated to a sale of the Note. If there is a change of the Loan Servicer, Borrower will be given notice of the change.*

Explanation

It is virtually always the case that when the Loan is sold into a mortgage backed securities' securitization, the trustee of the securitized pool will engage both (i) a "master servicer" who performs routine collections on behalf of the trustee with respect to acting as the agent of Lender relative to performing the day-to-day obligations of the Lender pursuant to the Loan Documents and (ii) a "special servicer" who takes over the servicing function (including foreclosure and negotiation of workout agreements) for any loans in the securitization pool that enter default status, or encounter a major situation like a loan restructuring, or a request by Borrower to sell the Mortgaged Property to a third-party subject to the Mortgage.

Borrower, who may have established some relationship with the employees of the originating Lender, finds that once the Loan is sold into a securitization, Borrower no longer has the same working relationship with the ultimate master servicer and/or special servicer. Many borrowers have found that this is not necessarily a positive development. Often times dealing with the master servicer and/or special servicer can feel like dealing with a bureaucracy. These servicers are not really invested in finding creative ways to be helpful in encouraging Borrower, particularly when and if Borrower needs to take some steps which require Lender's consent. At a minimum, it is often a time-consuming process to obtain such consents from the master servicer and/or the special servicer, and in other times it can feel as though these servicers will arbitrarily reject a Borrower's request for a needed consent. When and if a Loan goes into default, it often can be quite difficult to get the attention of the special servicer, and frequently the special servicer is not inclined to permit needed modifications to the Loan Documents to adjust to new circumstances which might otherwise permit the Mortgaged Property to perform better. Sometimes these difficulties arise because the Loan Servicers are subject to very complex and lengthy servicing agreements which create restrictions on their authority. Frequently, as a result of the securitization, the trustee has issued multiple tranches of debt to investors which is secured by the loans in the securitization pool. Often times the servicing agreement sets out standards of care with regard to the Loan Servicers which makes it confusing as to what they can and cannot do, particularly when one course of action might favor a certain tranche of securitization investors, but might be to the detriment of other securitization investors. Frequently, the easiest course for the Loan Servicers is not to take any action, and by doing so the special servicers will continue to collect a fee, even though nothing much is accomplished. By taking an action, the special servicers may expose themselves to litigation brought by Borrower, any of the investors in any of the multiple tranches of securitization that was issued by the trustee, or by other lenders who might be holding subordinated notes or participation interests or even mezzanine loans which are secured by pledges of equity interests in Borrower.

The above section in the Mortgage simply warns Borrower that a secondary-market transfer of the Loan may occur in the future, and that (with or without a secondary-market transfer) in the future there may be a change in the entities who provide servicing functions on behalf of Lender. There is no legal requirement that Borrower must be given a written notice that either of these events might happen, but it is quite common for these types of provisions to be included in the Loan Documents.

SECTION 35

Successors and Assigns Bound

Explanation

It is beneficial for both Borrower and Lender to have a provision in the Mortgage which clarifies that if either transfers their interests as they relate to the Mortgaged Property, their successors will be bound by the terms of the Mortgage. The following is a typical provision which provides this clarification:

> 35.1 *This Mortgage shall bind, and the rights granted by this Mortgage shall inure to, the respective successors and assigns of Lender and Borrower. However, a Transfer made by Borrower which is not permitted by Section 22 of this Mortgage shall be an Event of Default.*

Explanation

In the case where Lender assigns its interests in the Loan Documents to an assignee, under this provision, such assignee obtains all of the rights and benefits of Lender under the Loan Documents, and among other things becomes entitled to enforce Borrower's obligations thereunder. That is the essential purpose of the assignment of the Loan.

On Borrower's side, however, transfer of the Mortgaged Property raises a fascinating (and again, largely untested) question. Clearly, if the transferee of the real estate enters into an assumption agreement, Lender can enforce that agreement as a third-party beneficiary. *See* RESTATEMENT (THIRD) OF PROPERTY: MORTGAGES § 5.1(b)(3) and cmt. d (1997). However, suppose there is no assumption agreement. Is it possible for Lender to argue that the purchaser of the real estate nonetheless becomes automatically and personally liable on the covenants in the note and mortgage, on the ground that the covenants "run with the land"? The answer with respect to the covenant to pay the debt itself is clearly negative; it is well established that a non-assuming purchaser of the Mortgaged Property has no personal liability on the debt. *See* Schram v. Coyne, 127 F.2d 205 (6th Cir. 1942); RESTATEMENT (THIRD) OF PROPERTY: MORTGAGES § 5.2(d) and cmt. b (1997).

SECTION 36

Joint and Several Liability

Explanation

Many times there is more than one Borrower receiving the proceeds of the Loan. In such circumstances, Lender will typically want each Borrower to be fully liable for Borrower's obligations under the Loan Documents. Below is a typical Mortgage provision that deals with this:

> 36.1 *If more than one person or entity signs this Mortgage as Borrower, the obligations of such persons and entities shall be joint and several.*

Explanation

By making each Borrower jointly and severally liable for the obligations of Borrower under the Mortgage, this provision permits Lender to be able to sue each and/or all of the co-borrowers for the full Indebtedness. Hence, one co-borrower cannot prevent a suit for the full loan balance on the basis that the Lender must at the same time sue and attempt to recover from the other co-borrower. *See, e.g.*, Estate of Isaacson v. Hertz, 225 N.E.2d 106 (Ill. App. Ct. 1967). However, because liability is also "joint," if Lender has in fact recovered more than one-half of the total debt from one of the co-borrowers, that co-borrower can sue the other co-borrower for contribution of any amounts paid in excess of its share. *See, e.g.*, Shuttleworth v. Abramo, 1993 WL 104552 (Del. Ch. 1993); Estate of Leinbach v. Leinbach, 486 N.E.2d 2 (Ind. Ct. App. 1985).

The joint and several nature of the loan furthers the Lender's goal to recover the entire Indebtedness following an Event of Default as quickly and cheaply as possible. The provision also generally conforms to the co-borrowers' expectation that ultimately they will be responsible only for their share of the liability for the Loan. However, to the extent that the Mortgaged Property is inadequate to pay the debt and one of the co-borrowers has inadequate assets to pay its share of the debt, then it is the co-borrower who will absorb this loss (and the cost of suing other co-borrowers) rather than Lender.

SECTION 37

No Third-Party Beneficiary

Explanation

It is not uncommon for commercial real estate loans to be sold into a securitization where such loans are owned directly by the securitization's trustee, or are collateral for rated debt issued by the securitization trustee. As part of that structure, the trustee (who becomes Lender when purchasing such real estate loans) enters into servicing arrangements with one or more servicers. (See the provisions relating to master and special servicers set out in Part IV Section 34 of this Book.) Below is a Mortgage provision that has been utilized by Fannie Mae. This provision clarifies that third parties cannot look to Lender as a fiduciary for Borrower; and this provision also clarifies that any Loan Servicer engaged by Lender cannot claim any third-party beneficiary rights to receive benefits arising under the Servicing Agreement between Lender and the Loan Servicer.

37.1 *No creditor of any party to this Mortgage and no other person shall be a third-party beneficiary of this Mortgage or any other Loan Document. Without limiting the generality of the preceding sentence, (1) any arrangement (a "**Servicing Arrangement**") between the Lender and any Loan Servicer for loss sharing or interim advancement of funds shall constitute a contractual obligation of such Loan Servicer that is independent of the obligation of Borrower for the payment of the Indebtedness, (2) Borrower shall not be a third-party beneficiary of any Servicing Arrangement, and (3) no payment by the Loan Servicer under any Servicing Arrangement will reduce the amount of the Indebtedness.*

Explanation

Fannie Mae operates a Delegated Underwriting and Servicing (DUS) program under which some lenders have authority to underwrite and fund mortgage loans meeting certain guidelines, with the assurance that Fannie Mae will purchase the loans on the secondary market. Lenders who use this program can provide faster loan processing and avoid detailed scrutiny by Fannie Mae during the loan origination process. In return, however, these lenders must enter into a "loss sharing" agreement with Fannie Mae, under which the lenders will pay to Fannie Mae a portion of any shortfall in debt service payments made by their borrowers. The lender also services the loans under this arrangement.

In *Dacon Bolingbrook Associates Ltd. Partnership v. Federal National Mortgage Association*, 155 B.R. 467 (N.D. Ill. 1993), the lender entered into a DUS agreement with Fannie Mae. When the borrower defaulted in payments, the lender made up the deficiency as required by the agreement. Subsequently, when it became apparent that the borrower would not cure the default, Fannie Mae and the lender entered into a settlement agreement that refunded part of the payments the lender had made under the DUS agreement and terminated any further liability of the lender.

The borrower filed bankruptcy, and Fannie Mae was its only secured creditor. In addition to the unpaid principal, Fannie Mae asserted that it had a secured claim for accrued interest at a "default" rate, and that it was entitled to late fees. The borrower argued, by way of defense, that there had been no default because Fannie Mae had actually received all of the payments owed to it, even though it admitted that the lender had made the payments for a lengthy time period.

The court rejected the borrower's position. It pointed out that there was no agreement between the borrower and the lender—and no duty owed by the lender to the borrower—that compelled the lender to make the payments to Fannie Mae. The lender's payments, it held, "in no way constituted payment on behalf of the debtor so as to cure any default." The provision of the Mortgage discussed at the beginning of this Section 37 is designed to confirm and strengthen the court's holding in the *Dacon Bolingbrook* case, by emphasizing that the lender's duty under such a DUS agreement does not benefit the borrower.

SECTION 38

Severability; Amendments

Explanation

It is important to Lender to make it clear that if any particular provision of the Mortgage should be found to be invalid, that such invalidity will not invalidate all of the provisions of the Mortgage so as to make it impossible for Lender to enforce and foreclose the Mortgage. In addition, it is also important to Lender to clarify the manner in which the Mortgage can be amended. The following is a typical Mortgage provision which deals with these concerns:

> 38.1 *The invalidity or unenforceability of any provision of this Mortgage shall not affect the validity or enforceability of any other provision, and all other provisions shall remain in full force and effect. This Mortgage contains the entire agreement among the parties as to the rights granted and the obligations assumed in this Mortgage. This Mortgage may not be amended or modified except by a writing signed by the party against whom enforcement is sought.*

Explanation

The first sentence of the above Mortgage provision provides that in the event a portion of the Mortgage is found to be invalid, the remainder of the Mortgage will be enforced. This sentence, sometimes referred to as a "partial invalidity" clause, is important because it is possible that there are some unenforceable provisions among the hundreds of terms embodied in the Mortgage. One obvious example is the level of interest charged (including late charges and default interest) and the possibility that this might violate usury laws or constitute an unenforceable penalty.

The second sentence of the above Mortgage provision provides that the Mortgage reflects the complete agreement of the parties, and the third sentence states that no amendments to the Loan Documents will be effective unless they are in writing. The second sentence, to the extent relating to oral agreements made at or prior to the signing of the Loan Documents, is referred to as an "integration" clause. It is very helpful to clarify that the words contained in the Loan Documents constitute the entire agreement of the parties; doing so reduces the likelihood of fraud or misunderstanding as to the parameters of "the deal." Requiring that future modifications to the Loan be in writing serves the same function.

SECTION 39

Disclosure of Information

Explanation

The advent of widespread securitization of commercial mortgage loans has produced vast changes in borrowers' expectations of privacy and confidentiality. No longer can a borrower reasonably anticipate that the lender will keep secret the details of a loan transaction. The disclosure requirements of the securities laws dictate that, when a loan is placed in a securitized pool, prospective investors and those who represent them (REMIC trustees, servicers, and rating agencies) must receive complete access to all details of the transaction. Further, the borrower's performance under the loan (including delinquencies and any breaches of mortgage covenants) also becomes an open book.

Fannie Mae includes the following section in the Mortgage in order to warn Borrower of the required disclosure practices and to ward off any claim that such disclosures are violations of Borrower's privacy or confidentiality rights.

> 39.1 *Lender may furnish information regarding Borrower or the Mortgaged Property to third parties with an existing or prospective interest in the servicing, enforcement, evaluation, performance, purchase or securitization of the Indebtedness, including trustees, master servicers, special servicers, rating agencies, and organizations maintaining databases on the underwriting and performance of multifamily mortgage loans. Borrower irrevocably waives any and all rights it may have under applicable law to prohibit such disclosure, including any right of privacy.*

SECTION 40

Release

Explanation

If and when Borrower fully pays off the Indebtedness, it will want the Mortgage to provide for a procedure whereby Lender shall enter into needed documentation to release the Mortgage and other Loan Documents which are filed of record, and which will also require Lender to return the Note to Borrower. Below is a Mortgage provision which deals with this process:

> 40.1 *Upon payment of the Indebtedness, Lender shall enter into customary documentation so as to discharge and/or release of record this Mortgage, and any other Loan Documents previously filed on record; and shall release and deliver the Note to Borrower. Borrower shall pay Lender's reasonable costs incurred in releasing this Mortgage and Loan Documents previously filed of record.*

Explanation

The preceding Mortgage provision provides a procedure for the release of the Mortgage and other Loan Documents previously filed of record, and return of the Note, once the entire Indebtedness is satisfied. It is important to Borrower that the title records reflect that the Mortgage no longer encumbers the real estate; otherwise, it can be difficult for Borrower to obtain further financing on the property or to sell the Mortgaged Property in the future. It would be prudent for Borrower to require a discharge of the Mortgage in recordable form from Lender as a condition for making the final payment of the Indebtedness. Indeed, in the typical closing at a title company, the title company will not issue a clean title policy to the insured (a new owner or mortgage lender) unless the title company has received either such a recordable discharge from Lender or (if the Lender is a known institution) a payoff statement from Lender (a statement indicating what amount is owed and necessary to pay the loan off in full and the funds to satisfy any outstanding Indebtedness).

Unfortunately, sometimes this process does not work and, after closing and the payment in full of the Indebtedness, Lender fails to provide a recordable discharge of the Mortgage to the title company or Borrower. For this reason, many states have enacted statutes to require the issuance of a recordable discharge of the Mortgage or some other procedure to clear the satisfied Mortgage from the title records. *See, e.g.*, CAL. CIV. CODE § 2941 (statute (i) requires a release to be recorded within 30 days after satisfaction of debt and delivery of original note and mortgage to mortgagor upon mortgagor's written request, and (ii) contains a procedure by which a title company can record a release if the mortgagee fails to do so); 765 ILL. COMP. STAT. 905/4, 905/2 (requires mortgagee to execute a release upon receiving satisfaction of the lien and make a release available to mortgagor within one month).

Statutes also commonly provide for damages to the party who is harmed by the Lender's failure to comply with the requirements of the statute. *See, e.g.*, CAL. CIV. CODE § 2941 (violators of this statute are liable for all damages to persons affected by the violation and shall forfeit the sum of $500 to that person); UTAH CODE § 57-1-38 (3) (mortgagee or trustee who fails to release mortgage/deed of trust within 90 days after satisfaction is liable for greater of $1,000 or treble the actual damages suffered, plus attorneys' fees and court costs); 765 ILL. COMP. STAT. 905/4, 905/2 (mortgagee or trustee is liable for $200 plus reasonable attorneys' fees for violations of statute). Some courts have interpreted these statutes in a manner that is favorable to borrowers. For example, the court in *Hector, Inc. v. United Savings & Loan Association*, 741 P.2d 542, 547 (Utah 1987), interpreted the then-existing Utah statute to provide double damages (rather than simply damages) whether the borrower had initiated a lawsuit and obtained a judgment or not (the statute was ambiguous on this point). In addition, the court in *Hector* calculated damages based on a 10 percent rate of interest accruing on the value of the lots that the lender should have released for the period during which the lender failed to release the lots as required by the statute. *Id.* at 545. Although the court in *Hector* recognized a "good faith" defense for lenders, the court narrowly restricted this defense to the situation of a mistaken but honest belief that the secured debt has not been satisfied in full. *Id.*

Because the immediately preceding Mortgage Provision merely provides a basic procedure for the release of the Mortgage and return of the Note, there should not be any significant enforcement issues. It should be noted, however, that the issue of releasing the Mortgage once the Indebtedness is paid is typically governed by State statutes that may impose some limits on the costs Lender can recover for discharging the Mortgage.

In addition, there is a practical manner in which the problem of paid-off loans still appearing to encumber Mortgaged Property can be resolved. It is common for the title insurance company that paid the Lender based upon the payoff statement to provide a hold-harmless letter to the next title company that is asked to insure good title to the property. The title company will "use" the money it received to record the release to pay for the preparation of the hold-harmless letter.

SECTION 41

State-Specific Statutory Provisions

Explanation

Lenders and/or their counsel frequently use a form of Mortgage which contains language that is generally designed to apply to each Property Jurisdiction. However, since many States have Mortgage provisions which reflect matters that are customarily included in a Mortgage that is to be filed in that State's registry (either because these provisions are mandated by State law, or reflect what is the customary practice in such State), it is not uncommon for there to be one particular section of the Mortgage which is reserved to either modify prior sections of the Mortgage, or to include new provisions, which in each case will allow the Mortgage to have its provisions comply with what is either mandated by State law, or conform to what Lender's counsel believes to be customary practice for the Property Jurisdiction. The following is a typical Mortgage provision which would be the introduction to allowing Lender's counsel to include these State-specific provisions in the Mortgage [Note: Because this Book does not focus on any particular State, following the introductory language, we have not included any particular State-specific Mortgage provision language]:

> 41.1 *The following provisions are made applicable to this Mortgage: [specific state-by-state provisions that are necessary and/or customary in each State where the Mortgage is being recorded].*

Explanation

Typically each State has specific provisions relating to enforcement of remedies or other elements of the Mortgage, which need to be added in order for the Mortgage to comply with local law or conform with local practice.

SECTION 42

Waiver of Trial by Jury

Explanation

Typically a Mortgage will contain a provision which requires both Lender and Borrower to waive their right to a trial by jury. The following is a typical Mortgage provision relating to such waiver:

> 42.1 *Borrower and Lender each (a) covenants and agrees not to elect a trial by jury with respect to any issue arising out of this Mortgage or the relationship between the parties as Borrower and Lender that is triable of right by a jury and (b) waives any right to trial by jury with respect to such issue to the extent that any such right exists now or in the future. This waiver of right to trial by jury is separately given by each party, knowingly and voluntarily with the benefit of competent legal counsel.*

Explanation

Lenders desire this mutual waiver of the right to a jury trial because they fear that a jury will be more disposed to find in favor of "David" (i.e., Borrower) than "Goliath" (i.e., Lender) and to award larger verdicts to Borrower than a judge might award. This fear is based on certain infamous jury trial awards in the 1970s and 1980s. In addition, in some jurisdictions, when a party asserts the right to a jury trial, this can delay the case and lengthen the legal process. After Borrower defaults, Lender will want to exercise its remedies as quickly as possible to reduce deterioration to the Mortgaged Property and to mitigate its losses. Consequently, Loan Documents typically provide for a waiver of the right to a jury trial, similar to the one contained in the immediately preceding Mortgage provision.

Enforceability of jury trial waivers. Although the Seventh Amendment guarantees the right to a jury trial in civil cases, a contractual waiver of the right to a jury trial is effective if knowingly and voluntarily signed. *See, e.g., In re* Reggie Packing Co., 671 F. Supp. 571, 573 (N.D. Ill. 1987). In order to demonstrate that the waiver was "knowing" and "voluntary," the jury waiver provision should be so obvious that a person signing the document would readily notice it, and the provision must be explained to the party making the waiver. Heller Fin., Inc. v. Finch-Bayless Equip. Co., 1990 WL 103232, *1 (N.D. Ill.). Courts are divided as to which party bears the burden of proving whether an agreement to a waiver provision was knowing and voluntary. *See, e.g.,* Nat'l Equip. Rental, Ltd. v. Hendrix, 565 F.2d 255, 258 (2d Cir. 1977) (burden rests with party seeking to enforce waiver provision); *but see* K.M.C. Co., Inc. v. Irving Trust Co., 757 F.2d 752, 758 (6th Cir. 1985) (burden rests with party attempting to avoid enforcement of waiver provision).

Even though jury trial waivers are enforceable in theory, many courts, as one might expect, will indulge every reasonable presumption against such a waiver and place upon the lender a substantial burden in showing that the waiver was knowing, voluntary, and intentional. Aetna Ins. Co. v. Kennedy, 301 U.S. 389, 393 (1936). Connecticut courts, for example, look to the following factors in determining the validity of such waivers: (1) the conspicuousness of the waiver clause, including (a) its location relative to the signatures of the parties, (b) whether it was buried in the middle of a lengthy agreement, and (c) whether it was printed in a different typeface or font size than the remainder of the contract; (2) whether the party seeking to avoid enforcement was represented by counsel; (3) whether the same party had an opportunity to negotiate the terms of the agreement; and (4) whether the same party had been fraudulently induced into agreeing specifically to the jury trial waiver. *See, e.g.,* Happens, LLC v. Webster Bank, 1996 WL 589220, *2 (Conn. Super. Ct. 1996).

The immediately preceding Mortgage provision concerning the mutual waiver of trial by jury will be enforced if it can be shown that the waiver was intentionally, knowingly, and voluntarily made. The fact that the section is conspicuous (based on its location and font) and contains an acknowledgement by the parties that they consulted their own counsel with respect to the waiver increases the chances of its enforcement.

Form of Letter of Intent

____
____
____
____

__________, 20__

____
____
____
____

Re: ____________________ (the "**Project**")

Ladies and Gentlemen:

The undersigned is pleased to provide you with this letter of intent and to inform you that the undersigned may be interested in providing you or your affiliate ("**Borrower**") with a $__________ commercial real estate financing (the "**Loan**") for the captioned Project, which has as its address ______________. The undersigned currently contemplates that the Loan could have terms which are similar to those set out in the attached term sheet (the "Term Sheet"). Based on the information that you have provided to us to date, the undersigned, or an affiliate thereof (such entity, together with its assigns, agents, and successors, "**Lender**") hereby expresses its interest in proceeding to obtain additional information and to conduct such investigations regarding the business, operations, condition (financial or otherwise), and prospects of Borrower's parent, the Guarantor (as defined in the term sheet attached hereto as Exhibit A (the "**Term Sheet**")) and Borrower and to seek credit approvals for the Loan. This letter, together with the Term Sheet (collectively, this "**LOI**") does not purport to summarize all the terms, conditions, representations, warranties, and other provisions with respect to the transaction referred to herein and in the Term Sheet. Capitalized terms not otherwise defined herein have the meanings assigned thereto in the Term Sheet.

The terms which the undersigned proposes in this LOI are based upon our present understanding of the Project, Borrower, and the Guarantor. As additional or changed facts and circumstances become known to us, we may impose additional terms and conditions. The terms and conditions which shall ultimately be required with respect to Lender's closing the Loan are not limited to terms set forth herein and in the Term Sheet attached hereto. Those matters which are not covered by or made clear in this LOI are subject to mutual agreement by each of the parties hereto.

You understand that Lender has not completed its due diligence of Borrower, the Guarantor, and/or the Project, and that the conduct, performance, and satisfactory conclusion of such due diligence is a condition of and essential to any commitment on the part of Lender to enter into a transaction on the terms described herein. This LOI is provided for discussion purposes only, and is being provided solely to indicate the undersigned's current interest in the proposed transaction described herein. This LOI is neither an express nor implied commitment by the undersigned to lend or otherwise provide or arrange any financing in connection with the transactions contemplated herein or purchase any loans or securities in connection with the transactions contemplated hereby or to provide or assist in providing any loans. Any such commitment by the undersigned will be subject to, among other things, (i) satisfactory transaction structure and documentation, (ii) satisfactory completion of due diligence, including third-party reports and business plan, (iii) requisite Lender internal approvals, and (iv) other standard conditions for transactions of this type.

The parties acknowledge that it is their intention that the ultimate closing of the Loan will be conditioned upon Lender determining that the following conditions have been fully satisfied:

(a) Your making all payments required to be made prior to the closing of the Loan, as set forth in your Loan Application dated ____________ (the "**Loan Application**");

(b) The preparation, execution, and delivery of legal documentation (the "Loan Documentation"; and the loan documents comprising said documentation are herein collectively referred to as the "**Loan Documents**") in form and substance satisfactory to Lender and its counsel incorporating substantially the terms and conditions outlined or referred to in this LOI;

(c) The absence of any material adverse change in the financial condition, business, affairs, operations, or control of the special purpose entity which will serve Borrower and the Guarantor, or their respective principals since the date of their respective financial statements most recently delivered to Lender;

(d) The satisfaction of all conditions to be satisfied as a condition for the funding of the Loan as set forth in the Loan Documents;

(e) The absence of a disruption or adverse change in financial, banking, or capital markets generally, or in the market for new issuances of commercial real estate mortgage loans in particular, in each case that, in the judgment of Lender, could reasonably be expected to impair the syndication or sale of the Loan; and

(f) The absence of any material adverse change in any due diligence items relating to the Project, Borrower, and the Guarantor previously provided by you or any material adverse change in any new due diligence items hereafter reviewed by Lender or its counsel.

By your acceptance of this LOI, you agree to be responsible for all costs and expenses incurred by Lender including, but not limited to, legal fees and disbursements, environmental, engineering, and appraisal costs and other expenses incurred by Lender in connection with the processing of the Loan and your payment to Lender of the fees and other expenses which are required under the Loan Application.

You hereby represent and covenant (and it shall be a condition to our obligations under this commitment hereunder) that (a) all information (the "**Information**"), taken as a whole, either by or on behalf of you or any of your representatives is or will be, when furnished, complete and correct in all material respects and does not or will not, when furnished, contain any untrue statement of a material fact or omit to state a material fact necessary in order to make the statements contained therein not materially misleading in light of the circumstances under which such statements are made. You agree that if at any time prior to the closing of the Loan you become aware that any of the representations in the preceding sentence are incorrect, in any material respect, you will promptly supplement the Information so that such representations will be correct under those circumstances. You also acknowledge that in connection with determining whether or not to fund the Loan, we will be entitled to use and rely primarily on the Information without responsibility for independent verification thereof.

This LOI is not assignable by operation of law or otherwise without the prior written consent of Lender.

You agree (a) to indemnify and hold harmless Lender, and its affiliates and each of their respective officers, directors, employees, agents, advisors, controlling persons, members, and successors and assigns (each, an "**Indemnified Person**") from and against any and all losses, claims, damages, liabilities, and expenses, joint or several, to which any such Indemnified Person may become subject arising out of or in connection with this LOI, the Loan, or any related transaction or any claim, litigation, investigation, or proceeding relating to any of the foregoing, regardless of whether any such Indemnified Person is a party thereto (and regardless of whether such matter is initiated by a third party or by you or any of their respective affiliates), and to reimburse each such Indemnified Person upon demand for any reasonable legal or other expenses incurred in connection with investigating or defending any of the foregoing, provided that the foregoing indemnity will not, as to any Indemnified Person, apply to losses, claims, damages, liabilities, or related expenses to the extent they are found in a final, non-appealable judgment of a court of competent jurisdiction to have resulted from the willful misconduct or gross negligence of such Indemnified Person, and (b) to reimburse Lender, from time to time, upon presentation of a reasonably detailed statement, for all reasonable out-of-pocket expenses (including but not limited to expenses of Lender's due diligence investigation, consultants' fees, syndication expenses, travel expenses and fees, disbursements, and other charges of one firm of counsel for each of Lender, plus local counsel as required), in each case, incurred in connection with the Loan and the preparation, negotiation, and enforcement of this LOI, the definitive documentation for the Loan, and any ancillary documents or security arrangements in connection therewith. Notwithstanding any other provision of this LOI, no Indemnified Person shall be liable for any indirect, special, punitive or consequential damages in connection with its activities related to the Loan.

You acknowledge that the undersigned, Lender, and/or their respective affiliates may be providing debt financing, equity capital, or other services (including financial advisory services) to other companies in respect of which you may have conflicting interests regarding the transactions described herein or otherwise. Neither the undersigned nor any of our affiliates will use confidential information obtained from you by virtue of the transactions contemplated by this LOI or our other relationships with you in connection with the performance by us of services for other companies, and we will not furnish any such information to other companies. You also acknowledge that neither the undersigned nor any of our affiliates has any obligation to use in connection with the transactions contemplated by this LOI, or to furnish to you, confidential information obtained by us from other companies.

You further acknowledge and agree that (a) no fiduciary relationship between you and either the undersigned or the Lender is intended to be or has been created in respect of any of the transactions contemplated by this LOI, irrespective of whether Lender has advised or is advising you on other matters, (b) the undersigned or Lender, on the one hand, and you, on the other hand, have an arms-length business relationship that does not directly or indirectly give rise to, nor do you rely on, any fiduciary duty on the part of Lender, (c) you are capable of evaluating and understanding, and you understand and accept, the terms, risks, and conditions of the transactions contemplated by this LOI, (d) you have been advised that Lender is engaged in a broad range of transactions that may involve interests that differ from your interests and that Lender has no obligation to disclose such interests and transactions to you by virtue of any fiduciary, advisory, or agency relationship, and (e) you waive, to the fullest extent permitted by law, any claims you may have against Lender for breach of fiduciary duty or alleged breach of fiduciary duty and agree that Lender shall have no liability (whether direct or indirect) to you in respect of such a fiduciary duty claim or to any person asserting a fiduciary duty claim on behalf of or in right of you, including your stockholders, employees, or creditors.

The undersigned hereby notifies you that pursuant to the requirements of the USA PATRIOT Act, Title III of Pub. L. No. 107-56 (signed into law October 26, 2001) (as the same may be extended and in effect from time to time, the "**PATRIOT Act**"), the undersigned and Lender are each required to obtain, verify, and record information that identifies Borrower, which information includes the name, address, tax identification number, and other information regarding Borrower that will allow the undersigned and Lender to identify Borrower in accordance with the PATRIOT Act. This notice is given in accordance with the requirements of the PATRIOT Act and is effective as to Lender.

Any brokerage commission or finder's fee payable in connection with the securing of this LOI or the Loan shall be paid by Borrower. By acceptance of this LOI, Borrower hereby indemnifies Lender and its affiliates against claims of any brokers or finders arising in connection with this LOI or the consummation of the Loan contemplated herein.

Lender reserves the right, prior to or after the closing of Loan, to syndicate, assign, participate, or otherwise transfer (collectively, a "**Syndication**") all or any portion of the Loan and/or its remaining commitments hereunder, if any, to one or more banks, financial institutions, or other institutional lenders (together with Lender, the "**Syndicated Lenders**"). It is understood that Lender may commence Syndication efforts promptly upon the execution of this LOI, and you agree actively to assist Lender in completing a Syndication satisfactory to Lender, in its reasonable judgment. Such assistance shall include (i) direct contact between your senior management, representatives, and advisors and the proposed Syndicated Lenders, and (ii) your assistance in the preparation of any confidential information memorandum or similar disclosure document which we might prepare in connection with the syndication and other marketing materials to be used in connection with the Syndication. To assist us in our Syndication efforts, you agree promptly to prepare and provide to us all information with respect to Borrower and the other transactions contemplated hereby, including all Information, as we may reasonably request. You agree, at the request of Lender, to assist in the preparation of a version of any confidential information memorandum and other marketing materials and presentations to be used in connection with the Syndication of the Loan, including information and documentation that are either (a) publicly available or (b) not material with respect to Borrower, or any of its respective securities for purposes of foreign, United States Federal, and state securities laws. Any information and documentation that is not generally available to the public ("**Public Information**") is referred to herein as "**Private Information**." You further agree that each document provided by you to Lender in connection with the facilities or indebtedness hereunder or any Syndication thereof will, at the request of Lender, be identified by you as either (i) containing Private Information or (ii) containing solely Public Information.

Except as set forth herein, this LOI supersedes all other prior dealings of Borrower and its agents with Lender and its affiliates in connection with the Loan. Prior receipt of any document shall not constitute approval of that document unless expressly stated otherwise within this LOI.

EACH OF THE PARTIES HERETO IRREVOCABLY WAIVES THE RIGHT TO TRIAL BY JURY IN ANY ACTION, PROCEEDING, CLAIM, OR COUNTERCLAIM BROUGHT BY OR ON BEHALF OF ANY PARTY RELATED TO OR ARISING OUT OF THIS LOI OR THE PERFORMANCE OF SERVICES HEREUNDER.

The terms of this LOI may not be waived, modified, or in any way changed by implication, correspondence, or otherwise, unless such waiver, modification, or change is made in the form of an amendment to this LOI in writing and agreed to by all parties. However, Lender may at its option agree in writing to waive any of the conditions to closing.

If for any reason the Loan contemplated hereby does not close by __________, time being of the essence, this LOI shall lapse and shall be of no further force or effect unless Lender determines (in its sole discretion) that the time for closing should be extended and Lender provides you a written notice of such extension. Notwithstanding any such termination of this LOI, you shall remain liable for your obligations with respect to payment of all costs and expenses (including applicable fees payable to Lender and Lender's legal fees and expenses) and your indemnity with respect to brokers' or finders' fees, as set forth in this LOI and the Loan Application.

Except for the agreements and obligations contained in the immediately preceding fourteen (14) paragraphs of this LOI, you and the undersigned each acknowledge and agree that neither party shall be legally bound to the other by reason of this LOI (including the provisions set forth in the Term Sheet) or the acceptance hereof, nor shall any rights, liabilities, or obligations, express or implied, be created hereby. The undersigned currently contemplates that the Loan could have terms which are similar to those set out in the attached term sheet (the "Term Sheet"). It shall be and remain in the sole discretion of either party whether to enter into the transactions contemplated by this LOI (including the provisions set forth in the Term Sheet), and not until the parties and the Guarantor have each authorized, executed, and delivered each of the documents included in the Loan Documentation to be executed by such part or the Guarantor, as the case may be, and any conditions precedent to the effectiveness of such document have been satisfied will there be any legally binding obligations of the parties hereto with respect to the transaction contemplated herein, other than agreements and obligations contained in the immediately preceding fourteen (14) paragraphs of this LOI (it being understood that the parties hereto do intend to be legally bound with respect to the agreements and obligations contained in the immediately preceding fourteen (14) paragraphs of this LOI). This LOI supersedes all prior discussions or agreements, written or oral, between the parties regarding the transactions contemplated by this LOI (including the provisions set forth in the Term Sheet).

This LOI shall become effective only upon your written acceptance hereof which must be returned to Lender, not later than ___________________, time being of the essence.

Very truly yours,

____

By: ______________________________
Name:
Title:

ACCEPTED AND AGREED TO AS AN
INSTRUMENT UNDER SEAL
THIS _______ DAY OF ____________.

____

By: ______________________________
Name:
Title:

EXHIBIT A

TERM SHEET

_______________ FINANCING

This Term Sheet is neither an expressed nor implied commitment by ______ or an affiliate of __________ (such entity, together with its assigns, agents, and successors, "**Lender**") or any of its affiliates to provide any financing, to provide or purchase any loans or securities in connection with the transactions contemplated hereby or to provide or assist in providing any loans, which commitment, if any, shall only be as set forth in a separate commitment letter or other applicable type of agreement. This Term Sheet does not purport to summarize all the terms, conditions, representations, warranties, and/or other provisions with respect to the transactions referred to herein.

Property/ Project	The mortgaged land is located at ___________ (the "**Property**"). Located on the Property is a _ _________sf __ story office building and associated parking and other structures, and improvements located thereon (the "**Project**").
Sponsor	____________________
Borrower	_________________ ("**Borrower**"). Borrower must be a single-purpose limited liability company engaged in the rental and operation of the Project, which entity shall be governed by an operating agreement that complies with Lender's standard requirements for single-purpose entities.
Loan Amount	The total loan amount will be determined at closing and will be an amount (the "**Loan Amount**") equal to the lesser of (i) $____________ and (ii) 70% loan-to-value of the Project based on an as-complete appraisal ordered by Lender.
Interest Rate	One Month LIBOR plus a spread of 500bps (calculated for the actual number of days elapsed on the basis of a 365-day year), payable monthly in arrears, provided that LIBOR shall never be calculated at less than 0.00%.
Interest Rate Hedge	Borrower will purchase an interest rate swap or a cap, at Borrower's cost, at a level acceptable to Lender with a notional amount equal to the Loan Amount.
Default Interest Rate	A rate of interest per annum (computed upon a 365-day year and actual number of days elapsed) equal to 18%, <u>provided</u>, that such interest rate shall in no event exceed the maximum interest rate which Borrower may pay by law.
Maturity Date	__ months from the Closing Date, with two (2) twelve-month extensions, subject to Lender's customary conditions relating to loan extensions.
Breakage Costs	The Loan may be prepaid in full, subject to Borrower also paying all "breakage costs" associated with Borrower making a prepayment of any portion of the Loan. Such "breakage costs" shall approximate the costs that are payable to any counterparty pursuant to the applicable interest rate swap or a cap or cap agreement as a result of such prepayment of principal by Borrower.

Security	A senior mortgage with a lien encumbering the Property and the Project, and also granting a lien on all of the Project's leases and rents, and such additional collateral as is customary for loans made by Lender for the type of loans that is similar to the Loan.
Covenants	Usual and customary affirmative and negative covenants to be included in the definitive documents for the transaction contemplated hereby.
Defaults	Usual and customary defaults to be included in the definitive documents for the transaction contemplated hereby.
Closing Date	Closing will occur on or before ________, 20__ ("**Closing Date**").
Guarantor(s)	__________________ and/or other individuals or entity(ies) required by Lender, who shall be satisfactory to Lender (collectively, "**Guarantor**").
Guaranties / Indemnities	The definitive documentation for the Loan will provide customary and appropriate provisions relating to indemnity and related matters in a form reasonably satisfactory to Lender. Without limiting the generality of the foregoing, each Guarantor will provide the following guaranties and indemnities: - Non-Recourse Carve Out Guaranty; - Environmental Indemnity; and - Carry Guaranty (including interest on the Loan, property taxes, insurance, and other carry costs associated with the Project).

Conditions Precedent to Closing the Loan:

(i) Payment of the Origination Fee provided for in the Loan Application;

(ii) Receipt and satisfactory review of environmental assessment, appraisal, and physical needs assessment;

(iii) Receipt and approval of current title reports, covenants, restrictions, encumbrances, title insurance policies and surveys for the Project;

(iv) Satisfactory review of evidence that the zoning applicable to the Property permits the construction, development and operation of the Project as contemplated hereunder;

(v) Satisfactory review of judgment, lien, litigation, UCC, bankruptcy and related searches of Borrower, any members and/or principals thereof and each Guarantor;

(vi) Satisfactory review of all organizational documents of Borrower, the constituent members thereof and each Guarantor;

(vii) Evidence that Borrower, the constituent members thereof and each Guarantor is in compliance with applicable governmental rules and regulations (e.g., PATRIOT Act);

(viii) Receipt and satisfactory review of liability, builder's risk and property insurance for Borrower and the Property;

(ix) Satisfactory review of any management agreement, and the subordination of same to Lender;

(x) Receipt and satisfactory review of all governmental approvals, including, but not limited to, the certificate of occupancy for the Project;

(xi) Receipt and satisfactory review of any and all regulatory or other agreements pertaining to the Project with any governmental or quasi-governmental agency, including review and approval of deed restrictions or any ground leases;

(xii) Receipt and approval by Lender of financial information pertaining to each Guarantor, which may include, but not be limited to, financial statements and state and federal income tax returns (if applicable) and financing documents;

(xiii) Receipt and satisfactory review of executed leases with current tenants in the Project;

(xiv) Receipt and approval at least 10 business days prior to the Closing Date of all information required from Borrower and each Guarantor under "know-your-customer" and anti-money laundering rules and regulations, including the PATRIOT Act;

(xv) Satisfaction of any additional Property-related due diligence or documents required by Lender;

(xvi) Receipt of approval of the Loan from all applicable committees of Lender; and

(xvii) Lender satisfaction with due diligence review of the Sponsor, Borrower and the Project, including any third-party reports, business plan and budget.

Form of Note

NOTE

$________________________

________________, 20____

FOR VALUE RECEIVED, the undersigned, ______________, LLC ("**Borrower**") jointly and severally (if more than one) promises to pay to the order of ______________________________ ______________________________, a ______________________________, the principal sum of ______________________ Dollars ($______________________) (the "**Loan**"), with interest as it accrues on the unpaid principal balance of this Note (said Note, as the same may be amended, supplemented, extended, restated, or otherwise modified, from time to time; collectively, the "**Note**") at the Interest Rate.

1. **Defined Terms**. As used in this Note, (a) the term "**Lender**" means the holder of this Note, from time to time; (b) the term "**Indebtedness**" means the principal of, interest on, and all other amounts due and payable to Lender at any time, under this Note, the Security Instrument, or any other Loan Document, and all other Obligations, including prepayment premiums, late charges, default interest, and advances as provided in Section 6 of the Security Instrument to protect the security of the Security Instrument; and (c) the term "**Security Instrument**" has the meaning set forth in Section 4 of this Note. The definition of any capitalized term or word used herein can be found in this Note and, if not found in this Note, then found in the Security Instrument.
2. **Address for Payment**. All payments due under this Note shall be payable in immediately available funds at ____ ________________, or such other place as may be designated by written notice to Borrower from or on behalf of Lender.
3. **Payment of Principal and Interest**. Principal and interest shall be paid as follows:
   (a) Interest at the rate (the "**Interest Rate**") of either (i) Variable Rate or (ii) LIBOR Based Rate on the outstanding principal balance which is evidenced by this Note from time to time, as selected by Borrower pursuant to Section 6.1 (a) of the Security Instrument. Any remaining principal and interest which has not been paid by Borrower to Lender shall be due and payable on _________, 20__ or on any earlier date on which the entire unpaid principal balance evidenced by this Note becomes due and payable, by acceleration or otherwise (the "**Maturity Date**").
   (b) Solely for the purpose of calculating interest due, any regularly scheduled monthly installment of principal and interest that is received by Lender before the date it is due shall be deemed to have been received on the due date for that installment.
   (c) Interest charged on the outstanding principal balance which is evidenced by this Note from time to time shall be calculated based on a 360-day year and charged for the actual number of days elapsed.

(d) Notwithstanding any provision to the contrary in this Note, in no event shall the Interest Rate charged on the outstanding principal balance which is evidenced by this Note from time to time exceed the maximum rate of interest permitted under applicable state and/or federal usury law. Any payment of interest that would be deemed unlawful under applicable law for any reason shall be deemed received on account of, and will automatically be applied to reduce, the principal sum outstanding and any other sums (other than interest) due and payable to Lender under this Note, and the provisions hereof shall be deemed amended to provide for the highest rate of interest permitted under applicable law.

(e) Borrower agrees to pay said principal, and all accrued and unpaid interest thereon, as follows:

i. Beginning on _______________, and continuing on the 1st day of each succeeding month thereafter until the Maturity Date, Borrower shall pay all accrued interest.

ii. Beginning on ____________ [the 1st day of the month succeeding the date of this Note], and continuing on the 1st day of each succeeding month thereafter until the Maturity Date, Borrower shall make monthly payments of principal sufficient to amortize the outstanding principal balance over ____________ (__) years. A payment schedule for the payment of principal is attached to this Note.

iii. Interest not paid when due shall bear interest at 16% per annum (the "**Default Rate**).

4. **Security**. The Indebtedness is secured by, among other things, a Mortgage, Security Agreement, Assignment of Leases and Rents and Fixture Filing of even date (said mortgage, as the same may be amended, supplemented, extended, restated or otherwise modified, from time to time, collectively, the "**Security Instrument**"), and reference is made to the Security Instrument for other rights of Lender as to collateral for the Indebtedness.
5. **Application of Payments**. If at any time Lender receives, from Borrower or otherwise, any amount applicable to the Indebtedness that is less than all amounts due and payable at such time, Lender shall apply that payment to amounts then due and payable in the manner and in the order set forth in Section 6.2(d) of the Security Instrument. Neither Lender's acceptance of an amount that is less than all amounts then due and payable nor Lender's application of such payment in the manner authorized shall constitute or be deemed to constitute either a waiver of the unpaid amounts or an accord and satisfaction. Notwithstanding the application of any such amount to the Indebtedness, Borrower's obligations under this Note shall remain unchanged.
6. **Acceleration**. If any Event of Default occurs pursuant to Section 24 of the Security Instrument and the Indebtedness is accelerated as set forth in the Security Instrument, the entire unpaid principal balance, any accrued interest, and all other Indebtedness and amounts payable to Lender under this Note and any other Loan Document shall at once become due and payable. Lender may exercise this option to accelerate the Indebtedness regardless of any prior forbearance. Upon Lender's exercise of any right of acceleration under this Note, Borrower shall pay to Lender, in addition to the entire unpaid principal balance then evidenced by this Note outstanding at the time of the acceleration, all accrued interest and all other sums due Lender under the Loan Documents.
7. **Late Charge**. If any monthly amount payable under this Note or under the Security Instrument or any other Loan Document is not received by Lender within ten (10) days after the amount is due, Borrower shall pay to Lender, immediately and without demand by Lender, a late charge equal to ____ percent of the unpaid principal and interest due in such month. Borrower acknowledges that its failure to make timely payments will cause Lender to incur additional expenses in servicing and processing

the Loan, and that it is extremely difficult and impractical to determine those additional expenses. Borrower agrees that the late charge payable pursuant to this Section represents a fair and reasonable estimate, taking into account all circumstances existing on the date of this Note, of the additional expenses Lender will incur by reason of such late monthly payment.

8. **Exculpation**. Lender shall not be entitled to and shall not enforce the liability and obligation of Borrower to perform and observe the obligations contained in this Note, the Security Instrument, or in any of the other Loan Documents by any action or proceeding wherein a money judgment or personal liability shall be sought against Borrower or any members, beneficiaries, trustees, the economic and beneficial owner of Borrower or of any beneficial owners or trustees of Borrower or any managers, officers, shareholders, or directors thereof (collectively, the "**Released Parties**"), except that Lender may bring a foreclosure action, an action for specific performance, or any other appropriate action or proceeding in each case as set forth in the Security Instrument, to enable Lender to enforce and realize upon its interests under this Note, the Security Instrument, or the other Loan Documents or in the Mortgaged Property, or any other collateral given by Borrower pursuant to this Note and the other Loan Documents; provided, however, that, except as specifically provided herein, for purposes of enforcing Lender's rights under Section 28.1 of the Security Instrument, any judgment in any such action or proceeding shall be enforceable against Borrower only to the extent of Borrower's interest in the Mortgaged Property and/or in any other collateral given to Lender, and Lender, by accepting this Note, the Security Instrument, and the other Loan Documents, agrees that it shall not sue for, seek, or demand any deficiency judgment against Borrower or any of the Released Parties in any such action or proceeding under, or by reason of, or in connection with this Note, as specifically provided herein, for purposes of enforcing Lender's rights under Section 28.1 of the Security Instrument or the other Loan Documents. The provisions of this Section 8 shall not, however, (i) constitute a waiver, release, or impairment of any obligation evidenced or secured by this Note, the Security Instrument, or any of the other Loan Documents; (ii) impair the right of Lender to name Borrower as a party defendant in any action or suit for foreclosure and sale under the Security Instrument; (iii) affect the validity or enforceability of any guaranty made in connection with the Indebtedness or guaranty of liability for the acts specified below or any of the rights and remedies of the Lender thereunder; (iv) impair the right of Lender to obtain the appointment of a receiver; (v) impair the enforcement of the Assignment of Leases and Rents executed in connection herewith; or (vi) constitute a waiver of the right of Lender to enforce the liability and obligation of Borrower, by money judgment or otherwise, to the extent of any loss, damage excluding consequential exemplary and punitive damages, cost, expense, liability, claim, or other obligation incurred by Lender (including, without limitation, attorneys' fees and costs reasonably incurred) arising out of or in connection with the excluded matters specifically set forth in Section 28.1 of the Security Instrument. Should it become necessary to collect this Note through an attorney, all parties hereto, whether maker, endorser, surety, or guarantor, each severally agree to pay all costs of collecting this Note, including a reasonable attorney's fee, whether at trial, at any appellate level, or in any bankruptcy proceeding, whether collected by suit or otherwise. As used herein, *attorney's fees* shall include a separate award for paralegal or legal assistants' fees.

9. **Voluntary and Involuntary Prepayments**. This Note may be voluntarily prepaid in whole or in part by Borrower in accordance with the applicable provisions set forth in the Security Instrument.

10. **Costs and Expenses**. Borrower shall pay all expenses and costs, including reasonable fees and out-of-pocket expenses of attorneys and expert witnesses and costs of

investigation and litigation (including appellate), incurred by Lender as a result of any default under this Note or in connection with efforts to collect any amount due under this Note, or to enforce the provisions of any of the other Loan Documents, including those incurred in post-judgment collection efforts and in any bankruptcy proceeding (including any action for relief from the automatic stay of any bankruptcy proceeding) or judicial or non-judicial foreclosure proceeding.

11. **Forbearance**. Any forbearance by Lender in exercising any right or remedy under this Note, the Security Instrument, or any other Loan Document, or otherwise afforded by applicable law, shall not be a waiver of or preclude the exercise of any other right or remedy. The acceptance by Lender of payment of all or any part of the Indebtedness after the due date of such payment, or in an amount that is less than the required payment, shall not be a waiver of Lender's right to require prompt payment when due of all other payments on account of the Indebtedness or to exercise any right or remedy for any failure to make prompt payment. Enforcement by Lender of any security for the Indebtedness shall not constitute an election by Lender of remedies so as to preclude the exercise of any other right or remedy available to Lender.
12. **Waivers**. Presentment, demand, notice of dishonor, protest, notice of acceleration, notice of intent to demand or accelerate payment or maturity, presentment for payment, notice of nonpayment, grace, and diligence in collecting the Indebtedness are waived by Borrower.
13. **Loan Charges**. If any applicable law limiting the amount of interest or other charges permitted to be collected from Borrower in connection with the Loan is interpreted so that any interest or other charge provided for in any Loan Document, whether considered separately or together with other charges provided for in any Loan Document, violates that law, and Borrower is entitled to the benefit of that law, that interest or charge is hereby reduced to the extent necessary to eliminate that violation. The amounts, if any, previously paid to Lender in excess of the permitted amounts shall be applied by Lender to reduce the Indebtedness. For the purpose of determining whether any applicable law limiting the amount of interest or other charges permitted to be collected from Borrower has been violated, all Indebtedness that constitutes interest, as well as all other charges made in connection with the Indebtedness that constitute interest, shall be deemed to be allocated and spread ratably over the stated term of the Note. Unless otherwise required by applicable law, such allocation and spreading shall be effected in such a manner that the rate of interest so computed is uniform throughout the stated term of this Note.
14. **Commercial Purpose**. Borrower represents that the Indebtedness is being incurred by Borrower solely for the purpose of carrying on a business or commercial enterprise, and not for personal, family, or household purposes.
15. **Counting of Days**. Except where otherwise specifically provided, any reference in this Note to a period of "days" means calendar days, not Business Days.
16. **Governing Law; Consent to Jurisdiction and Venue**.
    (a) This Note, the Security Instrument, and the other Loan Documents shall be governed by the laws of the jurisdiction in which the Land is located (the "**Property Jurisdiction**").
    (b) Borrower agrees that any controversy arising under or in relation to this Note or the Security Instrument shall be litigated exclusively in the Property Jurisdiction. The state courts in the Property Jurisdiction shall have exclusive jurisdiction over all controversies which shall arise under or in relation to this Note, any security for the Indebtedness, or the Security Instrument. Borrower irrevocably consents to service, jurisdiction, and venue of such courts for any such litigation and waives any other venue to which it might be entitled by virtue of domicile, habitual residence, or otherwise.

17. **Rules of Construction**. The captions and headings of the Sections of this Note are for convenience only and shall be disregarded in construing this Note. Any reference in this Note to a "Section" shall, unless otherwise explicitly provided, be construed as referring, respectively, to a Section of this Note. Use of the singular in this Note includes the plural and use of the plural includes the singular. As used in this Note, the term "including" means "including, but not limited to."

18. **Notices**. All notices, demands, and other communications required or permitted to be given by Lender to Borrower or Borrower to Lender pursuant to this Note shall be given in accordance with Section 34 of the Security Instrument.

19. **WAIVER OF TRIAL BY JURY. BORROWER AND LENDER EACH**
    (A) **AGREES NOT TO ELECT A TRIAL BY JURY WITH RESPECT TO ANY ISSUE ARISING OUT OF THIS NOTE OR THE RELATIONSHIP BETWEEN THE PARTIES AS LENDER AND BORROWER THAT IS TRIABLE OF RIGHT BY A JURY;**
    (B) **WAIVES ANY RIGHT TO TRIAL BY JURY WITH RESPECT TO SUCH ISSUE TO THE EXTENT THAT ANY SUCH RIGHT EXISTS NOW OR IN THE FUTURE. THIS WAIVER OF RIGHT TO TRIAL BY JURY IS SEPARATELY GIVEN BY EACH PARTY, KNOWINGLY AND VOLUNTARILY WITH THE BENEFIT OF COMPETENT LEGAL COUNSEL; AND**
    (C) **AGREES THAT THE SCOPE OF THIS WAIVER IS INTENDED TO BE ALL-ENCOMPASSING OF ANY AND ALL DISPUTES THAT MAY BE FILED IN ANY COURT AND THAT RELATE TO THE SUBJECT MATTER OF THIS TRANSACTION, INCLUDING WITHOUT LIMITATION CONTRACT CLAIMS, TORT CLAIMS, BREACH OF DUTY CLAIMS, AND ALL OTHER COMMON LAW AND STATUTORY CLAIMS.**

    BORROWER ACKNOWLEDGES THAT THIS WAIVER IS A MATERIAL INDUCEMENT TO LENDER TO LOAN MONEY TO BORROWER.

20. **Miscellaneous Provisions**.
    (a) Borrower and each endorser and guarantor hereof each authorizes Lender to complete this Note if delivered incomplete in any respect. A photographic or other reproduction of this Note may be made by Lender, and any such reproduction shall be admissible in evidence with the same effect as the original itself in any judicial or administrative proceeding, whether or not the original is in existence.
    (b) Borrower will from time to time execute and deliver to Lender such documents, and take or cause to be taken, all such other further action, as Lender may request in order to effect and confirm or vest more securely in Lender all rights contemplated by this Note or any other loan documents related thereto (including, without limitation, to correct clerical errors) or to vest more fully in or assure to Lender the security interest in any collateral securing this Note or to comply with applicable statute or law.

[The balance of this page is intentionally left blank]

IN WITNESS WHEREOF, Borrower has signed and delivered this Note or has caused this Note to be signed and delivered by its duly authorized representative as of the date first above written.

[**SIGNATURES**]
[**Borrower name**]
________________________________, a
____

By: ____________________________
[Name and capacity of signatory]

Form of Carve Out Guaranty

GUARANTY AGREEMENT

THIS GUARANTY AGREEMENT (said agreement, as the same may be amended, supplemented, extended, restated, or otherwise modified, from time to time, collectively, this "Agreement"), dated as of ___________, 20__, by _____________ [and ___________] ([collectively,] the "Guarantor"), having an address at _________________, in favor of _______________________, having its principal place of business at _______________________ (together with its successors and assigns, "Lender").

WITNESSETH:

WHEREAS, __________________, a _______________ [Delaware] limited liability company (said entity, together with any successor corporation, association, partnership (general or limited), limited liability company, joint venture, trust, or other individual or organization formed as a result of any merger, reorganization, sale, transfer, assignment, devise, gift, or bequest of or by Borrower are, collectively, "Borrower") has obtained a loan in the principal amount of ____________________ Dollars ($_______________) (the "Loan") from Lender; and

WHEREAS, the Loan is evidenced by a note dated as of the date hereof (said note, as the same may be amended, supplemented, extended, restated, or otherwise modified, from time to time, collectively, the "Note") executed by Borrower and payable to the order of Lender in the stated principal amount of the Loan; and is secured by, among other things, a Security Instrument (as defined in the Note) encumbering Borrower's fee ownership interest in that certain real property described on Exhibit A attached hereto and incorporated herein by this reference (the "Land"), together with Borrower's fee ownership interest in the buildings, structures, fixtures, additions, parking facilities, enlargements, extensions, modifications, repairs, replacements, and improvements now or hereafter located thereon (the "Improvements"), collectively with the Land, and together with Borrower's interest in any assets related to such Land and Improvements (said Land, Improvements, and other Borrower assets, collectively, the "Mortgaged Property"); and this Guaranty, the Note, the Security Instrument, and the other documents and instruments listed on Exhibit B, as the same may from time to time be amended, consolidated, renewed, or replaced, being collectively referred to herein as the "Loan Documents"; and

WHEREAS, as a condition to making the Loan to Borrower, Lender has required that Guarantor guarantee payment to Lender of certain obligations and liabilities more particularly set out in this Guaranty; and

WHEREAS, Guarantor has a material financial interest in Borrower and in the extension of the Loan to Borrower (which Loan will be of substantial benefit to Guarantor) and, therefore, Guarantor desires to induce Lender to advance the Loan by entering into this Guaranty;

NOW, THEREFORE, in consideration of the above recitals and other good and valuable consideration, the receipt and sufficiency of which is acknowledged, Guarantor hereby represents, covenants, and agrees as follows (any capitalized term or word used herein without a specified definition shall be deemed to have the applicable specified definition for that term which is set forth in the Security Instrument):

1. INDEMNITY AND GUARANTY.

1.1. Guarantor hereby guarantees payment to Lender of, hereby agrees to pay, protect, defend, and save Lender harmless from and against, and hereby indemnifies Lender from and against any and all liabilities, monetary obligations, losses, damages, costs, and expenses (including, without limitation, reasonable attorneys' fees and disbursements), causes of action, suits, claims, demands, and judgments of any nature or description whatsoever (collectively, "Costs") which may at any time be imposed upon, incurred by, or awarded against Lender as a result of any of the following (collectively, the "Recourse Obligations"):

1.1.1. the failure of Borrower to account for security deposits, if any, or any other similar payment in lieu of a security deposit collected from any tenant demising space in the Improvements, from time to time;

1.1.2. a material misrepresentation made by Guarantor, Borrower, and/or the holders of beneficial or ownership interests in Borrower, in each case to Lender in connection with the financing evidenced by the Note, or as otherwise set forth in this Guaranty, the Note, the Security Instrument, and/or the other Loan Documents;

1.1.3. any attempt by Borrower to divert, misappropriate, or misapply, or otherwise cause to be diverted, misappropriated, or intentionally misapplied, any amounts payable by Borrower to Lender or which are to be paid by Borrower to Lender as set forth in any of the Loan Documents and are intended for the benefit of Lender;

1.1.4. the misappropriation or misapplication of insurance proceeds or condemnation awards payable to or obtained by Borrower relating to the Mortgaged Property or Borrower's failure to maintain the insurance policies or the insurance coverages required by the Security Instrument at all times in full force and effect;

1.1.5. any environmental matter(s) affecting the Mortgaged Property which is introduced or caused by Borrower or any beneficial owner of Borrower, or which is otherwise covered by the Environmental Indemnity (as defined in Exhibit B);

1.1.6. any waste of, or damage to, the Mortgaged Property caused by the willful misconduct or wanton acts or omissions of Borrower or its agents, officers, Affiliates, directors, equity owners, or employees;

1.1.7. any willful or grossly negligent material violation by Borrower of any law, ordinance, rule, or regulation applicable to Borrower or the Mortgaged Property;

1.1.8. any failure of Borrower to obtain Lender's prior written consent to any subordinate financing or other voluntary lien caused by Borrower or its agents encumbering the Mortgaged Property as required by the Security Instrument;

1.1.9. any failure on the part of Borrower, or of any Person acting by, through, or under Borrower, to pay charges for labor or materials that results in material liens on any portion of any of Borrower's interest in the Mortgaged Property;

1.1.10. any misappropriation of funds by Borrower in connection with the funding of the loan proceeds evidenced by the Note or otherwise in connection with the Indebtedness (as defined in the Security Instrument);

1.1.11. so long as an Event of Default exists, the failure of Borrower to deliver 100% of all net income (i.e., for any applicable period of time, all revenues directly or indirectly derived from the Mortgaged Property, net of all accrued operating expenses relating to the Mortgaged Property) received by Borrower, in accordance with the terms of the Security Instrument and/or any of the other Loan Documents;

1.1.12. any failure of Borrower to comply with separateness and bankruptcy-remoteness covenants in this Security Instrument and/or in the other Loan Documents; and

1.1.13. any material fraud committed by Borrower.

1.2. Guarantor hereby guarantees payment to Lender of, and hereby agrees to pay, 100% of the Indebtedness owed to Lender, should any of the following occur, and should Lender elect to give written notice to Borrower that some or all of the Indebtedness shall then be due and payable (collectively, the "Indebtedness Obligations," and together with the Recourse Obligations, collectively, the "Guaranteed Obligations"):

1.2.1. any failure of Borrower to obtain Lender's prior written consent to any Transfer;

1.2.2. the adjudication of Borrower or Guarantor as bankrupt as a result of:

1.2.2.1. any direct or indirect, voluntary Insolvency Activity caused or approved by Borrower or Guarantor and/or the holders of beneficial or ownership interests in Borrower or Guarantor or actions taken by any officer, director, or Person employed by Borrower or Guarantor (each a "Restricted Entity"); and/or

1.2.2.2. any direct or indirect, involuntary Insolvency Activity caused or approved by any other Person, if either (x) such Person was acting at the direction or request of, or in collusion with or by agreement with a Restricted Entity, or (y) if such Person caused any such Insolvency Activity to occur at the direction or request of, or in collusion or by agreement with a Restricted Person.

1.2.3. any adjudication of Borrower or Guarantor as bankrupt as a result of any formal filing in a legal proceeding by a Person who is not a Restricted Person, if Borrower or Guarantor, as the case may be, fails to oppose in court such filing in good faith, or Borrower, Guarantor, or any Restricted Entity of either of them otherwise consents to, acquiesces in, agrees with, files court papers in any way supportive of, or joins in such filing.

1.3. The Guarantor's liability with regard to its obligations in Sections 1.1 and 1.2 shall terminate and be released upon the indefeasible payment of the Indebtedness owed by Borrower or Guarantor pursuant to any of the terms set forth in by the Loan Documents, and Lender agrees to promptly provide reasonable written confirmation of such release upon receipt of a written request from Borrower or Guarantor.

1.4. Notwithstanding anything contained in this Guaranty to the contrary, Guarantor shall not be deemed to be a guarantor of any swap document if such Guarantor is not an "Eligible Contract Participant" as defined in § 1(a)(18) of the Commodity Exchange Act and the applicable rules issued by the Commodity Futures Trading Commission and/or the Securities and Exchange Commission (collectively, and as now or hereafter in effect, "the ECP Rules") to the extent that the providing of such guaranty by such Guarantor would violate the ECP Rules or any other applicable law or regulation. This paragraph shall not affect any obligations of a Guarantor other than as it relates to such swap document, nor shall it affect the obligations of any Guarantor who qualifies as an Eligible Contract Participant.

1.5. This is an irrevocable, absolute, continuing guaranty of payment and performance and not of collection. The liability of Guarantor under this Guaranty shall be direct and immediate and not conditional or contingent upon the pursuit of any remedies against Borrower or any other Person (including, without limitation, other guarantors, if any), nor against the collateral for the Loan. This Guaranty may not be revoked by Guarantor and shall continue to be effective with respect to any Guaranteed Obligations arising or created after any attempted revocation by Guarantor. The fact that at any time or from time to time the Guaranteed Obligations may be increased or reduced shall not release or discharge the obligation of Guarantor to Lender with respect to the Guaranteed Obligations. Guarantor waives any right to require that an action be brought against Borrower or any other Person or to require that resort be had to any collateral for the Loan or to any balance of any deposit account or credit on the books of Lender in favor of Borrower or any other Person. In the event, on account of the Bankruptcy Reform Act of 1994, as amended, or any other debtor relief law (whether statutory, common law, case law, or otherwise) of any jurisdiction whatsoever, now or hereafter in effect, which may be or become applicable, Borrower shall be relieved of one or more of the Guaranteed Obligations, Guarantor shall nevertheless be fully liable therefor. In the event of a default under the Loan Documents which is not cured within any applicable grace or cure period, Lender shall have the right to enforce its rights, powers, and remedies (including, without limitation, foreclosure of all or any portion of the collateral for the Loan) thereunder or hereunder, in any order, and all rights, powers, and remedies available to Lender in such event shall be non-exclusive and cumulative of all other rights, powers, and remedies provided thereunder or hereunder or by law or in equity. If the indebtedness and obligations guaranteed hereby are partially paid or discharged by reason of the exercise of any of the remedies available to Lender, this Guaranty shall nevertheless remain in full force and effect, and Guarantor shall remain liable for all remaining Guaranteed Obligations guaranteed hereby, even though any rights which Guarantor may have against Borrower may be destroyed or diminished by the exercise of any such remedy.

1.6. Guarantor shall, promptly (but no in event later than five [5] Business Days) after demand by Lender, and without presentment, protest, notice of protest, notice of non-payment, notice of intention to accelerate the maturity, notice of acceleration of the maturity, or any other notice whatsoever, pay any applicable amount due on the Guaranteed Obligations to Lender at Lender's address as set forth in the Security Instrument or as otherwise instructed by Lender. Such demand(s) may be made at any time coincident with or after the time for payment of all or any part of the Guaranteed Obligations, and may be made from time to time with respect to the same or different Guaranteed Obligations. Such demand shall be deemed made, given, and received in accordance with the notice provisions hereof.

1.7. Lender shall not be required (and Guarantor hereby knowingly, freely, irrevocably, and unconditionally waives any rights that Guarantor may have to require Lender), in order to enforce the obligations of Guarantor hereunder, first (i) to institute suit or otherwise exhaust its remedies against Borrower or any other Persons liable on the Loan or the Guaranteed Obligations, or against any other Person, (ii) to enforce Lender's rights against any collateral given to secure the Loan, (iii) to enforce Lender's rights against any other guarantors of the Guaranteed Obligations, (iv) to join Borrower or any other Persons liable on the Guaranteed Obligations in any action seeking to enforce this Guaranty, (v) to exhaust any available remedies against any collateral given to secure the Loan, or (vi) to resort to any other means of obtaining payment of the Guaranteed Obligations.

Lender shall not be required to mitigate damages or to take any other action to reduce, collect, or enforce the Guaranteed Obligations.

2. INDEMNIFICATION PROCEDURES.

2.1. If any action shall be brought against Lender (or any holder of an interest in the Loan) based upon any of the matters for which Lender is guaranteed or indemnified hereunder, Lender shall notify Guarantor in writing thereof and Guarantor shall promptly assume the defense thereof, including, without limitation, the employment of counsel by Guarantor which is reasonably acceptable to Lender and the negotiation of any settlement; provided, however, that any failure of Lender to notify Guarantor of such matter shall not impair or reduce the obligations of Guarantor hereunder. In the event of any conflict of interest that may arise in such joint representation, Lender shall have the right, at Borrower's expense, to employ separate counsel in any such action and to participate in the defense thereof. In the event Guarantor shall fail to discharge or undertake to defend Lender against any claim, loss, or liability for which Lender is indemnified hereunder, Lender may, at its sole option and election, defend or settle such claim, loss, or liability. The liability of Guarantor to Lender hereunder shall be conclusively established by such settlement, provided such settlement is made in good faith, the amount of such liability to include both the settlement consideration and the costs and expenses, including, without limitation, reasonable attorneys' fees and disbursements, incurred by Lender in effecting such settlement. In such event, such settlement consideration, costs, and expenses shall be included in Costs and Guarantor shall pay the same as hereinafter provided. Lender's good faith in any such settlement shall be conclusively established if the settlement is made on the advice of independent legal counsel for Lender.

2.2. Guarantor shall not, without the prior written consent of Lender: (i) settle or compromise any action, suit, proceeding, or claim or consent to the entry of any judgment that does not include as an unconditional term thereof the delivery by the claimant or plaintiff to Lender of a full and complete written release of Lender (in form, scope, and substance satisfactory to Lender in its sole discretion) from all liability in respect of such action, suit, proceeding, or claim and a dismissal with prejudice of such action, suit, proceeding, or claim; or (ii) settle or compromise any action, suit, proceeding, or claim in any manner that may adversely affect Lender or obligate Lender to pay any sum or perform any obligation.

2.3. All Costs incurred or accrued by Lender shall be immediately reimbursable to Lender when and as incurred or accrued and, in the event of any litigation, claim, or other proceeding, without any requirement of waiting for the ultimate outcome of such litigation, claim, or other proceeding, Guarantor shall pay to Lender any and all Costs within five (5) Business Days after written notice from Lender itemizing and providing documentation to support the amounts thereof incurred to the date of such notice. In addition to any other remedy available for the failure of Guarantor to periodically pay such Costs, such Costs, if not paid within said thirty (30)-day period, shall bear interest at the Default Rate (as defined in the Note) if, and to the extent and from the date that, Lender has paid or caused the payment of such Costs.

3. REINSTATEMENT OF OBLIGATIONS. IF PURSUANT TO ANY INSOLVENCY ACTION CONCERNING BORROWER OR GUARANTOR OR ANY OF THEIR AFFILIATES, (I) LENDER MUST RESCIND, RESTORE, OR RETURN ANY PAYMENT OR ANY PART THEREOF RECEIVED BY LENDER IN SATISFACTION (IN FULL OR IN PART) OF THE GUARANTEED OBLIGATIONS, AS SET FORTH HEREIN, AND (II) LENDER MAKES ANY SUCH REQUIRED PAYMENT OR ANY

PART THEREOF, THEN LENDER SHALL PROVIDE GUARANTOR WITH WRITTEN NOTICE THAT IT HAS MADE SUCH PAYMENT AND THE AMOUNT OF SUCH PAYMENT. UNLESS GUARANTOR ELECTS TO REIMBURSE LENDER BY PAYING TO LENDER THE AMOUNT OF ANY SUCH REQUIRED PAYMENT WITHIN FIVE (5) BUSINESS DAYS FOLLOWING THE GIVING OF ANY SUCH WRITTEN NOTICE, THEN ANY PRIOR RELEASE OR DISCHARGE FROM THE TERMS OF THIS GUARANTY GIVEN TO GUARANTOR BY LENDER SHALL BE WITHOUT EFFECT, AND THIS GUARANTY SHALL REMAIN IN FULL FORCE AND EFFECT AND BE DEEMED REINSTATED, ALL AS THOUGH SUCH PREVIOUS PAYMENT BY GUARANTOR HAD NEVER BEEN MADE. GUARANTOR ACKNOWLEDGES THAT GUARANTOR'S OBLIGATIONS HEREUNDER SHALL NOT BE DISCHARGED EXCEPT BY GUARANTOR'S OR ANY OTHER PERSON'S PERFORMANCE OF THE SAME AND THEN ONLY TO THE EXTENT OF SUCH PERFORMANCE. IN ADDITION, IF AT ANY TIME ANY PAYMENT OF PRINCIPAL, INTEREST, OR ANY OTHER AMOUNT PAYABLE BY BORROWER UNDER ANY LOAN DOCUMENT IS RESCINDED OR MUST BE RESTORED OR RETURNED PURSUANT TO AN INSOLVENCY ACTION CONCERNING BORROWER OR OTHERWISE, GUARANTOR'S OBLIGATIONS HEREUNDER WITH RESPECT TO SUCH PAYMENT SHALL BE FULLY REINSTATED AS THOUGH ANY SUCH RETURNED PAYMENT HAD NOT BEEN PAID.

4. WAIVERS BY GUARANTOR. TO THE EXTENT PERMITTED BY LAW, GUARANTOR HEREBY WAIVES AND AGREES NOT TO ASSERT OR TAKE ADVANTAGE OF:
    - 4.1. Any right to require Lender to proceed against Borrower or any other Person or to proceed against or exhaust any security held by Lender at any time or to pursue any other remedy in Lender's power or under any other agreement before proceeding against Guarantor hereunder;
    - 4.2. Any defense that may arise by reason of the incapacity, lack of authority, death or disability of any other Person or Persons or the failure of Lender to file or enforce a claim against the estate (in administration, bankruptcy, or any other proceeding) of any other Person or Persons;
    - 4.3. The dissolution or termination of existence of Borrower or the voluntary or involuntary liquidation, sale, or other disposition of all or substantially all of the assets of Borrower;
    - 4.4. Demand, presentment for payment, notice of nonpayment, protest, notice of protest, and all other notices (other than as may be expressly herein required) of any kind, or the lack of any thereof, including, without limiting the generality of the foregoing, notice of the existence, creation, or incurring of any new or additional indebtedness or obligation or of any action or non-action on the part of Borrower, Lender, any endorser or creditor of Borrower or of Guarantor or on the part of any other Person whomsoever under this or any other instrument in connection with any obligation or evidence of indebtedness held by Lender;
    - 4.5. Any defense based upon (i) an election of remedies by Lender or (ii) or suretyship defenses and defenses in the nature thereof;
    - 4.6. Any right or claim or right to cause a marshalling of the assets of Guarantor;
    - 4.7. The voluntary or involuntary receivership, insolvency, bankruptcy, assignment for the benefit of creditors, reorganization, assignment, composition, or readjustment of, or any similar proceeding affecting, Borrower or Guarantor, or any of Borrower's or Guarantor's properties or assets;
    - 4.8. Any principle or provision of law, statutory or otherwise, which is or might be in conflict with the terms and provisions of this Guaranty;

4.9. The damage, destruction, condemnation, foreclosure, or surrender of all or any part of the Mortgaged Property;

4.10. Any transfer by either Borrower or Guarantor of all or any part of the collateral encumbered by one or more of the Loan Documents;

4.11. Any duty on the part of Lender to disclose to Guarantor any facts Lender may now or hereafter know about Borrower or the Mortgaged Property, regardless of whether Lender has reason to believe that any such facts materially increase the risk beyond that which Guarantor intends to assume or have reason to believe that such facts are unknown to Guarantor or have a reasonable opportunity to communicate such facts to Guarantor, it being understood and agreed that Guarantor is fully responsible for being and keeping informed of the financial condition of Borrower, of the condition of the Mortgaged Property and of any and all circumstances bearing on the risk that liability may be incurred by Guarantor hereunder;

4.12. Any lack of diligence by Lender in collection, protection, or realization upon any collateral securing the payment of the indebtedness or performance of obligations hereby guaranteed;

4.13. Any lack of notice of disposition or of manner of disposition of any collateral for the Loan;

4.14. Any invalidity, irregularity, or unenforceability, in whole or in part, of any one or more of the Loan Documents;

4.15. Any lack of commercial reasonableness in dealing with the collateral for the Loan;

4.16. Any deficiencies in the collateral for the Loan or any deficiency in the ability of Lender to collect or to obtain performance from any Persons now or hereafter liable for the payment and performance of any obligation hereby guaranteed;

4.17. An assertion or claim that the automatic stay provided by 11 U.S.C. §362 (arising upon the voluntary or involuntary bankruptcy proceeding of Borrower) or any other stay provided under any other debtor relief law (whether statutory, common law, case law, or otherwise) of any jurisdiction whatsoever, now or hereafter in effect, which may be or become applicable, shall operate or be interpreted to stay, interdict, condition, reduce, or inhibit the ability of Lender to enforce any of its rights, whether now or hereafter acquired, which Lender may have against Guarantor or the collateral for the Loan;

4.18. Any failure of Lender to perfect any security or to extend or renew the perfection of any security;

4.19. Any exculpation of liability contained in the other Loan Documents;

4.20. Any modifications of the Loan Documents or any obligation of Borrower relating to the Loan by operation of law or by action of any court, whether pursuant to the Bankruptcy Reform Act of 1994, as amended, or any other debtor relief law (whether statutory, common law, case law, or otherwise) of any jurisdiction whatsoever, now or hereafter in effect, or otherwise; and

4.21. Without limiting the generality of the foregoing or of any other waivers or provisions set forth in this Guaranty, and to the extent permitted under applicable Legal Requirements Guarantor hereby knowingly, freely, irrevocably, and unconditionally waives and relinquishes (a) any defense arising because of an election made by Lender under Federal Bankruptcy Code ("FBC") Section 1111(b)(2) or based upon any borrowing or grant of a security interest by Borrower under FBC Section 364, (b) the defense of statute of limitations in any action hereunder or in any action for the collection of any indebtedness or the performance of any of Borrower's obligations under the Loan Documents, and (c) any defense that may arise by reason of the incapacity, lack of authority, death, or disability of any other person or persons, or the failure of Lender to file or enforce a claim against the estate (in administration, bankruptcy, or any other proceeding) of any other person or persons other than Guarantor.

5. Warranties and Representations. Guarantor warrants and represents to Lender for the express purpose of inducing Lender to enter into the security instrument, to advance loan proceeds, to accept this guaranty, and to otherwise complete the transactions contemplated by the security instrument, as follows:
   5.1. Incorporation by Reference. Each warranty and representation made by Guarantor in any of the Loan Documents is true, accurate, and complete and is incorporated herein by reference.
   5.2. Financial Information. True and complete copies of the balance sheet of Guarantor have been delivered to Lender and each of the same are true, accurate, and complete in all material respects and fairly present Guarantor's financial condition as of the dates thereof and no material and adverse change has occurred in Guarantor's financial condition or business since the respective dates thereof; and each balance sheet of Guarantor submitted in the future shall be true, accurate, and complete in all material respects and shall fairly present Guarantor's financial condition as of the dates thereof;
   5.3. No Violation. The payment and performance by Guarantor of Guarantor's obligations under the Security Instrument, this Guaranty, and the Environmental Indemnity do not and shall not constitute a violation of any law, order, regulation, contract, or agreement to which Guarantor is a party or by which Guarantor or Guarantor's property may be bound which might have consequences reasonably likely to materially and adversely affect the condition (financial or otherwise) or business of Guarantor or might have consequences reasonably likely to materially or adversely affect its performance hereunder;
   5.4. No Litigation. There is no material litigation now pending or, to the best of Guarantor's knowledge threatened in writing, against Guarantor which, if adversely decided could reasonably be expected to materially impair the ability of Guarantor to pay and perform Guarantor's obligations under this Guaranty or any of the other applicable Loan Documents. There is no litigation (whether or not material) pending, or threatened in writing, against Guarantor in which the amount in controversy exceeds $25,000.00 which is not either: (i) covered by adequate insurance, or (ii) previously disclosed in writing to Lender together with a written explanation of why such litigation is not material.
   5.5. Entity Matters. Guarantor is a duly organized, validly existing limited liability company organized and in good standing under the laws of ___________ [Delaware], has all requisite power and authority to conduct its business and to own its property as now conducted or owned, and is qualified to do business in all jurisdictions where the nature and extent of its business is such that such qualification is required by law.
   5.6. Valid and Binding. Each of the Loan Documents to which Guarantor is a party constitutes such Guarantor's legal, valid, and binding obligation in accordance with the respective terms thereof, subject to bankruptcy, insolvency, and similar laws of general application affecting the rights and remedies of creditors and with respect to the availability of remedies of specific enforcement subject to the discretion of the court before which proceedings therefor may be brought.
   5.7. Solvency. Guarantor is solvent and is not rendered insolvent by the obligations undertaken in this Guaranty. No Guarantor is contemplating either the filing of a petition or proceeding under any state or federal bankruptcy or insolvency or reorganization laws or the liquidating of all or a major portion of such Guarantor's

property, and no Guarantor has any knowledge of any such petition or proceeding being filed against such Guarantor.

5.8. Material Economic Benefit. The granting of the Loan to Borrower will constitute a direct material economic benefit to Guarantor.

5.9. No Lender Coercion. Neither Lender nor any other party has made any representation, warranty, or statement to Guarantor in order to induce the Guarantor to execute this Guaranty.

6. GENERAL PROVISIONS.

6.1. Fully Recourse. All of the terms and provisions of this Guaranty are recourse obligations of Guarantor and not restricted by any limitation on personal liability.

6.2. Rights and Remedies of Lender. Upon the occurrence of an Event of Default, Lender shall have the right to enforce its rights, powers, and remedies under the Loan Documents or hereunder or under any other agreement, document, or instrument now or hereafter evidencing, securing, or otherwise relating to the indebtedness evidenced by the Note or secured by the Loan Documents, in any order, and all rights, powers, and remedies available to Lender in such event shall be nonexclusive and cumulative of all other rights, powers, and remedies provided thereunder or hereunder or by law or in equity. Accordingly, Guarantor hereby authorizes and empowers Lender upon the occurrence of an Event of Default, at its sole discretion, to exercise any right or remedy which Lender may have, including, but not limited to, judicial foreclosure, exercise of rights of power of sale, acceptance of a deed or assignment in lieu of foreclosure, appointment of a receiver to collect rents and profits, exercise of remedies against personal property, or enforcement of any assignment of leases, as to any security, whether real, personal, or intangible (provided that Lender shall not set off or exercise prejudgment remedies as to any personal accounts of Guarantor without affording Guarantor five (5) Business Days prior notice). At any public or private sale of any security or collateral for any indebtedness or any part thereof guaranteed hereby, whether by foreclosure or otherwise, Lender may, in its discretion, purchase all or any part of such security or collateral so sold or offered for sale for its own account and may apply against the amount bid therefor all or any part of the balance due it pursuant to the terms of the Note, the Mortgage, or any other Loan Document without prejudice to Lender's remedies hereunder against Guarantor for deficiencies. If the Indebtedness guaranteed hereby is partially paid by reason of the election of Lender to pursue any of the remedies available to Lender, or if such indebtedness is otherwise partially paid, this Guaranty shall nevertheless remain in full force and effect, and Guarantor shall remain liable for the entire balance of the indebtedness guaranteed hereby even though any rights which Guarantor may have against Borrower may be destroyed or diminished by the exercise of any such remedy.

6.3. Survival. This Guaranty shall be deemed to be continuing in nature and shall remain in full force and effect and shall survive the exercise of any remedy by Lender under the Security Instrument or any of the other Loan Documents, including, without limitation, any foreclosure or deed in lieu thereof, even if, as a part of such remedy, the Loan is paid or satisfied in full; provided, however, that Lender shall not be entitled to recover against Guarantor under this Guaranty for an amount in excess of the amount of the Costs.

6.4. No Subrogation; No Recourse Against Lender. Notwithstanding the satisfaction by Guarantor of any liability hereunder, Guarantor shall not have any right of subrogation, contribution, reimbursement, or indemnity whatsoever or any right of recourse to or with respect to the assets or property of Borrower or to any collateral for the Loan unless and until Guarantor fully satisfies the payment of the Loan, all other amounts due under the Loan Documents, and the Costs. In connection with the foregoing, Guarantor expressly waives any and all rights of subrogation to Lender against Borrower (except as expressly provided above), and Guarantor hereby waives any rights to enforce any remedy which Lender may have against Borrower and any right to participate in any collateral for the Loan. In addition to and without in any way limiting the foregoing, Guarantor hereby subordinates any and all indebtedness of Borrower now or hereafter owed to Guarantor to all indebtedness of Borrower to Lender, and agrees with Lender that Guarantor shall not demand or accept any payment of principal or interest from Borrower, shall not claim any offset or other reduction of Guarantor's obligations hereunder because of any such indebtedness, and shall not take any action to obtain any of the collateral from the Loan. Further, Guarantor shall not have any right of recourse against Lender by reason of any action Lender may take or omit to take under the provisions of this Guaranty or under the provisions of any of the Loan Documents.

6.5. Reservation of Rights. Nothing contained in this Guaranty shall prevent or in any way diminish or interfere with any rights or remedies, including, without limitation, the right to contribution, which Lender may have against Borrower, Guarantor, or any other party under the Comprehensive Environmental Response, Compensation and Liability Act of 1980 (codified at Title 42 U.S.C. §9601 *et seq.*), as it may be amended from time to time, or any other applicable federal, state, or local laws, all such rights being hereby expressly reserved or under the Environmental Indemnity.

6.6. Financial Condition and Financial Statements. Guarantor hereby agrees, as a material inducement to Lender to make the Loan to Borrower, to maintain a [liquid][this is an issue for Borrower] net worth of not less than $____________. Guarantor hereby agrees, as a material inducement to Lender to make the Loan to Borrower, to furnish to Lender promptly upon demand by Lender (but not more often than two (2) times in any calendar year, except that during the continuance of an Event of Default the foregoing limitation shall not apply) current and dated financial statements detailing the assets and liabilities of Guarantor certified by Guarantor, in form and substance reasonably acceptable to Lender. Guarantor hereby warrants and represents unto Lender that any and all balance sheets, net worth statements, and other financial data which have heretofore been given or may hereafter be given to Lender with respect to Guarantor did or will as of the effective date thereof fairly and accurately present the financial condition of Guarantor.

6.7. Rights Cumulative; Payments. Lender's rights under this Guaranty shall be in addition to all rights of Lender under the Note, the Security Instrument, and the other Loan Documents. All rights and remedies of Lender shall be cumulative and may be exercised in such manner and combination as Lender may determine.

6.8. No Limitation on Liability. Guarantor hereby consents and agrees that Lender may at any time and from time to time without further consent from Guarantor do any of the following events, and the liability of Guarantor under this Guaranty shall be unconditional and absolute and shall in no way be impaired or limited by any of the following events, whether occurring with or without notice to Guarantor or with or without consideration: (i) any extensions of time for performance required by any of the Loan Documents or extension or renewal of the Note; (ii) any sale, assignment, or foreclosure of the Note, the Security Instrument, or any of the other Loan Documents or any sale or transfer of the Mortgaged Property; (iii) any change in the composition of Borrower, including, without limitation, the withdrawal or removal of Guarantor from any current or future position of ownership, management, or control of Borrower; (iv) the accuracy or inaccuracy of the representations and warranties made by Guarantor herein or by Borrower in any of the Loan Documents; (v) the release of Borrower or of any other Person or entity from performance or observance of any of the agreements, covenants, terms, or conditions contained in any of the Loan Documents by operation of law, Lender's voluntary act or otherwise; (vi) the release or substitution in whole or in part of any security for the Loan; (vii) Lender's failure to record, or to properly record, the Security Instrument or to file, or properly file, any financing statement, or to otherwise perfect, protect, secure, or insure any lien or security interest given as security for the Loan; (viii) the modification of the terms of one or more of the Loan Documents; (ix) any exculpatory, or nonrecourse, or limited recourse, provision in any of the Loan Documents limiting Lender's recourse to the Mortgaged Property encumbered by the Mortgage or to any other property or limiting Lender's rights to a deficiency judgment against Borrower or any other Person; (x) the filing of any bankruptcy or reorganization proceeding by or against Borrower, any owner of Borrower, or any subsequent owner of the Mortgaged Property; (xi) the invalidity or unenforceability of all or any portion of any of the Loan Documents as to Borrower, Guarantor, or any other Person; or (xii) the taking or failure to take any action of any type whatsoever. No such action which Lender shall take or fail to take in connection with the Loan Documents or any collateral for the Loan, nor any course or dealing with Borrower or any other Person, shall limit, impair, or release Guarantor's obligations hereunder, affect this Guaranty in any way, or afford Guarantor any recourse against Lender. Nothing contained in this Section shall be construed to require Lender to take or refrain from taking any action referred to herein.

6.9. Entire Agreement; Amendment; Severability. This Guaranty contains the entire agreement between the parties respecting the matters herein set forth and supersedes all prior agreements, whether written or oral, between the parties respecting such matters. Any amendments or modifications hereto, in order to be effective, shall be in writing and executed by the parties hereto. A determination that any provision of this Guaranty is unenforceable or invalid shall not affect the enforceability or validity of any other provision, and any determination that the application of any provision of this Guaranty to any Person or circumstance is illegal or unenforceable shall not affect the enforceability or validity of such provision as it may apply to any other Persons or circumstances.

6.10. Governing Law; Binding Effect; Waiver of Acceptance. This Guaranty shall be governed by and construed in accordance with the laws of the Property Jurisdiction except to the extent that the applicability of any of such laws may now or hereafter be preempted by Federal law, in which case such Federal law shall so govern and be controlling. To the fullest extent permitted by law, Guarantor hereby unconditionally and irrevocably waives any claim to assert that the law of any other jurisdiction governs this Guaranty. This Guaranty shall bind Guarantor and the heirs, personal representatives, successors, and assigns of Guarantor and shall inure to the benefit of Lender and the officers, directors, shareholders, agents, and employees of Lender and their respective heirs, successors, and assigns. Notwithstanding the foregoing, Guarantor shall not assign any of its rights or obligations under this Guaranty without the prior written consent of Lender, which consent may be withheld by Lender in its sole discretion; provided that any involuntary transfer or assignment caused by the death of Guarantor or any general partner, shareholder, joint venturer, trustee, manager, or beneficial owner of any Person holding any interest in Guarantor, any beneficial owner of Guarantor, or any trustee of Guarantor, as applicable, or if Guarantor is a partnership, any limited partner thereof, shall not be a default under this Guaranty nor require the prior written consent of Lender so long as Guarantor is reconstituted, if required, following such death and so long as (a) those Persons responsible for the management of the Mortgaged Property remain unchanged as a result of such death or any replacement management is approved by Lender, and (b) any such transferee or assignee is bound by the terms of this Guaranty. Guarantor hereby waives any acceptance of this Guaranty by Lender, and this Guaranty shall immediately be binding upon Guarantor.

6.11. Notice. All notices, demands, requests, or other communications to be sent by one party to the other hereunder or required by law, delivered in connection with the Loan, this Guaranty, or any of the other Loan Documents shall be in writing and shall be deemed to have been validly given or served by delivery of the same in person to the intended addressee, or by depositing the same with Federal Express or another reputable private courier service for next business day delivery to the intended addressee at its address set forth on the first page of this Guaranty or at such other address as may be designated by such party as herein provided, or by depositing the same in the United States mail, postage prepaid, registered or certified mail, return receipt requested, addressed to the intended addressee at its address set forth on the first page of this Guaranty or at such other address as may be designated by such party as herein provided. All notices, demands, and requests shall be effective upon such personal delivery, or one (1) business day after being deposited with the private courier service, or three (3) business days after being deposited in the United States mail as required above. Rejection or other refusal to accept or the inability to deliver because of changed address of which no notice was given as herein required shall be deemed to be receipt of the notice, demand, or request sent. By giving to the other party hereto at least fifteen (15) days' prior written notice thereof in accordance with the provisions hereof, the parties hereto shall have the right from time to time to change their respective addresses and each shall have the right to specify as its address any other address within the United States of America.

6.12. No Waiver; Time of Essence; Business Day. The delay or failure of any party hereto to enforce any right or remedy hereunder, or to promptly enforce any such right or remedy, shall not constitute a waiver thereof nor give rise to any estoppel against such party nor excuse any of the parties hereto from their respective obligations hereunder. Any waiver of such right or remedy must be in writing and signed by the party to be bound. This Guaranty is subject to enforcement at law or in equity, including actions for damages or specific performance. Time is of the essence hereof. The term "business day" as used herein shall mean a weekday, Monday through Friday, except a legal holiday or a day on which banking institutions in New York, New York, are authorized by law to be closed.

6.13. Captions for Convenience. The captions and headings of the sections and paragraphs of this Guaranty are for convenience of reference only and shall not be construed in interpreting the provisions hereof.

6.14. Attorneys' Fees. In the event it is necessary for Lender to retain the services of an attorney or any other consultants in order to enforce this Guaranty, or any portion thereof, Guarantor agrees to pay to Lender any and all costs and expenses, including, without limitation, reasonable attorneys' fees and disbursements, incurred by Lender as a result thereof and such costs, fees, and expenses shall be included in Costs.

6.15. Successive Actions. A separate right of action hereunder shall arise each time Lender acquires knowledge of any matter indemnified or guaranteed by Guarantor under this Guaranty. Separate and successive actions may be brought hereunder to enforce any of the provisions hereof at any time and from time to time. No action hereunder shall preclude any subsequent action, and Guarantor hereby waives and covenants not to assert any defense in the nature of splitting of causes of action or merger of judgments.

6.16. Reliance. Lender would not make the Loan to Borrower without this Guaranty. Accordingly, Guarantor intentionally and unconditionally enters into the covenants and agreements as set forth above and understands that, in reliance upon and in consideration of such covenants and agreements, the Loan shall be made and, as part and parcel thereof, specific monetary and other obligations have been, are being, and shall be entered into which would not be made or entered into but for such reliance.

6.17. SUBMISSION TO JURISDICTION; WAIVER OF JURY TRIAL. GUARANTOR, TO THE FULL EXTENT PERMITTED BY LAW, HEREBY KNOWINGLY, INTENTIONALLY, AND VOLUNTARILY, WITH AND UPON THE ADVICE OF COMPETENT COUNSEL, (i) SUBMITS TO PERSONAL JURISDICTION IN THE PROPERTY JURISDICTION OVER ANY SUIT, ACTION, OR PROCEEDING BY ANY PERSON ARISING FROM OR RELATING TO THIS GUARANTY, (ii) AGREES THAT ANY SUCH ACTION, SUIT, OR PROCEEDING IN RESPECT OF THIS GUARANTY MAY BE BROUGHT BY LENDER IN ANY STATE OR FEDERAL COURT OF COMPETENT JURISDICTION SITTING IN THE COUNTY WHERE THE IMPROVEMENTS ARE LOCATED, (iii) SUBMITS TO THE JURISDICTION OF SUCH COURTS, AND (iv) TO THE FULLEST EXTENT PERMITTED BY LAW, AGREES THAT GUARANTOR WILL NOT BRING ANY ACTION, SUIT, OR PROCEEDING IN ANY OTHER FORUM (BUT NOTHING HEREIN SHALL AFFECT THE RIGHT OF LENDER TO BRING ANY ACTION, SUIT, OR PROCEEDING IN ANY OTHER FORUM). GUARANTOR HEREBY WAIVES AND AGREES NOT TO ASSERT, AS A DEFENSE IN ANY ACTION, SUIT, OR PROCEEDING ARISING OUT OF OR RELATING TO THIS GUARANTY, THE NOTE, OR ANY OF THE OTHER LOAN DOCUMENTS, (a) THAT IT IS NOT SUBJECT TO SUCH JURISDICTION OR THAT SUCH ACTION, SUIT, OR PROCEEDING MAY NOT BE BROUGHT OR IS NOT MAINTAINABLE IN THOSE COURTS OR THAT THIS SECURITY INSTRUMENT, THE NOTE, AND/OR ANY OF THE OTHER LOAN DOCUMENTS MAY NOT BE ENFORCED IN OR BY THOSE COURTS OR THAT IT IS EXEMPT OR IMMUNE FROM EXECUTION, (b) THAT THE ACTION, SUIT, OR PROCEEDING IS BROUGHT IN AN INCONVENIENT FORUM, OR (c) THAT THE VENUE AND/OR FORUM OF THE ACTION, SUIT, OR PROCEEDING IS IMPROPER (BUT NOTHING HEREIN SHALL AFFECT THE RIGHT OF BENEFICIARY TO BRING ANY ACTION, SUIT, OR PROCEEDING IN ANY OTHER FORUM). GUARANTOR FURTHER CONSENTS AND AGREES TO SERVICE OF ANY SUMMONS, COMPLAINT, OR OTHER LEGAL PROCESS IN ANY SUCH SUIT, ACTION, OR PROCEEDING BY REGISTERED OR CERTIFIED U.S. MAIL, POSTAGE PREPAID, TO THE GUARANTOR AT THE ADDRESS SET FORTH HEREIN, AND CONSENTS AND AGREES THAT SUCH SERVICE SHALL CONSTITUTE IN EVERY RESPECT VALID AND EFFECTIVE SERVICE (BUT NOTHING HEREIN SHALL AFFECT THE VALIDITY OR EFFECTIVENESS OF PROCESS SERVED IN ANY OTHER MANNER PERMITTED BY LAW).

GUARANTOR AND LENDER EACH, TO THE FULL EXTENT PERMITTED BY LAW, HEREBY KNOWINGLY, INTENTIONALLY, AND VOLUNTARILY, WITH AND UPON THE ADVICE OF COMPETENT COUNSEL, WAIVE, RELINQUISH, AND FOREVER FORGO THE RIGHT TO A TRIAL BY JURY IN

ANY ACTION OR PROCEEDING BASED UPON, ARISING OUT OF, OR IN ANY WAY RELATING TO THIS GUARANTY OR ANY CONDUCT, ACT, OR OMISSION OF LENDER OR GUARANTOR, OR ANY OF ITS DIRECTORS, OFFICERS, PARTNERS, MEMBERS, EMPLOYEES, AGENTS, OR ATTORNEYS, OR ANY OTHER PERSONS AFFILIATED WITH LENDER OR GUARANTOR, IN EACH OF THE FOREGOING CASES, WHETHER SOUNDING IN CONTRACT, TORT, OR OTHERWISE.

6.18. Waiver by Guarantor. Guarantor covenants and agrees that, upon the commencement of a voluntary or involuntary bankruptcy proceeding by or against Borrower, Guarantor shall not seek or cause Borrower or any other Person to seek a supplemental stay or other relief, whether injunctive or otherwise, pursuant to 11 U.S.C. §105 or any other provision of the Bankruptcy Reform Act of 1978, as amended, or any other debtor relief law (whether statutory, common law, case law, or otherwise) of any jurisdiction whatsoever, now or hereafter in effect, which may be or become applicable, to stay, interdict, condition, reduce, or inhibit the ability of Lender to enforce any rights of Lender against Guarantor or the collateral for the Loan by virtue of this Guaranty or otherwise.

6.19. Assignments by Lender.

6.19.1. Lender may at its sole cost and expense, without notice to, or consent of, Guarantor, sell, assign, or transfer to or participate with any entity or entities all or any part of the indebtedness secured hereby, and each such entity or entities shall have the right to enforce the provisions of this Guaranty and any of the other Loan Documents as fully as Lender, provided that Lender shall continue to have the unimpaired right to enforce the provisions of this Guaranty and any of the other Loan Documents as to so much of the indebtedness secured hereby that Lender has not sold, assigned, or transferred. In connection with the foregoing, Lender shall have the right to disclose to any such actual or potential purchaser, assignee, transferee, or participant all financial records, information, reports, financial statements, and documents obtained in connection with this Guaranty and any of the other Loan Documents or otherwise.

6.19.2. In particular, Guarantor acknowledges and agrees that Lender and its successors and assigns may (i) sell the indebtedness secured hereby, this Guaranty, and each of the other Loan Documents to one or more investors as a whole loan, (ii) participate the indebtedness secured hereby, in whole or in part, to one or more investors, (iii) deposit this Guaranty and each of the Loan Documents with a trust, which trust may sell certificates to investors evidencing an ownership in the trust assets, or (iv) otherwise sell the indebtedness secured hereby or any interest therein to investors (the transactions referred to in clauses (i) through (iv) are hereinafter each referred to as a "Secondary Market Transaction"). In this regard, Guarantor shall make available to Lender all information concerning its business and operations that Lender may reasonably request. Lender shall be permitted to share such information with the investment banking firms, rating agencies, accounting firms, law firms, and other third-party advisory firms involved with the indebtedness secured hereby and the Loan Documents of the applicable Secondary Market Transaction. It is understood that the information provided by Guarantor to Lender may ultimately be incorporated into the offering documents for a Secondary Market Transaction and thus various investors may also have access to some or all of such information. Lender and all of the aforesaid third-party advisors and professional firms shall be entitled to rely on the information supplied by, or on behalf of, Guarantor, including but not limited to, any amendments, corrections, deletions, or additions to the Note, this Guaranty, and the other Loan Documents as is required by Lender and/or the prospective transferee; provided, however, that Guarantor shall not be required to do anything that has the effect of (a) changing the essential economic terms of the indebtedness secured hereby as set forth in the Loan Documents; or (b) imposing greater personal liability in connection with the indebtedness secured hereby than that currently set forth in the Loan Documents.

6.20. Counterparts; Reproductions. This Guaranty may be executed in any number of counterparts, each of which shall be effective only upon delivery and thereafter shall be deemed an original, and all of which shall be taken to be one and the same instrument, for the same effect as if all parties hereto had signed the same signature page. Any signature page of this Guaranty may be detached from any counterpart of this Guaranty without impairing the legal effect of any signatures thereon and may be attached to another counterpart of this Guaranty identical in form hereto but having attached to it one or more additional signature pages. This Guaranty and any documents, certificates, or instruments provided in connection with this Guaranty may be reproduced by the parties hereto by any photographic, photostatic, microfilm, microcard, digital, miniature photographic, or other similar process. To the extent permitted by applicable law, any such reproduction shall be admissible in evidence as the original itself in any judicial or administrative proceeding (whether or not the original is in existence and whether or not such reproduction was made in the regular course of business) and any enlargement, facsimile, or further reproduction of such reproduction shall likewise be admissible in evidence.

6.21. Parties Bound; Benefit. This Guaranty shall be binding upon Guarantor and Guarantor's respective successors, assigns, heirs, and personal representatives and shall be for the benefit of Lender, and of any subsequent holder of Lender's interest in the Loan and of any owner of a participation interest therein. In the event the interest of Lender under the Loan Documents is sold or transferred, then the liability of Guarantor to Lender shall then be in favor of both Lender originally named herein and each subsequent holder of Lender's interest therein, to the extent of their respective interests.

6.22. Partial Invalidity. Each of the provisions hereof shall be enforceable against Guarantor to the fullest extent now or hereafter not prohibited by applicable law. The invalidity or unenforceability of any provision hereof shall not limit the validity or enforceability of each other provision hereof.

6.23. Claims in Bankruptcy. In the event of an Insolvency Action involving Guarantor as debtor, Lender shall have the right to prove its claim in any such proceeding so as to establish its rights hereunder and receive directly from the receiver, trustee, or other court custodian dividends and payments which would otherwise be payable pursuant to or in satisfaction of Guarantor Claims. Guarantor hereby assigns any and all such dividends and payments to Lender. If Guarantor shall pay Lender an amount equal to all Obligations owed by Borrower to Lender, then Lender shall assign back to Guarantor all rights of Guarantor previously assigned to Lender pursuant to the first sentence of this Section 6.23.

6.24. Liens Subordinate; Standstill. Guarantor acknowledges and agrees that any liens, security interests, judgment liens, charges, or other encumbrances that Guarantor may have upon Borrower's assets securing payment by Guarantor of any sums owed to Lender pursuant to this Guaranty, to the extent permitted by applicable

Legal Requirements, shall be and remain inferior and subordinate to any liens, security interests, judgment liens, charges, or other encumbrances upon Borrower's assets securing payment of the Guaranteed Obligations, regardless of whether such encumbrances in favor of Guarantor or Lender presently exist or are hereafter created or attach. To the extent permitted by applicable Legal Requirements, Guarantor shall not (i) exercise or enforce any creditor's right it may have against Borrower, or (ii) foreclose, repossess, sequester, or otherwise take steps or institute any action or proceedings (judicial or otherwise, including, without limitation, the commencement of, or joinder in, any liquidation, bankruptcy, rearrangement, debtor's relief, or insolvency proceeding) to enforce any liens, mortgages, deeds of trust, security interests, collateral rights, judgments, or other encumbrances on assets of Borrower held by Guarantor.

6.25. Duration of Agreement. This Guaranty shall terminate and be of no further force or effect upon the indefeasible repayment of the Loan in full, and upon written request of Guarantor following such occurrence, Lender shall confirm such termination in writing, subject to the terms and conditions hereof.

[BALANCE OF PAGE INTENTIONALLY LEFT BLANK.]

IN WITNESS WHEREOF, Guarantor has executed this Indemnity and Guaranty under seal as of the day and year first above written.

GUARANTOR:

______________________________, a

____

By: ______________________________,
Name:
Title:

EXHIBIT A

Property Description

EXHIBIT B

Loan Document List

Form of Mortgage

<u>This instrument was prepared by and after recording return to:</u>

__________, Esq.
____
____
____

MORTGAGE, SECURITY AGREEMENT, ASSIGNMENT OF LEASES AND RENTS AND FIXTURE FILING

______________________, LLC,
Borrower

to

______________________________,
Lender

Dated as of ________, 20__

THIS INSTRUMENT CONSTITUTES A
FIXTURE FILING AND IS TO BE
INDEXED IN THE REAL PROPERTY RECORDS

Premises:

____

____

____

THIS MORTGAGE, SECURITY AGREEMENT, ASSIGNMENT OF LEASES AND RENTS AND FIXTURE FILING (this "**Mortgage and Security Instrument**") dated as of ___________, 20__ by ______________, LLC, a _______ limited liability company, having its principal office at ___________________________ ("**Borrower**") to _______________________, having its principal place of business at ___________________ ("**Lender**").

WITNESSETH:

To secure the payment of an indebtedness in the principal sum of ______________ Dollars ($______________), lawful money of the United States of America, to be paid with interest according to the terms of that certain Promissory Note (as hereinafter defined) and all other Indebtedness (as hereinafter defined), Borrower has agreed to enter into this Mortgage and Security Instrument.

NOW THEREFORE, for good and valuable consideration, the receipt of which is hereby acknowledged by Borrower, Borrower hereby agrees as follows:

SECTION 1: DEFINITIONS

"Affiliate" of any specified Person, shall mean any other Person directly or indirectly controlling or controlled by or under direct or indirect common control with such specified Person, and any immediate family member of such specified Person and/or any of their respective Affiliates. For the purposes of this definition, "control" when used with respect to any specified Person means the power to direct the management and policies of such Person, directly or indirectly, whether through the ownership of voting securities, by contract or otherwise; and the terms "controlling" and "controlled" have meanings correlative to the foregoing.

"Assignment of Leases and Rents" shall mean that certain Assignment of Leases and Rents dated as of the Closing Date between Borrower and Lender, as the same may be amended, restated, supplemented or otherwise modified from time to time.

"Assignment of Management Agreement" shall mean that certain Assignment of Management Agreement dated as of the Closing Date among Borrower, Lender and _______ [Manager], as the same may be amended, restated, supplemented or otherwise modified from time to time.

"Banking Day" as defined in Section 6.3(a) of this Mortgage. [Note: See Part IV Section 6 of this Book.]

"Borrower" means all persons or entities identified as "Borrower" in the first paragraph of this Mortgage, together with its successors and assigns.

"Borrower's Knowledge" means, with respect to any applicable representation and/or warranty provided for in any of the Loan Documents and which are subject to Borrower's Knowledge, such knowledge of applicable facts as _______ [Note: List applicable individuals] had with respect to any applicable matter as of the date any such representation and/or warranty shall be deemed to have been given pursuant to the express terms of the Loan Documents.

"Breakage Costs" as defined in Section 6.3(b) of this Mortgage. [Note: See Part IV Section 6 of this Book.]

"Cash Management Agreement" means any separate agreement between Borrower, Lender and an institutional bank or trustee, which is entered into for the purpose of, among other things, (i) establishing various reserves for the Mortgaged Property, (ii) collecting and depositing all revenues from the Mortgaged Property and (iii) dealing with the distribution of such revenues and deposits in the various reserves.

"Change in Law" means the occurrence, after the date of this Mortgage, of any of the following: (a) the adoption or taking effect of any Legal Requirement, (b) any change in any Legal Requirement or in the administration, interpretation, implementation or application thereof by any governmental authority, or (c) the making or issuance of any request, rule, guideline or directive (whether or not having the force of law) by any governmental authority; provided that notwithstanding anything herein to the contrary, (x) the Dodd-Frank Wall Street Reform and Consumer Protection Act and (y) all requests, rules, guidelines, or directives promulgated by Lender for International Settlements, the Basel Committee on Banking Supervision (or any successor or similar authority), or the United States or foreign regulatory authorities, in each case pursuant to Basel III regulations published by the Basel Committee on Banking Supervision, shall in each case be deemed to be a "Change in Law," regardless of the date enacted, adopted or issued.

"Closing Date" shall mean the date of this Mortgage.

"Default Rate" as defined in Section 23.2 of this Mortgage. [Note: See Part IV Section 23 of this Book.]

"Environmental Claim" as defined in Section 18.12 of this Mortgage. [Note: See Part IV Section 18 of this Book.]

"Environmental Inspections" as defined in Section 18.7 of this Mortgage. [Note: See Part IV Section 18 of this Book.]

"Environmental Permit" means any permit, license, or other authorization issued under any Hazardous Materials Law with respect to any activities or businesses conducted on or in relation to the Mortgaged Property which relates to the use, handling, storage and/or release of Hazardous Materials or other similar substances.

"ERISA" as defined in Section 8.1(g) of this Mortgage. [Note: See Part IV Section 8 of this Book.]

"ERISA Plan" as defined in Section 8.1(g) of this Mortgage. [Note: See Part IV Section 8 of this Book.]

"Event of Default" means the occurrence of any event listed in Section 24 of this Mortgage. [Note: See Part IV Section 24 of this Book.]

"Fixtures" means all property which is so attached to any portion of the Mortgaged Property so as to constitute a fixture under applicable state law in the State or Commonwealth where the Mortgaged Property is located, including: machinery, equipment, engines, boilers, incinerators, installed building materials; systems and equipment for the purpose of supplying or distributing heating, cooling, electricity, gas, water, air, or light; antennas, cable, wiring and conduits used in connection with radio, television, security, fire prevention, or fire detection or otherwise used to carry electronic signals; telephone systems and equipment; elevators and related machinery and equipment; fire detection, prevention and extinguishing systems and apparatus; security and access control systems and apparatus; plumbing systems; water heaters, ranges, stoves, microwave ovens, refrigerators, dishwashers, garbage disposers, washers, dryers and other appliances; light fixtures, awnings, storm windows and storm doors; pictures, screens, blinds, shades, curtains and curtain rods; mirrors; cabinets, paneling, rugs and floor and wall coverings; fences, trees and plants; swimming pools; and exercise equipment.

"Governmental Authority" means any board, commission, department or body of any municipal, county, state or federal governmental unit, or any subdivision of any of them, that has or acquires jurisdiction over the Mortgaged Property or the use, operation or improvement of the Mortgaged Property.

"Guarantor" as defined in Section 8.1(a) this Mortgage. [Note: See Part IV Section 8 of this Book.]

"Hazardous Materials" means petroleum and petroleum products and compounds containing them, including gasoline, diesel fuel and oil; explosives; flammable materials; radioactive materials; polychlorinated biphenyls (**"PCBs"**) and compounds containing them; lead and lead-based paint;

asbestos or asbestos-containing materials in any form that is or could become friable; underground or above-ground storage tanks, whether empty or containing any substance; any substance the presence of which on the Mortgaged Property is prohibited by any federal, state or local authority; any substance that requires special handling; and any other material or substance now or in the future defined as a "hazardous substance," "hazardous material," "hazardous waste," "toxic substance," "toxic pollutant," "contaminant," or "pollutant" within the meaning of any Hazardous Materials Law.

"Hazardous Materials Laws" means all federal, state, and local laws, ordinances and regulations and standards, rules, policies and other governmental requirements, administrative rulings and court judgments and decrees in effect now or in the future and including all amendments, that relate to Hazardous Materials and apply to Borrower or to the Mortgaged Property. Hazardous Materials Laws include, but are not limited to, the Comprehensive Environmental Response, Compensation and Liability Act, 42 U.S.C. Section 9601, et seq., the Resource Conservation and Recovery Act, 42 U.S.C. Section 6901, et seq., the Toxic Substance Control Act, 15 U.S.C. Section 2601, et seq., the Clean Water Act, 33 U.S.C. Section 1251, et seq., and the Hazardous Materials Transportation Act, 49 U.S.C. Section 5101, et seq., and their state analogs.

"Impositions" means any lien including any obligation owed by Borrower to any governmental and quasi-governmental liens entity as a periodic and on-going payment which is owed because of Borrower's ownership of the Mortgaged Property, which if not paid, would become a lien against the Mortgaged Property.

"Imposition Deposits" as defined in Section 10.1 of this Mortgage. [Note: See Part IV Section 10 of this Book.]

"Improvements" means the buildings, structures, improvements, and alterations now constructed or at any time in the future constructed or placed upon the Land, including any future replacements and additions.

"Interest Period" as defined in Section 6.4 of this Mortgage. [Note: See Part IV Section 6 of this Book.]

"Indebtedness" means the principal of, interest on, and all other amounts due and payable to Lender at any time under, the Note, this Mortgage or any other Loan Document, and all other Obligations, including prepayment premiums, late charges, default interest, and advances as provided in Section 6 to protect the security of this Mortgage.

"Insolvency Activities" as defined in Section 21.10 of this Mortgage. [Note: See Part IV Section 21 of this Book.]

"Initial Owners" as defined in Section 22.3(a) of this Mortgage. [Note: See Part IV Section 22 of this Book.]

"Key Principal" means the natural person(s) or entity identified as such in Exhibit __ of this Mortgage, and any person or entity who becomes a Key Principal after the date of this Mortgage and is identified as such in an amendment or supplement to this Mortgage.

"Land" means the land described in Exhibit A attached to this Mortgage.

"Leases" means all present and future leases, subleases, licenses, concessions or grants or other possessory interests now or hereafter in force, whether oral or written, covering or affecting the Mortgaged Property, or any portion of the Mortgaged Property (including proprietary leases or occupancy agreements if Borrower is a cooperative housing corporation), and all modifications, extensions or renewals.

"Legal Requirements" means all federal, state, city, municipal and other governmental statutes, laws, rules, orders, regulations, ordinances, judgments, decrees and injunctions of any governmental or quasi-governmental body or agencies affecting the acquisition, ownership, development, leasing, operation and/or use of the Mortgaged Property or any part thereof, whether now or hereafter enacted and in force, and all permits, licenses and authorizations and regulations relating thereto, and all covenants, agreements, restrictions and encumbrances contained in any instruments, at any time in force affecting the Mortgaged Property or any part thereof.

"Lender" means the entity identified as "Lender" in the first paragraph of this Mortgage and its successors and assigns, or any subsequent holder of the Note.

"LIBOR" as defined in Section 6.4(d) of this Mortgage. [Note: See Part IV Section 6 of this Book.]

"LIBOR Advance Rate" as defined in Section 6.4(e) of this Mortgage. [Note: See Part IV Section 6 of this Book.]

"LIBOR Based Rate" as defined in Section 6.4(f) of this Mortgage. [Note: See Part IV Section 6 of this Book.]

"LIBOR Rate" as defined in Section 6.4(d) of this Mortgage. [Note: See Part IV Section 6 of this Book.]

"Limited Liability Agreement" means that certain Operating Agreement dated _______, entered into by ________, which among other things constitutes the primary organizational document of Borrower, as the same may be amended, extended or modified from time to time.

"Loan" means the loan made by Lender to Borrower which is evidenced by the Note, and includes all obligations owed by Borrower to Lender pursuant to all guaranties, all indemnity agreements, the Note and all other Loan Documents. "

"Loan Advance" means each advance of proceeds of any portion of the Loan which shall be made from time to time by Lender to Borrower.

"Loan Agreement" means the loan agreement entered into on the date of this Mortgage between Borrower and Lender, which, among other things, provides for the funding of the Loan, as the same may be amended, extended or otherwise modified from time to time.

"Loan Documents" means the Note, this Mortgage, the Loan Agreement, all guaranties, the Cash Management Agreement, all indemnity agreements, other collateral agreements, O&M Programs, and any other documents now or in the future executed by Borrower, Key Principal, any guarantor or any other person in connection with the Loan evidenced by the Note, as each such document may be amended, modified or extended from time to time.

"Loan Servicer" as defined in Section 34.1 of this Mortgage. [Note: See Part IV Section 34 of this Book.]

"Maturity" as defined in Section 6.4(h) of this Mortgage. [Note: See Part IV Section 6 of this Book.]

"Maturity Date" as defined in Section 6.4(h) of this Mortgage. [Note: See Part IV Section 6 of this Book.]

"Mortgage" means this Mortgage and Security Agreement, which is entered into on the date hereof by Borrower for the benefit of Lender, as the same may be amended, extended or otherwise modified from time to time.

"Mortgaged Property" means all of the following, as applicable:

(1) the Land;
(2) the Improvements;
(3) the Fixtures, including goods, materials, supplies, chattels, furniture, fixtures, equipment and machinery now or later to be attached to, placed in or on, or used in connection with the use, enjoyment, occupancy or operation of all or any part of the Land

and/or the Improvements, whether stored on the Land and/or the Improvements or elsewhere, including all pumping plants, engines, pipes, ditches and flumes, and also all gas, electric, cooking, heating, cooling, air conditioning, lighting, refrigeration and plumbing fixtures and equipment, all of which shall be considered to the fullest extent of the law to be real property for purposes of this Mortgage; and any manufacturer's warranties with respect thereto;

(4) the Personalty;

(5) all current and future rights, including air rights, development rights, zoning rights and other similar rights or interests, easements, tenements, rights-of-way, strips and gores of land, streets, alleys, roads, sewer rights, waters, watercourses, and appurtenances related to or benefiting the Land or the Improvements, or both, and all rights-of-way, streets, alleys and roads which may have been or may in the future be vacated;

(6) all existing and future appurtenances, privileges, easements, franchises and tenements of the Land held by Borrower, from time to time, including all minerals, oil, gas, other hydrocarbons and associated substances, sulphur, nitrogen, carbon dioxide, helium and other commercially valuable substances which may be in, under or produced from any part of the Land, all development rights and credits, air rights, water, water rights (whether riparian, appropriative or otherwise, and whether or not appurtenant) and water stock, and any portion of the Land lying in the streets, roads or avenues, open or proposed, in front of or adjoining the Land and Improvements;

(7) all rights of Borrower to the payment of money, accounts, accounts receivable, reserves, deferred payments, refunds, cost savings, payments and deposits, whether now or later to be received from third parties (including all earnest money sales deposits) or deposited by Borrower with third parties (including all utility deposits and Imposition Deposits), contract rights, development and use rights, governmental permits and licenses, applications, architectural and engineering plans, specifications and drawings, as built drawings, chattel paper, instruments, documents, notes, drafts and letters of credit, which arise from or relate to construction on the Land and/or Improvements or to any business now or later to be conducted on it, or to the Land and/or Improvements generally; and any builder's or manufacturer's warranties with respect thereto;

(8) all insurance policies owned by Borrower pertaining to the Mortgaged Property and all proceeds payable to Borrower, including all claims to and demands for them, of the voluntary or involuntary conversion of any of the Land, Improvements or the other property described above into cash or liquidated claims;

(9) all proceeds paid or to be paid by any insurer of the Land, the Improvements, the Fixtures, the Personalty or any other part of the Mortgaged Property, whether or not Borrower obtained the insurance pursuant to Lender's requirement;

(10) all awards, payments and other compensation made or to be made by any municipal, state or federal authority with respect to the Land, the Improvements, the Fixtures, the Personalty or any other part of the Mortgaged Property, including any awards or settlements resulting from condemnation proceedings or the total or partial taking of the Land, the Improvements, the Fixtures, the Personalty or any other part of the Mortgaged Property under the power of eminent domain or otherwise and including any conveyance in lieu thereof;

(11) all contracts, options and other agreements for the sale of the Land, the Improvements, the Fixtures, the Personalty or any other part of the Mortgaged Property entered into by Borrower now or in the future, including cash or securities deposited to secure performance by parties of their obligations;

(12) all of Borrower's books and records pertaining to any and all of the property described above, including computer readable memory and any computer hardware or software necessary to access and process such memory;

(13) all proceeds from the conversion, voluntary or involuntary, of any of the above into cash or liquidated claims, and the right to collect such proceeds;
(14) all Rents and Leases;
(15) all earnings, royalties, accounts receivable, issues and profits from the Land, the Improvements or any other part of the Mortgaged Property, and all undisbursed proceeds of the loan secured by this Mortgage and, if Borrower is a cooperative housing corporation, maintenance charges or assessments payable by shareholders or residents;
(16) all Imposition Deposits;
(17) all refunds or rebates of Impositions by any municipal, state or federal authority or insurance company (other than refunds applicable to periods before the real property tax year in which this Mortgage is dated);
(18) all tenant security deposits which have not been forfeited by any tenant under any of the Leases;
(19) all proceeds of, additions and accretions to, substitutions and replacements for, and changes in any of the property of Borrower described above;
(20) all "Equipment," as that term is defined in the Uniform Commercial Code, owned by Borrower;
(21) all "Goods," as that term is defined in the Uniform Commercial Code, owned by Borrower;
(22) all Borrower's "Accounts," as that term is defined in the Uniform Commercial Code"; and
(23) all names under or by which any of the above Mortgaged Property may be operated or known, and all trademarks, trade names, and goodwill relating to any of the Mortgaged Property.

"Note"/"Promissory Note" means the Note described on page one of this Mortgage, and all schedules, riders, allonges and addenda, as such Note may be amended from time to time.

"Notice of Rate Selection" means a written notice, given by cable, tested telex, telecopier (with authorized signature), or by telephone if immediately confirmed by such a written notice, from ________ (or such other individual which in a written notice to Lender from Borrower is authorized to act in such capacity) which: (i) is irrevocable; (ii) is received by Lender not later than 10:00 A.M. Eastern Time: (a) if a LIBOR Based Rate is selected, at least three (3) Business Days prior to the first day of the Interest Period to which such selection is to apply, or (b) if a Variable Rate is selected, on the first day of the Interest Period to which it applies; and (iii) as to each selected interest rate option, sets forth the aggregate principal amount(s) to which such interest rate option(s) shall apply and the Interest Period(s) applicable to each LIBOR Advance.

"Obligation(s)" means, without limitation, all loans, advances, indebtedness, notes, liabilities, and amounts, liquidated or un-liquidated, owing by Borrower in connection with the Loan to Lender at any time, of each and every kind, nature and description, whether arising under this Mortgage or any of the other Loan Documents or otherwise, and whether secured or unsecured, direct or indirect (that is, whether the same are due directly by Borrower to Lender, or are due indirectly by Borrower to Lender as endorser, guarantor or other surety, or as borrower of obligations due third persons which have been endorsed or assigned to Lender, or otherwise), absolute or contingent, due or to become due, now existing or hereafter arising or contracted, provided any such debt or liabilities shall have arisen in connection with the Loan, including, without limitation, payment when due of all amounts outstanding from time to time under the Loan Documents. Said term shall also include (i) all interest and other charges chargeable to Borrower or due from Borrower to Lender from time to time and all costs and expenses referred to in this Mortgage or any of the other Loan Documents and (ii) any and all future advances made by Lender to protect or preserve the Mortgaged Property or the security interest created hereby on the Mortgaged Property, or for Taxes, assessments or insurance premiums as hereinafter provided or for performance of any of

Borrower's obligations hereunder or under the other Loan Documents (whether or not the original Mortgagor remains the owner of the Mortgaged Property at the time of such advances).

"O&M Program" as defined in Section 18.4 of this Mortgage. [Note: See Part IV Section 18 of this Book.]

"Permitted Encumbrances" means all matters of record set forth in Lender's title insurance policy which Lender received in connection with the closing of the Loan, together with any other title matters either approved by Lender, or expressly permitted to be entered into by Borrower pursuant to this Mortgage.

"Person" means an individual, partnership, limited liability company, corporation, trust or unincorporated organization.

"Personalty" means all furniture, furnishings, equipment, machinery, building materials, appliances, commercial tort claims, inventory, general intangibles, goods, supplies, tools, books, records (whether in written or electronic form), computer equipment (hardware and software) and other tangible personal property (other than Fixtures) which are used now or in the future in connection with the ownership, management or operation of the Land or the Improvements or are located on the Land or in the Improvements, and any operating agreements relating to the Land or the Improvements, and any surveys, plans and specifications and contracts for architectural, engineering and construction services relating to the Land or the Improvements and all other intangible property and rights relating to the operation of, or used in connection with, the Land or the Improvements, including all governmental permits relating to any activities on the Land.

"Prepayment Date" as defined in Schedule A to the Note. [Note: See Part IV Section 7 of this Book.]

"Prepayment Premium" as defined in Schedule A to the Note. [Note: See Part IV Section 7 of this Book.]

"Prime Rate" as defined in Section 6.4(i) of this Mortgage. [Note: See Part IV Section 6 of this Book.]

"Prohibited Activities or Conditions." as defined in Section 18.1 of this Mortgage. [Note: See Part IV Section 18 of this Book.]

"Property Jurisdiction" as defined in Section 32.1 of this Mortgage. [Note: See Part IV Section 32 of this Book.]

"Publicly-Held Corporation" as defined in Section 22.3(c) of this Mortgage. [Note: Part IV Section 22 of this Book.]

"RCRA" means the Resource Conservation and Recovery Act, 42 U.S.C. § 6901 *et seq.*, which imposes a rigorous "cradle-to-grave" scheme that regulates hazardous wastes from generation to final disposal or destruction.

"Remedial Work" as defined in Section 18.8 of this Mortgage. [Note: See Part IV Section 18 of this Book.]

"Rents" means all rents (whether from residential or non-residential space), revenues and other income of the Land or the Improvements, including parking fees, laundry and vending machine income and fees and charges for food, health care and other services provided at the Mortgaged Property, whether now due, past due, or to become due, and deposits forfeited by tenants.

"Servicing Arrangement" as defined in Section 37.1 of this Mortgage. [Note: See Part IV Section 37 of this Book.]

"Significant Lease" as defined in Section 5.6 of this Mortgage. [Note: See Part IV Section 5 of this Book.]

"Taxes" means all Impositions.

"Transfer" means (a) a sale, assignment, transfer or other disposition (whether voluntary, involuntary or by operation of law); (b) the granting, creating or attachment of a lien, encumbrance or security interest (whether voluntary, involuntary or by operation of law); (c) the issuance or other creation of an ownership interest in a legal entity, including a partnership interest, interest in a limited liability company or corporate stock; (d) the withdrawal, retirement, removal or involuntary resignation of a partner in a partnership or a member or manager in a limited liability company; or (e) the merger, dissolution, liquidation, or consolidation of a legal entity. "Transfer" does not include (i) a conveyance of the Mortgaged Property at a judicial or non-judicial foreclosure sale under this Mortgage or (ii) the Mortgaged Property becoming part of a bankruptcy estate by operation of law under the United States Bankruptcy Code. For purposes of defining the term "Transfer," the term "partnership" shall mean a general partnership, a limited partnership, a joint venture and a limited liability partnership, and the term "partner" shall mean a general partner, a limited partner and a joint venturer.

"UCC Collateral" as defined in Section 3.1 of this Mortgage. [Note: See Part IV Section 3 of this Book.]

"USTs" means underground storage tanks containing regulated substances, including petroleum products.

"Uniform Commercial Code" or "UCC" means the Uniform Commercial Code of __________ [the State or Commonwealth in which the Land is located], as the same may be amended and modified from time to time.

"Variable Rate" as defined in Section 6.4(j) of this Mortgage. [Note: See Part IV Section 6 of this Book.]

"Yield Rate" as defined in Schedule A to the Note. [Note: See Part IV Section 7 of this Book.]

SECTION 2: GRANT OF REAL ESTATE INTERESTS

2.1 **Mortgage**. For valuable consideration paid and for other good and valuable consideration, the receipt and sufficiency of which are hereby acknowledged, Borrower hereby irrevocably and unconditionally mortgages, grants, bargains, transfers, sells, conveys, sets over and assigns to Lender and its successors and assigns forever, with MORTGAGE COVENANTS, all of Borrower's right, title and interest in and to the "Mortgaged Property" more particularly defined below, to secure the prompt payment and performance of the Obligations, including, without limitation, all amounts due and owing and all obligations respecting the Note and all substitutions, modifications, extensions or amendments to any of the Loan Documents. The amount of principal obligations outstanding and evidenced by the Loan Documents and secured by this Mortgage total ________________ Dollars ($______________) as of the date of this Mortgage, but this Mortgage shall nevertheless secure payment and performance of all Obligations.

2.2 **Conditions to Grant**. Lender shall have and hold the above granted Mortgaged Property unto and to the use and benefit of Lender, and its successors and assigns, forever; provided, however, the conveyances, grants and assignments contained in this Mortgage are upon the express condition that, if Borrower (i) shall irrevocably and indefeasibly pay and perform each Obligation in full, including, without limitation, all principal, interest and premium thereon and other charges, if applicable, in accordance with the terms and conditions in the Loan Documents and this Mortgage, (ii) shall pay and perform every other Obligation and (iii) shall abide by and comply with each and every covenant and condition set forth herein and in the Loan Documents, the conveyances, grants and assignments contained in this Mortgage shall be appropriately released and discharged.

SECTION 3: GRANT OF PERSONAL PROPERTY INTERESTS

3.1 As a continuing security for the Obligations, Borrower hereby pledges, assigns and grants to Lender a security interest in any of the Mortgaged Property which, under applicable law, is deemed to be personal property or fixtures of Borrower, and all products and cash and non-cash proceeds thereof, whether acquired now or in the future (collectively, **"UCC Collateral"**). This Mortgage is and shall be deemed to be a security agreement and financing statement pursuant to the terms of the Uniform Commercial Code as to the UCC Collateral, such that Lender shall have all of the rights and remedies of a secured party under the Uniform Commercial Code with respect the UCC Collateral. This Mortgage shall also constitute a financing statement filed as a fixture filing under Section _____ of the Uniform Commercial Code. [Note: This is usually §9-502 of the Uniform Commercial Code covering any portion of the Mortgaged Property which now is or later may become a fixture, as determined by the laws of the State or Commonwealth in which the Land and Improvements are located.] Borrower agrees that it shall execute and deliver to Lender, upon Lender's request, financing statements, continuation statements and amendments, in such form as Lender may require to perfect or continue the perfection of this security interest, and Borrower hereby agrees and designates that Lender may execute any such financing statements, continuation statements and amendments on Borrower's or Lender's behalf, without the necessity of Borrower executing any such documentation. Borrower shall pay all filing costs and all costs and expenses of any record searches for financing statements that Lender may require. Without the prior written consent of Lender, Borrower shall not create or permit to exist any other lien or security interest in any of the UCC Collateral. If an Event of Default has occurred and is continuing, Lender shall have the remedies of a secured party under the Uniform Commercial Code, in addition to all remedies provided by this Mortgage or existing under applicable law. In exercising any remedies, Lender may exercise its remedies against the UCC Collateral separately or together, and in any order, without in any way affecting the availability of Lender's other remedies.

SECTION 4: ASSIGNMENT OF RENTS

4.1 As part of the consideration for the Obligations, Borrower absolutely and unconditionally assigns and transfers to Lender all Rents. It is the intention of Borrower to establish a present, absolute, unconditional and irrevocable transfer and assignment to Lender of all Rents and to authorize and empower Lender to collect and receive all Rents without the necessity of further action on the part of Borrower. Promptly upon request by Lender, Borrower agrees to execute and deliver such further assignments as Lender may from time to time require. Borrower and Lender intend this assignment of Rents to be immediately effective and to constitute a present absolute, unconditional and irrevocable assignment and not an assignment for additional security only. For purposes of giving effect to this present absolute, unconditional and irrevocable assignment of Rents, and for no other purpose, Rents shall not be deemed to be a part of the Mortgaged Property. However, if this present, absolute, unconditional and irrevocable assignment of Rents is not enforceable by its terms under the laws of the Property Jurisdiction, then the Rents shall be included as a part of the Mortgaged Property, and it is the intention of the Borrower that in this circumstance this Mortgage create and perfect a lien on Rents in favor of Lender, which lien shall be effective as of the date of this Mortgage.

SECTION 5: ASSIGNMENT OF LEASES; OTHER LEASE COVENANTS

5.1 **Assignment of Leases**. As part of the consideration for the Obligations, Borrower absolutely and unconditionally assigns and transfers to Lender all of Borrower's right, title and interest in, to and under the Leases, including Borrower's right, power and authority to modify the terms of any such Lease, or extend or terminate any such Lease. It is the intention of Borrower to establish a present absolute, unconditional and irrevocable transfer and assignment to Lender of all of Borrower's right, title and interest in, to and under the Leases. Borrower and Lender intend this assignment of the Leases to be immediately effective and to constitute a present absolute, unconditional and irrevocable assignment and not an assignment for additional security only. For purposes of giving effect to this absolute assignment of the Leases, and for no other purpose, the Leases shall not be deemed to be a part of the Mortgaged Property. However, if this present, absolute, unconditional and irrevocable assignment of the Leases is not enforceable by its terms under the laws of the Property Jurisdiction, then the Leases shall be included as a part of the Mortgaged Property, and it is the intention of the Borrower that in this circumstance this Mortgage create and perfect a lien on the Leases in favor of Lender, which lien shall be effective as of the date of this Mortgage.

5.2 **Borrower License to Exercise Landlord Rights**. Until Lender gives notice to Borrower of Lender's exercise of its rights under this Section 5.2 of the Mortgage, Borrower shall have all rights, power and authority granted to Borrower under any Lease (except as otherwise limited by this Section or any other provision of this Mortgage), including the right, power and authority to modify the terms of any Lease or extend or terminate any Lease. Upon the occurrence of an Event of Default, the permission given to Borrower pursuant to the preceding sentence to exercise all rights, power and authority under Leases shall automatically terminate. Borrower shall comply with and observe Borrower's obligations under all Leases, including Borrower's obligations pertaining to the maintenance and disposition of tenant security deposits.

5.3 **Borrower Recognition of Certain Lender Rights**. Borrower acknowledges and agrees that the exercise by Lender, either directly or by a receiver, of any of the rights conferred under this Section 5.3 of the Mortgage, shall not be construed to make Lender a mortgagee-in-possession of the Mortgaged Property so long as Lender has not itself entered into actual possession of the Land and the Improvements. The acceptance by Lender of the assignment of the Leases pursuant to this Section 5 of the Mortgage shall not at any time or in any event obligate Lender to take any action under this Mortgage or to expend any money or to incur any expenses. Lender shall not be liable in any way for any injury or damage to person or property sustained by any person or persons, firm or corporation in or about the Mortgaged Property. Prior to Lender's actual entry into and taking possession of the Mortgaged Property, Lender shall not (i) be obligated to perform any of the terms, covenants and conditions contained in any Lease (or otherwise have any obligation with respect to any Lease); (ii) be obligated to appear in or defend any action or proceeding relating to the Lease or the Mortgaged Property; or (iii) be responsible for the operation, control, care, management or repair of the Mortgaged Property or any portion of the Mortgaged Property. The execution of this Mortgage by Borrower shall constitute conclusive evidence that all responsibility for the operation, control, care, management and repair of the Mortgaged Property is and shall be that of Borrower, prior to such actual entry and taking of possession.

5.4 **Lender's Right to Assert Its Assignment Rights**. Upon delivery of notice by Lender to Borrower of Lender's exercise of Lender's rights under this Section 5.4 of this Mortgage at any time after the occurrence of an Event of Default, and without the necessity of Lender entering upon and taking and maintaining control of the Mortgaged Property directly, by a receiver, or by any other manner or proceeding permitted by the laws of the Property Jurisdiction, Lender immediately shall have all rights, powers and authority granted to Borrower under any Lease, including the right, power and authority to modify the terms of any such Lease, or extend or terminate any such Lease.

5.5 **Lender's Right to receive Leases**. Borrower shall, promptly upon Lender's request, deliver to Lender an executed copy of each Lease then in effect. All Leases which are not Significant Leases shall be on forms approved by Lender, and shall not include options to purchase, provided that any Lease which varies from the foregoing requirements shall require the prior written approval of Lender (which approval shall not be unreasonably withheld).

5.6 **Certain Limitations upon Borrower's Rights to deal with Leases**. Borrower shall not enter into a Lease of any portion of the Mortgaged Property in excess of_______ square feet (each a "**Significant Lease**"), except with the prior written consent of Lender and of the Tenant executing such Lease. Each Lease will be written on the approved Lease form which Borrower has previously delivered to Lender, or on another form approved in writing by Lender, in each case with such changes to the form as Lender shall approve in writing. Borrower shall not modify the terms of, or extend or terminate, any Significant Lease without the prior written consent of Lender. Borrower shall, without request by Lender, deliver an executed copy of each Lease to Lender promptly after such Lease is signed. All Leases, including renewals or extensions of existing Leases, shall specifically provide that (1) such Leases are subordinate to the lien of this Mortgage (unless waived in writing by Lender); (2) the tenant of such Lease shall attorn to Lender and any purchaser at a foreclosure sale, such attornment to be self-executing and effective upon acquisition of title to the Mortgaged Property by any purchaser at a foreclosure sale or by Lender in any manner; (3) the tenant of such Lease agrees to execute such further evidences of attornment as Lender or any purchaser at a foreclosure sale may from time to time request; (4) the Lease shall not be terminated by foreclosure or any other transfer of the Mortgaged Property; (5) after a foreclosure sale of the Mortgaged Property, Lender or any other purchaser at such foreclosure sale may, at Lender's or such purchaser's option, accept or terminate such Lease; and (6) the tenant shall, upon receipt after the occurrence of an Event of Default of a written request from Lender, pay all Rents payable under the Lease to Lender.

SECTION 6: INTEREST RATES

[Note: To be used when the Loan has a variable interest rate.]

6.1 Interest Rates.

(a) **Borrower's Options**. Principal amounts outstanding under the Loan shall bear interest at the following rates, at Borrower's selection, subject to the conditions and limitations provided for in this Mortgage or the Note: (i) Variable Rate or (ii) LIBOR Based Rate.

(b) **Selection to Be Made**. Borrower shall select, and thereafter may change the selection of, the applicable interest rate, from the alternatives otherwise provided for in this Mortgage, by giving Lender a Notice of Rate Selection: (i) prior to each Loan Advance, (ii) prior to the end of each Interest Period applicable to a LIBOR Advance or (iii) on any Business Day on which Borrower desires to convert an outstanding Bank Rate Advance to a LIBOR Advance; provided, however, if an Event of Default exists, Borrower's right to select interest rate options other than ones based upon Bank Rates shall cease.

(c) **If No Notice**. If Borrower fails to select an interest rate option in accordance with the foregoing prior to a Loan Advance, or prior to the last day of the applicable

Interest Period of an outstanding LIBOR Advance, any new Loan Advance made shall be deemed to be a LIBOR Advance.

(d) **Telephonic Notice**. Without any way limiting Borrower's obligation to confirm in writing any telephonic notice, Lender may act without liability upon the basis of telephonic notice believed by Lender in good faith to be from Borrower prior to receipt of written confirmation. In each case Borrower hereby waives the right to dispute Lender's record of the terms of such telephonic Notice of Rate Selection.

(e) **Limits on Options; One Selection per Month**. Each LIBOR Advance shall be in a minimum amount of $_00,000. At no time shall there be outstanding a total of more than three (3) LIBOR Advances at any time. If Borrower shall make more than one (1) interest rate selection in any thirty (30) day period, excluding conversions of outstanding advances made at the end of an applicable Interest Period of any previously outstanding LIBOR Advance, Lender may impose and Borrower shall pay a reasonable processing fee for each such additional selection.

6.2 <u>Payment of Interest and Principal</u>.

(a) **Payment and Calculation of Interest**. All interest shall be: (a) payable in arrears commencing [__________] 1, 20__ and on the same day of each month thereafter until the principal together with all interest and other charges payable with respect to the Loan shall be fully paid; and (b) calculated on the basis of a 360-day year and the actual number of days elapsed. Each change in the Prime Rate shall simultaneously change the Variable Rate payable under this Mortgage. Interest at the LIBOR Based Rate shall be computed from and including the first day of the applicable Interest Period to, but excluding, the last day thereof.

(b) **Prepayment**. The Loan or any portion thereof may be prepaid in full or in part at any time upon not less than [ten (10) days'] prior written notice to the holder of this Mortgage without premium or penalty other than any Breakage Costs. Any partial prepayment of principal shall first be applied to any installment of principal then due and then be applied to the principal due in the reverse order of maturity, and no such partial prepayment shall relieve Borrower of the obligation to pay each subsequent installment of principal when due.

(c) **Maturity**. At Maturity all accrued interest, principal and other charges due with respect to the Loan shall be due and payable in full and the principal balance and such other charges, but not unpaid interest, shall continue to bear interest at the Default Rate until so paid.

(d) **Application of Payments**. All payments shall be applied first to the payment of all fees, expenses and other amounts due to the Lender (other than principal and interest), then to accrued interest, and thereafter to outstanding principal; provided, however, [after] during any Event of Default, payments will be applied to the Obligations of Borrower in such order and manner as Lender determines in its sole discretion.

(e) **Make Whole Provision**. Borrower shall pay to Lender, immediately upon request and notwithstanding contrary provisions contained in any of the Loan Documents, such amounts as shall, in the conclusive judgment of Lender (in the absence of manifest error), compensate Lender for the loss, cost or expense which it may reasonably incur as a result of (i) any payment or prepayment, under any circumstances whatsoever, whether voluntary or involuntary, of all or any portion of a LIBOR Advance on a date other than the last day of the applicable Interest Period of a LIBOR Advance, (ii) the conversion, for any reason whatsoever, whether voluntary or involuntary, of any LIBOR Advance to a Bank Rate Advance on a date other than the last day of the applicable Interest Period, (iii) the failure of all or a portion of a Loan Advance which was to have borne interest at the LIBOR Based Rate pursuant to the request of Borrower to be made under the Loan Agreement (except as a result of a failure by Lender to fulfill Lender's obligations to fund), or (iv) the failure of Borrower to borrow in accordance with any request submitted by it for a LIBOR Advance. Such amounts payable by Borrower shall be equal to any reasonable administrative costs actually incurred plus any Breakage Costs.

6.3 **Certain Definitions and Provisions Relating To Interest Rate**.

(a) **Banking Day**. The term "Banking Day" means any day other than a Saturday, Sunday, legal holiday, or day on which banks are required or authorized by law to close in the city in which Lender's principal office is situated.

(b) **Breakage Costs**. The term "Breakage Costs" means any actual loss or expense (including, without limitation, actual lost profit) that Lender sustains or incurs as a direct consequence of any prepayment (whether optional or mandatory) other than on the last day of the applicable Interest Period of a portion of the Note bearing interest at the LIBOR Based Rate by Borrower on and after the date hereof and through the Maturity, including, but not limited to, any loss or any interest payable by Lender to lenders of funds obtained by it in order to make or maintain the Loan at the LIBOR Based Rate or as provided in the Swap Documents.

6.4 **Interest Period**.

(a) The term "Interest Period" means with respect to each LIBOR Advance: a period of one (1) month. Each such Interest Period shall commence on the Business Day so selected, or deemed selected, by Borrower and shall end on the numerically corresponding day in the first month thereafter, as applicable. Provided, however: (i) if there is no such numerically corresponding day, such Interest Period shall end on the last Business Day of the applicable month, (ii) if the last day of such an Interest Period would otherwise occur on a day which is not a Business Day, such Interest Period shall be extended to the next succeeding Business Day; but (iii) if such extension would otherwise cause such last day to occur in a new calendar month, then such last day shall occur on the next preceding Business Day.

(b) The term "Interest Period" shall mean with respect to each Bank Rate Advance consecutive periods of one (1) day each.

(c) No Interest Period may be selected which would end beyond the then Maturity Date of the Loan (as actually extended). If the last day of an Interest Period would otherwise occur on a day which is not a Business Day, such last day shall be extended to the next succeeding Business Day, except as provided above relative to a LIBOR Advance.

(d) **LIBOR Rate**. The term "LIBOR Rate" shall mean, as applicable to any LIBOR Advance, the rate per annum equal to the London Interbank Offered Rate administered by the ICE Benchmark Administration (or any other Person that takes over the administration of such rate) ("LIBOR"), as published by Reuters (or other commercially available source providing quotations of LIBOR as designated by Lender from time to time in a manner consistent with any such designation by Lender generally under substantially similar credit facilities for which it acts as a lender) at approximately 11:00 a.m. London time on the date that is two (2) London Banking Days preceding the applicable Interest Period, for Dollars (for delivery on the first day of such Interest Period) with a term equivalent to such Interest Period; provided, however, if the rate described above does not appear on the Reuters screen on any applicable interest determination date, the LIBOR Rate shall be the rate determined on the basis of the offered rates for deposits in U.S. Dollars for a one-month period which are offered by four major banks in the London interbank market at approximately 11:00 a.m. London time, on the day that is two (2) London Banking Days preceding the first day of such LIBOR Advance as selected by Lender. The principal London office of each of the four major London banks will be requested to provide a quotation of its U.S. Dollar deposit offered rate. If at least two such quotations are provided, the rate for that date will be the arithmetic mean of the quotations. If fewer than two quotations are provided as requested, the rate for that date will be determined on the basis of the rates quoted for loans in U.S. Dollars to leading European banks for a period of time comparable to such LIBOR Advance offered by major banks in New York City at approximately 11:00 a.m. New York City time, on the day that is two London Banking Days preceding the first day of such LIBOR Advance. In the event that Lender is unable to obtain any such quotation as provided above, it will be deemed that LIBOR Rate for a LIBOR Advance cannot be determined. In the event that the Board of Governors of the Federal Reserve System shall impose a Reserve Percentage with respect to LIBOR Rate deposits of Lender then for any period during which such Reserve Percentage shall apply, the LIBOR Rate shall be equal to the amount determined above divided by an amount equal to 1 minus the Reserve Percentage. "Reserve Percentage" shall mean the maximum aggregate reserve requirement (including all basic, supplemental, marginal and other reserves) which is imposed on member banks of the Federal Reserve System against "Euro-currency Liabilities" as defined in Regulation D.

(e) **LIBOR Advance**. The term "LIBOR Advance" means any principal outstanding under the Note which pursuant to this Mortgage bears interest at the LIBOR Based Rate.

(f) **LIBOR Based Rate**. The term "LIBOR Based Rate" means the per annum rate of interest equal to the applicable LIBOR Rate, plus 225 basis points.

(g) **London Banking Day**. The term "London Banking Day" means any Banking Day on which dealings in deposits in Dollars are transacted in the London interbank market and banks are open for business in London.

(h) **Maturity**. The term "Maturity" means ____, 20__ ("Maturity Date"), or upon acceleration of the Loan, if the Loan has been accelerated by Lender upon an Event of Default.

(i) **Prime Rate**. The term "Prime Rate" means the per annum rate of interest so designated from time to time by the Lender as its prime rate. The Prime Rate is a reference rate and does not necessarily represent the lowest or best rate being charged to any customer.

(j) **Variable Rate**. The term "Variable Rate" means a per annum rate equal at all times to the greater of (a) the Prime Rate or (b) the LIBOR Rate, plus __ basis points with changes therein to be effective simultaneously with any change in the Prime Rate without notice or demand of any kind.

(k) **Variable Rate Advance**. The term "Variable Rate Advance" means any principal amount outstanding under the Note which pursuant to this Mortgage bears interest at the Variable Rate.

6.5 <u>Additional Provisions Related to Interest Rate Selection</u>.

(a) **Increased Costs**. If, due to a Change in Law, there shall be an increase in the cost to Lender of agreeing to make or making, funding or maintaining LIBOR Advances, including without limitation changes which affect or would affect the amount of capital or reserves required or expected to be maintained by Lender, with respect to all or any portion of the Loan, or any corporation controlling Lender, on account thereof, then Borrower from time to time shall, upon written demand by Lender, pay Lender additional amounts sufficient to indemnify Lender against the increased cost. A certificate as to the amount of the increased cost and the reason therefor submitted to Borrower by Lender, in the absence of manifest error, shall be conclusive and binding for all purposes. Notwithstanding any provision hereof to the contrary, in no event shall Borrower be required to pay any amounts in respect of income or franchise taxes payable by Lender.

(b) **Illegality**. Notwithstanding any other provision of this Mortgage or the Note, if the introduction of or change in or in the interpretation of any law, treaty, statute, regulation or interpretation thereof shall make it unlawful, or any central bank or government authority shall assert by directive, guideline or otherwise, that it is unlawful, for Lender to make or maintain LIBOR Advances or to continue to fund or maintain LIBOR Advances then, on written notice thereof and demand by Lender to Borrower, (a) the obligation of Lender to make LIBOR Advances and to convert or continue any Loan Advances as LIBOR Advances shall terminate and (b) Borrower shall convert all principal outstanding under the Note into Variable Rate Advances.

(c) **Additional LIBOR Conditions**. The selection by Borrower of a LIBOR Based Rate and the maintenance of Loan Advances at such rate shall be subject to the following additional terms and conditions:

(d) **Availability**. If, before or after Borrower has selected to take or maintain a LIBOR Advance, Lender notifies Borrower that:

  (i) dollar deposits in the amount and for the maturity requested are not available to Lender in the London interbank market at the rate specified in the definition of LIBOR Rate set forth above, or

  (ii) reasonable means do not exist for Lender to determine the LIBOR Rate for the amounts and maturity requested,

then the principal which would have been a LIBOR Advance shall be a Variable Rate Advance.

(e) **Payments Net of Taxes**. All payments and prepayments of principal and interest under this Mortgage and the Note shall be made net of any taxes and costs first imposed after the date hereof resulting solely from having principal outstanding at or computed with reference to a LIBOR Based Rate. Without limiting the generality of the preceding obligation, illustrations of such taxes and costs are taxes, or the withholding of amounts for taxes, of any nature whatsoever including income, excise, interest equalization taxes (other than United States or state income taxes) as well as all levies, imposts, duties or fees whether now in existence or as the result of a change in or promulgation of any treaty, statute, regulation, or interpretation thereof or any directive guideline or otherwise by a central bank or fiscal authority (whether or not having the force of law) or a change in the basis of, or the time of payment of, such taxes and other amounts resulting therefrom.

(f) **Variable Rate Advances**. Each Variable Rate Advance shall continue as a Variable Rate Advance until Maturity of the Loan, unless sooner converted, in whole or in part, to a LIBOR Advance, subject to the limitations and conditions set forth in this Mortgage and the Note.

SECTION 7: INTENTIONALLY OMITTED

SECTION 8: REPRESENTATIONS AND WARRANTIES

8.1 **Representations and Warranties**.

Borrower warrants and represents to Lender for the express purpose of inducing Lender to enter into this Mortgage, to advance the proceeds of the Loan, and to otherwise complete all of the transactions contemplated hereby, that as of the date of this Mortgage:

(a) **Financial Information.**

True, accurate and complete, in all material respects, financial statements of Borrower [and each Person who shall have executed any guaranty or indemnity in favor of Lender, which shall be included as a Loan Document ("**Guarantor**")] have been delivered to Lender and the same fairly present the financial condition of Borrower and Guarantor as of the dates thereof and no material and adverse change has occurred in such financial condition since the dates thereof. All financial statements of Borrower and Guarantor hereafter furnished to Lender shall be true, accurate and complete in all material respects and shall fairly present the financial condition of Borrower and Guarantor as of the dates thereof.

(b) **No Violations.**

The consummation of the Loan and the subsequent payment and performance of the Obligations evidenced and secured by the Loan Documents shall not constitute a violation of, or conflict with, any law, order, regulation, contract, agreement or organizational document to which Borrower or Guarantor is a party or by which Borrower or Guarantor, or the Mortgaged Property, may be bound.

(c) **No Litigation.**

There is no material litigation now pending, or to Borrower's Knowledge threatened, against Borrower, Guarantor or the Mortgaged Property which if adversely decided could reasonably be expected to materially impair the ability of Borrower, Guarantor or the Mortgaged Property to pay and perform its obligations hereunder or under the other Loan Documents. There is no other litigation, whether or not material, pending, or to Borrower's Knowledge threatened, against Borrower, Guarantor or the Mortgaged Property.

(d) **Good Title and No Liens.**

Borrower is the lawful owner of the interest [and/or a leasehold interest] in the Mortgaged Property and of areas over, under or on which utility or passage easements are required to make use of the Improvements and parking as contemplated hereby and by the documents referred to herein, and is the lawful owner of the Improvements, free and clear of all liens and encumbrances of any nature whatsoever, except for the matters, if any, which are listed as permitted title exceptions in the Mortgage.

(e) **Loan Proceeds.**

The proceeds of the Loan shall be used solely and exclusively for the payment of costs relating to the closing of the Loan, refinancing of any prior mortgage loan encumbering the Mortgaged Property, or other relevant costs as set forth in answer to the project budget (as the same may be amended from time to time in accordance with this Mortgage or otherwise with Lender's prior written approval in each instance where such approval is required by the terms of this Mortgage). No portion of the proceeds of the Loan shall be used directly or indirectly, and whether immediately, incidentally or ultimately (i) to purchase or carry any margin stock, or to extend credit to others for the purpose thereof, or to repay or refund indebtedness previously incurred for such purpose, or (ii) for any purpose which would violate or is inconsistent with the provisions of regulations of the Board of Governors of the Federal Reserve System including, without limitation, Regulations G, T, U and X thereof.

(f) **Loan Documents Legal and Binding.**

Each of the Loan Documents constitute legal, valid and binding obligations of Borrower and, where applicable, Guarantor; in each case in accordance with the respective terms thereof, subject to bankruptcy, insolvency and similar laws of general application affecting the rights and remedies of creditors and, with respect to the availability of the remedies of specific enforcement, subject to the discretion of the court before which any proceeding therefore may be brought.

(g) **ERISA.**

Borrower does not have any pension, profit sharing, stock option, insurance or other arrangement or plan for employees covered by Title IV of the Employment Retirement Security Act of 1974, as now or hereafter amended ("**ERISA**") except as may be designated to Lender in writing by Borrower from time to time ("**ERISA Plan**") and no "Reportable Event" as defined in ERISA has occurred and is now continuing with respect to any such ERISA Plan. The granting of the Loan, the performance by Borrower of its obligations under the Loan Documents and Borrower's conducting of its operations do not and will not violate any provisions of ERISA.

(h) **No Material Adverse Change.**

There has been no material adverse change in the financial condition, business, affairs or control of Borrower or Guarantor since the date of their respective last financial statements most recently delivered to the Lender. No Default exists under any of the Loan Documents. There is no Default on the part of Borrower or Guarantor under this Mortgage or any of the other Loan Documents and no event has occurred and is continuing which could constitute a Default under any Loan Document. Borrower has filed all required federal, state and local tax returns and has paid all taxes due pursuant to such returns or any assessments against Borrower or the Mortgaged Property.

(i) **No Dealings with Brokers.**

Neither Borrower, nor Guarantor, nor anyone on behalf thereof, has dealt with any broker, finder or other person or entity who or which may be entitled to a broker's or finder's fee, or other compensation, payable by Lender in connection with this Loan.

(j) **Condemnation/Casualty.**

There are no condemnation proceedings or the like pending or, to Borrower's Knowledge, threatened in writing against the Mortgaged Property or any portion thereof nor has there occurred any casualty at the Mortgaged Property.

(k) **Special Assessments.**

Except as may be set forth in the Title Policy, as of the date hereof there are no pending, or to the Borrower's Knowledge, proposed special or other assessments for public improvements or otherwise affecting the Mortgaged Property.

(l) **Solvency.**

Neither Borrower nor any Guarantor is insolvent and neither Borrower nor any Guarantor will be rendered insolvent by the transaction contemplated under the Loan Documents.

(m) **Flood Zone.**

No portion of the Mortgaged Property is located in any special flood hazard area designated as such by any public authority.

(n) **Compliance with Anti-Terrorism, Embargo, Sanctions and Anti-Money Laundering Laws.**

Borrower and, to Borrower's Knowledge after having made diligent inquiry, (a) each Person owning an interest of 20% or more in Borrower, (b) each Guarantor, and (c) the property manager engaged by Borrower to manage the operation of the Mortgaged Property: (i) is not currently identified on OFAC List (as defined in Borrower's commitment letter), and (ii) is not a person with whom a citizen of the United States is prohibited to engage in transactions by any trade embargo, economic sanction, or other prohibition of United States law, regulation, or Executive Order of the President of the United States.

SECTION 9: TAXES; OPERATING EXPENSES

9.1 **Taxes; Operating Expenses.**

(a) Subject to the provisions of Section 5(c) and Section 9.1(d) of this Mortgage, Borrower shall pay, or cause to be paid, all Taxes when due and before the addition of any interest, fine, penalty or cost for nonpayment.

(b) Subject to the provisions of Section 5(c), Borrower shall pay the expenses of operating, managing, maintaining and repairing the Mortgaged Property (including insurance premiums, utilities, repairs and replacements) before the last date upon which each such payment may be made without any penalty or interest charge being added.

(c) As long as no Event of Default exists and Borrower has timely delivered to Lender any bills or premium notices that it has received, Borrower shall not be obligated to pay Taxes, insurance premiums or any other individual Imposition to the extent that sufficient Imposition Deposits are held in the deposit account controlled by Lender for the purpose of paying that specific Imposition pursuant to Section 10 of this Mortgage. If an Event of Default exists, Lender may exercise any rights Lender may have with respect to Imposition Deposits without regard to whether Impositions are then due and payable. Lender shall have no liability to Borrower for failing to pay any Impositions to the extent that any Event of Default has occurred and is continuing, insufficient Imposition Deposits are held by Lender at the time an Imposition becomes due and payable or Borrower has failed to provide Lender with bills and premium notices as provided above.

(d) Borrower, at its own expense, may contest by appropriate legal proceedings, conducted diligently and in good faith, the amount or validity of any Imposition other than insurance premiums, if (1) Borrower notifies Lender of the commencement or expected commencement of such proceedings, (2) the Mortgaged Property is not in danger of being sold or forfeited, (3) Borrower deposits with Lender reserves sufficient to pay the contested Imposition, if requested by Lender, and (4) Borrower furnishes whatever additional security is required in the proceedings or is reasonably requested by Lender, which may include the delivery to Lender of the reserves established by Borrower to pay the contested Imposition.

(e) Borrower shall promptly deliver to Lender a copy of all notices of, and invoices for, Impositions, and if Borrower pays any Imposition directly, Borrower shall promptly furnish to Lender receipts evidencing such payments.

SECTION 10: DEPOSITS FOR TAXES, INSURANCE AND OTHER CHARGES

10.1 Borrower shall deposit with Lender on the day monthly installments of principal or interest, or both, are due under the Note, until the Obligations are paid in full, an additional amount sufficient to accumulate in an escrow with Lender the entire sum required to pay, when due (based on estimates to be determined by Lender in accordance with provisions hereinafter set forth in this Section 10.1) the following: (1) any water and sewer charges which, if not paid, may result in a lien on all or any part of the Mortgaged Property, (2) the premiums for fire and other hazard insurance, rent loss insurance and such other insurance as Lender may require under Section 19 of the Mortgage, (3) Taxes, and (4) amounts for other charges and expenses which Lender at any time reasonably deems necessary to protect the Mortgaged Property, to prevent the imposition of liens on the Mortgaged Property, or otherwise to protect Lender's interests, all as reasonably estimated from time to time by Lender. The amounts to be deposited under the preceding sentence are collectively referred to in this Mortgage as the **"Imposition Deposits."** The amount of the Imposition Deposits shall be paid to

Lender monthly, and such monthly sums, as estimated by Lender, shall be in an amount so as to be sufficient to enable Lender to pay each of the Impositions before the date when such applicable Imposition shall first be due and payable.

Any waiver by Lender of the requirement that Borrower remit the Imposition Deposits to Lender must be by written notice given to Borrower, and may only be revoked by Lender, in Lender's discretion, at any time upon written notice given to Borrower.

10.2 Imposition Deposits when received by Lender shall be deposited in a deposit account. Lender shall apply the Imposition Deposits to pay Impositions so long as no Event of Default has occurred and is continuing. Unless applicable law requires, Lender shall not be required to pay Borrower any interest, earnings or profits on the Imposition Deposits. Borrower hereby pledges and grants to Lender a security interest in the Imposition Deposits and the account in which they are being deposited as additional security for all of Borrower's obligations under this Mortgage and the other Loan Documents. Any amounts deposited with Lender under this Section 10.2 shall not be trust funds, nor shall they operate to reduce the Indebtedness, unless applied by Lender for that purpose.

10.3 If Lender receives a bill or invoice for an Imposition, Lender shall pay the Imposition from the Imposition Deposits held by Lender. Lender shall have no obligation to pay any Imposition to the extent it exceeds Imposition Deposits then held by Lender. Lender may pay an Imposition according to any bill, statement or estimate from the appropriate public office, insurance company or other vendor without inquiring into the accuracy of the bill, statement or estimate or into the validity of the Imposition.

10.4 If at any time the amount of the Imposition Deposits held by Lender for payment of a specific Imposition exceeds the amount reasonably deemed necessary by Lender, the excess shall be credited against future installments of Imposition Deposits. If at any time the amount of the Imposition Deposits held by Lender for payment of a specific Imposition is less than the amount reasonably estimated by Lender to be necessary, Borrower shall pay to Lender the amount of the deficiency within 15 days after notice from Lender.

10.5 If an Event of Default has occurred and is continuing, Lender may apply any Imposition Deposits, in any amounts and in any order as Lender determines, in Lender's discretion, to pay any Impositions or as a credit against the Indebtedness. Upon payment in full of the Indebtedness, Lender shall refund to Borrower any Imposition Deposits held by Lender.

SECTION 11: APPLICATION OF PAYMENTS

11.1 If at any time Lender receives, from Borrower or otherwise, any amount applicable to the Indebtedness which is less than all amounts due and payable at such time, then Lender may apply that payment to amounts then due and payable in any manner and in any order determined by Lender, in Lender's discretion. Neither Lender's acceptance of an amount which is less than all amounts then due and payable nor Lender's application of such payment in the manner authorized shall constitute or be deemed to constitute either a waiver of the unpaid amounts or an accord and satisfaction. Notwithstanding the application of any such amount to the Indebtedness, Borrower's obligations under this Mortgage and the Note shall remain unchanged.

SECTION 12: COMPLIANCE WITH LAWS

12.1 Borrower shall comply with all laws, ordinances, regulations and requirements of any Governmental Authority and all recorded lawful covenants and agreements relating to or affecting the Mortgaged Property, including all laws, ordinances, regulations, requirements and covenants pertaining to health and safety, construction of improvements on the Mortgaged Property, fair housing, zoning and land use, and Leases. Borrower also shall comply with all applicable laws that pertain to the maintenance and disposition of tenant security deposits. Borrower shall at all times maintain records sufficient to demonstrate compliance with the provisions of this Section. Borrower shall take appropriate measures to prevent, and shall not engage in or knowingly permit, any illegal activities at the Mortgaged Property that could endanger tenants or visitors, result in damage to the Mortgaged Property, result in forfeiture of the Mortgaged Property, or otherwise materially impair the lien created by this Mortgage or Lender's interest in the Mortgaged Property. Borrower represents and warrants to Lender that no portion of the Mortgaged Property has been or will be purchased with the proceeds of any illegal activity.

SECTION 13: USE OF PROPERTY

13.1 Unless required by applicable law, Borrower shall not (a) except for any change in use approved by Lender, allow changes in the use for which all or any part of the Mortgaged Property is being used at the time this Mortgage was executed, (b) initiate or acquiesce in a change in the zoning classification of the Mortgaged Property, or (c) establish any condominium or cooperative regime with respect to the Mortgaged Property.

SECTION 14: INSPECTION

14.1 Lender, its agents, representatives, and designees may make or cause to be made entries upon and inspections of the Mortgaged Property (including environmental inspections and tests) during normal business hours, or at any other reasonable time.

SECTION 15: BOOKS AND RECORDS; FINANCIAL REPORTING AND OTHER REPORTS

15.1 Borrower shall keep and maintain at all times at the Mortgaged Property or the management agent's offices, and upon Lender's request shall make available at the Mortgaged Property, complete and accurate books of account and records (including copies of supporting bills and invoices) adequate to reflect correctly the operation of the Mortgaged Property, and copies of all written contracts, Leases, and other instruments which affect the Mortgaged Property. The books, records, contracts, Leases and other instruments shall be subject to examination and inspection at any reasonable time by Lender.

15.2 Borrower shall furnish to Lender all of the following:

(a) within 120 days after the end of each fiscal year of Borrower and Guarantor, financial statements of Borrower and Guarantor, which in the case of Borrower will include a statement of income and expenses for Borrower's operation of the Mortgaged Property for that fiscal year, a statement of changes in financial position of Borrower relating to the Mortgaged Property for that fiscal year and a balance sheet showing all assets and liabilities of Borrower relating to the Mortgaged Property as of the end of that fiscal year, all prepared in accordance with GAAP, and reviewed by a certified public accountant reasonably acceptable to Lender;

(b) within 120 days after the end of each fiscal year of Borrower, and at any other time upon Lender's request, a rent schedule for the Mortgaged Property showing the name of each tenant, and for each tenant, the space occupied, the lease expiration date, the rent payable for the current month, the date through which rent has been paid, and any related information requested by Lender;

(c) within 120 days after the end of each fiscal year of Borrower, and at any other time upon Lender's request, an accounting of all security deposits held pursuant to all

Leases, including the name of the institution (if any) and the names and identification numbers of the accounts (if any) in which such security deposits are held and the name of the person to contact at such financial institution, along with any authority or release necessary for Lender to access information regarding such accounts;

(d) within 20 days following the end of each calendar quarter, (i) an operating statement showing the results of operation of the Mortgaged Property for the prior quarter and on a year-to-date basis for the period just ended; (ii) a detailed, current rent roll of the Mortgaged Property, containing such details as Lender may reasonably request, (iii) cash flows from the Mortgaged Property for the quarter just ended, (iv) leasing reports for the quarter just ended, and (v) aging and accounts receivables report for the Mortgaged Property for the quarter just ended;

(e) concurrently with the filing thereof, complete copies of all federal and state tax returns and supporting schedules of Borrower; and

(f) within a reasonable period of time and from time to time such other financial data or information as Lender may reasonably request with respect to the Mortgaged Property, or Borrower, including, but not limited to, rent rolls, aged receivables, aged payables, leases, budgets, forecasts, reserves, cash flow projections, physical condition of the Mortgaged Property, pending lease proposals, evidence of payment of all real estate taxes due from time to time and to the extent in Borrower's possession or reasonably available to Borrower such other financial data or information as Lender may reasonably request.

15.3 Each of the statements, schedules and reports required by this Section 15.3 shall be certified to be complete and accurate by an individual having authority to bind Borrower, and shall be in such form and contain such detail as Lender may reasonably require. Lender also may require that any statements, schedules or reports be audited at Borrower's expense by independent certified public accountants acceptable to Lender.

15.4 If Borrower fails to provide in a timely manner the statements, schedules and reports required by this Section 15, Lender shall have the right to have Borrower's books and records audited, at Borrower's expense, by independent certified public accountants selected by Lender in order to obtain such statements, schedules and reports, and all related costs and expenses of Lender shall become immediately due and payable and shall become an additional part of the Indebtedness.

15.5 If an Event of Default has occurred and is continuing, Borrower shall deliver to Lender upon written demand all books and records relating to the Mortgaged Property or its operation.

SECTION 16: LIENS; ENCUMBRANCES

16.1 Borrower acknowledges that, to the extent provided in Section 22 of the Mortgage, the grant, creation or existence of any mortgage, deed of trust, deed to secure debt, security interest or other lien or encumbrance (a "Lien") on the Mortgaged Property (other than the lien of this Mortgage) or on certain ownership interests in Borrower, whether voluntary, involuntary or by operation of law, and whether or not such Lien has priority over the lien of this Mortgage, is a "Transfer" which constitutes an Event of Default.

SECTION 17: PRESERVATION, MANAGEMENT AND MAINTENANCE OF THE MORTGAGED PROPERTY

17.1 Borrower (1) shall not commit waste or permit impairment or deterioration of the Mortgaged Property, (2) shall not abandon the Mortgaged Property, (3) shall restore or repair promptly, in a good and workman-like manner, any damaged part of the Mortgaged

Property to the equivalent of its original condition, or such other condition as Lender may approve in writing, whether or not insurance proceeds or condemnation awards are available to cover any costs of such restoration or repair, (4) shall keep the Mortgaged Property in good repair, including the replacement of Personalty and Fixtures with items of equal or better function and quality, (5) shall provide for professional management of the Mortgaged Property by a property manager satisfactory to Lender under a management contract approved by Lender in writing, and (6) shall give notice to Lender of and, unless otherwise directed in writing by Lender, shall appear in and defend any action or proceeding purporting to affect the Mortgaged Property, Lender's security or Lender's rights under this Mortgage. Borrower shall not (and shall not permit any tenant or other person to) remove, demolish or alter the Mortgaged Property or any part of the Mortgaged Property except in connection with the replacement of tangible Personalty.

17.2 If, in connection with the closing of the Loan or at any later date, Lender waives in writing the requirement of Section 17.1(5) above that Borrower enter into a written contract for management of the Mortgaged Property and if, after the date of this Mortgage, Borrower intends to change the management of the Mortgaged Property, Lender shall have the right to approve in writing such new property manager and the written contract for the management of the Mortgaged Property and to require that Borrower and such new property manager enter into an Assignment of Management Agreement on a form approved by Lender. If required by Lender (whether before or after an Event of Default), Borrower will cause any Affiliate of Borrower who shall serve as property manager of the Mortgaged Property to enter into an agreement with Lender, in a form approved by Lender, providing for subordination of the fees of the Affiliate of Borrower and such other provisions as Lender may require.

SECTION 18: ENVIRONMENTAL HAZARDS

18.1 Except for matters covered by an O&M Program or matters described in Section 18.4 below, Borrower shall not cause or permit any of the following:

(a) the presence, use, generation, release, treatment, processing, storage (including storage in above ground and underground storage tanks), handling, or disposal of any Hazardous Materials on or under the Mortgaged Property or any other property of Borrower that is adjacent to the Mortgaged Property;

(b) the transportation of any Hazardous Materials to, from, or across the Mortgaged Property;

(c) any occurrence or condition on the Mortgaged Property or any other property of Borrower that is adjacent to the Mortgaged Property, which occurrence or condition is or may be in violation of Hazardous Materials Laws; or

(d) any violation of or noncompliance with the terms of any Environmental Permit with respect to the Mortgaged Property or any property of Borrower that is adjacent to the Mortgaged Property.

The matters described in subsections (a) through (d) above are referred to collectively in this Section as "**Prohibited Activities or Conditions**."

18.2 Prohibited Activities and Conditions shall not include the safe and lawful use and storage of quantities of (1) pre-packaged supplies, cleaning materials and petroleum products customarily used in the operation and maintenance of comparable multifamily properties; (2) cleaning materials, personal grooming items and other items sold in pre-packaged containers and used by tenants and occupants of demised spaces within the Mortgaged Property; and (3) petroleum products used in the operation and maintenance of motor vehicles from time to time located on the Mortgaged Property's parking areas, so long as all of the foregoing are used, stored, handled, transported and disposed of in compliance with Hazardous Materials Laws.

18.3 Borrower shall take all commercially reasonable actions (including the inclusion of appropriate provisions in any Leases executed after the date of this Mortgage) to prevent its employees, agents, and contractors, and all tenants and other occupants from causing or permitting any Prohibited Activities or Conditions. Borrower shall not lease or allow the sublease or use of all or any portion of the Mortgaged Property to any tenant or subtenant for any use by any user that, in the ordinary course of its business, would cause or permit any Prohibited Activity or Condition.

18.4 If a Borrower establishes a program pursuant to a written protocol approved by Lender which sets out a plan of training, cleaning, work practices, and surveillance to deal with and/or maintain Hazardous Materials (an "**O&M Program**"), then Borrower shall comply in a timely manner with, and cause all employees, agents, and contractors of Borrower and any other persons present on the Mortgaged Property to comply with, the O&M Program. All costs of performance of Borrower's obligations under any O&M Program shall be paid by Borrower, and Lender's out-of-pocket costs incurred in connection with the monitoring and review of the O&M Program and Borrower's performance shall be paid by Borrower upon demand by Lender. Any such out-of-pocket costs of Lender which Borrower fails to pay promptly shall become an additional part of the Indebtedness as provided in Section __.

18.5 Borrower represents and warrants to Lender that, except as previously disclosed by Borrower to Lender in writing:

(a) Borrower has not at any time engaged in, caused or permitted any Prohibited Activities or Conditions;

(b) to the best of Borrower's knowledge after reasonable and diligent inquiry, no Prohibited Activities or Conditions exist or have existed;

(c) except to the extent previously disclosed by Borrower to Lender in writing, the Mortgaged Property does not now contain any underground storage tanks, and, to the best of Borrower's knowledge after reasonable and diligent inquiry, the Mortgaged Property has not contained any underground storage tanks in the past. If there is an underground storage tank located on the Property which has been previously disclosed by Borrower to Lender in writing, that tank complies with all requirements of Hazardous Materials Laws;

(d) Borrower has complied with all Hazardous Materials Laws, including all requirements for notification regarding releases of Hazardous Materials. Without limiting the generality of the foregoing, Borrower has obtained all Environmental Permits required for the operation of the Mortgaged Property in accordance with Hazardous Materials Laws now in effect and all such Environmental Permits are in full force and effect;

(e) no event has occurred with respect to the Mortgaged Property that constitutes, or with the passing of time or the giving of notice would constitute, noncompliance with the terms of any Environmental Permit;

(f) there are no actions, suits, claims or proceedings pending or, to the best of Borrower's knowledge after reasonable and diligent inquiry, threatened that involve the Mortgaged Property and allege, arise out of, or relate to any Prohibited Activity or Condition; and

(g) Borrower has not received any complaint, order, notice of violation or other communication from any Governmental Authority with regard to air emissions, water discharges, noise emissions or Hazardous Materials, or any other environmental, health or safety matters affecting the Mortgaged Property or any other property of Borrower that is adjacent to the Mortgaged Property.

The representations and warranties in this Section 18.5 shall be continuing representations and warranties that shall be deemed to be made by Borrower throughout the term of the loan evidenced by the Note, until the Indebtedness has been paid in full.

18.6 Borrower shall promptly notify Lender in writing upon the occurrence of any of the following events:

(a) Borrower's discovery of any Prohibited Activity or Condition;

(b) Borrower's receipt of or knowledge of any complaint, order, notice of violation or other communication from any Governmental Authority or other person with regard to present or future alleged Prohibited Activities or Conditions or any other environmental, health or safety matters affecting the Mortgaged Property or any other property of Borrower that is adjacent to the Mortgaged Property; and

(c) If any representation or warranty in this Section 18 becomes untrue after the date of this Mortgage.

Any such notice given by Borrower shall not relieve Borrower of, or result in a waiver of, any obligation under this Mortgage, the Note, or any other Loan Document.

18.7 Borrower shall pay promptly the costs of any environmental inspections, tests or audits (**"Environmental Inspections"**) required by Lender in connection with any foreclosure or deed in lieu of foreclosure, or as a condition of Lender's consent to any Transfer under Section 22 of this Mortgage, or required by Lender following a reasonable determination by Lender that Prohibited Activities or Conditions may exist. Any such costs incurred by Lender (including the fees and out-of-pocket costs of attorneys and technical consultants whether incurred in connection with any judicial or administrative process or otherwise) which Borrower fails to pay promptly shall become an additional part of the Indebtedness. The results of all Environmental Inspections made by Lender shall at all times remain the property of Lender and Lender shall have no obligation to disclose or otherwise make available to Borrower or any other party such results or any other information obtained by Lender in connection with its Environmental Inspections. Lender hereby reserves the right, and Borrower hereby expressly authorizes Lender, to make available to any party, including any prospective bidder at a foreclosure sale of the Mortgaged Property, the results of any Environmental Inspections made by Lender with respect to the Mortgaged Property. Borrower consents to Lender notifying any party (either as part of a notice of sale or otherwise) of the results of any of Lender's Environmental Inspections. Borrower acknowledges that Lender cannot control or otherwise assure the truthfulness or accuracy of the results of any of its Environmental Inspections and that the release of such results to prospective bidders at a foreclosure sale of the Mortgaged Property may have a material and adverse effect upon the amount which a party may bid at such sale. Borrower agrees that Lender shall have no liability whatsoever as a result of delivering the results of any of its Environmental Inspections to any third party, and Borrower hereby releases and forever discharges Lender from any and all claims, damages, or causes of action, arising out of, connected with or incidental to the results of, the delivery of any of Lender's Environmental Inspections.

18.8 If any investigation, site monitoring, containment, clean-up, restoration or other remedial work (**"Remedial Work"**) is necessary to comply with any Hazardous Materials Law or order of any Governmental Authority that has or acquires jurisdiction over the Mortgaged Property or the use, operation or improvement of the Mortgaged Property under any Hazardous Materials Law, Borrower shall, by the earlier of (1) the applicable deadline required by Hazardous Materials Law or (2) 30 days after notice from Lender demanding such action, begin performing the Remedial Work, and thereafter diligently prosecute it to completion, and shall in any event complete the work by the time required by applicable Hazardous Materials Law. If Borrower fails to begin on a timely basis or diligently prosecute any required Remedial Work, Lender may, at its option, cause the Remedial Work to be completed, in which case Borrower shall reimburse Lender on demand for the cost of doing so. Any reimbursement due from Borrower to Lender shall become part of the Indebtedness.

18.9 Borrower shall cooperate with any inquiry by any Governmental Authority and shall comply with any governmental or judicial order which arises from any alleged Prohibited Activity or Condition.

18.10 Borrower shall indemnify, hold harmless and defend (i) Lender, (ii) any prior owner or holder of the Note, (iii) the Loan Servicer, (iv) any prior loan servicer, (v) the officers, directors, shareholders, partners, employees and trustees of any of the foregoing, and (vi) the heirs, legal representatives, successors and assigns of each of the foregoing (collectively, the **"Environmental Indemnitees"**) from and against all proceedings, claims, damages, penalties and costs (whether initiated or sought by Governmental Authorities or private parties), including fees and out-of-pocket expenses of attorneys and expert witnesses, investigatory fees, and remediation costs, whether incurred in connection with any judicial or administrative process or otherwise, arising directly or indirectly from any of the following:

(a) any breach of any representation or warranty of Borrower in this Section 18 of this Mortgage;

(b) any failure by Borrower to perform any of its obligations under this Section 18 of this Mortgage;

(c) the existence or alleged existence of any Prohibited Activity or Condition;

(d) the presence or alleged presence of Hazardous Materials on or under the Mortgaged Property or any property of Borrower that is adjacent to the Mortgaged Property; and

(e) the actual or alleged violation of any Hazardous Materials Law.

18.11 Counsel selected by Borrower to defend Environmental Indemnitees shall be subject to the approval of those Environmental Indemnitees. However, any Environmental Indemnitee may elect to defend any claim or legal or administrative proceeding at the Borrower's expense.

18.12 Borrower shall not, without the prior written consent of those Environmental Indemnitees who are named as parties to a claim or legal or administrative proceeding (an **"Environmental Claim"**), settle or compromise the Environmental Claim if the settlement (1) results in the entry of any judgment that does not include as an unconditional term the delivery by the claimant or plaintiff to Lender of a written release of those Environmental Indemnitees, satisfactory in form and substance to Lender; or (2) may materially and adversely affect Lender, as determined by Lender in its discretion.

18.13 Lender agrees that the indemnity under this Section 18 shall be limited to the assets of Borrower and Lender shall not seek to recover any deficiency from any natural persons who are general partners of Borrower.

18.14 Borrower shall, at its own cost and expense, do all of the following:

(a) pay or satisfy any judgment or decree that may be entered against any Environmental Indemnitee or Environmental Indemnitees in any legal or administrative proceeding incident to any matters against which Environmental Indemnitees are entitled to be indemnified under this Section of the Mortgage;

(b) reimburse Environmental Indemnitees for any expenses paid or incurred in connection with any matters against which Environmental Indemnitees are entitled to be indemnified under this Section of the Mortgage; and

(c) reimburse Environmental Indemnitees for any and all expenses, including fees and out-of-pocket expenses of attorneys and expert witnesses, paid or incurred in connection with the enforcement by Environmental Indemnitees of their rights under this Section of the Mortgage, or in monitoring and participating in any legal or administrative proceeding.

18.15 In any circumstances in which the indemnity under this Section of the Mortgage applies, Lender may employ its own legal counsel and consultants to prosecute, defend or negotiate any claim or legal or administrative proceeding and Lender, with the prior written consent of Borrower (which shall not be unreasonably withheld, delayed or conditioned), may settle or compromise any action or legal or administrative proceeding. Borrower shall reimburse Lender upon demand for all costs and expenses incurred by Lender, including all costs of settlements entered into in good faith, and the fees and out-of-pocket expenses of such attorneys and consultants.

18.16 The provisions of this Section of the Mortgage shall be in addition to any and all other obligations and liabilities that Borrower may have under applicable law or under other Loan Documents, and each Indemnitee shall be entitled to indemnification under this Section 18 of this Mortgage without regard to whether Lender or that Indemnitee has exercised any rights against the Mortgaged Property or any other security, pursued any rights against any guarantor, or pursued any other rights available under the Loan Documents or applicable law. If Borrower consists of more than one person or entity, the obligation of those persons or entities to indemnify the Environmental Indemnitees under this Section 18 of this Mortgage shall be joint and several. The obligation of Borrower to indemnify the Environmental Indemnitees under this Section 18 of this Mortgage shall survive any repayment or discharge of the Indebtedness, any foreclosure proceeding, any foreclosure sale, any delivery of any deed in lieu of foreclosure, and any release of record of the lien of this Mortgage.

<u>SECTION 19</u>: PROPERTY AND LIABILITY INSURANCE

19.1 Borrower shall keep the Improvements insured at all times against such hazards as Lender may from time to time require, issued by companies authorized to do business in the State of _______, having a Best's Rating of not less than A-VIII and otherwise reasonably acceptable to Lender in its sole discretion and which insurance shall include but not be limited to the following:

(a) commercial property insurance on an all-risk or Special Causes of Loss basis without exception (including, without limitation, flood, required if Mortgaged Property is in a "Special Flood Hazard Area" A or V, pursuant to the Federal Flood Disaster Protection Act of 1973, as amended, vandalism and malicious mischief, flood, earthquake, windstorm, collapse, boiler explosion, machinery breakdown, sprinkler leakage coverage, cost of demolition, increased costs of construction and the value of the undamaged portion of the building and soft costs coverage) covering all the real estate, fixtures and personal property to the extent of the full insurable value thereof, having replacement cost valuation and no coinsurance, with deductibles not in excess of $100,000 (or as otherwise reasonably acceptable to the Lender). If at any time the Property and Collateral are undergoing construction or renovation, the property insurance required herein shall be written on a builder's risk/course of construction non-reporting form prior to completion and a Permission to Occupy Endorsement, if not otherwise covered under the borrower commercial property insurance; and

(b) rent loss or business interruption insurance in an amount equal to one year's projected rentals then being derived by the Mortgaged Property, plus an extended period of indemnity of no less than 180 days.

Borrower acknowledges and agrees that Lender's insurance requirements may change from time to time throughout the term of the Indebtedness. If Lender so requires, such insurance requirements, to the extent applicable, shall also include sinkhole insurance, mine subsidence insurance and, if the Mortgaged Property does not conform to applicable zoning or land use laws, building ordinance or law coverage.

19.2 Borrower shall at all times provide and maintain the following additional insurance coverages issued by companies authorized to do business in the State of the Property Jurisdiction, having a Best's Rating of not less than A-VIII:

(a) commercial general liability insurance, with not less than $1,000,000 per occurrence and $2,000,000 in the aggregate, per location or such other amounts as may be determined by Lender from time to time;

(b) automobile liability insurance (including non-owned automobile) with a coverage of $1,000,000 per occurrence;

(c) worker's compensation, employer's liability and other insurance required by law;

(d) excess liability insurance in an amount no less than $50,000,000 each occurrence and in the aggregate; and

(e) such other insurance coverages in such amounts as Lender may request consistent with the customary practices of prudent developers and owners of similar properties.

All premiums on insurance policies required under this Section 19.2 shall be paid by Borrower. All such policies shall also be in a form approved by Lender. All policies of property damage insurance shall include a non-contributing, non-reporting mortgage clause in favor of, and in a form approved by, Lender.

19.3 An actual insurance policy or certified copy thereof, or a binder, certificate of insurance, or other evidence of property coverage in the form of Acord 27 (Evidence of Property Coverage), Acord 25 (Certificate of Insurance), or a 30-day binder in form acceptable to Lender with an unconditional undertaking to deliver the policy or a certified copy within sixty (60) days, shall be delivered at closing of the Loan. Lender shall be named as first mortgagee on policies of all-risk-type insurance on the Mortgaged Property, as loss payee on the Improvements and its contents, and as first mortgagee on rent-loss or business interruption coverages related thereto. Except with respect to commercial general liability insurance, as to which Lender shall be named as an additional insured, on forms acceptable to the Lender, with respect to the Mortgaged Property, all other required insurance coverages shall have a so-called Mortgagee's endorsement or "Lender's loss-payable endorsement," in form and substance reasonably satisfactory to Lender.

19.4 Borrower shall comply with all insurance requirements and shall not permit any condition to exist on the Mortgaged Property that would invalidate any part of any insurance coverage that this Mortgage requires Borrower to maintain.

19.5 In the event of a casualty loss which damages any portion of the Mortgaged Property, Borrower shall give immediate written notice to the insurance carrier and to Lender. Borrower hereby authorizes and appoints Lender as attorney-in-fact for Borrower to make proof of loss, to adjust and compromise any claims under policies of property damage insurance, to appear in and prosecute any action arising from such property damage insurance policies, to collect and receive the proceeds of property damage insurance, and to deduct from such proceeds Lender's expenses incurred in the collection of such proceeds. This power of attorney is coupled with an interest and therefore is irrevocable. Subject to the provisions contained in Section 19.5 of this Mortgage, Lender may, at Lender's option, (1) hold the balance of such proceeds to be used to reimburse Borrower for the cost of restoring and repairing the Mortgaged Property to the equivalent of its original condition or to a condition approved by Lender (the "Restoration"), or (2) apply the balance of such proceeds to the payment of the Indebtedness, whether or not then due. To the extent Lender determines to apply insurance proceeds to Restoration, Lender shall do so in accordance with Lender's then-current policies relating to the restoration of casualty damage on similar multifamily properties.

19.6 Notwithstanding the foregoing provisions of Section 19.6 of this Mortgage to the contrary, Lender shall not exercise its option to apply insurance proceeds and/or condemnation awards to the payment of the Indebtedness if all of the following conditions are met:

(a) no Event of Default (or any event which, with the giving of notice or the passage of time, or both, would constitute an Event of Default) has occurred and is continuing;

(b) Lender determines, in its discretion, that there will be sufficient funds from the proceeds or awards that are paid pursuant to the applicable insurance, or are otherwise paid to Lender by Borrower, in either case to complete the Restoration;

(c) Lender determines, in its discretion, that the rental income from the Mortgaged Property after completion of the Restoration will be sufficient to meet all operating costs and other expenses, Imposition Deposits, deposits to reserves and loan repayment obligations relating to the Mortgaged Property;

(d) Lender determines, in its discretion, that the Restoration will be completed before the earlier of (A) one year before the maturity date of the Note or (B) one year after the date of the loss or casualty;

(e) to the extent plans and specifications are customarily prepared in connection with implementing the repairs necessary to complete the Restoration ("**Cost To Repair**"), Lender shall have approved, in its discretion, in writing any such plans and specifications;

(f) Borrower shall have provided to Lender such waivers of lien, architect's certificates, contractor's sworn statements and other evidence of payments required to be made, from time to time, until the Restoration has been fully completed, as Lender shall reasonably require; and

(g) upon Lender's request, Borrower provides Lender evidence of the availability during and after the Restoration of the insurance required to be maintained by Borrower pursuant to this Mortgage.

19.7 If the aggregate actual cost of making the necessary repairs, restorations or replacement needed to complete the Restoration does not exceed $100,000, the insurance proceeds or condemnation award shall be released to Borrower to pay for the Costs To Repair, but only to the extent of such costs, as estimated by Lender. Otherwise, funds shall be released upon final completion of the Restoration, unless Borrower requests earlier funding, in which event partial monthly disbursements equal to 90% of the value of the work completed shall be made prior to final completion of the repair, restoration or replacement and the balance of the disbursements shall be made upon full completion and the receipt by Lender of satisfactory evidence of payment and release of all liens. Notwithstanding the foregoing, Lender will release the portion of such retained amount being held with respect to any contractor, subcontractor or materialman engaged in the Restoration as of the date upon which Lender has determined that such contractor, subcontractor or materialman has satisfactorily completed all work and has supplied all materials in accordance with the provisions of such contractor's, subcontractor's or materialman's contract, such contractor, subcontractor or materialman delivers the lien waivers and evidence of payment in full of all sums due to such contractor, subcontractor or materialman as may be reasonably requested by Lender or by the title company issuing Lender's title insurance policy.

SECTION 20: CONDEMNATION

20.1 Borrower shall promptly notify Lender of any action or proceeding relating to any condemnation or other taking, or conveyance in lieu thereof, of all or any part of the Mortgaged Property, whether direct or indirect (a "Condemnation"). Borrower shall appear in and prosecute or defend any action or proceeding relating to any Condemnation unless otherwise directed by Lender in writing. Borrower authorizes and appoints Lender as attorney-in-fact for Borrower to commence, appear in and prosecute, in Lender's or Borrower's name, any action or proceeding relating to any Condemnation and to settle or compromise any claim in connection with any Condemnation. This power of attorney is coupled with an interest and therefore is irrevocable. However, nothing contained in this Section 20.1 shall require Lender to incur any expense or take any action. Borrower hereby transfers and assigns to Lender all right, title and interest of Borrower in and to any award or payment with respect to (i) any Condemnation, or any conveyance in lieu of Condemnation, and (ii) any damage to the Mortgaged Property caused by governmental action that does not result in a Condemnation.

20.2 Except for those provisions expressly provided for in Section 19 of this Mortgage (which require Lender to allow the awards or proceeds of any such Condemnation to be applied to pay for applicable costs of Restoration), Lender may apply such awards or proceeds, after the deduction of Lender's expenses incurred in the collection of such amounts, to the payment of the Indebtedness, with the balance, if any, to be paid to Borrower. Unless Lender otherwise agrees in writing, any application of any awards or proceeds to the Indebtedness shall not extend or postpone the due date of any monthly installments referred to in the Note, or change the amount of such installments. Borrower agrees to execute such further evidence of assignment of any awards or proceeds as Lender may require.

SECTION 21: BORROWER BANKRUPTCY REMOTENESS; SEPARATENESS COVENANTS

21.1 Until the Indebtedness is paid in full, Borrower (a) shall not acquire any real or personal property other than the Mortgaged Property and personal property related to the operation and maintenance of the Mortgaged Property; and (b) shall not operate any business other than the management and operation of the Mortgaged Property.

21.2 Borrower will not engage in any business or activity, other than the ownership, operation and maintenance of the Mortgaged Property and activities incidental thereto, including, without limitation, Borrower's obtaining of the Loan from Lender.

21.3 Borrower will not acquire, own, hold, lease, operate, manage, maintain, develop or improve any assets other than the Mortgaged Property and such Personalty as may be necessary for the operation of the Mortgaged Property and will conduct and operate its business as presently conducted and operated.

21.4 Borrower will preserve its existence as an entity duly organized, validly existing and in good standing (if applicable) under the laws of the jurisdiction of the State of Delaware and will do all things necessary to observe organizational formalities.

21.5 Borrower will not merge or consolidate with any other Person.

21.6 Borrower will not take any action to dissolve, wind-up, terminate or liquidate in whole or in part; to sell, transfer or otherwise dispose of all or substantially all of its assets; to change its legal structure; transfer or permit the direct or indirect transfer of any partnership, membership or other equity interests, as applicable, other than Transfers permitted under this Mortgage; issue additional partnership, membership or other equity interests, as applicable, or seek to accomplish any of the foregoing.

21.7 if Borrower is a limited partnership, each general partner of Borrower must be a Person who is not an individual and must either be a corporation or a single-member Delaware limited liability company, in each case which must (x) have two (2) independent directors, and (y) must hold direct equity interests as a general partner in Borrower of not less than __ [1]%.

21.8 if Borrower is a corporation, Borrower shall at all times have at least two independent directors on its board.

21.9 if Borrower is a limited liability company, Borrower shall at all times remain organized under the laws of the State of Delaware; and Borrower (A) must have at least __ [1] independent director(s) serving as special independent manager(s) of Borrower, (B) shall not take any bankruptcy related action or shall not cause or permit the members or managers of Borrower to take any bankruptcy related action, unless its independent director(s), then serving as special independent manager(s) of Borrower, shall have consented in writing to such action, and (C) must have two natural individuals, or one entity that is not a member of Borrower, enter into the limited liability company agreement of Borrower, which shall contain a provision that under the terms of such limited liability agreement, such individuals or entity, as the case may be, shall become a member of Borrower immediately prior to withdrawal or dissolution of the last remaining member of Borrower.

21.10 Borrower will not, without the prior unanimous written consent of all of Borrower's partners, members, or shareholders, as applicable, and, if applicable, the prior unanimous written consent of 100% of the members of the board of directors or of the board of Managers of Borrower, take any of the following actions ("**Insolvency Actions**"):

(a) File any insolvency, or reorganization case or proceeding, to institute proceedings to have Borrower be adjudicated bankrupt or insolvent.

(b) Institute proceedings under any applicable insolvency law.

(c) Seek any relief under any law relating to relief from debts or the protection of debtors.

(d) Consent to the filing or institution of bankruptcy or insolvency proceedings against Borrower.

(e) File a petition seeking, or consent to, reorganization or relief with respect to Borrower under any applicable federal or state law relating to bankruptcy or insolvency.

(f) Seek or consent to the appointment of a receiver, liquidator, assignee, trustee, sequestrator, custodian, or any similar official for Borrower or a substantial part of its property.

(g) Make any assignment for the benefit of creditors of Borrower.

(h) Admit in writing Borrower's inability to pay its debts generally as they become due.

21.11 Borrower will not amend or restate its organizational documents if such change would cause the provisions set forth in those organizational documents not to comply with the requirements set forth in this Section 21 of this Mortgage.

21.12 Borrower will not own any subsidiary or make any investment in, any other Person.

21.13 Borrower will not commingle its assets with the assets of any other Person and will hold all of its assets in its own name.

21.14 Borrower will not incur any debt, secured or unsecured, direct or contingent (including guaranteeing any obligation), other than, (A) the Indebtedness (and any further indebtedness as expressly permitted in this Mortgage) and (B) customary unsecured trade payables incurred in the ordinary course of owning and operating the Mortgaged Property provided the same are not evidenced by a promissory note, do not exceed, in the aggregate, at any time a maximum amount of two percent of the original principal amount of the Indebtedness and are paid within 60 days of the date incurred.

21.15 Borrower will maintain its records, books of account, bank accounts, financial statements, accounting records and other entity documents separate and apart from those of any other Person and will not list its assets as assets on the financial statement of any other Person; provided, however, that Borrower's assets may be included in a consolidated financial statement of its Affiliate provided that (A) appropriate notation will be made on such consolidated financial statements to indicate the separateness of Borrower from such Affiliate and to indicate that Borrower's assets and credit are not available to satisfy the debts and other obligations of such Affiliate or any other Person and (B) such assets will also be listed on Borrower's own separate balance sheet.

21.16 Except for capital contributions or capital distributions permitted under the terms and conditions of its organizational documents, Borrower will only enter into any contract or agreement with any general partner, member, shareholder, principal or Affiliate of Borrower or any Guarantor, or any general partner, member, principal or Affiliate thereof, upon terms and conditions that are commercially reasonable and substantially similar to those that would be available on an arm's-length basis with third parties.

21.17 Borrower will not maintain its assets in such a manner that will be costly or difficult to segregate, ascertain or identify its individual assets from those of any other Person.

21.18 Borrower will not assume or guaranty (excluding any guaranty that has been executed and delivered in connection with the Note) the debts or obligations of any other Person, hold itself out to be responsible for the debts of another Person, pledge its assets to secure the obligations of any other Person or otherwise pledge its assets for the benefit of any other Person, or hold out its credit as being available to satisfy the obligations of any other Person.

21.19 Borrower will not make or permit to remain outstanding any loans or advances to any other Person except for those investments permitted under the Loan Documents and will not buy or hold evidence of indebtedness issued by any other Person (other than cash or investment-grade securities).

21.20 Borrower will file its own tax returns separate from those of any other Person, except to the extent that Borrower is treated as a "disregarded entity" for tax purposes and is not required to file tax returns under applicable law, and will pay any taxes required to be paid under applicable law.

21.21 Borrower will hold itself out to the public as a legal entity separate and distinct from any other Person and conduct its business solely in its own name, will correct any known misunderstanding regarding its separate identity and will not identify itself or any of its Affiliates as a division or department of any other Person.

21.22 Borrower will maintain adequate capital for the normal obligations reasonably foreseeable in a business of its size and character and in light of its contemplated business operations and will pay its debts and liabilities from its own assets as the same become due.

21.23 Borrower (1) has paid and will pay its debts and liabilities as the same become due; (2) has maintained and will maintain adequate capital; (3) will at all times remain solvent; (4) will pay its debts and liabilities (including a fairly allocated portion of any personnel and overhead expenses shared with any affiliate); and (5) will maintain adequate capital for the normal operations reasonably foreseeable in a business of its size and character in light of its business operations.

21.24 Borrower will allocate fairly and reasonably shared expenses with Affiliates (including shared office space) and use separate stationery, invoices and checks bearing its own name.

21.25 Borrower will not acquire obligations or securities of its partners, members, shareholders, or Affiliates, as applicable.

21.26 Except as contemplated or permitted by the property management agreement with respect to the Property Manager, Borrower will not permit any Affiliate or constituent party independent access to its bank accounts.

21.27 If Borrower is a single-member limited liability company, it must satisfy each of the following conditions:

(a) Have either one springing member that is a corporation whose stock is 100% owned by the sole member of Borrower and that satisfies the requirements for a corporate springing member set forth below in this Section or two springing members who are natural persons;

(b) Otherwise comply with criteria for single-member limited liability companies (including the delivery of Delaware single-member limited liability company opinions acceptable in all respects to Lender and to the Rating Agencies), as established by Standard & Poor's Ratings Services. If the springing member is a corporation, such springing member will at all times comply, and will cause Borrower to comply, with each of the representations, warranties and covenants contained in Section 21 of this Mortgage as if such representation, warranty or covenant were made directly by such corporation. If there is more than one springing member, only one springing member will be the sole member of Borrower at any one time, and the second springing member will become the sole member only upon the first springing member ceasing to be a member.

(c) At all times Borrower will have one and only one member.

SECTION 22: TRANSFERS OF THE MORTGAGED PROPERTY INTERESTS IN BORROWER

22.1 The occurrence of any of the following events shall constitute an Event of Default under this Mortgage:

(a) a Transfer of all or any part of the Mortgaged Property or any interest in the Mortgaged Property;

(b) a Transfer of a Controlling Interest in Borrower;

(c) a Transfer of a Controlling Interest in any entity which owns, directly or indirectly through one or more intermediate entities, a Controlling Interest in Borrower;

(d) a Transfer of all or any part of Key Principal's ownership interests (other than limited partnership interests) in Borrower, or in any other entity which owns, directly or indirectly through one or more intermediate entities, an ownership interest in Borrower;

(e) if Key Principal is an entity, (A) a Transfer of a Controlling Interest in Key Principal, or (B) a Transfer of a Controlling Interest in any entity which owns, directly or indirectly through one or more intermediate entities, a Controlling Interest in Key Principal;

(f) if Borrower or Key Principal is a trust, the termination or revocation of such trust; and

(g) a conversion of Borrower from one type of legal entity into another type of legal entity, whether or not there is a Transfer.

Lender shall not be required to demonstrate any actual impairment of its security or any increased risk of default in order to exercise any of its remedies with respect to an Event of Default under this Section.

22.2 The occurrence of any of the following events shall not constitute an Event of Default under this Mortgage, notwithstanding any provision of this Section to the contrary:

(a) a Transfer to which Lender has consented in writing;

(b) a Transfer that occurs by devise, by descent, or by operation of law upon the death of a natural person, so long as the transferee is reasonably satisfactory to Lender;

(c) a Transfer of obsolete or worn out Personalty or Fixtures that are contemporaneously replaced by items of equal or better function and quality, which are free of liens, encumbrances and security interests other than those created by the Loan Documents or consented to by Lender;

(d) the grant of an easement, if before the grant Lender determines in writing that the easement will not materially affect the operation or value of the Mortgaged Property or Lender's interest in the Mortgaged Property, and Borrower pays to Lender, upon demand, all costs and expenses incurred by Lender in connection with reviewing Borrower's request; and

(e) the creation of a tax lien or a mechanic's, materialman's or judgment lien against the Mortgaged Property which is bonded off, released of record or otherwise remedied to Lender's satisfaction within 30 days of the date of creation.

22.3 For purposes of this Section, the following terms shall have the meanings set forth below:

(a) "**Initial Owners**" means, with respect to Borrower or any other entity, the persons or entities who on the date of the Note own in the aggregate 100% of the ownership interests in Borrower or that entity.

(b) A Transfer of a "Controlling Interest" shall mean, with respect to any entity, the following:

(i) if such entity is a general partnership or a joint venture, a Transfer of any general partnership interest or joint venture interest which would cause the Initial Owners to own less than 51% of all general partnership or joint venture interests in such entity;

(ii) if such entity is a limited partnership, a Transfer of any general partnership interest;

(iii) if such entity is a limited liability company or a limited liability partnership, a Transfer of any membership or other ownership interest which would cause the Initial Owners to own less than 51% of all membership or other ownership interests in such entity;

(iv) if such entity is a corporation (other than a Publicly-Held Corporation) with only one class of voting stock, a Transfer of any voting stock which would cause the Initial Owners to own less than 51% of voting stock in such corporation;

(v) if such entity is a corporation (other than a Publicly-Held Corporation) with more than one class of voting stock, a Transfer of any voting stock which would cause the Initial Owners to own less than a sufficient number of shares of voting stock necessary to have the power to elect the majority of directors of such corporation; and

(vi) if such entity is a trust, the removal, appointment or substitution of a trustee of such trust other than (A) in the case of a land trust, or (B) if the trustee of such trust after such removal, appointment or substitution is a trustee identified in the trust agreement as approved by Lender.

(c) "**Publicly-Held Corporation**" shall mean a corporation, the outstanding voting stock of which is registered under Section 12(b) or 12(g) of the Securities and Exchange Act of 1934, as amended.

22.4 Lender shall consent, without any adjustment to the rate at which the Loan secured by the Note bears interest or to any other economic terms of the Loan, to a one time Transfer during the term of the Loan that would otherwise violate this Section, if, prior to the Transfer, Borrower has satisfied each of the following requirements:

(a) the submission to Lender of all information required by Lender to make the determination required by this Section;

(b) the absence of any Event of Default;

(c) the transferee meets all of the eligibility, credit, management and other standards (including any standards with respect to previous relationships between Lender and the transferee and the organization of the transferee) customarily applied by Lender at the time of the proposed Transfer to the approval of borrowers in connection with the origination or purchase of loans secured by similar mortgages, deeds of trust or deeds to secure debt on commercial real estate properties which are being used for similar purposes as Mortgaged Property;

(d) in the case of a Transfer of all or any part of the Mortgaged Property, or direct or indirect ownership interests in Borrower or Key Principal (if an entity), if transferor or any other person has obligations under any Loan Document, the execution by the transferee or one or more individuals or entities acceptable to Lender of a written assumption agreement that is acceptable to Lender and that, among other things, requires the transferee to perform all obligations of transferor or such person set forth in such Loan Document, and may require that the transferee comply with any provisions of this Mortgage or any other Loan Document which previously may have been waived by Lender;

(e) if a guaranty has been executed and delivered in connection with the Note, this Mortgage or any of the other Loan Documents, Borrower causes one or more individuals or entities acceptable to Lender to execute and deliver to Lender a similar guaranty in a form acceptable to Lender;

(f) the transferring Borrower ("Transferee") assumes and agrees to pay (subject to the non-recourse provisions of this Section 22 hereof) all the service payments payable under the Note and to perform all other obligations of Borrower arising under the Note, this Mortgage and the other Loan Documents and (provided that Borrower shall be relieved of such obligations from and after the date of such Transfer and Lender shall execute and deliver to such Borrower at the time of the Transfer a release to such effect) prior to or concurrently with the closing of such Transfer, the Transferee, as a condition to proceeding with such Transfer, shall execute, without any cost or expense to Lender, such documents and agreements as Lender shall reasonably require to evidence and effectuate said assumption and shall deliver such legal opinions (including a nonconsolidation opinion in substantially the same form as that delivered in connection with the closing of the Loan evidenced by the Note) as Lender may reasonably require;

(g) Transferee and Borrower authorize the filing of, without any cost or expense to Lender, new financing statements or financing statement amendments and any additional documents reasonably requested by Lender;

(h) Borrower shall cause to be delivered to Lender, without any cost or expense to Lender, such endorsements to Lender's title insurance policy, hazard insurance endorsements or certificates and other similar materials as Lender may deem necessary at the time of the Sale, all in form and substance reasonably satisfactory to Lender, including, without limitation, an endorsement or endorsements to Lender's title insurance policy insuring that the lien of this Mortgage constitutes a first lien on the Mortgaged Property subject only to the Permitted Exceptions, extending the effective date of such policy to the date of execution and delivery (or, if later, of recording) of the assumption agreement referenced above in sub-subsection (f) of this Section 22.4 and insuring that fee simple title to the Mortgaged Property is vested in the Transferee, or, in lieu thereof, such other documents or evidence as Lender may reasonably require in order to confirm the priority of this Mortgage;

(i) Borrower shall execute and deliver to Lender, without any cost or expense to Lender, a release of Lender, its officers, directors, employees and agents, from all claims and liability relating to the transactions evidenced by the Note, this Mortgage, and any of the other Loan Documents through and including the date of the closing of the Transfer, which agreement shall be in form and substance satisfactory to Lender and shall be binding upon the Transferee; and

(i) Lender's receipt of all of the following:
(ii) a non-refundable review fee in the amount of $______ and a transfer fee equal to one percent (1%) of the outstanding Indebtedness immediately prior to the Transfer.
(iii) In addition, Borrower shall be required to reimburse Lender for all of Lender's out-of-pocket costs (including reasonable attorneys' fees) incurred in reviewing the Transfer request.

22.5 Any Transfer shall not be construed so as to relieve any current guarantor or indemnitor (collectively "**Indemnitor**") of its obligations under any existing guaranty or indemnity agreement, in favor of Lender which is in effect immediately prior to any such Transfer, as being part of the Loan Documents; and each such Indemnitor at the time of any such Transfer, as a condition to Lender's consenting to such Transfer, shall execute, without any cost or expense to Lender, such documents and agreements as Lender shall reasonably require to evidence and implement the ratification of each such guaranty or indemnity; provided that if any beneficial owner of, or related party to, the Transferee shall be approved by Lender in Lender's sole but reasonable discretion, not to be unreasonably withheld or delayed, and any such entity (which approval shall be deemed granted so long as Lender receives (1) a certified financial statement of such beneficial owner of Transferee showing that such entity has a liquid net worth of not less than $___________, and (2) a certification of such beneficial owner of Transferee, in form and substance reasonably satisfactory to Lender, which certifies that at no time during the ten (10) year period immediately prior to the date of such Transfer (A) has such entity been convicted of a felony, or (B) has such entity been adjudicated bankrupt or insolvent or filed, consented to or acquiesced in any petition of bankruptcy, reorganization or arrangement pursuant to any federal bankruptcy law, or any similar federal or state law), executes, without any cost or expense to Lender, each indemnity and guaranty, in form substantially the same as executed in connection with the execution of the original Loan Documents, then Lender shall execute and deliver to the current Indemnitor or, concurrently with such transaction, a full release of the current Indemnitor from all obligations related to, or arising under, the Loan Documents in connection with occurrences which happen from and after the closing of such Transfer.

SECTION 23: PROTECTION OF LENDER'S SECURITY

23.1 If Borrower fails to perform any of its obligations under this Mortgage or any other Loan Document, or if any action or proceeding is commenced which purports to affect the Mortgaged Property, Lender's security or Lender's rights under this Mortgage, including eminent domain, insolvency, code enforcement, civil or criminal forfeiture, enforcement of Hazardous Materials Laws, fraudulent conveyance or reorganizations or proceedings involving a bankrupt or decedent, then Lender at Lender's option may make such appearances, disburse such sums and take such actions as Lender reasonably deems necessary to perform such obligations of Borrower and to protect Lender's interest, including (1) payment of fees and out-of-pocket expenses of attorneys, accountants, inspectors and consultants, (2) entry upon the Mortgaged Property to make repairs or secure the Mortgaged Property, (3) procurement of the insurance required by Section 19 of this Mortgage, and (4) payment of amounts which Borrower has failed to pay under other Section(s) of this Mortgage.

23.2 Any amounts disbursed by Lender under this Section, or under any other provision of this Mortgage or the other Loan Documents, shall be added to, and become part of, the principal component of the Indebtedness evidenced by the Note, shall be immediately due and payable and shall bear interest from the date of disbursement until paid at the "**Default Rate**" as defined in the Note.

23.3 Nothing in this Section 23 of this Mortgage shall require Lender to incur any expense or take any action.

SECTION 24: EVENTS OF DEFAULT

24.1 The occurrence of any one or more of the following shall constitute an Event of Default under this Mortgage:

(a) any failure by Borrower to pay or deposit when due any amount required by the Note, this Mortgage or any other Loan Document;

(b) any failure by Borrower to maintain the insurance coverage required by Section 19 of the Mortgage;

(c) any failure by Borrower to comply with the bankruptcy remote special purpose provisions of Section 21 of the Mortgage;

(d) Breach of any representations or warranties contained in this Mortgage or any of the other Loan Documents;

(e) the existence of any collusion, fraud, dishonesty or bad faith by or with the acquiescence of Borrower, which in any material way relates to or affects the Loan or reduces the value of the Collateral;

(f) any breach by Borrower of its obligations with respect to Transfer set forth in Section 22 of this Mortgage;

(g) any failure by Borrower to perform any of its obligations as and when required under any Loan Document other than this Mortgage which continues beyond the applicable express cure period, if any, specified in that Loan Document;

(h) any failure by Borrower to perform any of its obligations under this Mortgage (other than those specified in the immediately preceding subsections (a) through (g)), as and when required, which continues for a period of 30 days after written notice of such failure by Lender to Borrower, but no such notice or grace period shall apply in the case of any such failure which could, in Lender's judgment, absent immediate exercise by Lender of a right or remedy under this Mortgage, result in harm to Lender, impairment of the Note or this Mortgage or any other security given under any other Loan Document;

(i) any exercise by the holder of any other debt instrument secured by a mortgage, deed of trust or deed to secure debt on all or any part of the Mortgaged Property, or a pledge of equity interests in Borrower, in each case of a right to declare all amounts due under that debt instrument immediately due and payable.

(j) if Borrower:

(i) shall file a voluntary petition in bankruptcy or for arrangement, reorganization or other relief under any chapter of the federal bankruptcy code or any similar Law, now or hereafter in effect;

(ii) shall file an answer or other pleading in any proceedings admitting insolvency, bankruptcy, or inability to pay its debts as they mature;

(iii) within sixty (60) days after the filing against it of any involuntary proceedings under the federal bankruptcy code or similar Law, now or hereafter in effect, such proceedings shall not have been vacated;

(iv) have an order issued appointing a receiver, trustee or liquidator for it or for all or a major part of its property or the Land which is not vacated within sixty (60) days following entry thereof;

(v) shall be adjudicated a bankrupt;

(vi) shall make an assignment for the benefit of creditors or shall admit in writing its inability to pay its debts generally as they become due or shall consent to the appointment of a receiver or trustee or liquidator of all or the major part of its property, or the Land;

(vii) shall for any reason cease to exist; or

(k) one or more final, unappealable judgments are entered against Borrower in amounts aggregating in excess of $200,000, and said judgments are not stayed or bonded over within thirty (30) days after entry and not otherwise fully insured; or

(l) if Borrower shall fail to pay any debt owed by it or is in default under any agreement with Lender or any other party and such failure or default continues after any applicable grace period specified in the instrument or agreement relating thereto.

SECTION 25: ACCELERATION; REMEDIES

25.1 At any time during the existence of an Event of Default, Lender, at Lender's option, may declare the Indebtedness to be immediately due and payable without further demand, and may invoke the power of sale and any other remedies permitted by the laws of the Property Jurisdiction or provided in this Mortgage or in any other Loan Document. Borrower acknowledges that the power of sale granted by this Mortgage may be exercised by Lender without prior judicial hearing. Borrower has the right to bring an action to assert that an Event of Default does not exist or to raise any other defense Borrower may have to acceleration and sale. Lender shall be entitled to collect all costs and expenses incurred in pursuing such remedies, including attorneys' fees and costs of documentary evidence, abstracts and title reports.

25.2 If the applicable laws of the Property Jurisdiction permit the holder of a mortgage to invoke power of sale remedies, and Lender invokes the power of sale, Lender shall deliver a copy of a notice of sale to Borrower in the manner prescribed by the applicable laws of the Property Jurisdiction. In addition, Lender shall give public notice of the sale, to the extent such public notice is mandated by the applicable laws of the Property Jurisdiction, in the manner prescribed by such law, and in all events Lender shall sell the Mortgaged Property in accordance with the applicable provisions of the laws of the Property Jurisdiction. To the extent permitted by applicable law, Lender, without demand on Borrower, shall sell the Mortgaged Property at public auction to the highest bidder at the time and place and under the terms designated in the notice of sale in one or more parcels and in such order as Lender may determine. Lender may postpone the sale of all or any part of the Mortgaged Property by public announcement at the time and place of any previously scheduled sale or by advertising in accordance with the applicable laws of the Property Jurisdiction. Lender or Lender's designee may purchase the Mortgaged Property at any sale.

SECTION 26: REMEDIES CUMULATIVE

26.1 Each right and remedy provided in this Mortgage is distinct from all other rights or remedies under this Mortgage or any other Loan Document or afforded by applicable law, and each shall be cumulative and may be exercised concurrently, independently, or successively, in any order:

(a) Upon the occurrence and during the continuation of any Event of Default, Lender may take such action, without notice or demand, as it deems advisable to protect and enforce its rights against Borrower and in and to the Mortgaged Property, subject to applicable law, including, but not limited to, the following actions, each of which may be pursued concurrently or otherwise, at such time and in such order as Lender may determine, in its sole discretion, without impairing or otherwise affecting the other rights and remedies of Lender:

(i) declare the entire Indebtedness to be immediately due and payable;

(ii) institute proceedings for the complete foreclosure of this Mortgage in which case the Mortgaged Property or any interest therein may be sold for cash or upon credit in one or more parcels or in several interests or portions and in any order or manner;

(iii) with or without entry, to the extent permitted and pursuant to the procedures provided by applicable law, institute proceedings for the partial foreclosure of this Mortgage for the portion of the Indebtedness then due and payable, subject to the continuing lien of this Mortgage for the balance of the Indebtedness not then due;

(iv) sell for cash or upon credit the Mortgaged Property or any part thereof and all estate, claim, demand, right, title and interest of Borrower therein and rights of redemption thereof, pursuant to power of sale or otherwise, at one or more sales, as an entity or in parcels, at such time and place, upon such terms and after such notice thereof as may be required or permitted by law;

(v) institute an action, suit or proceeding in equity for the specific performance of any covenant, condition or agreement contained herein or in the Note;

(vi) recover judgment on the Note either before, during or after any proceedings for the enforcement of this Mortgage;

(vii) apply for the appointment of a trustee, receiver, liquidator or conservator of the Mortgaged Property, without notice and without regard for the adequacy of the security for the Indebtedness and without regard for the solvency of the Borrower, any guarantor or of any person, firm or other entity liable for the payment of the Indebtedness;

(viii) enter into or upon the Mortgaged Property, either personally or by its agents, servicers, nominees or attorneys and, to the extent Borrower is in occupancy of the Mortgaged Property, dispossess Borrower and its agents and servants therefrom, and thereupon Lender (or any receiver appointed pursuant to subsection (vii) above) may do or permit one or more of the following, successively or concurrently: (a) enter upon and take possession and control of any and all of the Mortgaged Property; (b) take and maintain possession of all documents, books, records, papers and accounts relating to the Mortgaged Property; (c) exclude Borrower and its agents, servants and employees wholly from the Mortgaged Property; (d) manage and operate the Mortgaged Property; (e) preserve and maintain the Mortgaged Property; (f) make repairs and alterations to the Mortgaged Property; (g) complete any construction or repair of the Improvements, with such changes, additions or modifications of the plans and specifications or intended disposition and use of the Improvements as Lender may, in its sole discretion, deem appropriate or desirable to place the Mortgaged Property in such condition as will, in Lender's sole discretion, make it or any part thereof readily marketable or rentable; (h) if the Lease has been terminated, conduct a marketing or leasing program with respect to the Mortgaged Property, or employ a marketing or leasing agent or agents to do so, directed to the leasing or sale of the Mortgaged Property under such terms and conditions as Lender may, in its sole discretion, deem appropriate or desirable; (i) employ such contractors, subcontractors, materialmen, architects, engineers, consultants, managers, brokers, marketing agents, or other employees, agents, independent contractors or professionals, as Lender may, in its sole discretion, deem appropriate or desirable to implement and effectuate the rights and powers herein granted; (j) execute and deliver, in the name of Lender as attorney-in-fact and agent of Borrower or in its own name as Lender, such documents and instruments as are necessary or appropriate to consummate authorized transactions; (k) affirm or modify any lease of any real property interest constituting a part of the Mortgaged Property, or enter such other leases, whether of real or personal property, or tenancy agreements, under such terms and conditions as Lender may, in its sole discretion, deem appropriate or desirable; (l) collect and receive the Rents from the Mortgaged Property; (m) eject tenants or repossess personal property, as provided by law, for breaches of the conditions of their leases or other agreements; (n) sue for unpaid Rents, payments, income or proceeds in the name of Borrower or Lender; (o) maintain actions in forcible entry and detainer, ejectment for possession and actions in distress for rent; (p) compromise or reduce Rents, payments, income or proceeds that may become due; (q) delegate or assign any and all rights and powers given to Lender by this Mortgage; and (r) do any acts which Lender, in its sole discretion, deems appropriate or desirable to protect the security hereof and use such measures, legal or equitable, as Lender may, in its sole discretion, deem appropriate or desirable to implement and effectuate the provisions of this Mortgage. Borrower hereby constitutes and appoints Lender, its assignees, successors, transferees and nominees, as Borrower's true and lawful attorney-in-fact and agent, with full power of substitution in the Mortgaged Property, in Borrower's name, place and stead, during an Event of Default, to do or permit any one or more of the foregoing described rights, remedies, powers and authorities, successively or concurrently, and said power of attorney shall be deemed a power coupled with an interest and irrevocable so long as any portion of the Indebtedness is outstanding. Any money advanced by Lender in connection with any action taken under this subsection (viii), together with interest thereon at the Default Rate from the date of making such advancement by Lender until actually paid by Borrower, shall be a demand obligation owing by Borrower to Lender and shall be secured by this Mortgage and by every other instrument securing all or any portion of the Indebtedness;

(ix) with or without taking possession of the Mortgaged Property, sue or otherwise collect the Rents, including those past due and unpaid; and

(x) exercise any other right or remedy available hereunder, under any of the other Loan Documents or at law or in equity.

In the event of a sale, by foreclosure or otherwise, of less than all of the Mortgaged Property, this Mortgage shall continue as a lien on the remaining portion of the Mortgaged Property.

(b) To the fullest extent permitted by law, the proceeds of any sale under this Mortgage shall be applied, to the extent funds are so available, to the following items in such order as Lender in its discretion may determine:

(i) To payment of the reasonable costs, expenses and fees of taking possession of the Mortgaged Property, and of holding, operating, maintaining, using, leasing, repairing, improving, marketing and selling the same and of otherwise enforcing Lender's rights and remedies hereunder and under the other Loan Documents, including, but not limited to, receivers' fees, court costs, attorneys', accountants', appraisers', managers' and other professional fees, title charges and transfer taxes.

(ii) To payment of all sums expended by Lender under the terms of any of the Loan Documents and not yet repaid, together with interest on such sums at the Default Rate.

(iii) To payment of the interest, principal, the Prepayment Consideration and all other obligations secured by this Mortgage, including, without limitation, interest at the Default Rate, in any order that Lender chooses in its sole discretion.

(iv) The remainder, if any, of such funds shall be disbursed to Borrower or to the person or persons legally entitled thereto.

(c) To the extent permitted by applicable law, Lender may adjourn from time to time any sale by it to be made under or by virtue of this Mortgage by announcement at the time and place appointed for such sale or for such adjourned sale or sales; and, except as otherwise provided by any applicable provision of law, Lender, without further notice or publication, may make such sale at the time and place to which the same shall be so adjourned.

(d) Upon the completion of any sale or sales made by Lender under or by virtue of this Section, Lender or an officer of any court empowered to do so, shall execute and deliver to the accepted purchaser or purchasers a good and sufficient instrument, or good and sufficient instruments, conveying, assigning and transferring all estate, right, title and interest in and to the property and rights sold. Any such sale or sales made under or by virtue of this Section shall operate to divest all the estate, right, title, interest, claim and demand whatsoever, whether at law or in equity, of Borrower in and to the properties and rights so sold, and shall be a perpetual bar both at law and in equity against Borrower and against any and all persons claiming or who may claim the same, or any part thereof from, through or under Borrower.

(e) Upon any sale made under or by virtue of this Section, Lender may bid for and acquire the Mortgaged Property or any part thereof and in lieu of paying cash therefor may make settlement for the purchase price by crediting upon the Indebtedness the net sales price after deducting therefrom the expenses of the sale and costs of the action and any other sums which Lender is authorized to deduct under this Mortgage.

(f) No recovery of any judgment by Lender and no levy of an execution under any judgment upon the Mortgaged Property or upon any other property of Borrower shall affect in any manner or to any extent the lien of this Mortgage upon the Mortgaged Property or any part thereof, or any liens, rights, powers or remedies of Lender hereunder, but such liens, rights, powers and remedies of Lender shall continue unimpaired as before.

SECTION 27: FORBEARANCE

27.1 Lender may (but shall not be obligated to) agree with Borrower, from time to time, and without giving notice to, or obtaining the consent of, or having any effect upon the obligations of, any guarantor or other third-party obligor, to take any of the following actions: extend the time for payment of all or any part of the Indebtedness; reduce the payments due under this Mortgage, the Note, or any other Loan Document; release anyone liable for the payment of any amounts under this Mortgage, the Note, or any other Loan Document; accept a renewal of the Note; modify the terms and time of payment of the Indebtedness; join in any extension or subordination agreement; release any Mortgaged Property; take or release other or additional security; modify the rate of interest or period of amortization of the Note or change the amount of the monthly installments payable under the Note; and otherwise modify this Mortgage, the Note, or any other Loan Document.

27.2 Any forbearance by Lender in exercising any right or remedy under the Note, this Mortgage, or any other Loan Document or otherwise afforded by applicable law, shall not be a waiver of or preclude the exercise of any other right or remedy. The acceptance by Lender of payment of all or any part of the Indebtedness after the due date of such payment, or in an amount which is less than the required payment, shall not be a waiver of Lender's right to require prompt payment when due of all other payments on account of the Indebtedness or to exercise any remedies for any failure to make prompt payment. Enforcement by Lender of any security for the Indebtedness shall not constitute an election by Lender of remedies so as to preclude the exercise of any other right available to Lender. Lender's receipt of any awards or proceeds under Sections 19 and/or 20 of this Mortgage shall not operate to cure or waive any Event of Default.

SECTION 28: EXCULPATION

28.1 Lender shall not be entitled to and shall not enforce the liability and obligation of Borrower to perform and observe the obligations contained in this Mortgage, the Note or in any of the other Loan Documents by any action or proceeding wherein a money judgment or personal liability shall be sought against Borrower or any members, beneficiaries, trustees, the economic and beneficial owner of Borrower or of any beneficial owners or trustees of Borrower or any managers, officers, shareholders or directors thereof (collectively, the "Released Parties"), except that Lender may bring a foreclosure action, an action for specific performance or any other appropriate action or proceeding to enable Lender to enforce and realize upon its interests under the Note, this Mortgage or the other Loan Documents or in the Mortgaged Property, or any other collateral given by Borrower pursuant to this Mortgage and the other Loan Documents; provided, however, that, except as specifically provided herein, for purposes of enforcing Lender's rights under this Section 28, any judgment in any such action or proceeding shall be enforceable against Borrower only to the extent of Borrower's interest in the Mortgaged Property and in any other collateral given to Lender, and Lender, by accepting this Mortgage, the Note and the other Loan Documents, agrees that it shall not sue for, seek or demand any deficiency judgment against Borrower or any of the Released Parties in any such action or proceeding under, or by reason of, or in connection with this Mortgage, the Note or the other Loan Documents. The provisions of this Section 28.1 shall not, however, (i) constitute a waiver, release or impairment of any obligation evidenced or secured by this Mortgage, the Note or any of the other Loan Documents; (ii) impair the right of Lender to name Borrower as a party defendant in any action or suit for foreclosure and sale under this Mortgage; (iii) affect the validity or enforceability of any guaranty made in connection with the Debt or guaranty of liability for the acts specified below or any of the rights and remedies of the Lender thereunder; (iv) impair the right of Lender to obtain the appointment of a receiver; (v) impair the enforcement of the Assignment of Leases and Rents executed in connection herewith; or (vi) constitute a waiver of the right of Lender to enforce the liability and obligation of Borrower, by money judgment or otherwise, to the extent of any loss, damage excluding consequential exemplary and punitive damages, cost, expense, liability, claim or other obligation incurred by Lender (including, without limitation, attorneys' fees and costs reasonably incurred) arising out of or in connection with the following:

(a) the misappropriation or conversion of Rents, if any, or any other similar payment collected, received or held by or on behalf of Borrower under any Lease;

(b) after notice of an uncured Event of Default and during the continuance of such Event of Default, the failure of Borrower to apply 100% of any and all income derived from the Mortgaged Property, and received by Borrower, to the repayment of the Indebtedness (except to the extent that Borrower did not have the legal right, because of a bankruptcy, receivership or similar judicial proceeding, to direct disbursement of such sums or payments);

(c) a material misrepresentation made by Borrower, or the holders of Controlling beneficial or ownership interests in Borrower, in connection with the Mortgaged Property, or the financing evidenced by the Note, this Mortgage or the other Loan Documents ("Control" shall mean, with respect to any Person, the possession, directly or indirectly, of the power to direct or cause the direction of the management and policies of such Person, whether through the ownership of voting securities or other beneficial interests, by contract or otherwise, and Control shall not be deemed absent solely because another Person shall have veto power with respect to major decisions. The terms "Controlled" and "Controlling" shall have correlative meanings);

(d) the misappropriation or misapplication of insurance or condemnation proceeds obtained by Borrower relating to the Mortgaged Property;

(e) any violation of an Environmental Law or any release or contamination affecting the Mortgaged Property, which is introduced or caused by Borrower or the holders of Controlling beneficial or ownership interests in Borrower or any parties Controlled by or under common Control therewith;

(f) any physical waste of or damage to the Mortgaged Property caused by the willful or wanton acts or omissions of Borrower or its agents;

(g) the failure of Borrower to comply with special purpose entity provisions contained in Section 21 of this Mortgage;

(h) Borrower fails to obtain Lender's prior written consent to any subordinate financing or other voluntary lien caused by Borrower or its agent encumbering the Mortgaged Property as required by this Mortgage;

(i) Borrower fails to obtain Lender's prior written consent to any Transfer if and to the extent required by this Mortgage;

(j) Borrower permits monthly Rent to be paid more than one (1) month in advance without depositing such Rent in an account earmarked for payment of the Debt;

(k) the failure of Borrower to cause the required insurance policies which Borrower is required to maintain pursuant to this Mortgage to at all times remain in full force and effect and to cause all Taxes and Premiums to be paid prior to delinquency thereof;

(l) the commission of any fraud by Borrower or the holders of beneficial or ownership interests in Borrower;

(m) the adjudication of Borrower, or any guarantor or indemnitor who shall have executed a guarantee or an indemnity for the benefit of Lender and which are part of the Loan Documents, as bankrupt as a result of any voluntary filing by Borrower, such guarantor or such indemnity, as the case may be; and

(n) Borrower, such guarantor or such indemnitor conspires with others to cause an involuntary filing of a bankruptcy proceeding against Borrower, such guarantor or such indemnitor, as the case may be.

Notwithstanding anything to the contrary in this Mortgage, the Note or any other Loan Documents, Lender shall not be deemed to have waived any right which Lender may have under Sections 506(a), 506(b), 1111(b) or any other provisions of the Bankruptcy Code to file a claim for the full amount of the Indebtedness secured by this Mortgage or to require that all collateral shall continue to secure all of the Indebtedness owing to Lender.

<u>SECTION 29</u>: WAIVER OF MARSHALING

29.1 Notwithstanding the existence of any other security interests in the Mortgaged Property held by Lender or by any other party, Lender shall have the right to determine the order in which any or all of the Mortgaged Property shall be subjected to the remedies provided in this Mortgage, the Note, any other Loan Document or applicable law. Lender shall have the right to determine the order in which any or all portions of the Indebtedness are satisfied from the proceeds realized upon the exercise of such remedies. Borrower and any party who now or in the future acquires a security interest in the Mortgaged Property and who has actual or constructive notice of this Mortgage waives any and all right to require the marshaling of assets or to require that any of the Mortgaged Property be sold in the inverse order of alienation or that any of the Mortgaged Property be sold in parcels or as an entirety in connection with the exercise of any of the remedies permitted by applicable law or provided in this Mortgage.

SECTION 30: FURTHER ASSURANCES

30.1 Borrower shall execute, acknowledge, and deliver, at its sole cost and expense, all further acts, deeds, conveyances, assignments, estoppel certificates, financing statements, transfers and assurances as Lender may require from time to time in order to better assure, grant, and convey to Lender the rights intended to be granted, now or in the future, to Lender under this Mortgage and the Loan Documents.

SECTION 31: ESTOPPEL CERTIFICATE

31.1 Within 10 days after a request from Lender, Borrower shall deliver to Lender a written statement, signed and acknowledged by Borrower, certifying to Lender or any person designated by Lender, as of the date of such statement, (i) that the Loan Documents are unmodified and in full force and effect (or, if there have been modifications, that the Loan Documents are in full force and effect as modified and setting forth such modifications); (ii) the unpaid principal balance of the Note; (iii) the date to which interest under the Note has been paid; (iv) that Borrower is not in default in paying the Indebtedness or in performing or observing any of the covenants or agreements contained in this Mortgage or any of the other Loan Documents (or, if the Borrower is in default, describing such default in reasonable detail); (v) whether or not there are then existing any setoffs or defenses known to Borrower against the enforcement of any right or remedy of Lender under the Loan Documents; and (vi) any additional facts requested by Lender.

SECTION 32: GOVERNING LAW; CONSENT TO JURISDICTION AND VENUE

32.1 This Mortgage, and any Loan Document which does not itself expressly identify the law that is to apply to it, shall be governed by the laws of the jurisdiction in which the Land is located (the **"Property Jurisdiction"**).

32.2 Borrower agrees that any controversy arising under or in relation to the Note, this Mortgage, or any other Loan Document shall be litigated exclusively in the Property Jurisdiction. The state and federal courts and authorities with jurisdiction in the Property Jurisdiction shall have exclusive jurisdiction over all controversies which shall arise under or in relation to the Note, any security for the Indebtedness, or any other Loan Document. Borrower irrevocably consents to service, jurisdiction, and venue of such courts for any such litigation and waives any other venue to which it might be entitled by virtue of domicile, habitual residence or otherwise, and agrees that all litigation relating to the Loan shall be conducted in the state and federal courts which are located in the state which contains the Property Jurisdiction.

SECTION 33: NOTICES

33.1 All notices, demands, requests, or other communications (each a "**notice**") to be sent by one party to the other hereunder or required by law to be delivered in connection with the Loan, this Mortgage or any of the other Loan Documents shall be in writing and shall be deemed to have been validly given or served by delivery of the same in person to the intended addressee, or by depositing the same with Federal Express or another reputable private courier service for next business day delivery to the intended addressee at its address set forth on the first page of this Mortgage or at such other address as may be designated by such party as herein provided, or by depositing the same in the United States mail, postage prepaid, registered or certified mail, return receipt requested, addressed to the intended addressee at its address set forth on the first page of this Mortgage or at such other address as may be designated by such party as herein provided. All notices, demands, and requests shall be effective upon such personal delivery, or one (1) business day after being deposited with the private courier service, or three (3) business days after being deposited in the United States mail as required above. Rejection or other refusal to accept or the inability to deliver because of changed address of which no notice was given as herein required shall be deemed to be receipt of the notice, demand, or request sent. By giving to the other party hereto at least fifteen (15) days' prior written notice thereof in accordance with the provisions hereof, the parties hereto shall have the right from time to time to change their respective addresses and each shall have the right to specify as its address any other address within the United States of America.

SECTION 34: SALE OF NOTE; CHANGE IN SERVICE

34.1 The Note or a partial interest in the Note (together with this Mortgage and the other Loan Documents) may be sold one or more times without prior notice to Borrower. A sale may result in a change of the parties who service the loan (collectively the "**Loan Servicer**"). There also may be one or more changes of the Loan Servicer unrelated to a sale of the Note. If there is a change of the Loan Servicer, Borrower will be given notice of the change.

SECTION 35: SUCCESSORS AND ASSIGNS BOUND

35.1 This Mortgage shall bind, and the rights granted by this Mortgage shall inure to, the respective successors and assigns of Lender and Borrower, and of any subsequent holder of Lender's interest in the Loan and of any owner of a participation interest therein. However, a Transfer made by Borrower which is not permitted by Section 22 of this Mortgage shall be an Event of Default.

SECTION 36: JOINT AND SEVERAL LIABILITY

36.1 If more than one person or entity signs this Mortgage as Borrower, the obligations of such persons and entities shall be joint and several.

SECTION 37: NO THIRD-PARTY BENEFICIARY

37.1 No creditor of any party to this Mortgage and no other person shall be a third-party beneficiary of this Mortgage or any other Loan Document. Without limiting the generality of the preceding sentence, (1) any arrangement (a **"Servicing Arrangement"**) between the Lender and any Loan Servicer for loss sharing or interim advancement of funds shall constitute a contractual obligation of such Loan Servicer that is independent of the obligation of Borrower for the payment of the Indebtedness, (2) Borrower shall not be a third-party beneficiary of any Servicing Arrangement, and (3) no payment by the Loan Servicer under any Servicing Arrangement will reduce the amount of the Indebtedness.

SECTION 38: SEVERABILITY; AMENDMENTS

38.1 The invalidity or unenforceability of any provision of this Mortgage shall not affect the validity or enforceability of any other provision, and all other provisions shall remain in full force and effect. This Mortgage contains the entire agreement among the parties as to the rights granted and the obligations assumed in this Mortgage. This Mortgage may not be amended or modified except by a writing signed by the party against whom enforcement is sought.

SECTION 39: DISCLOSURE OF INFORMATION

39.1 Lender may furnish information regarding Borrower or the Mortgaged Property to third parties with an existing or prospective interest in the servicing, enforcement, evaluation, performance, purchase or securitization of the Indebtedness, including trustees, master servicers, special servicers, rating agencies, and organizations maintaining databases on the underwriting and performance of multifamily mortgage loans. Borrower irrevocably waives any and all rights it may have under applicable law to prohibit such disclosure, including any right of privacy.

SECTION 40: RELEASE

40.1 Upon payment of the Indebtedness, Lender shall enter into customary documentation so as to discharge and/or release of record this Mortgage, and any other Loan Documents previously filed on record; and shall release and deliver the Note to Borrower. Borrower shall pay Lender's reasonable costs incurred in releasing this Mortgage and Loan Documents previously filed of record.

SECTION 41: STATE-SPECIFIC STATUTORY PROVISIONS

41.1 The following provisions .are made applicable to this Mortgage: [specific state-by-state provisions which are necessary and/or customary in each State where the Mortgage is being recorded].

SECTION 42: SUBMISSION TO JURISDICTION; WAIVER OF TRIAL BY JURY

42.1 BORROWER AND LENDER EACH, TO THE FULL EXTENT PERMITTED BY LAW, HEREBY KNOWINGLY, INTENTIONALLY, AND VOLUNTARILY, WITH AND UPON THE ADVICE OF COMPETENT COUNSEL, (i) SUBMITS TO PERSONAL JURISDICTION IN THE PROPERTY JURISDICTION OVER ANY SUIT, ACTION, OR PROCEEDING BY ANY PERSON ARISING FROM OR RELATING TO THIS MORTGAGE, (ii) AGREES THAT ANY SUCH ACTION, SUIT, OR PROCEEDING IN RESPECT OF THIS MORTGAGE MAY BE BROUGHT BY LENDER IN ANY STATE OR FEDERAL COURT OF COMPETENT JURISDICTION SITTING IN THE COUNTY OF ______________ IN THE CITY OF ____________ IN THE PROPERTY JURISDICTION, (iii) SUBMITS TO THE JURISDICTION OF SUCH COURTS, AND, (iv) TO THE FULLEST EXTENT PERMITTED BY LAW, AGREES THAT BORROWER WILL NOT BRING ANY ACTION, SUIT, OR PROCEEDING IN ANY OTHER FORUM (BUT NOTHING HEREIN SHALL AFFECT THE RIGHT OF LENDER TO BRING ANY ACTION, SUIT, OR PROCEEDING IN ANY OTHER FORUM). BORROWER HEREBY WAIVES AND AGREES NOT TO ASSERT, AS A DEFENSE IN ANY ACTION, SUIT, OR PROCEEDING ARISING OUT OF OR RELATING TO THIS MORTGAGE, THE NOTE OR ANY OF THE OTHER LOAN DOCUMENTS, (A) THAT IT IS NOT SUBJECT TO SUCH JURISDICTION OR THAT SUCH ACTION, SUIT, OR PROCEEDING MAY NOT BE BROUGHT OR IS

NOT MAINTAINABLE IN THOSE COURTS OR THAT THIS SECURITY INSTRUMENT, THE NOTE, AND/OR ANY OF THE OTHER LOAN DOCUMENTS MAY NOT BE ENFORCED IN OR BY THOSE COURTS OR THAT IT IS EXEMPT OR IMMUNE FROM EXECUTION, (B) THAT THE ACTION, SUIT, OR PROCEEDING IS BROUGHT IN AN INCONVENIENT FORUM, OR (C) THAT THE VENUE AND/OR FORUM OF THE ACTION, SUIT, OR PROCEEDING IS IMPROPER (BUT NOTHING HEREIN SHALL AFFECT THE RIGHT OF BENEFICIARY TO BRING ANY ACTION, SUIT, OR PROCEEDING IN ANY OTHER FORUM). BORROWER FURTHER CONSENTS AND AGREES TO SERVICE OF ANY SUMMONS, COMPLAINT, OR OTHER LEGAL PROCESS IN ANY SUCH SUIT, ACTION, OR PROCEEDING BY REGISTERED OR CERTIFIED U.S. MAIL, POSTAGE PREPAID, TO THE BORROWER AT THE ADDRESS SET FORTH HEREIN, AND CONSENTS AND AGREES THAT SUCH SERVICE SHALL CONSTITUTE IN EVERY RESPECT VALID AND EFFECTIVE SERVICE (BUT NOTHING HEREIN SHALL AFFECT THE VALIDITY OR EFFECTIVENESS OF PROCESS SERVED IN ANY OTHER MANNER PERMITTED BY LAW).

42.2 BORROWER AND LENDER EACH, TO THE FULL EXTENT PERMITTED BY LAW, HEREBY KNOWINGLY, INTENTIONALLY, AND VOLUNTARILY, WITH AND UPON THE ADVICE OF COMPETENT COUNSEL, WAIVES, RELINQUISHES, AND FOREVER FORGOES THE RIGHT TO A TRIAL BY JURY IN ANY ACTION OR PROCEEDING BASED UPON, ARISING OUT OF, OR IN ANY WAY RELATING TO THIS MORTGAGE OR ANY CONDUCT, ACT, OR OMISSION OF LENDER OR BORROWER, OR ANY OF ITS DIRECTORS, OFFICERS, PARTNERS, MEMBERS, EMPLOYEES, AGENTS, OR ATTORNEYS, OR ANY OTHER PERSONS AFFILIATED WITH LENDER OR BORROWER, IN EACH Of THE FOREGOING CASES, WHETHER SOUNDING IN CONTRACT, TORT, OR OTHERWISE.

[The remainder of this page is intentionally left blank.]

IN WITNESS WHEREOF, Borrower and Lender hereto have executed this Mortgage by its duly authorized representative as of the date first written above.

BORROWER:

______________________________, a

____

By: ______________________________,
Name:
Title:

LENDER:

______________________________, a

____

By: ______________________________,
Name:
Title:

STATE OF ____________________________
COUNTY OF __________________________
On this _____ day of ________________, 20____, before me, personally appeared __________ ____, to me known to be the person described in and who executed the foregoing instrument, and who acknowledged that he/she/they executed the same as his/her/their free act and deed.

____

Notary Public
Print Name: ______________________________________
My Commission Expires: __________________________

STATE OF ____________________________
COUNTY OF __________________________
On this _____ day of ________________, 20____, before me, personally appeared __________ ____, to me known to be the person described in and who executed the foregoing instrument, and who acknowledged that he/she/they executed the same as his/her/their free act and deed.

____

Notary Public
Print Name: ______________________________________
My Commission Expires: __________________________

Index

C

F

J

K

L

M

N

O

P

R

T

U

V

W

Y